D1067542

The Anointed

The Anointed

Evangelical Truth in a Secular Age

Randall J. Stephens

Karl W. Giberson

The Belknap Press of
Harvard University Press
Cambridge, Massachusetts
London, England
2011

Printed in the United States of America

Library of Congress Cataloging-in-Publication Data

Stephens, Randall J., 1973–

The anointed : evangelical truth in a secular age / Randall J. Stephens, Karl W. Giberson.

p. cm.

Includes bibliographical references (p.) and index.

ISBN 978-0-674-04818-8 (alk. paper)

1. Evangelicalism—United States. 2. Intellect—Religious aspects—Christianity. 3. Christian conservatism—United States. 4. Conservatism—Religious aspects—Christianity. 5. Christianity and politics—United States. 6. Church and state—United States. 7. Christianity and culture—United States. 8. United States—Church history. I. Giberson, Karl. II. Title.

BR1642.U5S73 2011

277.3′082—dc23 2011019826

Contents

The Anointed

Introduction

I disagree with these experts," said Don McLeroy, the intense, balding chair of the Texas State Board of Education, speaking at a distinctly non-Texan clip. The board was in the middle of a massive revision of the state's public school social studies and science curriculum. Texas conservatives, many of them evangelicals like McLeroy, had been focusing on three simple words, "strengths and weaknesses," around which their wagons were now circling in a final act of confrontation. The three words were all that remained after decades of legal wrangling had steadily pushed the biblical story of Creation from America's public schools. Many of the country's millions of creationists considered this a scientific, cultural, and moral disaster. And, adding economic insult to intellectual injury, it had been paid for with their tax dollars.

Since the late 1980s, in an effort to mollify Texas creationists, state curriculum guidelines had mandated the teaching of the "strengths and weaknesses" of evolution. Teaching that the godless theory of evolution had "weaknesses" at least offered hope that the creationist beliefs of Texas schoolchildren might not be completely destroyed by the public schools. McLeroy, like many Texas evangelicals, enthusiastically endorsed young earth creationism. He believed that the *best* scientific evidence—the sort provided by *real* experts—pointed to Earth's being 6,000 to 10,000 years old, just as the Bible taught, not 4.5 billion years, as the scientific community contended.[1] Moreover, evolution was not a fact; it was just a theory.

In March 2009, McLeroy and other board members had heard several scientists testify that the board needed to take the theory of evolution seriously. The word "theory," as used in the scientific community, these experts emphasized, meant more than "hunch"—a popular misuse of the term commonly employed to great effect by critics. Brown University biology professor Kenneth Miller warned that the idea that evolution is riddled with weaknesses "does Texas a disservice" by implying a false sense of uncertainty in evolutionary science.[2]

The self-assured McLeroy was a dentist. His expertise resided in areas far removed from the science of human origins, though he consistently presumed to pass judgments on the conclusions of the scientific community. He invoked "other" authorities that he thought were more credible and certainly more congenial to his faith. A similar controversy swirled around American history, a subject that also came under the board's watchful eye, and that was even further from McLeroy's field of knowledge. Nevertheless, he was convinced that he had a legitimate concern about the teaching of history, just as he did about science. For too long, he and his fellow conservatives complained, students had been taught a distorted, liberal version of American history. Teachers intentionally made students feel bad about America's many crimes from its checkered past—slavery, the treatment of Native Americans, and the oppression of women. Yet children knew little about the triumphs of the new conservatism from the early 1960s to the present. They knew even less about the entrepreneurial heroes of industry like Carnegie and Rockefeller, who embodied America's greatness. Why were they not as celebrated as Babe Ruth, the hero of America's national pastime? Most important for McLeroy, Texas students were not learning about America's godly heritage. "Christianity has had a deep impact on our system," he told the *New York Times.* "The men who wrote the Constitution were Christians who knew the Bible."[3] McLeroy made this claim with the support of fellow Texans like David Barton, an amateur Christian historian, popular speaker, and Republican leader. The self-taught Barton suggested to the board that students should understand that Christianity was the key to American exceptionalism. America's founding principles and even the Constitution were rooted in a biblical understanding of the Fall and human sinfulness. The public school curriculum, advised Barton and others, should emphasize that Christianity is a force for good and the reason for America's strength among nations. Barton and other presumed expert advisors also questioned the liberal focus of textbooks. In their estimation, civil rights leaders like the labor organizer César Chávez and Supreme Court Justice Thurgood Marshall received too much attention given their meager achievements.[4]

These were no small changes that McLeroy, his committee, and their advisors were demanding. Their impact would be felt, they hoped, well beyond the classroom. A change in the Lone Star State's history standards would mark a change in society. "The philosophy of the classroom in one generation," commented a Christian activist on the board, "will be the philosophy of the government in the next."[5]

In May 2010 the board approved the new curriculum, with its conservative tone, by a party-line vote of nine to five, a decision reaching potentially five million Texas schoolchildren. Since Texas purchases so many textbooks—some forty-eight million in a typical year—the change could even influence the national market, affecting children around the country.[6]

No board members had claimed professional expertise on these subjects, but that did not daunt them, for they had their own authorities, like David Barton, guiding them. "Somebody's gotta stand up to experts," blurted McLeroy at the March 2009 meeting, by which he meant the conventionally accredited experts in the academy.[7] McLeroy stated that he had, in fact, thought seriously about others' views on history and science, including the academic leadership in these fields, and he was prepared to do battle with them. He had discussed these matters with his second cousin, a master's student at Harvard University, as he researched the issues and found the academic approach wanting. Texas State Democratic Senator Kirk Watson was incredulous at this comment. Speaking for so many who had been watching the proceedings, he asked McLeroy: "And you're relying on her as you make up the curriculum as opposed to Nobel laureates and scientists that might be working at the University of Texas?"[8]

McLeroy's confidence that liberal, secular experts at leading universities should retreat in the face of his campaign to educate children with traditional Christian principles is a widespread and quintessential feature of conservative American culture. On Main Street, where McLeroy worships, shops, and runs his dental business, the insights of honest citizens, regardless of their education, are often valued above those of credentialed, experienced experts. By these populist lights, so-called experts have their own prejudices and agendas that are seemingly at odds with the traditional values that these Christians believe have defined America from its founding.

The concerns animating McLeroy and the millions of Texans cheering him on are greatly heightened by their deeply held religious sensibilities. Many, perhaps most, evangelical Christians from Maine to California would share the concerns of their fellow believers in Texas that a secular, liberal, elitist minority held sway in the public schools and jettisoned a traditional, God-honoring, and patriotic curriculum for one that undermined their values and corroded their faith. A godly leader challenging this state of affairs might seem heroic and quickly gain their support. A secular leader would engender mistrust.

McLeroy's confidence in his alternative curriculum testifies to the power and inspiration of evangelical leaders like Barton and others who have challenged secular knowledge and authority. Such leaders—

and evangelicalism has many of them—have undermined the academic status quo in such a way that a multitude of lay Christians are comfortable standing up to the "experts," confident that there really are two sides to these questions. That McLeroy and his committee were able to persuade textbook companies to negotiate the content of their publications testifies to the remarkable political, cultural, and economic power of American evangelical Christianity today and its influence on public life.

Heavily reported stories like the textbook controversy in Texas project a public face for evangelicalism in America. This face, for the most part, looks like the politically monolithic "Christian Right," a simple textbook "fundamentalism" led by often dubious leaders. Journalists painting with broad brush strokes describe it as a unified subculture that elected George W. Bush, opposes gay marriage and evolution, and promotes apathy about global warming and other environmental concerns. This one-dimensional caricature glosses over powerful *internal* intellectual tensions and even contradictions within evangelicalism, where a small but growing minority of evangelicals even consider themselves liberal. Some of the voices raised in alarm over the textbook controversy in Texas belonged to evangelicals; some of the most strident criticisms of David Barton's revisionist history have come from evangelical historians; and most evangelical scientists embrace evolution within the framework of their belief that God is ultimately the creator of all that is. But their voices are strangely muted when raised against people like McLeroy.[9]

Populist and often woefully uninformed sentiments dominate, like the belief that Earth is a few thousand years old. In the realm of ideas debated in the public square, high-profile, media-savvy evangelical "experts" rally millions of believers to common causes by carefully donning mantles of great authority. Such leaders promote elaborate and well-articulated worldviews that often run counter to contemporary scholarship, public opinion, and even the best-informed voices within evangelicalism.[10] Millions of evangelicals like Don McLeroy look to such Christian experts for advice and leadership on issues as diverse as human origins, psychology and family counseling, theology, and American history. Evangelicals who turn to such authorities believe that any expert must first and foremost have an unquestioning belief in the literal truth of the Bible.

Evangelical Christians are arrayed along a broad spectrum of believers, ranging from conservative to liberal, with considerable diversity even under those labels. Most believe that Christians must undergo conversion, a life-changing experience in which a seeker enters into a relationship with Jesus Christ and is saved from sin—sin that is "original" and, if not addressed, condemns one to an eternity in hell.

Since World War II, evangelicals of all stripes have looked to leaders like the evangelist Billy Graham and the Christian author C. S. Lewis for guidance on how to live according to the Bible, which they understand to be God's Word. Religious labels are notoriously slippery and vague, and many evangelicals can be found in mainline and even Catholic churches. Some may identify themselves as liberal Protestants, the very tradition out of which evangelicalism arose in opposition. Others, such as those within the Pentecostal or holiness tradition, stress works of the Holy Spirit beyond conversion, including speaking in tongues, miraculous help from God, or achieving a state of sinless perfection known as entire sanctification.

Fundamentalists, on the conservative end of the evangelical spectrum, believe the Bible was essentially dictated by God and is thus without any error. They emphasize the importance of correct biblical doctrines and dispute the claims of secularism and liberalism, including most scientific explanations of origins, like evolution and the Big Bang theory. The late Southern preacher and political leader Jerry Falwell, the most visible fundamentalist in modern America, defined a fundamentalist as an evangelical who is angry about something. That definition captures the disputatious character of fundamentalism.

Some evangelicals, and most fundamentalists, stress individual salvation and attempt to separate themselves from a wicked world. But certain evangelicals, like Jim Wallis of *Sojourners,* think in terms of social sin and work to reform the world through charity, poverty relief, and social justice campaigns. All evangelicals, however, believe in the power of Jesus to transform the world and, in their own way, work to live out and communicate that message.

The American evangelical community, numbering roughly one hundred million people, represents a kind of "parallel culture" that, in its extreme forms, aims to establish its own beliefs as the only worthwhile ones.[11] Most recent analyses of evangelicalism have focused on the movement's political objectives, as if evangelicalism can be reduced to conservative politics and a quest for political power. Yet political diatribes against extreme conservatism tell us little about the intellectual climate of evangelicalism, reveal almost nothing about why the various positions are important, and offer no explanation as to why Christians listen to certain leaders while ignoring better-informed but equally evangelical alternatives. Political accounts cannot illuminate the reasons evangelicals might typically be found endorsing a certain position on, say, global warming or genetic testing that might not seem connected in any meaningful way to their faith.

High-profile leaders who attract great followings, and who are, in the vocabulary of their constituents (and themselves), "anointed" by God to speak for him to Christians, resemble the biblical prophets of old who spoke as God's official messengers. This anointing has two meanings for Christians: The literal meaning refers to a relatively common practice of placing a small quantity of oil on the forehead to symbolize a prayer request for God's intervention in a personal matter, such as an illness. A parishioner newly diagnosed with cancer, for example, might kneel at the front of his or her church and be anointed with oil by the pastor while fellow church members gather around in prayerful support. The figurative meaning of anointing refers to the process by which God sends his spirit in a special way to a person, empowering that person to speak and lead other Christians. Many evangelical leaders, like Oral Roberts, Jerry Falwell, and Billy Graham, believe the success of their ministries derives from a special anointing they received from God that empowered them to accomplish great things they could not have accomplished on their own. Anointing, though it brings great authority, is typically unrelated to intellectual credibility. A winsome preacher who can quote the Bible and tell heart-warming stories of God's blessings may possess more authority on global warming for believers than an informed climatologist with 100 publications and a doctorate from Harvard.

Evangelicalism tends to be antielitist, sometimes in ways that are admirable and authentically democratic. God, believers like to quote from the Bible, is no "respecter of persons." Jesus' disciples were humble fishermen who went on to do great things. Moses lacked confidence that he could be a leader. Baptist and Methodist preachers blazing trails on America's nineteenth-century frontier put this egalitarianism into practice, ridiculing overeducated ministers and their presumed "credentials." Humble evangelical preachers led a movement that emphasized conversion and charisma and had little time for the life of the mind. Eager to spread a simple gospel message as widely as possible, they embraced and often mastered new media—newspapers, magazines, radio, and then television—but continued to cast a suspicious eye on higher education and professional elites. One of the most famous preachers of late nineteenth- and early twentieth-century America railed to great applause, "We have been clamoring for fifty years for an educated ministry and we have got it to-day, and the church is deader than it ever has been in its history." Educated divines, hooted the colorful revivalist, were little more than the sum of their degrees: "A.B.'s, Ph.D.'s, D.D.'s, LL.D.'s, and A.S.S.'s."[12]

The culture wars that occupied the faithful in the twentieth century—prohibition campaigns, antievolution crusades, anticommunist movements, and the reaction to cultural liberation in the 1960s—made evangelicals even more suspicious of academic expertise. In the eyes of many of the faithful, psychologists seemed to counsel self-fulfillment at the expense of godliness. Biologists and physicists made little or no room for divine action in their materialist descriptions of nature. Historians, especially after the tumultuous upheaval of the 1960s, appeared to disdain the Founding Fathers, question the intentions of presidents, and cast doubt on the integrity of all dead white males. Millions of evangelicals began asking what had happened to their country. For numerous stalwarts, the decadence and secularism of the modern age pointed to satanic conspiracies and even to the coming of the Apocalypse. Conservative evangelicals looked to their leaders for wisdom in understanding how their world had spun out of control.

The conservative wing of American evangelicalism grows both larger and more autonomous even as the religious movement evolves in new directions. Perceived conservative excesses spawn moderate responses from within the larger arena of traditional and authentic evangelicalism. Increasing numbers of young Christian believers, for example, are more likely to engage causes of social justice than to embrace controversial moral issues. Christian college students across the country are raising their voices on behalf of the poor and disenfranchised, setting aside more stereotypical concerns like homosexuality and abortion that preoccupied their parents. The evangelical geneticist and head of the Human Genome Project Francis Collins launched the BioLogos Foundation to counter the antiscience message of the creationists and the intelligent design movement, both driven almost entirely by evangelicals. Nevertheless, these responses are quite modest and get submerged beneath the much larger projects to which they are reacting.[13]

Genuine intellectual engagement with controversial ideas or challenges to tradition is difficult within the parallel culture of evangelicalism. In the fall of 2010 two faculty members at Calvin College found their jobs threatened for publishing an inquiry about the historicity of

Adam and Eve.[14] There are barriers to such engagement—no matter how scholarly—in the world of Christian higher education. Most evangelical colleges require faculty to affirm or even sign faith statements, an act that many, including the American Association of College and University Professors and even Phi Beta Kappa, consider incompatible with academic freedom. They also have conservative donors, boards, and constituencies that become alarmed when faculty speak out against adherence to still popular but fully discredited ideas. Richard Colling lost his job teaching chemistry at Olivet Nazarene University because of his efforts to help the university's students make peace with evolution.[15]

Credentials that endow evangelicals with cachet in the secular academy often do not impress their rank-and-file brethren, many of whom are cut off from the larger intellectual world, intentionally or otherwise. Some even view secular credentials with suspicion, as the product of a liberal education considered to be corrosive to faith. Evangelicalism is a vast and robust parallel culture and one that often has little need for interaction with the secular world on the "outside." That insular character allows ideas to flourish long after the larger intellectual community and even the more educated wing of evangelicalism have abandoned them. This insularity gives rise to powerful tensions between evangelicals and those who move in mainstream intellectual circles.[16]

The intellectual isolation of evangelicals has led to their near universal rejection of evolution, to take the most dramatic example. Fewer than 10 percent of Americans *in toto* accept evolution in the purely naturalistic sense, insisting on no role for God in the process. But what is most remarkable is the *alternative* account of origins embraced by almost half the population of America, and almost all who call themselves evangelical. A 2005 Pew Research Center survey revealed that almost two-thirds of evangelicals believed that "humans and other living things have existed in their present form only."[17]

Known as young earth creationism or simply creationism, this unconventional "theory" entails the belief that Earth is less than 10,000 years old, a sharp contrast to the 4.5 billion years determined by the scientific community. Against mountains of evidence from geology, physics, biology, astronomy, and other sciences, creationists insist confidently that their estimate is correct, despite being unimaginably smaller than that of the scientific community. The current chief leader of this movement is Ken Ham, a protégé of Henry Morris, who started the movement a half-century ago, at a time when far fewer evangelicals rejected the scientifically determined age of Earth.

Ham heads a large, multimillion-dollar ministry known as Answers in Genesis (AIG). He interprets the Genesis Creation account completely literally, insisting that it provides a perfect explanation of the available scientific data on origins. The tall, stern, Australian-born Ham has the most limited of scientific credentials—an undergraduate degree in applied science from the Queensland Institute of Technology and a Diploma of Education from the University of Queensland. He has never published a scientific paper or presented at a recognized scientific conference. And yet Ham's message is warmly embraced by millions of evangelicals. His radio show *Answers in Genesis* broadcasts daily on over 1,000 stations worldwide. His website is overrun with traffic; his glossy color magazine *Answers* boasts almost 70,000 subscribers; and in June 2007 his 27-million-dollar Creation Museum opened in Petersburg, Kentucky, and received more than 250,000 visitors in its first six months of operation.

Ham does not speak for all Christians, of course, and his strongest critics include some of his fellow evangelicals. Detractors are understandably dismayed at his success in convincing people that Christianity must be at war with science. Respected and deeply religious scientists—like Francis S. Collins or Nobel laureate William Phillips—are certainly not at war with science and have tried to encourage evangelicals to put down their arms. Yet Collins and Phillips have nothing approaching Ham's popular influence, though Collins's public role in heading the National Institutes of Health (NIH) may change that. Neither Phillips nor Collins sits at the helm of a media empire or has enough clout with conservative groups to counter the simple and straightforward appeal of leaders invoking biblical authority for their positions, no matter how suspect.[18]

The antievolutionism of Ham and other creationist leaders receives the lion's share of media attention because the teaching of origins in America's taxpayer-supported high schools is so contentious. Most famously in the Scopes Monkey Trial, and most recently in the Dover Intelligent Design Trial, origins has been on America's front page almost since Darwin's controversial theory arrived on this continent. Creationist leaders making careers out of bashing evolution have long been fixtures in American culture and have even supplied Hollywood with stock, if caricatured, villains like Matthew Harrison Brady in *Inherit the Wind* (1960). But Christian pundits can also be found in other areas with comparable influence. The late amateur American historian Peter Marshall and the late Christian celebrity pastor D. James Kennedy joined David Barton in challenging mainstream history just as Ham has challenged science. They have convinced millions that America is a "Christian nation," using the same rhetorical strategies as the creationists. Kennedy, like most prominent evangelical preachers, was also a staunch creationist, using his powerful media empire, Coral Ridge Ministries, to fight evolution.

Just as Ham and the creationists reject contemporary science and offer in its place a faith-friendly alternative, so Barton and his fellow Christian revisionist historians reject much of conventional history in favor of a Christianized reading of America's beginnings. It matters little to their followers that no one in the American historical profession supports their claims about the Founding Fathers. Nevertheless, homeschooling parents and teachers in evangelical high schools, unaware of criticism or misrepresentations, have embraced the historical work of Barton and teach it to millions of young people. If these youths learn their lessons well, they will graduate believing that Buddhists, Hindus, Muslims, secularists, and even Roman Catholics are outside the mainstream of American culture and, in some sense, do not belong.[19]

Barton has convinced many that the doctrine of church/state separation is a lie foisted on the nation by an unscrupulous Supreme Court. He devotes much of his writing and many of his speaking engagements to the subject. Americans, he demands, need to see clearly that secular historians and liberal judges have reframed the country's past. But the subject is nuanced and not adequately treated with simple black-and-white formulas. Pennsylvania Senator Arlen Specter made this point while challenging Barton's abilities as a historian and a legal authority. "All of this pseudoscholarship would hardly be worth discussing, let alone disproving," says Specter, "were it not for the fact that it is taken so very seriously by so many people." Delegates at the Iowa State Republican Convention in 1994 booed Specter when he challenged Barton's views on the separation of church and state. "Led by the firebrands of the 'far right,'" worries Specter, "millions apparently believe that a conspiracy involving some combination of the left, modern U.S. Supreme Courts, the Jewish element in the ACLU, homosexuals, nonbelievers, enemies of God, atheistic secular humanists, the antifamily movement, non-Christian people and atheistic people, and infidels has been unleashed to rape the Constitution and rape the churches by misinterpreting the First Amendment."[20] Barton's millions of fans, however, do not see him as a "firebrand of the far right." They are drawn to him because he speaks their language, appeared often on Glenn Beck's once popular Fox News program, invokes their faith, and wants to help them take back "their" country from liberals and secularists.

Not surprisingly, many evangelicals are attracted to alternate visions of the social sciences—reconstructions that restore traditional interpretations of social problems. Christians have always viewed society through the lens of good versus evil. Followers of Christ, seeking his will and living godly lives, have, since the first century, understood that they share their world with those who reject Christ and act under the influence of Satan. Social problems in this context invite explanation in terms of sin and righteousness. Supernatural, often demonic, forces have been and still are invoked. Seventeenth-century Puritans blamed some of their problems on witchcraft and executed nineteen members of their community as a result. Nineteenth-century racists rationalized the plight of African Americans because, in their view, Noah's son Ham, the progenitor of the black race, had been cursed by God for seeing his father naked and not covering him. The late Henry Morris, America's greatest champion of creationism, said that evolution was a tool of Satan to destroy belief in God.[21] Similarly, some evangelicals consider AIDS to be God's punishment on the gay community for a sinful lifestyle.[22]

Evangelicals are strongly committed to the traditional nuclear family as the foundation of society. If heterosexual, born-again Christian parents raise their children properly according to biblical principles, they believe, social problems will retreat and even disappear. In their view the problems of society are spiritual, not social, economic, or cultural. The solution is to follow God's law as laid down in the Bible, not to create programs conceived in the minds of secular academics or policy makers. Many evangelicals thus reject the social and behavioral sciences and their solutions for problems they encounter in raising their children or living in community with people holding different values, preferring instead the ancient wisdom of biblical perspectives. James C. Dobson, founder of the vast Focus on the Family organization, offers just such an approach. Dobson, possibly the most influential psychologist in America, presided over a multimillion-dollar empire in Colorado Springs, where he and his staff counseled followers on the importance of avoiding sexual impropriety, encouraging Christian entertainment and hobbies, and learning self-discipline. In pursuit of their aims, Dobson promotes spanking children, overcoming and preventing homosexuality with prayer and discipline, and following biblical mandates about wives' submission to their husbands' authority.[23]

The American Medical Association, the American Psychiatric Association, and the American Association of Marriage and Family Therapy have long rejected many of Dobson's views. Social science research on child development, marriage, and human sexuality published in mainstream scholarly journals has explicitly undermined Dobson's claims about the importance of spanking, the nature of homosexuality, and gender roles, in particular. His approach to the family, rooted in a literal reading of the Bible, is dramatically out of step with the modern world. But Dobson's organization has an answer: "Gradually, science dethroned Scripture, first in epistemological matters (the nature of knowledge), and then in moral matters." Scripture, an absolute authority, must not be compromised by fallible science: "Reading the Bible at face value reveals its expectation that people need to adjust to it rather than allowing for it to adjust to new discoveries, desires and trends."[24]

Some psychologists at evangelical colleges across the country oppose Dobson's ideas. David Myers, author of several major textbooks used by millions of students at secular universities nationwide, challenges Dobson's claim that his views are essentially Christian. Myers has written broadly on the integration of traditional Christianity and contemporary psychology and speaks openly about his faith. By the lights of contemporary scholarship, he is far more qualified than Dobson. This, however, means little to Dobson's supporters, who prefer Dobson's homey biblical approach and confident assertions that God has a blueprint for society. Once again, the intellectual fault lines appear in the social sciences as in the natural sciences and history. Evangelicals seeking to reconcile their faith with the best of contemporary scholarship have a genuine alternative to simply rejecting secular knowledge in favor of homegrown in-house biblical alternatives. But

Dobson's message resonates so deeply with their values that they see no need to look elsewhere.[25]

The enduring appeal of leaders like Ham, popular historians D. James Kennedy and Peter Marshall, and others is enhanced by the way they stitch their personal worldviews into the fabric of biblical prophecy, in essence transforming themselves into actors in God's cosmic drama. In so doing they capitalize on the conviction of many evangelicals that they are living in the end-times. This apocalyptic paradigm leads enthusiasts to interpret contemporary events in the light of biblical prophecies. Stories on the front page, especially about Israel, nuclear weapons, the clash of Islam and Christianity, or the United Nations, become portents of Apocalypse, hinting at an impending great confrontation between the forces of good and evil foretold in the Bible. The back cover of Ham's classic antievolutionary text, *The Lie,* contains these words, referencing the book of 2 Peter in the New Testament: "The Bible prophetically warns that in the last days false teachers will introduce destructive lies among the people. Their purpose is to bring God's Truth into disrepute and to exploit believers by telling them made-up and imagined stories. Such a Lie is among us. That Lie is Evolution."[26]

Absolutely nothing in the referenced biblical passage suggests that the message of these "false teachers" is evolution, of course, but Ham's framing of prophecy in this way effectively endows him and his movement with a cosmic significance. He is fighting the greatest of battles against the most powerful and evil forces in the universe. In similar fashion, Barton speaks with alarmist language about the academy's secularization of American history. On his organization's website he warns of a "War on God in America." "God is no longer visible in American history," laments Barton, "and His absence is now construed as a mandate for secularism." In the face of secular militants undermining America's Christian identity, he cautions, evangelicals have become complacent and directionless. Dobson interprets setbacks at Focus on the Family in the context of the war between good and evil. Protesting a 1995 Beijing United Nations Conference on Women, Dobson identified the chief culprit in the secular organization. The event, according to Dobson, was "Satan's trump card if I have ever seen it."[27]

In the conservative evangelical and deeply biblical worldviews of revered figures like Marshall, Dobson, Barton, and Ham, tolerant liberal pluralism signals utter chaos, or worse, the end of the world, as prophesied in the Bible. They unite in opposing it, for its true source is Satan. Some anticipate that the Anti-Christ will emerge, perhaps soon, to lead a vast army of secular infidels against the faithful as history draws to a close. In the wake of 9/11 Barton drew critical lessons from current events: "In recent decades schools and public arenas have moved toward a completely inclusive pluralism, teaching that all of the 1700 different religions are equal and therefore deserve equal acceptance and respect." That was a tragic misconception, Barton observed. Non-Christian religions did not deserve the same respect as Christianity. Prominent Christian historian Peter Marshall went further, seeing in such cataclysm the end of history. "Many years ago I came to the conclusion that God's time clock for world history had reached the period the Bible calls the 'last days,' or 'the end of the age,'" he told visitors to his website. Since the rebellious 1960s, America had been on the road to Sodom: "the Watergate scandal, and the disgrace of an American president; the tragic withdrawal in defeat from South Vietnam; the explosion of homosexuality and the subsequent AIDS epidemic . . . the pornography plague; the rise of gambling addiction," all pointed to the approaching Apocalypse.[28]

End-times prophecy is mesmerizing and has always had its devotees. Jesus' followers in the New Testament thought the Apocalypse was imminent. Luther thought the pope was the Anti-Christ. Within the last century Hitler, Mussolini, and even Henry Kissinger have been identified as the Anti-Christ. Some end-times stalwarts at the moment speculate that Barack Obama may even be the Anti-Christ.[29]

The most remarkable teacher of end-time prophecy is the best-selling author Tim LaHaye, who has been an authority for evangelicals for half a century. LaHaye is a powerful contemporary prophet, perhaps the most overtly fundamentalist character in the evangelical pantheon. Books in his *Left Behind* series have sold an astonishing sixty million copies, their popularity deriving from the widespread belief that cataclysmic scenarios unfolding on the world scene today are actually predicted in the Bible. Using the same creative, speculative, and popular literalistic approach as Ham, Barton, and Dobson, LaHaye reads current events into the book of Revelation and other difficult portions of scripture. The end product is a dramatic and exciting popular theology with apocalyptic glosses on everything from the emergence of Israel and the fall of communism to the acceptance of evolution and the AIDS outbreak. LaHaye fervently believes he is simply interpreting the Bible with integrity, as led by the spirit of God. Asked why the majority of biblical studies scholars challenge his views, LaHaye retorts, "These are usually liberal theologians that don't believe the Bible literally."[30]

LaHaye and other like-minded authorities stake much on America's connection to Israel, a relationship that looms large for those awaiting the return of Jesus. The link with Israel creates an end-times role for the United States, which even the most creative enthusiasts have trouble finding in the Bible. LaHaye's wildly popular approach has, not surprisingly, met with strong criticism from scholars of every theological stripe. The respected New Testament scholar and leading evangelical N. T. Wright, the former bishop of Durham in the United Kingdom, has puzzled over the success of the *Left Behind* novels and their theology: "Few in the U.K. hold . . . that there will be a literal 'rapture' in which believers will be snatched up to heaven, leaving empty cars crashing on freeways and kids coming home from school only to find that their parents have been taken to be with Jesus while they have been 'left behind.'" It struck Wright as a "pseudo-theological version of

Home Alone" that frightened young people into a distorted faith. It was not the product of careful biblical scholarship.[31]

Such opposition has done little, though, to dissuade the swelling ranks of LaHaye's followers, who, like generations of Christians before them, believe they are living in the end-times and that the events unfolding around them are plotted out in the Bible. Such a view is exciting, like being transported directly into the plot of a great Hollywood disaster movie, but with the confidence that you are on the winning side.

The apocalyptic paradigm unites and synergizes the programs of Marshall, Ham, and LaHaye. If the world is best understood in terms of spiritual warfare, and a cosmic confrontation looms on the horizon, then the secularization of schools, the de-Christianization of American history, the promotion of evolution, and the emergence of nontraditional versions of the family are all part of the same Satanic plan to destroy faith in God. According to this worldview, a great secular army will be conscripted for the battle of the end-times, led by charismatic leaders who have alerted their faithful followers to what is transpiring.

The anointed warn of impending battles and teach constituents how to spot false prophets and maniacal academics. The anointed are, in fact, linked in various ways, both professionally and personally; they see each other as allies in the same battle. Barton's WallBuilders' website contains a link to Ham's Answers in Genesis. LaHaye founded Christian Heritage College where the Institute for Creation Research was located when Ham worked there. Dobson enthusiastically promotes Barton's Christian history and Ham's young earth creationism. Gatherings of prominent evangelical leaders, like the popular "Worldview Weekends," will often feature two or more of these individuals on the program together. Their overlapping agendas are facets of the same conservative evangelical approach to America's problems at the dawn of a new millennium—an approach that remains enormously popular, even as it is challenged by both a grassroots movement with different priorities and an internal scholarly critique claiming that it is, quite simply, wrong.

Despite such challenges, however, the parallel culture of American evangelicalism provides a rich soil in which anointed leaders can grow. The present authorities will certainly be replaced by different popular leaders who will rise to power on the same winds that lofted their predecessors. The agenda may remain the same, as it did when Ken Ham succeeded Henry Morris as America's leading creationist. Or it may change, as new issues draw the attention of a younger generation. Regardless of the context, however, leaders speaking directly to and for God will continue to have an authority far beyond that obtained by those who have earned doctorates, won Nobel Prizes, become tenured at Ivy League universities, or otherwise acquired professional and secular acclaim. We need to look more closely at how evangelical experts emerged to discover just why this is the case.

1 The Answer Man

Highway 20 runs across northern Kentucky and ends in the small river town of Petersburg in Boone County, named for Kentucky's legendary hero Daniel Boone. The highway cuts through rock formations revealing countless layers of limestone alternating with shale; the stacked patterns are often visible from a car window. The rocks are part of a famous formation called the "Cincinnatian" that contains some of the richest fossil beds in the world.

Cincinnatian fossils date from a half-billion-year-old geological epoch called the Ordovician, named for the Welsh tribe known as the Ordovices. Major extinctions bracketed the period, which is not unusual; nor are the generations of steadily evolving animals preserved in the layers of limestone and shale. The sequence of their fossilized skeletons shows evolution at work, as natural selection pruned the varying offspring of each generation and rewarded the fittest with enhanced reproduction.

Ordinary-looking rocks unearthed in the construction of local roads and buildings provide evidence for this ancient story. Sharp-eyed amateurs can pick up a rock at the edge of the road and see fossils of trilobites, shellfish, and other ancient and extinct life forms. Successive layers of rock tell the tale of life in the Ordovician era: one species giving way to another—shells growing ever thicker, teeth getting larger, claws getting sharper. Transitional fossils connect newer species to their ancestors; extinctions note the loss of species, gone forever from Earth. Tens of millions of years of geological history lie exposed in these layers—chapters in the almost four-billion-year story of life on this planet.

Motorists traveling down Highway 20, however, have little interest in the story told by the rocks outside their car windows. Their attention is focused on the road ahead, as it should be. But a surprising number of these motorists are en route to Boone County's premier tourist destination, a "Creation Museum" that proclaims a completely different message from that contained in the rocks along the highway.

The Creation Museum opened in the spring of 2007 and now sees thousands of visitors a month streaming through its turnstiles, happily paying the nearly twenty-five-dollar entrance fee (fifteen dollars for children) to experience their preferred version of natural history, one that affirms their faith and is "based on the Bible," but that contrasts dramatically with the version scientists read from the rocks along Highway 20. "The Creation Museum," announces the souvenir booklet handed to visitors, "places Biblical history within the context of the greater issue: Why should we trust the Bible?" Introducing a theme reiterated throughout the museum, and deeply appreciated by the target audience, the booklet asserts, "Our conclusions about the world are affected by the decision to trust either the words of the eternal, perfect God or the words of temporal, fallible men."[1]

Passing under the watchful eyes of metallic stegosauruses atop the entrance gate, a tyrannosaur amid the trees, and sauropods lining the lobby, visitors have no idea they are entering anything other than a typical garden-variety museum of natural history. This museum, however, is based on the young earth creationism model of natural history, which teaches that God created everything in six days, less than 10,000 years ago, and that Adam and Eve and their descendents were contemporary with every biological family of animals that ever lived ("family" is the creationist equivalent of the biblical "kind"). Inside the museum, visitors view children playing by a waterfall, with dinosaurs nearby, filling out the carefully constructed diorama suggesting a scientifically informed re-creation of their actual habitat.

The depicted scene represents Earth, just thousands of years ago, shortly after Adam and Eve sinned and were expelled from the Garden of Eden, as described in Genesis, the first book in the Bible. Earth is declining rapidly, having been cursed by God for Adam's sin, which brought "death and corruption into the creation."[2] The curse affects all of creation: Gentle herbivores are turning into monstrous carnivores, barbs and thorns are sprouting on plants, nature is becoming red in tooth and claw. And all living things, including humans, are being sentenced to die eventually, because of Adam's sin, which "explains the catastrophes, disease, suffering, and death in the present world."[3]

"The Creation Museum," wrote one enthusiastic reviewer, "shows that the problems in our culture aren't the disease—they are merely symptoms of a much more serious cultural infection . . . Mankind broke God's law, cursing all of creation and staining the human race with sin forever. The museum shows the vast array of evil that has blossomed as a result of that single act of rebellion thousands of years ago."[4]

Henry Morris (1918–2006) was the intellectual godfather of the worldview on display in the Creation Museum, with significant inspiration from his mentor George McCready Price. A prolific fundamentalist engineer, Morris wrote more about the scientific implications of the Genesis story of Adam and Eve's fall from grace than anyone else. Morris describes it like this: "Because Adam had the sentence of death imposed as an actual operational feature of his biological life, his descendents also have inherited a life principle which involved a built-in death principle. The moment a child is conceived he begins to die."[5] The Genesis narrative reports that human sin steadily increased, helped along by mysterious giants and supernatural creatures. Genesis 6:4 tells us, "There were giants in the earth in those days; and also after that, when the sons of God came in unto the daughters of men, and they bear children to them, the same became the mighty men of old." Morris argued that the Hebrew word translated as *giants* here suggests the presence of demons that spread until almost the entire human race was corrupted and God could stand it no longer: "Hordes of the monstrous offspring of these unlawful unions" spread across the planet until the recently created world became "intolerable even to a God of compassion and long-suffering."[6]

So God destroyed Earth in a great flood that, we learn in the museum, occurred around 2348 B.C. Noah, as the familiar story goes, built an ark that saved his family and two of every "kind." "This global catastrophe," museum visitors are told, "resulted in fossils all over the earth." Virtually all the fossils on the planet, including those in the rocks along Highway 20, were created in the violent hydrodynamic cataclysm of Noah's Flood.[7] Life-sized dioramas in the museum show paleontologists digging up fossils created by the Flood. Videos based on the 1980 eruption of Mount St. Helens show how receding floodwaters carved out the entire Grand Canyon in a few weeks after the deluge. Fossil-rich layers visible along the highway outside would have been the work of a few days, and certainly not the half-billion years asserted so confidently by geologists at the universities in nearby Cincinnati. Andrew Snelling, Ph.D., a geologist affiliated with the museum, sees all this as evidence for the Flood: "The countless billions and billions of fossils in these graveyards, in many cases exquisitely preserved, testify to the rapid burial of once-living plants and animals on a global scale in a watery cataclysm and its immediate aftermath."[8]

The museum is fascinating and persuasive to its target audience of American evangelicals, with their deeply rooted instinct that the Bible is the most important source of truth. But the museum does not tell the *scientific* story of natural history, despite the dinosaurs that greet visitors outside, the authoritative ambience of the displays, and the impressions made on its many patrons; in fact, it disputes, albeit elegantly, almost everything science has learned about natural history in the past two centuries. The alternative story—based on the Bible instead of a suspect and over-reaching "reason"—is told in more than 160 remarkable exhibits in the museum, sprawling over an acre and a half. Patrick Marsh, who designed the Jaws and King Kong attractions at Universal Studios in Florida, created the exhibits. Marsh, like everyone working at the museum, accepts the story that unfolds in its exhibits. "The Creation Museum," he says, "will tell the history of the Earth from the perspective of the Bible. Our perspective is that the Bible is true and we will show that God created the Earth in six literal days, and that man and dinosaurs roamed the Earth together."[9]

The museum presents much more than just natural history, which is treated almost as an incidental backdrop to the larger religious narrative being unfolded. Everything is here, divided into a sequence of epochal events called the "Seven C's": creation, corruption, catastrophe, confusion, Christ, cross, and consummation. A visitor's journey starts with a presentation about God *creating* a world that is soon *corrupted* by sin—visible in the "Cave of Sorrows." God finds this intolerable and responds with the *catastrophe* of the Flood. After the Flood, humans begin work on an ambitious tower to reach into the heavens, which, in their cosmology, are not all that far away. They seek to be exalted like God. This building project—the Tower of Babel—upsets God again, so he *confuses* human language. The monolingual human race splinters into languages and cultures and spreads around the globe, in a diaspora some four thousand years ago. Two thousand years later *Christ* appears, dying on the *cross* to save the human race, and departs with a promise to return at the end of time to *consummate* human history and take the faithful to heaven.

Museum tours end at the Last Adam Theater, where visitors learn of Jesus' sacrifice and receive a call to repent of their sins. An adjacent chapel is staffed with volunteers eager to pray with those wanting to be saved. The message of salvation in Christ, says Ken Ham, who made it all possible, is the "ultimate motivation for the Creation Museum." He reprinted a letter from a woman rejoicing that a young man, after visiting the museum, not only "accepted Christ as his Savior" but also "broke up with his agnostic girlfriend."[10] This repentance is the true reason for the museum, where displays of dinosaurs and paleontologists at work sit alongside dioramas of Moses and Paul, the two formative intellects of the Judeo-Christian tradition. Martin Luther even makes a cameo, calling Christians back to the Bible, away from an errant and insufficiently biblical Catholicism.

Ham's message has been a consistent one. On the last page of his book *The Lie: Evolution,* published in 1987, he acknowledges that he is waging a battle on behalf of Creation and asks, rhetorically, "Why?" He answers: "because we know that those who do not trust the Lord will spend eternity separated from Him."[11] Two decades later, in his "letter to museum guests," he writes: "We hope you'll return often to hear the redemption story, and gain a deeper understanding of the Savior who loves you and gave himself for you."[12]

At the ceremony opening the museum, Ham spoke of repairing the damage done to Christianity eighty-two years ago when Clarence Darrow humiliated William Jennings Bryan at the Scopes Trial. "It was the first time the Bible was ridiculed by the media in America, and that was a downward turning point for Christendom," he told the enthusiastic crowd. "We are going to undo all of that here at the Creation Museum. We are going to answer the questions Bryan wasn't prepared to, and show that belief in every word of the Bible can be defended by modern science."[13]

In the celebrated confrontation at Dayton, immortalized (and caricatured) in *Inherit the Wind,* the agnostic Darrow challenged Bryan on issues of biblical interpretation. Bryan, whose knowledge of the Bible was considerable though not scholarly, was put off guard on the stand, just as the wily Darrow had intended. Darrow lobbed countless challenges to a simple reading of the Bible at Bryan, who struggled to find adequate answers to questions the Bible did not address. In response to the challenge of reconciling the story of Creation in six days with the findings of modern geology, Bryan suggested that the days of Genesis were not literal days but long periods of time—geological epochs. But all this was secondary and irrelevant to the Great Commoner, who was far more interested in ensuring that biblical truth was not trumped by science. In a phrase that worked well on the lecture circuit, Bryan put geology in its place by saying, "It is better to trust in the Rock of Ages, than to know the age of the rocks."[14]

What little Bryan knew about connecting Genesis to geology he had learned from the writings of an eccentric and largely self-taught Seventh-day Adventist from the backwoods of eastern Canada, George McCready Price (1870–1963). Price's book *The New Geology,* published in 1923, defended a six-day Creation, relying on Noah's Flood to produce the fossil layers in a remarkable act of rapid and catastrophic sedimentation. Geologists inferring from the fossil layers that Earth is billions of years old got it completely wrong. *The New Geology* articulated ideas that would, decades later, come to be known as scientific creationism, continuing into the present only slightly modified. Ham's museum mirrors the geology Price worked out a century ago. The geological layers that reveal the sequence of past epochs—the so-called geological column at the heart of the modern science of geology—are, quite simply, a fantasy, according to Price, Morris, and now Ham.

Price's "new geology" assaulted the "old geology" for being so filled with inexplicable anomalies that it could not be trusted. Lining up fossils in order of their stacking in rock layers was a fool's errand, and there was simply no evidence for the geological sequences presented in the textbooks of the day: This alleged historical order of the fossils is clearly a scientific blunder, for unequivocal evidence proves that this supposedly historical order must be a mistake. There is no possible way to prove that the Cretaceous dinosaurs were not contemporary with the late Tertiary mammals; no evidence whatever that the trilobites were not living in one part of the ocean at the very same time that the ammonites and the nummulites were living in other parts of the ocean; and no proof whatever that all these marine forms were not also contemporary with the dinosaurs and the mammals.[15]

Scientifically uninformed readers like Bryan loved Price's arguments against the theory of evolution, although they often did not buy his reworking of geological history as the result of the Great Flood of Noah. The scientific community, not surprisingly, occasionally heaped ridicule on Price, but mostly it ignored him. But this community was coming to be viewed with suspicion anyway.[16] In opposition to Price, most evangelicals, including Bryan, accepted the great antiquity of Earth and were content to believe that the days of Genesis were geological epochs, or could be dealt with some other way. And many were satisfied that the Great Flood of Noah was a local affair, not Price's global catastrophe, and certainly not the source of all the geological features on Earth. Price's relevance largely stemmed from his authority to refute evolution—he had written a book, after all—but, despite evolution's having supposedly "won" in some cultural sense at the Scopes Trial, populist sentiment opposed Darwin's theory after the trial, just as it had before. As a result, coverage of evolution continued to recede from high school textbooks, as nervous publishers pandered to scientifically uninformed school boards, a quasi-intellectual skirmish that continues unabated into the present.[17]

Evolution's prospects in the public schools improved in the late 1950s. Worried that the Soviet Union had beaten them into space with the 1957 launch of *Sputnik,* American educators scrutinized science education, and curricular reform began in earnest. The updated biology texts that appeared in the early 1960s reflected the central role that evolution was now playing in the field of biology.[18] Awareness of evolution had steadily increased, generating widespread negative reactions from fundamentalists who were looking for a new antievolutionary messiah to succeed William Jennings Bryan. That messiah appeared in 1961 with a book that would come to define creationism in America, and eventually make it possible for an organization to raise twenty-seven million dollars to build a creation museum.

The book was *The Genesis Flood: The Biblical Record and Its Scientific Implications.* It greatly influenced evangelicals, perhaps as much as any text on any topic in the second half of the twentieth century. When we consider how many court cases were inspired by its vision, how many Christian schools were created to teach its curriculum, how many books recasting its central ideas were written, it is hard to imagine another book with anywhere near its cultural impact. Coauthored by Old Testament scholar John Whitcomb and hydraulics engineer Henry Morris, it and its literary offspring have defined antievolution in America since its publication.[19]

The Genesis Flood authoritatively defends a literal reading of the biblical accounts of the Creation, Fall, and Flood. Whitcomb, the biblical half of the creationist duo, worried that Christians had gone too far in accommodating the biblical text to contemporary science, mistakenly ignoring the work of George McCready Price. Convinced that the Bible should be given more authority than science, he believed that better science was needed—science in harmony with scripture.

Enter Morris. Like Whitcomb he was a biblical literalist and young earth creationist. But his credentials were in hydraulics and he understood enough about the power of water and floods to defend Price's *New Geology,* although he knew it had not been an effective book. Morris was certain that, if biblical scholars had not caved in to secular science, then Christian geologists would have developed alternative scientific models that harmonized with the Bible, rather than embracing alternative interpretations that were compatible with science. After all, God had provided a "head start" for science: "The creation chapters of Genesis are marvelous and accurate accounts of the actual events of the primeval history of the universe. They give data and information far beyond those that science can determine." Morris was dismayed by the widespread belief that the biblical Flood inundated only Noah's local area and little else, when the biblical record was so clear on this point. Why, asked Morris, would Noah build an ark when he, his family, and the local animals could have gone on safari and returned when the Flood was over?[20]

Unlike the self-taught Price, Morris was an academic, with a Ph.D. in hydraulic engineering from the University of Minnesota and a faculty appointment at Virginia Tech. He had publications in peer-reviewed scientific journals. Morris understood floods in the real world, and Whitcomb understood them in ancient Near Eastern literature, like the book of Genesis. The argument born of their collaboration proved formidable, a whole greater than the sum of its parts. Millions of conservative Christians holding other positions on origins migrated to this articulate young earth creationism, which became something of an "orthodoxy" for mainstream evangelicals.[21]

The Genesis Flood contained two arguments woven together, a logical double helix. The first was Price's flood geology, energized, updated, documented, and decoupled from its suspicious Seventh-day Adventist heritage. The second was an assault on a "compromised" biblical interpretation, calling the faithful to a stance on scripture known as "plenary verbal" inspiration, and a hermeneutic of "plain reading." By these lights, the original manuscripts of the Bible were flawless, inerrant communications from God. The biblical writers were basically careful scribes who wrote down the precise words given to them by God, with no possibility of human error.

The Genesis Flood elaborates a far-reaching challenge to the standard scientific picture of Earth history, seeking "to orient the data" of the relevant sciences—anthropology, geology, hydrology—"within this Biblical framework."[22] Described in exhaustive detail in Whitcomb and Morris's text and summarized in countless subsequent, more accessible works, the model is charming in its simplicity, convincing in its argument, and encouraging in its confident message that the Bible need not be undermined by science.

God created everything in six twenty-four-hour days using supernatural processes no longer operating, effectively making the study of origins an exclusively *theological* exercise, outside the purview of science. The world before Noah's Flood, even after the Fall, was a global greenhouse with a delightful climate maintained everywhere by a thick layer of water vapor above the sky. Like the venerable Methuselah, people lived for centuries (as the first chapters of Genesis record), and animals grew to grand sizes in the paradisiacal climate, shielded by the vapor canopy from harmful ultraviolet rays. Noah's Flood was precipitated by the collapse of this vast canopy, supplemented by additional waters from the "great deep." According to this model, "colliding plates produced new mountains in a time period of days, and rapidly moving Flood waters then eroded them in weeks."[23] The fossil record contains the story of the global destruction of life during the Flood.[24]

The argument in *The Genesis Flood* is comforting to evangelicals raised to view the Bible as authoritative and inclined to interpret it literally. If the Bible contains God's actual words—as opposed to human reflections on religious experiences—then one should read it as literally as possible and not put one's own "creative" interpretation on it. In the introduction to *The Genesis Flood,* the authors write: "We desire to ascertain exactly what the Scriptures say. . . . We do this from the perspective of full belief in the complete divine inspiration of perspicuity of Scripture, believing that a true exegesis thereof yields determinative Truth in all matters with which it deals."[25]

The Genesis Flood criticized Christians who used the conclusions of science to modify their interpretations of the Bible, such as the nineteenth-century geologist Charles Lyell, who strongly influenced Darwin, or the eighteenth-century natural historian Georges Louis de Buffon, who turned the "days" of Genesis into epochs to accommodate the great age of Earth. Such manipulations of the conventional understanding, wrote Whitcomb and Morris, turned geology into "a pseudoscience composed of a patchwork of circular reasoning, Procrustean interpretations, pure speculation and dogmatic authoritarianism."[26] The duo turned the science-trumps-scripture approach around, starting with the most "natural" interpretation of the Bible and making science fit that interpretation. Science that did not fit would be rejected and sent out for repair.

The Genesis Flood convinced many readers, who found themselves drawn to its articulate argument, presented by credentialed scholars, that the Bible and science were in perfect accord. The suggestion that Bible-believing scientists could develop a "creation model" that would successfully challenge the "evolution model" was inspirational to evangelicals nervous that science was attacking their worldview. Creation "research" centers emerged, tapping into an important undercurrent in the evangelical psyche. A robust market for the new argument began to grow. Was it really possible that the science that had been undermining the Bible for over a century was doing an about-face?

Many of the new "research" centers were of dubious credibility and were run by uncredentialed amateurs like Carl Baugh, who claims to have multiple doctorates and is listed by the Trinity Broadcasting Network as the "foremost doctor on creation science."[27] Baugh hosts the show *Creation in the 21st Century*.[28] His degrees are from unaccredited institutions, one of which lists him as the president.[29] His claims include the odd proposition that, before Noah's Flood, "radio stars would have sung to man each morning."[30] In a unique reading of the Genesis account of the "firmament" (Hebrew *raqia*), Baugh suggests that "thin metal sheets" made of compressed hydrogen originally surrounded Earth, creating a planetwide tropical climate.[31]

Another popular creationist, Kent "Dr. Dino" Hovind, presides over a significant creation ministry in Florida, including a dinosaur theme park, from a jail cell in Edgefield, South Carolina.[32] Hovind, whose son

Eric heads the ministry now, is serving a ten-year sentence for tax evasion and related crimes.[33] Dr. Dino, before being incarcerated, was an enthusiastic speaker and debater, claiming 700 appearances a year. He carried a check for $250,000 that he said he would give to anyone who could provide any evidence for evolution. Like Baugh, Hovind has bogus educational credentials, including a doctorate from Patriot University, where he wrote a dissertation riddled with misspelled words. In it he claimed that the snake in the Garden of Eden taught Adam and Eve about evolution and that St. Augustine was a theistic evolutionist.[34]

Baugh and Hovind are typical of the fundamentalists who put "Dr." in front of their names, pretend to have training that informs their crusades, and grow large ministries. In dramatic contrast, some serious creationist organizations do actual scientific research. The most sophisticated is the Geoscience Research Institute at the Seventh-day Adventist Loma Linda University in Loma Linda, California. A few miles away the more theologically conventional Institute for Creation Research (ICR) aspired to be a significant research center. ICR was launched at Christian Heritage College in San Diego, which had been started by Morris and Tim LaHaye, who went on to great fame as the best-selling coauthor of the wildly popular end-of-the-world *Left Behind* novels.

ICR, which moved to Dallas, Texas, in 2008, did its best to hire credentialed science instructors in the relevant areas and developed a master's degree program that the state of California refused to license in 1988. ICR sued in federal district court and won—not on the merits of its academic program but on due process grounds. One of California's criticisms was that ICR's program did not measure up to those of accredited institutions, and it was not accredited by the Western Association of Colleges and Schools, or WASC.[35] ICR ingeniously resolved this public relations problem by helping to launch an alternative accrediting agency, the Transnational Association of Christian Colleges and Schools (TRACS), which, not surprisingly, found ICR's program entirely worthy of accreditation. ICR energetically promoted creationism with a monthly newsletter, a publisher that spun out books and video materials, a program of workshops, lectures, and debates, college courses, and even some actual research on a creation model that could accommodate the data as well as the evolution model could. The latter project was an utter failure. After four decades of effort, ICR scientists have discovered nothing of scientific value, and the creation model is little changed from that put forth in *The Genesis Flood,* which was basically what Price had outlined before the Scopes Trial.

Morris's original vision was bold, sincere, and ambitious. Convinced that the Bible provided an outline for a young-earth, worldwide-flood model of origins, he optimistically worked to raise up a generation of fundamentalist scientists who would topple evolution from its scientific pinnacle. It was not to be. The creation science model seemed stalled from the beginning, as if tethered to the starting gate. No publications ever made it into established scientific journals, and the creationists had to start their own journals to explore their ideas and create the impression that they were doing science.[36] Even the well-intentioned peer-review processes they employed did not work well, since in many fields there were simply no experts to serve as peers. The best-credentialed creationist, Kurt Wise, a Harvard Ph.D. in paleontology, earned praise from Richard Dawkins for being an "honest creationist" when he exposed the shoddy work published in the leading creationist journal *Creation Ex Nihilo.*[37] One of the more thoughtful young earth creationists, Paul Nelson, has admitted that the evidence against his position is "overwhelming" and that "most recent [young earth] creationists are motivated by religious concerns."[38] Defeats in the courts also compromised the creationist cause.[39] In the most devastating setback, at Little Rock, Arkansas, in 1982, the courts determined scientific creationism to be a set of religious ideas masquerading as science and, as such, inappropriate for teaching in public schools.[40]

In marked contrast to its failures on the scientific front, creationism succeeded outside the academy, especially at the grassroots level, with polls indicating that half of all Americans accepted the young earth model of origins. And almost all Americans agreed that creationist ideas deserved a hearing in the public schools.[41] Creationist books poured off evangelical presses, recycling arguments and speculations from *The Genesis Flood* as if they had been confirmed rather than refuted in the intervening years. Leading evangelicals like Charles Colson, Rick Warren, Al Mohler, and D. James Kennedy went on the record against evolution. Even President George W. Bush lent his support, remarking that he "wouldn't be a bit surprised if the Biblical account of creation and the scientific evidence of the origins of the universe will yet find common ground."[42]

The popularity of creationism did not derive from its scientific arguments. If anything, it succeeded *despite* its weak science. Moreover, while creationism was certainly attractive in the way it embraced and buttressed biblical literalism, its success cannot be located there, or it would have flourished in the early twentieth century, when the fundamentalist movement was getting under way. Creationism's popular appeal derived largely from a powerful *social* argument, namely, that America's worrisome slide into immorality, liberalism, and unbelief was caused by the widespread acceptance of evolution and its pernicious influence in areas like education, law, sexual mores, politics, and so on.

This threefold character of creationism was articulated in 1996 when ICR's publishing arm brought out *The Modern Creation Trilogy.* Coauthored by Henry Morris and his son John, who was being groomed to succeed his father at ICR, the volumes were titled *Scripture and Creation, Science and Creation,* and *Society and Creation.* Volume 3 is the only one that opens with a Bible verse: "Be not deceived; evil communications corrupt good manners." The evil communication, of course, is evolution: "The evolutionary deception and its evil influences have, indeed, corrupted every area of human life on this planet, and this fact in itself should be enough to demonstrate its ultimate satanic source."[43] In a similar vein, Ken Ham illustrated the opening of chapter 8 of his book *The Lie: Evolution* with a drawing of bricks labeled "Abortion," "Pornography," "Homosexuals," and "Lawlessness," all resting on a foundation labeled "Evolution." The chapter was titled, simply, "The Evils of Evolution."[44] In *Darwin's Plantation,* Ham argues that "racism has been fertilized by the theory of evolution."[45]

This message was seductive. For a century, evangelicals had watched a society they once thought of as their own "slouching toward Gomorrah," as conservative jurist Robert Bork titled one of his books.[46] Prayer and Bible reading had disappeared from the public schools, replaced by drugs, sex education, and demands for the tolerance of homosexuality. Standards of dress, obscene language in public, teenage pregnancy, and promiscuity ominously pointed to a culture in decline. Even nativity scenes and traditional Christmas greetings were under attack. "Concerned citizens" were sounding alarms, wrote Morris, but to no avail, since they had "compromised with the evolutionary concepts that are behind it all."[47]

Of the three messages about evolution in the trilogy—it's false, it's unbiblical, it's responsible for much of what's wrong with the world—the third one gained the most traction. Proving evolution false was not going well, and for those who kept up with the project, the efforts were discouraging.[48] Plus, scientific research is expensive and demands expertise that was in short supply within the creationist community. Biblical scholarship could also be disappointing as well-credentialed scholars, even those with so-called high views of scripture who published with evangelical presses, challenged the creationists' claims that their literal reading of the biblical texts was the most faithful.[49] But the claim that evolution was a source of great evil, or, as Morris titled his influential book, *The Long War Against God,* played well and was easy to communicate.

This state of affairs created a strategic challenge for the antievolution movement. What was the best way to fight evolution? Should resources be allocated to scientific research projects that, if successful, would create arguments that the secular academy would take seriously? Could evolution be refuted on its own scientific ground and its influence removed in this way, just as Marxism had been undermined by its many failures in the twentieth century, or nineteenth-century racism undermined by developments in genetics? Or should antievolutionary arguments be addressed to evangelicals attracted to the claim that evolution caused America's social decay? Arguments of this last sort were easier to produce than their scientific counterparts. Conservatives fretting about the growing acceptance of homosexuality, divorce, or promiscuity, for example, were a ready audience for enthusiastic, simplistic proclamations that evolution was responsible. In contrast, explanations for how changes in the ozone layer at the time of Noah's Flood might have affected nuclear decay rates and thus undermined radioactive dating methods would have many people's eyes glazing over.

ICR struggled with this challenge. Its mission, clearly stated on its website, emphasized the scientific aspects of the antievolutionary agenda: "ICR equips believers with evidence of the Bible's accuracy and authority through scientific research, educational programs, and media presentations, all conducted within a thoroughly biblical framework." The "evolution is evil" message, while appealing, was secondary.

The ICR's different strategies for fighting evolution led to the departure in 1994 of Ken Ham, one of the organization's most popular speakers. Ham left to start his own creation ministry, aimed at popular audiences and driven by fidelity to a simple, literal reading of the Bible, rather than by the development of scientific models that could accommodate a young earth. Ham focused on the importance of Creation for Christian laypeople who considered the Bible to be an ultimate and inerrant authority on whatever topics it addressed. Ham's departure ultimately led to a reorientation of creationism, away from a scientific emphasis that at least paid lip service to the importance of research, and toward the populist promotion of creationism in the absence of a scientific model. The mission statement of the ministry he founded, Answers in Genesis, emphasizes "providing answers to questions surrounding the book of Genesis . . . We also desire to train others to develop a biblical worldview, and seek to expose the bankruptcy of evolutionary ideas."[50] The bankruptcy of evolution was simply assumed, even in the absence of a creation model to explain the scientific observations.

With the death of Morris in 2006, leadership of ICR passed to his son John, who proved unable to fill his father's shoes. The grand vision of ICR as an accredited graduate school doing creation research and sending educated creation scientists out into the scientific community was never realized by either father or son, although the institute remained active. Henry Morris III wrested control from his brother John in 2007 and moved ICR to Texas. He made himself its CEO. John retained the title "president" but stayed behind in California.

Texas should have been more receptive to ICR than California had been, but the promising move only brought further problems. The questionable creationist TRACS accrediting agency was not recognized by Texas, and so ICR applied to the Southern Association of Colleges and Schools to accredit its master's programs. The application was turned down, a decision ICR appealed, only to be rejected a second time. In the response, the state of Texas invoked its legal obligation to "prevent deception of the public resulting from the conferring and use of fraudulent or substandard college and university degrees."[51]

Concurrently with ICR's Texas troubles, Ken Ham's ministry, Answers in Genesis, flourished. Its charismatic founder and leader became an international figure, heading a creation ministry with an annual budget in the tens of millions of dollars, a glossy magazine with a circulation of 70,000, a popular website, and a 27-million-dollar museum in Boone County, Kentucky, containing displays of children playing with dinosaurs.

Ham was born in Queensland, Australia, in 1951, into a deeply religious fundamentalist family that, in his words, "brought me up to love the Lord, His Word, and uphold the authority of the Word and defend the Christian faith."[52] The family was actively involved in starting Sunday schools and other outreach ministries in Queensland.

Ham's formal education consists of a bachelor's degree in applied science from the Queensland Institute of Technology and a Diploma of Education from the University of Queensland. The latter secured him a job teaching high school biology, which he did for five years starting in 1974. Queensland was considered by many at that time to be "corrupt and socially backward."[53] Science education, in particular, was in such disarray that *both* evolution and creationism were required topics in the public schools.[54] Ham was fine with this situation and happily morphed into an antievolutionary evangelist on the weekends, honing his skills as a public speaker in area churches. The entrepreneurial and mission-minded Ham noted that materials did not exist for the effective teaching of young earth creationism in the public schools. To fill that gap, he and fellow schoolteacher John Mackay started Creation Science Educational Media Services and made money selling such materials to state-funded schools.

Elsewhere in Australia, Dr. Carl Wieland had begun the Creation Science Association (CSA), with its first chapter in Adelaide, South Australia, in 1977. Wieland, a medical doctor, had been inspired, like Ham, by Whitcomb and Morris's book *The Genesis Flood.* In 1980 Ham and Mackay merged their organization with Wieland's and became the Creation Science Foundation (CSF), which would eventually evolve into Answers in Genesis, the largest creationist organization in Australia.[55]

Because Ham had resigned from teaching in 1979 and was thus a "full-time creationist," the newly formed CSF turned over its magazine, *Ex Nihilo,* to him (from the Latin, "out of nothing"). *Ex Nihilo,* renamed *Creation Ex Nihilo* and eventually just *Creation,* reflected Ham's populist inclinations.

Under Ham's charismatic and capable leadership, CSF flourished, growing steadily in influence. In 1984 CSF launched another magazine, a more technical, research-oriented journal titled *Ex Nihilo Technical Journal,* now the *Journal of Creation.* Shortly after, in 1987, Ham had a bizarre conflict with John Mackay, his long-time colleague. Mackay and Ham, like most fundamentalists, believed strongly in the existence of Satan, demons, demonic possession, and witches and witchcraft. Mackay claimed that Ham's personal secretary, Margaret Buchanan, was a witch. He said she was the incarnation of the Old Testament figure Jezebel and accused her of having had sex with her dead husband. Mackay claimed that Buchanan had attended séances and satanic orgies, and could cast demons into cats and dogs and even inanimate objects. Associates were encouraged to gather any presents they had received from Buchanan and burn them, lest the demons come out and lead them astray.[56]

Mackay's accusations got him kicked out of the Redlands Baptist Church and dropped from the CSF.[57] His crusade against Ham's secretary may have been motivated by money, jealousy, and a desire to take control of the struggling organization, or he may simply have believed his own bizarre claims about witchcraft. In 1987 the legal requirement to teach creationism in Queensland was dropped, eliminating much of CSF's revenue. At the same time, Ham was setting his sights on the far larger creationist audience—and market—in America. Despite his strange and censured behavior, Mackay continues to circulate in the creationist world and, in late 2007, was interviewed by Richard Dawkins for a Channel 4 UK special aired in 2008.[58]

Convinced that God wanted them in America, Ham and Mally, his wife of fifteen years, came to the United States in 1987, the same year that the U.S. Supreme Court declared the teaching of creationism in public schools unconstitutional. "He just showed up on our doorstep," said Institute for Creation Research Senior Vice President Duane Gish.[59]

Functioning as a "missionary" on loan from the Creation Science Foundation in Australia, Ham took a position at ICR in San Diego. His primary activities included speaking and writing to nonscientists about the importance of young earth creationism to Christianity and the damage that evolution was doing to society. He spent no time in research, but established a solid reputation as a speaker at events geared toward laypeople, like weekend seminars in churches and radio appearances.

Ham's 1987 publication *The Lie: Evolution* was indicative of his style. Filled with cartoons, caricatures, and simplistic generalizations, the book offered an easy, accessible, and entertaining presentation of the evils of evolution. Cute characters standing on the Bible showed the importance of a biblical foundation for life. Ham's rhetoric, both in person and in his writings, was militant: "There is a war going on in society—a very real battle. The war is Christianity versus humanism, but we must wake up to the fact that, at the foundational level, it's really creation versus evolution."[60]

In 1989 Ham started his popular "Back to Genesis" initiative, inaugurating what would become the central focus of his ministry. In articles in the ICR monthly newsletter *Acts & Facts,* seminars around the country, and other outlets Ham argued persuasively that God provided a blueprint for society in Genesis—the book of beginnings—presenting the proper understanding of the family, nature, politics, and so on: "Genesis is the only book that provides an account of the origin of all the basic entities of life and the universe: the origin of life, of man, of government, of marriage, of culture, of nations, of death, of the chosen people, of sin, of diet and clothes, of the solar system . . . the list is almost endless."[61]

Ham's presence at ICR transformed the organization. Before his arrival in 1987, ICR representatives—with the exception of the superstars, Morris and Gish—spoke to crowds that sometimes measured only in the dozens, making dry technical presentations about problems with radioactive dating, transitional fossils, biochemical challenges to life, and so on. ICR had pretensions, as its name and charter suggested, of doing real science and spreading a real scientific message. However, it was ICR's staged debates with prominent evolutionists—highly entertaining affairs—that drew crowds of consequence. Not surprisingly, ICR was operating on a shoestring. Ham brought the equivalent of a fire-and-brimstone message about the dangers of evolution, what one critic has called a "good hate and fear line."[62] Ham attracted crowds numbering in the thousands and money began to flow to ICR, allowing the organization to pay off existing mortgages and fund new projects. The missionary from Australia was a real contributor.

In 2004, Liberty University recognized Ham with an honorary doctorate of literature, fifteen years after it had awarded one to his mentor, Henry Morris. Chancellor Jerry Falwell, America's most prominent fundamentalist at the time, had long been an eager supporter of Ham, praising him in his newsletter and looking forward to the opening of the Creation Museum, which would "skillfully address the issues of Genesis and further defend the foundations of the Bible."[63] Falwell's son and heir, Jonathan, would later describe Ham's museum as a "godsend."[64]

Ham's message resonated with conservatives in late twentieth-century America and was reminiscent of William Jennings Bryan's anti-evolution crusade at the beginning of the century. Not coincidentally, Bryan and Ham shared the same alarmist opinion of Darwin's theory, as a worldview corroding the foundations of a healthy society. Evolution, in this view, should be opposed not just because it is *untrue*, although it certainly was. Evolution should be countered because "it has been used as the pseudo-scientific justification for almost every deadly philosophy and every evil practice known to man."[65] Bryan and Ham bookend a century that witnessed an astonishing populist rejection of biology's central theory and the vilification of the previous century's most famous scientist, Charles Darwin.

After his remarkable seven-year stint as a "creationism missionary," Ham left ICR to start his own ministry. His departure fit a familiar pattern that had long characterized creationist organizations and evangelical organizations in general, which tend to be personality-driven. Fighting evolution—or any of the other perceived social evils that agitate evangelicals—is an idiosyncratic enterprise with widespread disagreement about how it should be done. Most of the organizations are "one-man shops" with a single charismatic leader at the helm. Ham and Morris, while clearly on the same side, had different ideas about the best way to combat the forces of evolution. Morris's original vision was to work from the top down, developing a scientific model that the academy would embrace to replace evolution and a biblical model that Christians would embrace to replace errant old earth readings. Ham's approach was bottom up. He would convince millions of ordinary people to reject evolution in the hopes that this grassroots groundswell would change society and work its way up, or at least marginalize the apostate eggheads at the top.

In 1994, with some help from his old shop in Australia, now called Creation Ministries International, Ham started what would soon become the world's most influential creation ministry, Answers in Genesis. Flush with success from his tenure at ICR, he wasted no time setting up popular media outreaches aimed at children, teenagers, lay adults, and religious leaders. Little to nothing was spent on research, although scientific rhetoric and authority were constantly invoked.

Ham took two ICR colleagues with him and, with the blessing of Morris, who provided a gracious endorsement and a donation, laid plans for his new organization. After resolving initial uncertainties about the exact name, the management of Australian creationist magazines looking for an American outlet, and the relation between the new organization and its Australian counterpart, Ham launched Answers in Genesis in early 1994. In March of that year he and his partners from ICR moved to northern Kentucky, a geographically central location chosen as the ideal site for a future Creation Museum.

Ham's new ministry sprinted out of the starting gate. Generous donors provided funds; attendance at creation seminars was strong; and sales of media were beyond expectations. AIG's second newsletter reported that 6,200 people attended the first major creation conference, held in Denver, Colorado, the same month that Ham moved to Kentucky and the first newsletter was mailed out. The free newsletter, containing articles, announcements, news, and advertisements, has a wide, but closely guarded, circulation.

Six months later the *Answers . . . with Ken Ham* radio program began airing on 45 stations. This popular show, featuring 90 seconds of creationist commentary by Ham, was broadcast on over 1,000 stations by 2008. By the end of the first year more than 85,000 people had attended "teaching events" and almost 150 radio stations were carrying Ham's short program.

Ham launched a website in 1995 that, like his other initiatives, was enormously popular, winning the "Ministry Website of the Year" award from National Religious Broadcasters in 2006. Web traffic to the AIG site grew to 25,000 visitors per day by 2008.

AIG's staff grew rapidly, from just over 100 in 2004 to almost 300 by 2008. AIG seminars have grown steadily in popularity with more than 300 events per year, and a typical "event" often encompasses five or six lectures to different audiences.

The big event, of course, was the opening of the Creation Museum in the spring of 2007. Once again, Ham's managerial Midas touch worked its magic, and the multimillion-dollar project was completed without a mortgage, funded entirely by donations and revenue from the organization. Within six months more than a quarter-million people had visited. In the spring of 2008, the hours were extended to accommodate the growing crowds.

AIG is an astonishing success story. A media empire dedicated to the proposition that we should get our science from the Bible has been created, *ex nihilo,* in less than two decades. At its center is an affable, quirky, passionate Australian who came to America as a "creation missionary" just two decades ago. Ham is now a major public figure, a populist pied piper with millions of eager followers. The late Jerry Falwell described AIG as "one of the most important Christian ministries in the world."[66] In his *Falwell Confidential* newsletter he praised AIG for "equipping the church with answers so that we can defend the faith and challenge the church concerning compromise."[67] Ham appeared on D. James Kennedy's widely popular radio program *Truths That Transform.*

Secular media regularly features Ham when the stories involve creationism. He has appeared on *CBS News, NBC Nightly News, The PBS News Hour with Jim Lehrer, Nightline,* CNN, and the BBC. PBS featured him prominently in the concluding episode of its seven-part series *Evolution.*

AIG, which has always had an international presence in the English-speaking world, is developing strategies to branch out overseas. With its multimillion-dollar budget, over thirteen million in 2005 and currently estimated at over twenty million, AIG dwarfs other organizations.[68]

Ham's simple message resonates with fundamentalist Christians in America and around the world. Their faith is under attack by evolution. By undermining faith in God's word, particularly Genesis, modern science is destroying the foundations of civil—meaning "Christian"—society. The result is widespread anarchy, immorality, and nihilism.

Ham's rudimentary biblical literalism, rejection of biology's central theory as well as key ideas from physics and cosmology, and pandering anti-intellectual presentation style have alarmed educated evangelicals.

His message includes ideas that were debated by conservative Christians more than a century ago and rejected. Ham's literal reading of the Genesis story of Creation is a case in point. Nineteenth-century geology established, to the satisfaction of most educated people, including Christians, that Earth was very old. Geologists, most of them Christians, developed strategies for harmonizing these conclusions with the Bible.

There was limited controversy on this topic, even among the leaders of the emerging fundamentalist movement. This project began in 1909 to identify the "fundamental" ideas of Christianity. Concerned that new approaches to the Bible were undermining the central ideas of the faith, some wealthy Christian businessmen underwrote a series of widely circulated pamphlets called *The Fundamentals,* from which the movement took its name.

In *The Fundamentals,* leading conservatives defined the beliefs they considered essential to Christianity: the reality of God, the divinity of Christ, the authority of the Bible, and so on. Their list did *not* include a rejection of evolution, and, although it appeared in about 20 percent of the essays, nowhere was it presented as incompatible with the Christian faith, despite the efforts of a few conservatives to have it portrayed as such.[69] Evolution was not celebrated, of course, and the founder of *The Fundamentals* series noted that he felt "a repugnance to the idea that an ape or an orangutan was my ancestor." Nevertheless, he was willing "to accept the humiliating fact, if proved."[70] Darwin's theory was still on shaky scientific ground, however, so many Christians saw little need to work too hard at accommodating a theory that might die shortly of natural causes. Some were hopeful that the theory could be partially accommodated—nonhuman evolution, for example—with what one scholar called "judicious modifications of traditional formulations of Christian doctrine."[71]

Many educated Christians shared this attitude. Creationism, while popular at the grassroots, was rarely the dominant view within any evangelical academic organization. The American Scientific Affiliation (ASA), an organization of evangelical scientists, fits this pattern. Members of ASA, which was launched in the 1940s, between the Scopes Trial and the publication of *The Genesis Flood,* affirm the following: "I believe in the whole Bible as originally given, to be the inspired word of God, the only unerring guide of faith and conduct. Since God is the Author of this book, as well as the Creator and Sustainer of the physical world about us, I cannot conceive of discrepancies between statements in the Bible and the real facts of science."[72]

Virtually all antievolutionary creationists, including Morris and Ham, hold exactly this position on scripture. Incensed that evangelicals with this same view could be at peace with evolution, Ham referred to such compromising Christians as "shepherds in our churches who are really leading the sheep astray."[73] Morris tried for years to bring the ASA around to young earth creationism but eventually gave up, demoralized by the "complete capitulation of the ASA to evolutionism."[74]

In 1949 the ASA launched the *Journal of the American Scientific Affiliation,* a scholarly publication now called *Perspectives on Science and Christian Faith.* No topic has received more attention than the relationship between evolution and the opening chapters of Genesis. In an effort to be inclusive, the journal gave space to the young earth creationist viewpoint, but the majority of the articles were from perspectives that embraced, rather than rejected, the generally accepted conclusions of the scientific community about evolution.

Contrary to the view popularized by the creationists, no compelling case can be made that the Bible "teaches" young earth creationism, in any sense other than a simple, decontextualized reading in English. The influential fourth-century theologian St. Augustine rejected this simplistic reading of Genesis on the grounds that it was anthropomorphic to suppose that God would create the world in a human workweek and then "rest," as if the task had tired him out. Fifteen centuries later, when geologists like William Buckland and Adam Sedgewick, who were

Bible-believing Christians like Ham, discovered that Earth was very old, they easily squared their discoveries with the Bible.[75] And even Darwin's theory, destined eventually to be at the center of a storm of religious controversy, could be reconciled with various readings of Genesis.[76] Many people, of course, hoped that the controversial new theory would die on its own. Others hoped that evolutionary mechanisms consistent with divine purpose might rise to the surface. Decades would pass before mutation and natural selection would elbow aside more theologically congenial options. Widespread hostility to evolution grew slowly, and a couple of generations of thinkers would pass before strong opposition to *The Origin of Species* would really get going.

The relevant interpretative issues are fascinating. For example, only a simple reading of Genesis in English supports the conclusions drawn by the creationists. According to their view, God dictated the story of Creation to the biblical author with the intention that it be read as literal history—a literary form that didn't even exist at the time. While the creationists maintain that their view of scripture is "high" because they don't contaminate God's message with human interpretation, it would be more accurate to say that their view of scripture is not informed by scholarship. They pay almost no attention to the nuances of the original languages, the worldview of the likely authors, genre, literary structure, and similar matters. In the final episode of the PBS *Evolution* series, Ham is pictured confidently telling his fundamentalist audience, "I don't interpret scripture; I just read it."[77] While such statements play well to lay audiences who warm to claims that we should "take God at his word" or "trust the clear message of God" rather than the "interpretation of men," in fact it is simply not possible to do so with an ancient text derived from an oral tradition in a different language. To read such a text—any text—*is* to interpret it. In fact, the mere act of *translating* such a text into English involves interpretation.

All this is well understood by biblical scholars. In fact, many of the world's leading scholars of biblical languages and cultures are evangelicals with a "high" view of scripture and a confidence that it is inspired by God, though there is no consensus on exactly what "inspired" means. Scholarship in this area does not, in fact, destroy one's confidence in the Bible.

Many educated evangelicals, informed by biblical scholarship, have thus concluded that the Genesis story of Creation is simply not literal history. The word translated as "Adam" in the story is the generic Hebrew term for "man." "Eve" means "mother of all living." God's behavior—strolling in the garden in the evening with Adam and Eve—is distinctly anthropomorphic. Talking snakes, Adam's naming all the animals on the planet, Eve's being made from Adam's side and identified as a subordinate "helpmate"—the story simply does not look like history from any reasonable literary perspective. This conclusion is powerfully reinforced when this Hebrew story is compared with its contemporary analogs in other cultures.

The modern scholarly approach to Genesis transforms the story into a myth in the best sense of that word—a story with a powerful meaning that may or may not be tenuously rooted in history. The opening chapters of Genesis affirm that God is the creator, that humans were created for fellowship with God, and that they are "fallen" or separated from God in some way. None of these conclusions demands either a rejection of biological evolution or an abandonment of the Bible as authoritative. They simply require that the Bible be read from an informed perspective, which is not the naïve assumption that God dictated it to an uncomprehending scribe in twenty-first-century prose.

Because fundamentalism, by nature, is aggressive and polemical—"evangelicalism with an attitude" is a common description—it is easy for its leaders to shout loudly and be heard. The message is confident, without nuance, persuasive and comprehensible at first pass; the accompanying concerns about social anarchy add layers of interest and attract well-intentioned donors; the ground being defended is far removed from the sinister precincts roamed by well-defined enemies of the faith like Richard Dawkins, Sam Harris, and Christopher Hitchens.

Evangelical alternatives to the fundamentalist message, by contrast, are often conflicted and irenic. They share ground with a fully secularized science. Dissenting nonfundamentalist evangelicals are often academics working at secular schools. Fundamentalists eye such institutions with suspicion.

Evangelical alternatives to Ham's creationism are not comparable package deals where everything fits nicely together. The alternatives recognize complexity and acknowledge that there is much we don't know, about both the Bible and the natural world. These viewpoints, in the words of one evangelical leader, have "come to peace with science," but this science is, of course, the much-maligned Darwinian evolution celebrated by Dawkins for enabling an "intellectually fulfilled atheism."[78] This is the same Darwinism vilified by Morris, Ham, and most other biblical literalists.

The sheer number of leading scientists who reject creationism while affirming Christian beliefs makes a strong argument for the compatibility of evolution and Christianity. The academic stature of this group dwarfs that of leaders like Ham, and, taken collectively, they represent a significant movement. They also outnumber, by a wide margin, adherents of the tiny but more visible and politically active intelligent design movement. But they are almost invisible because they are not united in any cause and are not funded by any deep pocket. Their influence is restricted because, with few exceptions, most of them have professional lives far removed from the creation-evolution controversy.

Owen Gingerich, of Harvard University, to take but one example, is a devout Mennonite with a reputation as both a historian of science and a successful science popularizer. His scholarly work has illuminated the controversy over heliocentricity in the sixteenth and seventeenth centuries. He has spent countless hours in the archives of

Europe's great libraries, researching the earliest manuscripts of Copernicus's revolutionary book, trying to understand how sixteenth-century readers responded to the radical suggestion that the Earth moved around the sun—the sixteenth-century precursor to the evolution controversy of today. He does not write children's books about dinosaurs or build creation museums. Only in retirement has Gingerich begun to put considerable effort into addressing issues related to science and religion. But his efforts are nowhere near the scale of Ham's Answers in Genesis campaigns.[79] Gingerich is just one of many leading intellectuals who see no reason for Christians to reject contemporary science. But this message has taken a back seat to a career focused on more traditional scholarly topics.

By far the most significant evangelical scientist is Francis Collins, director of the Human Genome Project up to its completion in 2003, now head of the National Institutes of Health, and one of the most influential scientific leaders in the world. Collins, a prolific author and engaging speaker, is emerging as a conceivable counter to Ham, at least for the educated wing of the evangelical world.

Collins had remarkably humble beginnings. Homeschooled on a Shenandoah Valley farm in Virginia, he studied chemistry at the University of Virginia and earned a Ph.D. at Yale University in 1974. A biochemistry course sparked his interest in the molecules that make up the language of life: DNA and RNA. Scientists correctly anticipated that these molecules would soon be at the heart of a major scientific revolution.

Advances in genetics would have far-reaching implications for medicine because so many diseases were genetically based. Passionate about the anticipated benefits of gene therapies, Collins completed an M.D. and then returned to Yale, where he was named a Fellow in Human Genetics from 1981 to 1984. At Yale he developed ingenious approaches to finding useful information on long strings of DNA. He soon had a national reputation as the "Indiana Jones" of the genome project, seemingly able to find any needle he wanted in that great biochemical haystack we call human genes.

In 1989, Collins and his team identified the gene for cystic fibrosis, then Huntington's disease, neurofibromatosis, one type of adult acute leukemia, and more. The original vision of genetically based therapies to alleviate suffering began to take shape on the scientific horizon, inspiring Collins and other scientists. In 1993 Collins became head of the National Center for Human Genome Research, overseeing an ambitious quest he said "beats going to the moon or splitting the atom." The obvious practical applications of mapping the genome created worldwide interest in the project, and Collins quickly became one of the most public members of America's scientific community.

Progress was rapid: In June 2000 a first draft of the genome was ready to be announced. President Clinton declared it a "day for the ages." After years of effort, the three billion DNA letters of the human genome had been mapped. "Without a doubt," said Clinton, "this is the most important, most wondrous map ever produced by humankind." On his left in the East Room of the White House stood Collins, who had been working frantically with Clinton's speechwriter to figure out the best way to make the announcement, to give the speech the right tone to note the sobering achievement. "Today," said Clinton, "we are learning the language in which God created life. We are gaining ever more awe for the complexity, the beauty, and the wonder of God's most divine and sacred gift." That same year, the A&E Network gave Collins its "Biography of the Year" award. His initial version of the genomic sequence was published in the prestigious *Nature* magazine a few months later. The article ran over sixty pages and was the longest piece that *Nature* had ever published.[80]

On April 14, 2003, Collins and his team announced that the project was completed. The date coincided with the fiftieth anniversary of the discovery of DNA by Watson and Crick. The genome was mapped, ahead of schedule, under budget, and with the enthusiastic participation of laboratories around the world. Its winsome director, elected to the National Academy of Science ten years earlier, had become a fixture on the national and international science scene.

Collins was now one of America's leading public intellectuals. His boyish face, mop-top haircut, and trademark motorcycle were everywhere, from the cover of *Time* to the Colbert Report. In 2005 *US News and World Report* and the Harvard Center for Public Leadership honored Collins as one of "America's Best Leaders." President Bush awarded him the Presidential Medal of Freedom, the nation's highest civilian award, in 2007. In 2008 he resigned his post at the NIH to create time for additional projects, particularly writing, and creating the BioLogos Foundation, a multifaceted project aimed at helping evangelicals conquer their fear of evolution. In 2009 he resigned from BioLogos when Barack Obama asked him to head the NIH.

Collins emerged as a controversial public man of faith in 2006 with the publication of *The Language of God: A Scientist Presents Evidence for Belief.* The book was, on one level, just another volume on science and religion, not all that different from similar books that evangelical and other presses had been putting out for years, generally by less well-known scholars from small evangelical colleges.[81] But the author of *The Language of God* was not obscure. He was the head of the Human Genome Project, not a faculty member at a tiny college. The publisher was the Free Press, not an evangelical house like InterVarsity or Zondervan. The jacket sported blurbs from Archbishop Desmond Tutu, singer Naomi Judd, Nobel laureate William Phillips, and Robert Schuller of the Crystal Cathedral. *The Language of God* was launched into a cultural strata entirely different from that of other evangelical publications.

Like many popular evangelical books, *The Language of God* celebrated its author's dramatic conversion, at age twenty-seven, from atheism to Christianity. Collins's Christian faith was personally satisfying, intellectually fulfilling, and complementary to the best understanding of science. Impressed by the power of faith in the lives of his dying patients, Collins started to read C. S. Lewis, the author of *The Chronicles of Narnia.* Many evangelicals consider Lewis's classic work of apologetics, *Mere Christianity,* to be the most important text written in the twentieth century. Collins identified strongly with Lewis's own faith journey from agnosticism to Christianity and soon found himself on the same path, and eventually in the same place: "On a beautiful day, as I was hiking in the Cascade Mountains . . . the majesty and beauty of god's creation overwhelmed my resistance. As I rounded a corner and saw a beautiful and unexpected frozen waterfall, hundreds of feet high, I knew the search was over. The next morning, I knelt in the dewy grass as the sun rose and surrendered to Jesus Christ."[82]

The existence of God, says Collins, is implied by the Big Bang, which "cries out for a divine explanation."[83] The fine-tuning for life of the laws of physics "provides an interesting argument in favor of a Creator."[84] The "digital elegance of DNA" is "deeply satisfying," "aesthetically pleasing," and "artistically sublime." For religious believers these are reasons to be "more in awe, not less."[85]

Collins says his faith in a personal creator enlarges his sense of what it means to discover something for the first time: "to see things that God knew before, and now you get to see them too," Collins told PBS reporter Bob Abernethy, is "exhilarating."[86] Likewise, Collins's faith informs his ethical decisions. "Bioethics," he argues, "rests on the foundation of the moral law."[87]

The Language of God was reviewed in the prestigious pages of *Scientific American, Science,* and other leading journals. The reviews were often critical, but Collins's stature as an important and influential member of the scientific community was not challenged. Only the agnostic curmudgeon Sam Harris, in a strikingly mean-spirited review titled "The Language of Ignorance," was disrespectful of Collins as a scientist, claiming that his comments on religion indicated that he lacked a "scientific frame of mind," an odd claim to make about a member of the National Academy of Science.[88]

Collins speaks openly about his faith, affirming his belief in the Bible, the resurrection of Jesus, and the virgin birth. On these key central tenets, he is as orthodox as one can be, and essentially identical to Ken Ham. Collins has come out publicly and identified with the evangelical community by writing forewords and jacket blurbs for books by other evangelicals; he has spoken at evangelical colleges and conservative churches, including Southern Baptist ones. Evangelical publications have interviewed him.[89] *Christianity Today,* a magazine for educated, conservative evangelicals, recognized *The Language of God* as a "book of the year" for 2007.[90]

Collins carries the evangelical message into the secular world in ways that fundamentalists could only dream of. John Horgan interviewed him in *National Geographic,* probing him about the viability of religion in an age of science.[91] The liberal online magazine *salon.com* challenged Collins on biblical miracles like the virgin birth and resurrection of Jesus, and he responded simply: "If you believe in God, and if God is more than nature, then there's no reason that God could not stage an invasion into the natural world, which—to our limited perspective—would appear to be a miracle."[92]

However, despite the authenticity of his credentials as a leading scientist and faithful Christian, many conservative evangelicals have rejected Collins because he believes in evolution and does not read the first chapters of Genesis literally. In *The Language of God* he recalls speaking at a national gathering of Christian physicians. Some in attendance walked out "shaking their heads in dismay" when he confessed to being an evolutionist.[93] People have stormed out of Southern Baptist churches when they discovered that he accepted evolution. Others came to the microphone after his talk and implied that, in accepting evolution, he was "under the influence of the devil." And, though Collins regularly receives critical email from nonbelievers, the "nastiest" messages come from fellow Christians, "infuriated that someone who claims to be a believer could say these things about the truth of the evolutionary process." He has even been "excommunicated" a couple of times, which, given that he is Protestant, is technically impossible.[94]

"We need to come back to where the center of our faith really is," says Collins. "I'm very fond of noting what Christ said: 'The first and greatest commandment is to love the Lord with all your heart, with all your soul, and all your mind and all your strength.'" He notes that Jesus, who was quoting an Old Testament passage from Deuteronomy, added "mind" to the list.[95]

The different responses to Collins expose the great fault line that runs through American evangelicalism. Antievolutionism is so widespread that the majority of evangelicals simply assume that no Christian could believe in Darwin's evil theory. When Collins takes the pulpit in a Southern Baptist church, his audience no more expects endorsements of evolution than endorsements of pornography, theft, or illegal drug use.

Evangelical critics see Collins as a compromiser—someone who has caved in to secular anti-God pressures and abandoned a faithful reading of the Bible in order to curry favor with the academy. In a review for *Answers in Genesis,* Joseph Kezele, a medical doctor who heads the Arizona Origin Science Association, excoriates Collins for accepting the Big Bang "as if it were observed fact, and not a presupposition." Kezele vents that Collins "dismisses Genesis as history."[96]

Kezele even takes aim at Collins's credentials: "Most disappointing to me as a physician are the repetitions of disproved evolutionary canards regarding human anatomy. Research has confirmed that the design of the retina *is* ideal, that the spine *is* well designed for optimum flexibility and weight bearing, and that the appendix *does* have extremely important functions as part of the immune system in the earlier years of life." Kezele employs a well-worn creationist argument. He uses his marginally relevant medical degree to validate a set of sweeping and undocumented dismissals of generally accepted positions in the mainstream scientific community.

Without expertise in navigating the complex scientific literature, how would a layperson—even a well-educated one—figure out that Kezele's medical degree provides him with almost no expertise to make this claim? How would they know that the "research" being referenced is not from peer-reviewed scientific literature? How would they know that the "evolutionary canards" have not been disproven at all but are, in fact, affirmed constantly in leading scientific journals?

The most remarkable charge in the review, however, would have to be the strange *ad hominem* claim that "Dr. Collins, of all people, should know that initially the human genome was free of the accumulated burden of mutations—but he ignores this because of his presupposition that Adam and Eve were the continuation of some pre-Adamic race, an idea necessitated by Collins' belief in evolution."[97] This argument is traditional creationist fare—a potent and persuasive mix of falsehoods, innuendo, and half-truths. No evidence of any sort even hints that the human genome was ever "free of the . . . burden of mutations." Yet we are told that this is something that Collins, as an expert geneticist, should know, as though it were standard information in introductory textbooks. But Kezele suggests that he *does* know this but chooses to ignore it because of a presupposition.

This particular argument captures the complexity of the controversy and illustrates the central creationist logic: The position one holds on origins derives, not from consideration of *evidence,* but from one's starting *assumptions.* If Collins began with different assumptions—specifically, acceptance of the literal truth of the Bible instead of an overconfidence in science—he would clearly see the truth of creationism. But since he starts with the unsupported assumption that evolution is true, he is forced to reject obvious truths like the purity of the original human genome, the young earth, and the veracity of Genesis.

For creationists like Kezele and his allies at Answers in Genesis, Collins's compromises lead to far more than minor reinterpretations of secondary parts of the Bible. To suggest that death and suffering preceded the sin of Adam is to blame these defects of the created order on God. The Bible states in Romans 6:23, "The wages of sin is death." Death is not a tool of natural selection, used by God to winnow out the less fit en route to homo sapiens. When Collins suggests that Adam must not be a literal historical figure, he undermines the New Testament references to Christ as a "last Adam" undoing the damage of the first Adam. "When Scripture refers to Jesus as the last Adam," Kezele asks rhetorically, "should Christ also be taken allegorically?"

In the theological framework of fundamentalism, the acceptance of evolution forces compromises on the Bible that ultimately undermine the reality of Christ. That is why the stakes are so high.

Kezele concludes his review with an ominous warning for Collins to "rethink his interpretation of Scripture, for one day we all will have to stand before the Lord and account for our treatment of His Word."[98]

Ham and Collins are prominent evangelical leaders. They share many religious beliefs. When asked about Ham, who has dedicated his life to nurturing the chilly climate that he encounters in many religious settings, Collins even told the *Christian Post,* "As a born again Christian, I regard Ken Ham as my brother in faith and I have no doubt of the complete sincerity of his position." He was quick to add, of course, that "as a working scientist who has studied the intricacies of human DNA as my life's profession, I have arrived at very different conclusions on the basis of the facts in front of me."[99]

Collins understates his qualifications. Instead of calling himself "a working scientist who has studied DNA," he could have said, with less humility but no less truth, that he was "a world-class expert on genetics."

And what of Ham's credentials? He last brushed up against science at the high school level in Australia before the Cold War ended. He has never published a scientific paper nor written a single sentence for a scholarly journal. He writes for uneducated readers and children, and gives his books titles like *D Is for Dinosaur* or *The Answers Book.* He has no stature within the scientific community and his work, such as it is, has been solidly refuted.[100] His approach to the origins controversy has been lampooned on *The Simpsons, Family Guy,* and *Saturday Night Live.*[101]

Could informed evangelicals take their cues from Collins? To be sure, much of the educated leadership of the evangelical community has done that, but many have not. The leaders of the intelligent design movement, for example, are working hard to undermine Collins's influence, and one of their senior fellows negatively reviewed his book in the *Weekly Standard.*[102] But when it comes to millions of rank-and-file evangelicals, Ham's simple message remains comforting and attractive. For now at least, evangelicals continue to attend creation seminars where Buddy Davis, the AIG creationist song evangelist, leads them in antievolutionary choruses: "I don't believe in evolution, I know creation is true / I believe that God above created me and you."[103]

Ken Ham videos are shown regularly in adult Sunday school classes across America. Sometimes those classes have well-educated academics in them, and sometimes those academics walk out in frustration. For an educated person to listen to Ham is to be transported into a scientific Land of Oz, where modern science does not exist and alternative explanations for everything from stars to starfish hold sway.

Ham's organization, Answers in Genesis, is a media juggernaut with almost unlimited access to America's vast evangelical subculture. Collins and others like him may have scientific credentials and the respect and support of the scientific community, and "truth" in some sense may be on their side. Those seem like limited assets, however, alongside the mighty resources of Answers in Genesis. Collins does not have a collection of colorful children's books to be placed in church libraries, curricula for vacation bible schools, or a library of popular-level books and DVDs. He does not have a syndicated radio broadcast or a glossy magazine or a small army of like-minded zealots to accept the many speaking engagements he cannot. No museum enshrines his personal vision of natural history.

Grassroots organizations like Answers in Genesis are powerful shapers of popular opinion in America's vast evangelical subculture. Unburdened by the need to do expensive and time-consuming scientific research, undistracted by the task of dealing with ongoing scientific work done by others, they are free to package and promote their message as they see fit. Since they already know the answers, they can speak with confidence, unfettered by nuances that might make them seem tentative and unsure. They can easily dismiss critics like Richard Dawkins and Daniel Dennett as infidels seeking to destroy belief in God, and malign critics like Francis Collins and evangelical institutions like Wheaton College as "compromisers." They can brandish their Bibles and proclaim loudly that they "take God at his word"; that they "just read the Bible"; that they trust in the "infallible and enduring truth of revelation" rather than the limited and changing opinions of sinful men.

In a world where so many people long for simple, comfortable answers, it is easy to be seduced by those inviting us to abandon the complicated middle ground that is so gray and mysterious. For millions of American evangelicals convinced that the world is black and white, Ken Ham is most certainly wearing white.

2 The Amateur Christian Historian

In 2006 conservative Virginia congressman J. Randy Forbes voiced concerns about America's godlessness. "Day by day," he lamented, "the spiritual foundations of America are being pushed out of our lives." Some lawmakers had issues with the phrase "under God" in the Pledge of Allegiance, and secularists wanted to ban God from public life. Just studying the religion of the Founding Fathers in public schools had become "controversial." Forbes complained to his constituents that Christianity was under attack and that under the false banner of "tolerance" some Americans were turning the country into a secular wasteland.[1]

The agitated Forbes, well placed to lead an army of prayer warriors, founded the Congressional Prayer Caucus in 2005, which gathered conservative Christian representatives together to pray for the nation and to use legislation to support public prayer. A true-blue evangelical, Forbes had taught Sunday school for twenty years at Great Bridge Baptist Church and had received a 100 percent profamily rating from the Christian Coalition. Forbes's Prayer Caucus took 2 Chronicles 7:14 as its guide: "If my people, who are called by my name, shall humble themselves, and pray, and seek my face, and turn from their wicked ways; then will I hear from heaven, and will forgive their sin, and will heal their land." Dozens of congressmen joined Forbes each week in the Capitol building, praying for America and resolving to protect the Christian rights of citizens. Members urged their constituents to form similar prayer groups in their communities. "We deal with all kinds of problems in Congress," said one member, "but I'm still like a little kid in Sunday School. Jesus is always the answer." Another called on America to "glorify the name of Jesus Christ."[2]

In Forbes's judgment America had not glorified Jesus. References to God on national monuments and in exhibitions were being obscured. A huge new $621 million Capitol Visitor Center had room for everything except God. A replica of the House Speaker's rostrum no longer carried the words "In God We Trust." The center recognized "E Pluribus Unum"—not "In God We Trust"—as the nation's official motto. Planners restored the deleted phrases following protests, but in Forbes's view this episode was yet another in a long series of misrepresentations and revisions of American history. Neither the Franklin Delano Roosevelt Monument (1997) nor the World War II Monument (2004) contained references to God.[3]

In 2007 evangelicals, feeling scorned by such omissions, challenged a rule banning mention of "God" from official commendatory certificates sent to constituents. "Those of us old enough to remember life under a predominantly liberal worldview," lamented one woman to a national newspaper, "remember with pain the complete marginalization and denigration of evangelicals. . . . We remember our essay papers being marked down by teachers intolerant of any worldview other than the liberal one; we remember family members calling us 'cultists' and peers mocking us openly for our faith. Christians developed an 'underground' mentality, removing ourselves from the public forum." Forbes acknowledged this marginalization and addressed it directly in the hope of bringing the nation back to its Christian foundation.[4]

David Barton, an evangelical amateur historian and political activist from Texas, praised Forbes as an able politician, a champion of American history, and a proponent of moral issues and biblical values. Barton had become the leading "Christian America" historian by the 1990s. He spoke and published widely and appeared often on Christian radio stations and in videos; he was a ubiquitous evangelical authority. His influential WallBuilders organization was launched to refute the erroneous idea that church and state should be separated and to convince Americans that the nation had genuinely Christian roots. He resonated with Forbes: "I really look at him and think of the sons of Issachar in 1 Chronicles 12:32 . . . [The Bible says] that they understood the times and knew what to do." Barton hosted Forbes often on his radio program, *WallBuilders Live,* to talk about his vision for America. He compared him to King David, because he doesn't act "until he checks with God on what to do." "We took a little wisdom from Solomon," said Forbes of the Congressional Prayer Caucus: If Americans prayed, the country could be straightened out. So much threatened the godly republic: the liberal media, Hollywood immorality, sex education, stem cell research, and activist judges bent on sanctioning gay marriage. But Forbes was most irked by the rewriting of the nation's sacred history.[5]

On December 18, 2007, Forbes introduced a resolution on the House floor, "affirming the rich spiritual and religious history of our Nation's founding and subsequent history." In the coming months ninety cosponsors joined Forbes to reassert America's godly heritage and recover the narrative of the country's Christian past, which had been suppressed by heavy-handed secularists. Forbes and many of his compatriots considered this divine history to be an unambiguous, self-evident truth.[6]

Forbes found allies outside the Beltway, as tens of thousands of evangelicals supported his campaign to rescue the nation from secularists. His view of American history drew heavily on David Barton and on WallBuilders' extensive library of valuable primary sources. The resulting resolution charted the Christian faith and heroic deeds of the country's great men from the American Revolution to the Reagan Revolution. "Congress adopted (and has reaffirmed on numerous subsequent occasions) the National Seal with its Latin motto 'Annuit Coeptis,' meaning 'God has favored our undertakings,'" read his resolution. It insisted that "political scientists have documented that the most frequently-cited source in the political period known as The Founding Era was the Bible." In addition, the all-seeing eye atop the pyramid on U.S. currency symbolized "the many signal interpositions of Providence in favor of the American cause." The country had suffered from a secularist amnesia. The resolution called for an "American Religious History Week" in May to commemorate and educate citizens about Christianity's role in the nation's history.[7] The struggle to do so provoked a battle about the past that lined up experts on each side of a great divide.

A national lobby for secularists, atheists, and humanists called the Secular Coalition for America cried foul. The coalition promotes reason and science as "the most reliable methods for understanding the universe and improving the human condition." Members of the group responded to the resolution by cataloging Christian intolerance and brutality through the centuries. They warned of historical fabrication and shot back: "If we don't stop it, next thing you know they'll be trying to teach the Immaculate Conception in biology class." Journalist Chris Hedges lambasted the resolution's falsehoods and anachronistic logic, reiterating themes from his unsubtly titled book *American Fascists: The Christian Right and the War on America* (2007). The resolution, he claimed, revealed the "frightening populism" of angry Christians remaking the country in their own image. Other leading moderates and left-liberals weighed in, calling for people to condemn the phony "Christian nation" version of American history.[8]

Forbes's resolution riled professional historians, both Christian and secular, whose studies of America's past rested on research and scholarship. Barton and like-minded amateurs, by contrast, denied the validity of historical scholarship that did not give a primary place to a literal reading of the Bible. Instead, they lauded Forbes's challenges to the prevailing view of history and celebrated America's conservative Protestant roots. In their view, God chose America for a special purpose. They followed the logic of seventeenth-century Puritans, who proclaimed their new settlement a City on a Hill, a righteous example for the rest of the world to follow. Divinely appointed, America had a special role to play among the nations. Richard G. Lee brazenly mixed providence, Christianity, and nationalism in the richly illustrated *American Patriot's Bible* (2009). Stories of faith, piety, and American heroism enlivened Lee's New King James Version. Quotes from Ronald Reagan, Henry Ward Beecher, Helen Keller, and Robert E. Lee were interspersed with chapters from the book of Acts. Along with a table of biblical books was a list of U.S. presidents. The presentation offended even some evangelical critics. One called it a whitewash of American history, "saturated with this nationalistic, 'fight-for-God-and-country,' mindset."[9] Nonetheless, many other politicians, speakers, and authors agreed with the God-and-country principles Lee illustrated. Assuming authority to speak on such matters, they boldly asserted America's sacred origins on Fox News and Christian television. "America was and is a covenant nation. God has not chucked that out," said one bestselling popular historian on the Christian Broadcasting Network. America needed to be reclaimed for Christ. Prolific amateur historians produced DVD documentaries on the Founders' faith, served as expert witnesses for court cases, created websites promoting their cause, and advised the nation's largest state boards of education on public school history curricula.[10]

Professional historians, however, had long argued that describing the founding and subsequent history of the United States as "Christian" ignored the nonsectarian ideals of the Founders. The Christian origins view, they argued, projects contemporary political and religious notions back onto the eighteenth century, distorting the Founders by making them into twenty-first-century born-again Christians. Gordon Wood, America's leading Revolutionary era historian, put the matter bluntly. "It is one of the striking facts of American history that the American Revolution was led by men who were not very religious," he countered in an essay published as energized evangelicals helped elect Ronald Reagan. "At best the Founding Fathers only passively believed in organized Christianity and at worst they scorned and ridiculed it."[11]

Martin Marty, the dean of American church history, agrees. He notes that references to God came up occasionally in debates about the Constitution, though not in biblical terms. Those who hashed out the issues of the day rarely referred to Christ or to Christian salvation. In fact they discussed matters of church and organized religion so rarely that one would hardly know Americans of the time were churchgoers. "Whether the general absence of God is intentional or reflects the habits of the Enlightenment," Marty argued, "it is significant."[12]

Religion, of course, was important to the Founders. Revolutionary era believers and skeptics across the spectrum shared basic religious principles: human sinfulness, virtue, a creator God who guaranteed human rights, the importance of religious disestablishment, and the belief that God worked through nations. But there was also much diversity.[13] Thomas Jefferson, the principal author of the Declaration of Independence, intended to represent the consensus of Congress when he wrote that the United States would "assume the separate and equal station to which the Laws of Nature and Nature's God entitle them." Founders like Jefferson were careful about words like "God" because of the baggage they carried. Deistic writers often described the workings of "the Author of Our Being" or "the Creator," a disengaged God of nature and not the personal God of evangelicalism. Such details contradict the view that evangelical Christians founded America. But conservatives like Barton and Forbes disagree and accuse academic historians of secular revisionism.[14]

Until the late nineteenth century most American historians did indeed see divine intervention and the steady hand of God in human history. The German historian who founded the modern critical historical enterprise, Leopold von Ranke, regularly invoked God to explain how things happened. The rise and fall of empires, the fortunes of men, and the persistence of war revealed "the hand of God," "the work of God," and "the judgment of God." Like many early nineteenth-century intellectuals, Ranke believed in a divinely ordered world. Historians could decipher the "holy hieroglyph" and show God's designs in history.[15]

Romantic age historians charted a similar course. Harvard professors and amateur historians alike chronicled the divine guidance of the American republic. No major historians were agnostic, and several were clergymen. The "fortunes of a nation are not under the control of blind destiny," George Bancroft wrote in the year of America's centennial. Rather, "a favoring Providence, calling our institutions into being, has conducted our country to its present happiness and glory."[16]

On such matters Bancroft and his contemporaries stood closer to the Puritan divine Cotton Mather than to post–Civil War era historians. Half of the history textbooks published from 1800 to 1860 mentioned God in the preface. The widely used *Abridged History of the United States* (1844) begins with a religion-infused nationalism: "The government of the United States is acknowledged by the wise and good of other nations, to be the most free, impartial, and righteous government of the world." The author goes on to warn that "all agree, that for such a government to be sustained many years, the principles of truth and righteousness, taught in the Holy Scriptures must be practised. *The rulers must govern in the fear of God, and the people obey the laws.*"[17]

Historians could assume that students were acquainted with the King James Version of the Bible. The definition of God, however, was typically Unitarian, vague, or nonsectarian, a divine presence in the grandeur of history, not the God invoked today by the Religious Right. Still, the skilled student and teacher could detect the hand of

God in the past. Absolute truths and universal principles guided these prewar historians. Bancroft had little patience for secularized historicism: "They speak falsely who say that truth is the daughter of time; it is the child of eternity, and as old as the Divine mind."[18]

By the time historians began professionalizing their discipline near the end of the nineteenth century, many had rejected what they referred to as the "fables and precious pieties" of Bancroft's generation. Inspired by the German passion for accurate and unbiased history, American historians of the new era pursued a *science* of the past. Speculative or philosophical history was out; rational, plodding, and particular history was in. In 1884 professional and amateur scholars created the American Historical Association (AHA), which soon embodied this new approach. Its leaders encouraged members to implement scientific methods. In 1910 an early AHA president asked, "did not Darwin spend twenty years in accumulating data, and in selecting typical phenomena, before he so much as ventured a generalization?" Why shouldn't historians be as fastidious, as scientific as their colleagues in the hard sciences? Historians were to be careful methodological agnostics, constantly aware of biases and preconceptions that might cloud their judgments.[19]

To the dismay of many Americans, the acids of professional history eroded the myths of an enchanted past. Late nineteenth-century biblical criticism applied the science of history and textual analysis to God's word. Conservative Protestants feared this would undo the faith. "Higher" questions of culture, interpretation, authorship, editing, and revision now dominated the work of biblical scholars and historians. Denominations held heresy trials for errant views of scripture. A Union Seminary Old Testament professor faced the wrath of the Presbyterians after claiming that the Bible should be read and studied much as other ancient texts were. "The Bible is not an infallible book," wrote Washington Gladden, a leading Protestant minister in the early 1890s. For him, the discrepancies and outright contradictions of the Bible proved that its writers "were not miraculously protected" from historical inaccuracy.

Such outright assaults on the Bible were followed by vigorous counterattacks on all fronts. The early twentieth-century celebrity preacher Billy Sunday actually linked German higher criticism with the conflagrations of the day. "Never will I try to rearrange God's plan," he pledged. "How do I not know that he isn't using the Allies to punish Germany for higher criticism and heresies?" he mused as the battles of World War I raged. For Sunday and millions of others like him the 1925 Scopes Trial put the Bible to the test. The higher critics, it seemed, won the day. That dramatic showdown embarrassed fundamentalists and proved to many that they, too, would lose in the court of public opinion. Late nineteenth- and early twentieth-century researchers, applying despised critical methods to America's own sacred documents, questioned the vaunted ideals of the country's Founders. Were not the signers of the Constitution motivated by property concerns? Did not these men hope to secure the privileges of elites?[20]

Early twentieth-century Protestantism fractured along conservative and liberal lines. A conservative critic warned that liberal theology bore so little relation to Christianity that it belonged in a distinct category. The cohesion of Protestantism disintegrated under the pressures of new scientific discoveries, theological innovation, and an ever-changing culture. From the time of the Scopes Trial to the 1960s, the evangelical side of the Protestant fracture remained largely absent from national and local politics. Unconcerned about disputes over modern history, evangelicals focused on denominational matters, evangelism, and doctrinal debates instead.[21]

By the end of the twentieth century, however, many conservative Christians worried that they had lost ground to liberal adversaries, and had even been booted from the public square. Politicized amateur historians responded by reasserting America's Christian heritage. With a greater stake in the political process after the tumultuous 1960s and

1970s, they laid claim to the country's past after decades of disinterest in professional historical scholarship, and even less interest in politics.[22]

AT MID-CENTURY A FEW vocal preachers rose to fame as fierce opponents of communism, a brightly lit ideological candle that attracted all kinds of moths. The cause energized a new sense of America's history and destiny. Curiously, perhaps, enthusiastic evangelists preaching a fast-approaching Apocalypse joined this crusade, despite the suspicious eye they usually cast on political activity. But "godless communism" posed a threat that evangelicals could not ignore. Earlier involvement in Sabbath legislation, temperance, anti-Masonry, and antislavery served as a guide for political action. The communist menace at home and abroad conjured grand conspiracies and shadow organizations in the evangelical imagination. Those speculations fit neatly with apocalyptic visions of the faithful, looking for Jesus' imminent return. Communist leaders naturally loomed large in the pantheon of Anti-Christs predicted by evangelicals.[23]

In the 1950s and 1960s the Iowa-based Christian Anti-Communism Crusade and the Christian Crusade in Tulsa rallied tens of thousands of followers. The latter's monthly magazine warned its 90,000 readers that atheistic communists and their naïve sympathizers had Christian America under siege. The Christian Crusade's leader, Billy James Hargis, viewed America as God's last hope against worldwide socialism and the "last stronghold of Christianity." "Satan knows this," Hargis assured readers, explaining why the Devil fought his ministry so fiercely.[24]

The John Birch Society—the most influential right-wing, anticommunist organization in the country—painted Eisenhower red and made national headlines. Fellow cold warrior Hargis published a book titled *Communist America—Must It Be?* and scored with an American public feeling menaced by the Soviet Union. In 1960 his first edition quickly sold 15,000 copies, and a second printing sold 10,000. Hargis's good-versus-evil diatribe called on Christians to oppose an activist Supreme Court, the United Nations, wicked public officials, secular liberals, and public schools that had fallen into the hands of Marxists. Godly citizens, Hargis argued, needed to wake up and lay claim to their country. "Our founding fathers did not intend to establish a government that did not recognize God and Jesus Christ," the Oklahoma preacher lamented. He wrote about the Christian origins of the nation and the perils of the present. As we face the satanic Soviet forces, Hargis asked, "Are we ashamed of our nation? Are we ashamed of our flag? Are we ashamed of our God? Are we ashamed of the faith of our fathers?"[25]

Billy Graham, America's most celebrated preacher, was not ashamed. And while never as strident as Hargis, he had been fighting communism and calling America back to its Christian roots since he first made national headlines in the late 1940s. Backed by news mogul William Randolph Hearst, the Florida native and graduate of Wheaton College took to the national stage. His popular revival meetings—which eventually aired on television—drew millions. Graham toured the country preaching judgment on a nation in the grip of gambling, alcohol, lewd entertainment, and infidelity. He assured reporters eager for his pronouncements that he avoided political and theological bickering. As the Cold War heated up, however, the threat of communism captured his attention. All might be well, he preached, in one of the most reassuring voices ever to emerge from behind a pulpit, if Americans returned to the untarnished Christianity of the nation's early history.[26]

That was the theme of one of Graham's 1947 sermons. Following a preaching tour in Europe, he reflected on the role the United States played on the world stage. Might the country go the way of Babylon, Rome, and other great fallen empires? "The wages of a nation's sin, the wages of an organization's sin, the wages of individual sin," he thundered, "is death." America's foundations lay squarely on the Bible. Its

Founding Fathers exemplified Christian virtue. But now the enemies at the gates—higher criticism, climbing divorce rates, atheism—threatened that holy legacy. "America as we know it today," worried the evangelist, "cannot possibly reach 1975."[27]

Graham, like so many evangelicals in these years, was ambivalent about partisan politics. When asked about the 1963 civil rights march on Washington, he responded, "Only when Christ comes again will little white children of Alabama walk hand in hand with little black children." Other evangelicals looking for an early return of Jesus also harbored grave suspicions about politics and social change. In the 1960s Jerry Falwell—the most influential right-wing Christian of the late twentieth century—also hesitated when it came to direct political action. He criticized the tactics and principles of the civil rights movement, which made pulpits into political stumps. "Preachers are not called to be politicians," he declared, "but to be soul winners."[28]

When future attorney general John Ashcroft first contemplated going into politics, he had no role models in his Assemblies of God church. He knew only one other member of his denomination who had run for public office, J. Roswell Flower. And Flower was only a Springfield, Missouri, city councilman. (As a councilman he energetically worked to convince residents that the fluoridation of water was a communist plot.) In a 1988 interview, Ashcroft pondered the evangelical tradition's opposition to "government—almost as a worldly thing—in the same way that we shunned formal education for a long time."[29]

The social and cultural tumult of the 1960s changed everything, however, and conservative Christians entered the political arena in force. Editorials in *Christianity Today* highlighted left-wing revolutionary zeal and moral turpitude. Student protesters, campus radicals, and disheveled, pot-smoking rock icons looked like harbingers of the end of civilization. "As respect for law and order wanes, violence and crime rise to new heights," warned a writer in evangelicalism's premier magazine. "Today paganism is baring its vicious spirit as part of the contemporary American soul," he announced. "Civil society seems to be falling apart." Paul Weyrich, architect of the new Christian Right, spoke of the "bitter fruit of liberalism." The leftward turn of the 1960s and "policies which are anti-family, anti-religion, and devoid of respect for traditional values" energized Christian activists.[30]

Years later Jerry Falwell commented that the 1973 *Roe v. Wade* decision legalizing abortion thrust him into the political realm, but the evidence points in another direction. In the 1970s the Carter-appointed head of the Internal Revenue Service proposed that private Christian academies and schools, primarily in the South, should have to prove that they were not segregated, or they would lose tax-exempt status. Conservative critics—most of them attending all-white churches—stormed in opposition to this state intervention and gathered around a common cause of Christian rights. In ever-greater numbers evangelicals were voting and participating in politics.[31]

At the same time, born-again Christianity was growing. The liberal mainline denominations—Methodist, Presbyterian, Episcopal, and Congregational—suffered membership losses from 1970 to 1985 while the Southern Baptists grew by 23 percent. Pentecostal and holiness churches thrived. These believers wanted to claim their country's godly heritage, wrote an author in the popular evangelical magazine *Christian Life* in 1971. He proclaimed the sacred cause: "When God needed a navigator to discover this great land, He had Columbus ready!" "When He needed an author for the finest declaration of human rights the world has ever seen, He had Jefferson ready!" If secular colleges and universities would not teach America's godly history, others must step up. Opening its doors in 1968, a small Nazarene college in the suburbs of Kansas City adopted an "American Heritage" theme. As protests raged on most of the nation's campuses, students at MidAmerica Nazarene College were encouraged to honor the flag, remember the sacrifices of America's fallen heroes, and reflect on the motto "In God

We Trust." American eagle statues dotted the campus on the edge of the prairie. Less than a decade later, *Newsweek* proclaimed 1976 "The Year of the Evangelical." As Americans celebrated the country's bicentennial, evangelical presses rolled out books with titles like *One Nation under God; America: God Shed His Grace on Thee;* and *Faith, Stars and Stripes.*[32]

God and country were on the radar that year and writers became inspired. America had been a "Christian" nation since its founding, a minister declared in *Preacher's Magazine.* Only in recent years had that sacred truth been questioned. For example, "Now there are those who like to prohibit singing Christmas carols, since there are 'minorities' who do not believe in Christ." Things needed to change. "Bible-believing Christians can stop wringing their hands with a guilty feeling because they are Americans and love Old Glory," wrote a former missionary. America needed redemption. Since the 1960s liberal social planners had tried to enslave passive citizens. The missionary found strength in the Christian heritage of the Pilgrims while she pondered God's judgment in these "last days." "Will Godly men and women pray about running for office this year?" Others marked the bicentennial by lamenting the state of the nation and calling on Christians to take action and reclaim their history. Evangelical intellectual and key shaper of the movement Carl F. H. Henry echoed those sentiments in *Christianity Today,* a publication he founded in 1956 at the urging of Billy Graham. Why were Americans, and Christians in particular, ashamed to be blue-blooded patriots? Even third-world communists celebrated their nation's achievements. Of course, Henry acknowledged that Watergate and Vietnam had disillusioned Americans, but Christians were duty-bound to love their country and respect their rulers. Believers needed to look to the nation's past, even though secular historians routinely ignored "divine providence" and the religious roots of the country. Across America evangelicals were waking up to new possibilities, rubbing their eyes as a bright new sun rose on the political horizon.[33]

"Could it be that we Americans, as a people, had been given a mission by Almighty God?" asked Peter Marshall and David Manuel in 1975 as they pondered the connections between their faith and their country. Marshall, who died in September 2010, was a Yale graduate, the son of Peter Marshall, United States chaplain to the Senate, and Catherine Marshall, whose best-selling biography of her husband, *A Man Called Peter,* became a popular film. Manuel, a conservative Christian editor at Doubleday and fellow Yalie, heard Marshall talk about America's sacred history at a Cape Cod church in the mid-1970s. Marshall asked those present to reconsider their country's history. Wasn't Christopher Columbus inspired by the Holy Spirit as he sailed west? Weren't the Pilgrims who landed on New England's rocky shores driven by divine purpose? "We as a people have thrown away our Christian heritage," Marshall declared from the pulpit.[34]

Marshall and Manuel were horrified at the direction America had taken in recent years. Sexual promiscuity swept across the country like wildfire. Communist forces at home and overseas undermined whatever was left of the American dream. Divorce rates climbed and homosexuals demanded new rights. At the same time New Left historians and revisionists denounced the crimes of America's Founders. In 1975 historian Francis Jennings wrote a book to uncover the lies and hypocrisies of European colonizers. Columbus was in it for the money. The Puritan Massachusetts Bay Colony's governor John Winthrop was a liar. "The Watergate deceits," Jennings argued, "do not seem to be a very new thing in history."[35]

Marshall and Manuel teamed up to rewrite America's history. In contrast to the secular accounts, God would play a central role in their story, restoring optimism to a nation crippled by doubts and fears. Marshall has recalled that neither he nor Manuel "had ever done any serious research after our student days." Yet they "had prayed earnestly about it, and we felt that God would have us proceed." What Marshall discovered about America's divine origins, he later claimed, he did not learn as a history major at Yale in the late 1950s and early 1960s. Indeed, history professors were boring moral equivocators. Marshall and Manuel scoured university and public libraries in New England in search of God's work in ages past. If they could show "God's hand in our nation's beginnings," they thought, perhaps they could rekindle Americans' patriotism and sense of purpose.[36]

Their book, *The Light and the Glory* (1977), chronicled the nation's lofty Christian past. Like the Israel of the Old Testament, America was in a covenant with God. If Christians could only see that clearly, they could act accordingly. America's history was a divine drama, as good and evil constantly played off each other. They argued that God directed Columbus's ships. God even made the Massachusetts Bay Colony a "City on a Hill." God led the Continental Army to victory in the American Revolution. Satan, always in opposition, won his fair share of battles, too, but God triumphed overall. The Devil—through witchcraft, the occult, Quakers, and unruly preachers like Anne Hutchinson and Roger Williams—occasionally plagued God's people. Yet those episodes were brief, and the faithful dealt appropriately with all manner of demons and troublemakers.[37]

The book was a stunning success and spawned a children's edition. Marshall and Manuel developed homeschooling curricula and videos based on it. Homeschoolers and private Christian academies made it an enormous hit. The book sold almost a million copies, making it one of the best-selling nonfiction Christian books of all time.[38] It also launched the Peter Marshall Ministries website, which sold books, advertised trips to historical sites in New England, announced upcoming lectures, and served as a virtual podium for the fiery Marshall. *The Light and the Glory* gave Marshall a platform to speak as a historian and an expert, making him a force to be reckoned with. As a Christian authority, he took on what he imagined to be clueless secular historians. In 2005 Marshall reflected on the sorry state of affairs in academic history. It was a "sad truth today about this lie about the Founding Fathers all being a bunch of deists," he lamented in a documentary interview. He blamed "secularist professors in our universities and colleges, who don't do much original research." Out-of-touch historians, he reasoned, "don't want to be disturbed by . . . the reality of this situation to find out they've been teaching wrong."[39]

Just as Marshall was certain that the Founders were not deists and that God guided the nation in ages past, he was also sure that God's anger burned hot when the country careened into a moral abyss. Marshall read natural disasters as divine punishment, logged the moral decay of America's colleges and universities, and blasted Democrats and gays with equal fury. God, he said, allowed Hurricane Katrina to devastate the Gulf Coast to shake Americans out of their spiritual lethargy. The Virginia Tech shooting of 2007 was payback for legalization of abortion. The 2007 wildfires that consumed acres of California real estate may have been divine punishment for that state's runaway political correctness and progay legislation. God, however, could bring wonder from disasters such as Barack Obama's shocking election in November 2008. That, said Marshall, was clearly a sign of God's judgment on America. "Until we come to repentance—both individually and corporately," he warned, "I believe that things will continue to get worse." He assured readers of his blog, "I can say this with confidence because of what I know about God's plan for this nation, and His hand in our history."[40]

All this was nothing new, said Marshall. From the days of the Puritans God has chastised Americans with calamities. Christians should respond by reclaiming America. In 1996 Marshall asked at a Christian Coalition meeting: "What is a Christian's primary responsibility?" Was it to evangelize or to get involved in government? As the crowd mulled it over, Marshall responded that it was the latter. For far too long the saints had ceded politics and American history to their liberal adversaries.[41] Marshall's explanation of upheaval and Christians' duty to reclaim their country found a warm reception among believers who felt that secular elites and the curriculum of public schools, colleges, and universities did not represent their interests.

The new political message Marshall adopted appealed to other evangelists, too, like Francis Schaeffer. A self-styled intellectual, the irascible Schaeffer battled secular demons by writing popular history and philosophy. His best-selling 1976 book *How Should We Then Live: The Decline of Western Thought and Culture* reads like a born-again version of Will Durant's *Story of Civilization,* minus the scholarly apparatus. Schaeffer chronicled the horrors of the modern West from Søren Kierkegaard and Marcel Duchamp to the Beatles. Westerners had lost their moral bearing, he sermonized, and had replaced the Christian God with cheap materialism and sham philosophies. The book sold over a million copies in the decades that followed and was made into a popular film series.[42] Once again history became a story of moral decay that only God could correct. This was a message that evangelicals welcomed and that reinforced their faith.

Schaeffer and his son, Franky, took up the prolife cause in the 1970s and rubbed shoulders with America's conservative political elite—including Congressman Jack Kemp and Surgeon General C. Everett Koop. By the early 1980s, *Newsweek* called Francis Schaeffer a fundamentalist guru. The Schaeffers hoped to get Christians engaged in politics. Believers, they argued, needed to know how high the stakes were. Evangelicals must own America's Christian heritage. The nation was founded on the principles of the Bible and the Reformation, the elder Schaeffer declared in *A Christian Manifesto* (1981), a battle plan for the Christian Right. The book argued that the Founders "understood that they were founding the country upon the concept that goes back into the Judeo-Christian thinking that there is Someone there who gave inalienable rights." Those principles had vanished in the twentieth century, and the government was now in the hands of materialists and humanists, fumed Schaeffer. Within a year *A Christian Manifesto* had sold approximately 300,000 copies. Falwell distributed it to viewers of his television program. The book inspired Christian Right activists for years. Among them was Katherine Harris, former Florida attorney general and a U.S. representative. Her time spent at L'Abri, Francis Schaeffer's European evangelical retreat center, and the impression Schaeffer made on her deeply informed her religious and political outlook, she states.[43]

The Schaeffers had embarked on a bold campaign, joining Marshall to reclaim America for Christ. In an extreme form, such views have come to be called Reconstructionism, or Dominionism. This controversial theology of religious-political dominion takes its cue from Genesis 1:26: "And God said, Let us make man in our image, after our likeness: and let them have dominion over the fish of the sea, and over the fowl of the air, and over the cattle, and over all the earth, and over every creeping thing that creepeth upon the earth." Dominionists claim that America has a special relationship with God and that society must be rebuilt on that principle. Mixing flag-waving nationalism and Old Testament legal codes, this relatively small group places great emphasis on America's holy origins.

The late Rousas John Rushdoony—son of Armenian immigrants, Calvinist theologian, conservative historian, homeschooling advocate, and critic—founded the movement. Schaeffer studied Rushdoony's work in the 1960s and even based a L'Abri seminar on one of his books on American history. Rushdoony's stern Calvinism and forceful challenge to secularism enlivened conservative believers like Schaeffer. His 1973 tome, *The Institutes of Biblical Law,* was fierce, promoting limited government and advocating brutal punishments for personal sins. The death penalty, claimed Rushdoony, should be meted out for murder, adultery, incest, homosexuality, and witchcraft. "Predestination is an inescapable concept," he told students at the conservative Hillsdale College in 1973; "it is simply a declaration that somewhere an ultimate law, force, cause, power, or direction governs all things." And in his estimation, "every law order is a religious establishment; the important question is, of which religion?" Rushdoony denounced statist governments as pagan and upheld America's Founders as exemplars of Christian virtue. Thomas Jefferson and Benjamin Franklin were not deists, he insisted. Their thought was, quite the contrary, infused with Calvinistic predestination and providentialism. Unlike the secular—and disastrous—French Revolution, the American Revolution was rooted in biblical Christianity and notions of divine law.[44]

Americans could look to their heritage to make real changes, thought Rushdoony. Unlike premillennial fundamentalists—who wait for Jesus to rescue them from a wrecked world before a thousand years of peace—he and his followers were avowedly postmillennial, like many mid-nineteenth-century evangelicals. Rushdoony assumed that the labors of Christians would eventually enable the return of Christ after world governments had come under his authority. National progress is simply working out the plans of God. "The American sense of destiny, from colonial times to well into the 19th century," he asserted, "was a Christian sense of mission and calling." But some Americans did not fit the pattern. Indians, for instance, were "heedless of the future" and wasteful of their resources. Their removal was a blessing.[45]

Rushdoony toiled in obscurity. His work on God, Indians, law, and the Founders was unknown even in his lifetime. *Christianity Today,* the most influential evangelical magazine of the twentieth century, seldom mentioned him or his work. But his extreme ideas would get a dramatic hearing through the efforts of D. James Kennedy. This high-profile television and radio preacher carried Rushdoony's ideas about history, politics, and providence to mass audiences throughout the 1980s and 1990s. In doing so, Kennedy, for decades one of America's leading preachers, shaped conservative Christianity as few others had. By the time he died in 2007 Kennedy had established a vast, powerful media empire.[46]

Kennedy woke one Sunday morning in 1953 to a shouting radio

preacher's sermon. "Suppose you were to die today and stand before God," the minister's voice crackled over the speaker. "'What right do you have to enter into My heaven?'—what would you say?" Believing this was God calling him, Kennedy soon after entered the ministry. In 1959 he became senior minister of Coral Ridge Presbyterian Church in Fort Lauderdale. His original congregation consisted of forty-five members but grew to ten thousand by the time of his death. He built on that numerical success, writing more than fifty books, founding Knox Theological Seminary and a K–12 school, managing a media empire, and broadcasting his sermons daily on television and radio.[47]

Kennedy was a powerful presence in the Christian Right. His Ph.D. in religious education from New York University lent him a credibility that others lacked. In 2005 he ranked alongside Billy Graham and megachurch pastor and evangelical leader Rick Warren as one of the ten most trusted spokespersons for Christianity, according to a Barna Group poll. Even after his death, coralridge.org remained a thriving website, rebroadcasting his sermons. His broadcasts also run on the Armed Forces Network and Trinity Broadcast Network, reaching over three million viewers in the United States and abroad.

American history dominated Kennedy's agenda. Some of his most popular books and DVDs explored historical themes.[48] "What one individual would you identify as the virtual founder of America?" Kennedy asked readers of his ministry's bulletin in 2007. Washington? Jefferson? Franklin? Paine? No. According to Kennedy, it should, in fact, be John Calvin, Protestant reformer and leader of Geneva's sixteenth-century theocracy. George Bancroft, whom Kennedy called the "great American historian," claimed as much about Calvin. "If we are to get back to the principles that made America great," Kennedy mused, "I believe we must get back to the principles of John Calvin, because it was precisely his principles that made this nation great." The sovereignty of God, the authority of scripture, and the reality of sin mattered most to that stern reformer and, by extension, to the colonists.[49]

Kennedy hammered on typical themes found in books like his popular work *What If America Were a Christian Nation Again?* God had blessed the Founders and American Christians—including Abraham Lincoln—over the centuries. Like Marshall, Kennedy had no trouble tracking the footprints of divine providence across the wilderness of history. God had thwarted the efforts of the Catholic nations of Spain and France. He favored the Pilgrims and the Puritans. Through General Washington God had orchestrated America's victory over British tyranny. "America would be a free nation," wrote Kennedy, "and it would be that Puritan and evangelical form of Christianity that would give birth to our nation."[50]

Americans were losing their way, however, just like the Old Testament Hebrews who strayed off the path of righteousness. To get the country back on track, Kennedy established the Center for Reclaiming America for Christ in 1996. The center now serves as a model for "reclamation" efforts around the country. In 1996 the first Reclaiming America for Christ conference in Fort Lauderdale attracted eight hundred politicians, conservative activists, and church leaders from thirty-nine states. Participants attended minicourses on Christian civics, economics, and constitutional law. Keynote speaker Edwin Meese, Ronald Reagan's attorney general, read from the Mayflower Compact about the "religious antecedents of our country." He concluded by quoting the militant hymn "Onward Christian Soldiers." At that event and the annual conferences that followed, leading conservative politicians spoke to believers, frustrated that the American establishment was ignoring the sacred roots of the nation and secularizing the public sphere.[51]

At the 2005 Reclaiming America for Christ conference, Katherine Harris urged her audience to "win back America for God." Also present was the two-and-a-half-ton Ten Commandments monument that Judge Roy Moore had installed in the Alabama Supreme Court building. Since a federal judge had ordered the removal of the granite behemoth, supporters had taken "Roy's Rock" on a cross-country tour. Conference attendees posed for pictures next to that symbol of defiance. Moore's avid Christian Americanism and flouting of federal laws inspired Kennedy's flock. Harris told a Baptist newspaper in 2006 that God chose the nation's rulers and only Christian politicians could stem the legislation of sin. Too many conservative Christians believed they should not be involved in politics. That, she said, was a "lie we have been told."[52]

In 2005 Kennedy explained the goal of Reclaiming America for Christ to Terry Gross on NPR. Gross asked if Kennedy ever considered how that title might sound to a Jew, Muslim, Buddhist, or Hindu. Unapologetic, Kennedy reminded her that America's Christian past was not up for debate. Lofting Founders' quotes at Gross, he argued that America's real history had been forgotten: "The Christian foundation of America has been expurgated from all of our textbooks and our schools." But he was addressing that problem, with the help of experts like Rushdoony and David Barton, who had both appeared on his radio program, men who could be depended upon for authoritative history.[53]

BY THE 1990S BARTON was the premier Christian historian. He was also leading the assault on the separation of church and state. Though Marshall and Schaeffer sold more books, Barton more than matched them as a tireless lecturer, conservative advocate, and media personality. With a B.A. in religious education from Oral Roberts University, an Honorary Doctorate of Letters from Pensacola Christian College, and a winsome Southern charm, Barton rose to prominence out of relative obscurity. In the 1980s he taught and coached at a fundamentalist K–12 school in Aledo, Texas. He later became its principal. WallBuilders, his grassroots organization, now shapes public and private school curricula and educates Americans about the nation's righteous heritage. WallBuilders is a reference to Israel's rebuilding of its walls in the Old Testament book of Nehemiah. Just as the wayward Israelites reconstructed the walls of Jerusalem and returned to the faith of their fathers, Barton said, modern believers could rebuild on the foundations of America's Christian past.

Barton's message falls on welcome ears, and his close ties to the nation's conservative political establishment make him well-placed to deliver it. For many years he was cochair of the Texas Republican party, and in 2004 the GOP enlisted him to speak to church groups in Ohio about the upcoming election. Averaging 250 public lectures each year, he has spoken about America's Christian roots to thousands of children, pastors, politicians, and housewives. Many of his lectures are flawlessly delivered verbatim from memory, and his encyclopedic recall dazzles his audiences. With a perpetually young, boyish face looking out from under a trademark cowboy hat, and sporting an American-flag shirt, the articulate Barton inspires churchgoers around the country.[54]

Despite his amateur status and marginal credentials, Barton has served as an expert witness for Supreme Court cases, spoken to U.S. lawmakers on the divine presence in history, and helped develop public school curricula for several states. In 2005, Senate Majority Leader Bill Frist invited Barton to lead a spiritual heritage tour. One hundred senators and their families were promised "a Fresh Perspective on Our Nation's Capitol" by "a historian noted for his detailed research." The project made no sense to Senate Minority Leader Dick Durbin. "I would have to ask Sen. Frist why he feels this man has any professional expertise explaining what the U.S. Capitol is all about," said the skeptical Durbin. Rob Boston of Americans United for Separation of Church and State considered Barton a poor choice for Frist's tour. Barton "is to American history what the fundamentalist creationist is to science," claimed Boston.[55]

Others shared that disdain. Barton and his organization wielded too much influence and misinformed Americans, they thought. WallBuilders sold over 100,000 videotapes on America's Christian heritage by 1994. At $19 apiece, they helped build the organization. A disturbed American Civil Liberties Union (ACLU) responded with a video of its own. A Virginia ACLU director lamented that Barton sent "a misleading message, ringing throughout the religious right, that seek[s] to create a state religion."[56]

In the eyes of his supporters, of course, Barton's enthusiasm for spreading the good news about the religiosity of the Revolutionary generation was warranted. Public school and college textbooks did, even in the eyes of secular historians, downplay religion or treat it episodically. Rarely was it related to the larger national narrative. Yet in his rush to make his case, Barton consistently stumbled. He employed secondary and tertiary sources to mine key quotes, to take one example. Critics from Americans United for Separation of Church and State dogged Barton for using a dozen unverified quotations. WallBuilders eventually published a list of "Unconfirmed Quotations" on its website and Barton had to revise his publications accordingly. Still, he argued that WallBuilders' standards for scholarship were actually higher than those of the academy.[57] A James Madison scholar from the University of Richmond could not have disagreed more, upbraiding Barton for using unconfirmed quotes and for misrepresenting evidence. "Barton's claims have no relationship to truth," he wrote, "but can be floated easily to support political agendas concerning school prayer."[58]

Like many conservative Christians, Barton thinks that the twentieth-century Supreme Court has chipped away at the nation's religious foundations. He finds parallels between errant Old Testament Israelites and wayward modern liberals. He lambasts the 1947 *Everson v. Board of Education* decision, which first applied the doctrine of separation of church and state to the states. Similarly, the *Engel v. Vitale* (1962) decision banning official school prayer proved to Barton that "the Court had affronted the traditional interpretation of the First Amendment." The equally maddening case of *School District of Abington v. Schempp* (1963) forbade the required reading of scripture in public schools. Graphs in Barton's book *Original Intent* illustrated the results of these disastrous cases: a rise in violence, crime, and sexual immorality and a decline in family stability and SAT scores.[59]

Barton says that church and state should never have been separated. "'Separation of church and state' currently means almost exactly the opposite of what it originally meant," he challenges, contending that few Americans know much about history or America's legal apparatus. "American history today has become a dreary academic subject," he laments on the WallBuilders website. In his estimation "history is presented in such an edited, revised, and politically-correct manner that God's hand is rarely visible." Academics are especially to blame. Barton claims that the peer-review process and the heavy interpretive component of professional history make it unreadable and unreliable. He thinks young scholars making their way to seminary face a similarly depressing situation. "Do you actually study the Bible or do you study only higher criticism?" he asks. He dismisses complaints about his credentials by referring to the unvarnished truth of the primary sources he employs. Conservative talk show host Glenn Beck, one of Barton's chief promoters, makes the same point: "historians have been going back and trying to piece things together and bring in their own ideas instead of going back to the original sources, and that's really the problem." The claim is reminiscent of the longstanding fundamentalist directives to read the Bible *unmediated* by scholars or priests.[60]

So what do we learn from the unmediated documents of American history? On WallBuilders' website and in its books Barton details the astonishing acts of God in American history and the Christian faithfulness of individuals as diverse as John Adams, Thomas Jefferson, and

Benjamin Franklin. Barton's online pieces offer up the wisdom of the Founders on any given subject: "Was George Washington a Christian?"; "The Founding Fathers on Jesus, Christianity and the Bible"; "The Founding Fathers and Slavery"; and, fittingly for current culture wars, "The Founding Fathers on Creation and Evolution." Seemingly contradictory evidence like the Treaty of Tripoli, 1796–1797, which stated that "the Government of the United States of America is not, in any sense, founded on the Christian religion," is laboriously dismantled by Barton. As of 2008 two of Barton's books—*America's Godly Heritage* and *Original Intent*—had sold 58,000 and 150,000 copies respectively. Barton has also sold hundreds of thousands of other books, tapes, and videos.[61]

In 2010 Barton reached his largest audience by becoming a regular guest on Glenn Beck's Fox News program as well as Beck's radio show. According to a 2009 Harris poll, Beck was America's second-favorite television personality, after Oprah Winfrey. Beck's patronage, like Winfrey's, could make a career or sell millions of copies of a book.[62] Barton received a dramatic lift for his message after appearing on the *Glenn Beck Program.* Barton's day as America's historian had come, said Beck: "my gut tells me you are one of the most important men in America for this message today." Though Beck had barely started college himself, he launched his online Beck University in 2010 to explore ideas of Faith, Hope, and Charity. He appointed Barton, "an expert in historical and constitutional issues," as one of the school's "professors." Barton also joined Beck for the August 28 Restoring Honor gathering, held at the Lincoln Memorial in the capital. Scheduled on the anniversary of Martin Luther King's famous march on Washington, the event sought to awaken Americans to the need for a dramatic change in government leadership and to honor the country's heroes and heritage. The night before the Restoring Honor rally, Beck held a kickoff event at the Kennedy Center. Speakers at the event—more religious revival than political crusade—included Barton, J. Randy Forbes, action star Chuck Norris, and the conservative Texas pastor and Christian Zionist John Hagee.[63]

In Barton's view, America is a Christian nation—not Muslim, Buddhist, Hindu, or secular. Not surprisingly, Barton questioned the 2007 unofficial swearing-in ceremony of the first Muslim congressman, Keith Ellison of Minnesota. The use of the Koran in that ritual, said Barton, was out of place and went against American tradition. He also opposed a Hindu prayer that opened a July 2007 session of the Senate.

Barton moves easily from history to science. As a representative evangelical and an expert witness on the evangelical view of global warming, he addressed members of Congress in 2007. "From the beginning, God warned about elevating nature and the environment over man and his Creator," he remarked. Besides, he went on, there was no clear scientific consensus that global warming was a reality.[64]

He has had a more significant impact as a chief advisor for the National Council on Bible Curriculum in Public Schools (NCBCPS). In 2010 the organization boasted that 555 school districts in 38 states used their materials and that over 360,000 students had taken their courses.[65] Critics of the curriculum note that it encourages creationist pseudoscience and runs counter to prevailing currents in biblical studies, history, and archeology. Indeed, archeologist J. O. Kinnaman, one of the "respected scholars" on which the curriculum relies, claims to have personally seen Jesus' school records in India and argues that Jesus and Paul ventured to Great Britain. He has made even more bizarre claims about the lost continent of Atlantis and the pyramid of Giza. A Southern Methodist University religious studies scholar concludes, not surprisingly, that the NCBCPS materials are "filled with factual errors, tabloid scholarship, and plagiarism, as well as religious claims and presuppositions that cause them to run afoul of pertinent court rulings."[66]

Barton's work with the NCBCPS puts him in strange, notorious company. But it has also allowed him to present his version of American history to over 100,000 public school students. The council declares, "The Bible was the foundation and blueprint for our Constitution, our Declaration of Independence, our educational system, and our entire history until the last twenty to thirty years." The NCBCPS recommends WallBuilders videos and other materials for exploring America's holy past. Barton's Christian Americanism runs throughout the curriculum.[67]

Such efforts were dwarfed by other opportunities to shape the nation's public school curriculum. Both Marshall and Barton lent their expertise to the Texas State Board of Education, which made national and international headlines in 2009 and 2010 for its conservative revamping of the history curriculum. Approved in May 2010, the new curriculum made numerous changes. Thomas Jefferson was removed from a list of Enlightenment thinkers. Students would now learn more about conservative individuals and groups. Pupils would "describe the causes and key organizations and individuals of the conservative resurgence of the 1980s and 1990s, including Phyllis Schlafly, the Contract with America, the Heritage Foundation, the Moral Majority, and the National Rifle Association."[68] There was public uproar as Marshall and Barton proposed to eliminate key figures of the civil rights era like César Chávez and Thurgood Marshall. They also wanted textbooks to highlight tensions between the Christian West and the Islamic East. In that simplistic view the Barbary Wars in the early nineteenth century marked the "original war against Islamic Terrorism." Critics howled. Marshall and Barton were not historians, wrote John Fea, a professor of history at Messiah College, a leading evangelical school. History, wrote Fea, should not have to conform to the political or religious whims of the present. "The board has made these standards political and had little academic discussion about what students need to learn," said a dissenter on the board, ashamed of what the curriculum overhaul would do to education in her state.[69] The American Historical Association also registered its displeasure, urging the Texas board to rethink major omissions and revisions in the interest of "historical accuracy."[70]

EVEN BEFORE BARTON emerged as a nationally recognized, highly controversial figure, he had ascended to great heights in the evangelical world. In 2005 *Time* magazine named him one of the twenty-five most influential evangelicals in America, along with James Dobson, Chuck Colson, and Rick Warren. Evangelical historian Mark Noll, one of Barton's critics, also made the list.[71]

With a Ph.D. from Vanderbilt University, Noll taught for twenty-seven years at Wheaton College in Illinois, America's premier evangelical school, before accepting the Francis A. McAnaney Chair of history at the University of Notre Dame. Noll is a major scholar. The *Atlantic Monthly* called his 2002 book *America's God: From Jonathan Edwards to Abraham Lincoln* "almost certainly the most significant work of American historical scholarship" of the year. That richly detailed volume was much like dozens of Noll's other books, essays, and editorial pieces published with leading university presses, evangelical publishers, and opinion magazines. In 2006 President George W. Bush awarded Noll the National Humanities Medal.[72]

Intellectual historian Mark Lilla has commented on the work of Noll and Barton and "the effort to reinterpret history to give religion a more central place in America's past—and, perhaps, in its future." Lilla praises the serious scholarship of Noll and another evangelical historian, George Marsden, who "counter the tendency in American historiography to rummage through the past for anticipations of our secular, egalitarian, multicultural present." Their work is a "useful corrective and reminds us that the role of religion in American life was large and the separation of church and state less clear than today." In marked contrast, states Lilla, is the "schlock history written by religious propagandists like David Barton, the author of the bizarre pastiche *The Myth of Separation,* who use selective quotations out of context to suggest that the framers were inspired believers who thought they were founding a Christian nation."[73]

Noll also finds Barton's work problematic. "Barton is a very hardworking researcher," Noll told the *New York Times* in 2005, "but what I guess I worry about is the collapsing of historical distance, and the effort to make really anybody fit directly into the category of the early 21st century evangelicals." Noll later remarked, "History done to prove a thesis in the present is going to be bad history." And prove a thesis in the present it does. Under Barton's influence the 2004 platform of the Republican Party of Texas read: "The Republican Party affirms that the United States of America is a Christian nation, and the public acknowledgement of God is undeniable in our history."[74]

Noll's work, informed by primary sources and recent scholarship, contrasts dramatically with Barton's pop, pseudo-history. Noll distinguishes between "ordinary" history and "providential history." The former limits itself to the material evidence that historians work with and traces causes and effects without resorting to metaphysical explanations. In his early research on Revolutionary America Noll concluded that providential history was bogus. Patriot ministers in the 1770s, for example, proclaimed that the Revolution was God's work. But what is a historian, even a Christian one, to make of this? "I came to the conclusion that this was hopeless," said Noll. "If you use Christian standards, it is very hard to say God brought the Revolution." Patriots labeled their Loyalist opponents, many of whom emigrated peacefully to Canada, godless agents of evil. Providentialist logic did not hold together, Noll thought.[75]

What can evangelicals say about "Christian America"? No nation, says Noll, can claim to be "God's new Israel." In his estimation, that conceit is a kind of idolatry. And though Americans in ages past firmly believed their country was in a covenant with God—much like seventeenth-century Puritans did—there is no good reason to believe that now. Historian Gordon Wood made a similar point in 2006 in discussing the uses and abuses of history for religious and political purposes. "We can't solve our current disputes over religion by looking back to the actual historical circumstances of the Founding," he wrote. A revival of the Founders' eighteenth-century religious views—diverse as they were, yet biased heavily toward Protestant Christianity—could not meet the needs of a complex, pluralistic twenty-first-century society. Noll acknowledges that Christian motives produced great good in America, though he also warns that the nation has seen great evil, often perpetrated in the name of Christ: "If we really believed the notion of a special manifestation of divine benevolence to America, we would end with a twisted view of God." How could Christians reconcile the ethics of Jesus with the slaughter of Native Americans? Could God ordain America's system of black slavery? It is almost equally incredible, Noll argues, that God would sanction the exploitation of workers or the degradation of the environment. Providential history, which assumes a special relationship between God and America, leads to awkward, even tortured, conclusions.[76]

Still, Noll contends that we can talk about "Christian America." The United States is not messianic, he emphasizes. But some aspects of the country's history comport with Christian principles. America's tradition of democratic liberty matches the Bible's teachings on the dignity of all peoples. At times, America has been a liberating force in the world. Americans have played significant roles in modern missionary and humanitarian movements. Even these conclusions, however—amounting to what Noll calls a "weak view" of Christian America—must be open to challenge and modification.[77]

Noll's measured approach is far from the popular work of those on both the right and the left. Some leftists distort the historical record to privilege secularism or pluralism. Susan Jacoby, Brooke Allen, and Christopher Hitchens present early American history in a revised, humanist fashion. Noll describes their work as "a little more sophisticated [than Barton's] just because the individuals who do that sort of thing tend to have had a different education." But he sees Christian Americanist history and its secular analog as "two peas in the same pod." In Noll's estimation Barton is no worse than those who say that the Founding Fathers believed in separation of church and state just as contemporaries do. The image of Revolutionary America as a God-free utopia of enlightened freethinkers is as distorted as the counterview of a theocratic founding.[78]

Many evangelicals, and sympathetic scholars in the academy, have questioned politically driven, uncritical, providentialist history. These historians and religious studies scholars have addressed intellectual problems that plague evangelicalism. Noll, Nathan Hatch, and George Marsden published a book in the 1980s to counter the first wave of Christian America popularizers. "We feel that a careful study of the facts of history shows that early America does not deserve to be considered uniquely, distinctly or even predominantly Christian," they concluded, "if we mean by the word 'Christian' a state of society reflecting the ideals presented in Scripture." In their view Marshall and Manuel's book *The Light and the Glory* differed little from seventeenth-century Puritan history and contained numerous blind spots. The deathtrap colony of Jamestown—racked by famine, disease, and violence—received short shrift, as did Baptists, Anglicans, and any groups and individuals who did not match the authors' rosy sacred story.[79]

Not long after Schaeffer's *Christian Manifesto* hit the shelves of Christian bookstores, evangelical historians in the academy dismissed the author's history as poorly researched, thinly veiled propaganda. Schaeffer was clearly not a scholar, Noll told *Newsweek* when several evangelical historians waged a war of words with the aging fundamentalist patriarch and his obstreperous son, Franky. Writing in *Christian Century,* one scholar called the Schaeffers to task for reading contemporary political values into the eighteenth century. The Founders' civil religion may have drawn on the ideals of theism, but this hardly made the country they were founding into a Christian nation. Noll thought it odd that Schaeffer, who spent his life defending biblical inerrancy, would sanctify Jefferson and Franklin—men who challenged the authority of scripture. Marsden and Noll told Schaeffer that the Founders' work was not distinctly biblical nor even Christian. A rankled Franky likened these critics to "weak Christians" and "revisionists."[80]

Other evangelical historians have criticized the anachronisms ubiquitous in Christian histories. Judging from such work, argues Randall Balmer, one would think that America was founded solely for religious purposes. This revisionism, he notes, "has also given rise to rather comic attempts to transform people like Thomas Jefferson, Thomas Paine, James Madison, and Abraham Lincoln into something like fundamentalists." The collapse of historical distance is grossly ahistorical.[81]

How do Christian Nation historians answer their challengers? On critiques of his credentials, Barton is unconcerned. His thorough knowledge of the lives of America's founding generation and the laws they enacted, he says, trumps any dusty pedigree. When he attributed false or suspect quotes to Benjamin Franklin, Abraham Lincoln, James Madison, Thomas Jefferson, and Patrick Henry, outside researchers called him to task. He is unshaken by such trials. Doubters represent the "kind of misportrayals and mischaracterizations" to which he has grown accustomed. Indeed, Barton and other Christian Americanists view such persecutions as the sign of a special calling.[82]

As the culture wars rage on, history and national identity will continue to exercise believers and nonbelievers alike. Barton, Marshall, and other amateur historians have pressed history into the service of politics and religion. Franky Schaeffer admitted as much in the early 1980s. History needed to serve the greater cause, he insisted. "Some evangelical historians quibble about which had more influence on America's founding fathers—the French Enlightenment or European Reformation," he scoffed. "Meanwhile, in the *real* nonevangelical world, the *culture goes down the tubes.*"[83]

In the light of popular perceptions of American history, Franky Schaeffer's anxiety seems misplaced. In the first decade of the twenty-first century, many Americans accept Barton and Marshall's vision of the past. A national survey in 2007 revealed that 55 percent of Americans believed that the Constitution established a Christian nation even though God is not mentioned in that founding document. In addition, 65 percent of those surveyed thought that the Founding Fathers intended the United States to be a Christian country. In 2006 the Pew Forum on Religion in Public Life conducted a similar poll that showed that "Americans overwhelmingly consider the U.S. a Christian nation: Two-in-three (67%) characterize the country this way, down just slightly from 71% in March 2005." A decade earlier, fewer Americans tied the nation's history to Christianity. Sixty-nine percent of those surveyed in 2006 also thought that liberals had gone too far "in trying to keep religion out of the schools."[84]

With such views prevailing, J. Randy Forbes pushed for his "America's Spiritual Heritage Week" resolution again in May 2009. He reintroduced the bill on the National Day of Prayer. James Dobson came to Washington, D.C., to lend his support, and Focus on the Family called the resolution "one of the more amazing bills ever to have been introduced in Congress." Forbes's efforts won him the Distinguished Christian Statesman Award from the D. James Kennedy Center for Christian Statesmanship. But the bill gained even fewer cosponsors than it had before and was referred to the House Committee on Oversight and Government Reform, a legislative purgatory. It was the thought that counted, though. The bill raised the issue of America's divine history to the national level. A Republican congressman from Ohio expressed the gratitude of many when he praised Forbes's "research and facts" as "exemplary and truthful regarding our nation's Judeo-Christian heritage."[85]

Ideas about America's sacred roots, its covenant with God, or its providential place in world history seem as much a part of its enduring character as frontier legends and stories of the railroad. Like other Americans exploring the marketplace of ideas, evangelicals are no more bound to one historian than another or to one view of history than another. Evangelicalism is a diverse movement, and its conversation with the past is no exception. As the profile of public figures like Barton rises, ever greater numbers of evangelical historians publish history books with major university presses and teach at top-tier research universities. Serious professional historians, both inside and outside evangelicalism, cannot help being troubled by the uncritical approach of Christian popularizers and their attempt to force evidence into a predetermined framework. The historical work of Barton, Marshall, Schaeffer, and Kennedy is simplistic and free from the ambiguities and complicated moral questions that make the more serious work of evangelical historians in the academy so dynamic and interesting. Such historians will not have Barton's appeal. They won't be consulted on state school curricula or climate science. Few will appear on Fox News. And they certainly will not head up media empires.

For millions of America's evangelicals, a comforting story—a myth—about how "your" country was founded by people like you is too good not to be true. The complicated and alienating alternatives, especially when critiqued by an approachable fellow believer like David Barton, seem confusing and unsettling.

3 The Family of God

I'm a psychologist," James Dobson told Larry King in 2002, as the popular CNN host chatted with the nation's premier Christian child-rearing expert, chief evangelical counselor, and political powerbroker. Dobson headed Focus on the Family, one of the largest Christian organizations in the nation. He wrote books that sold in the millions and hosted one of America's most popular radio programs. King asked Dobson's opinion on religious and ethical matters: the end of the world, the nature of Islam, war, the death penalty, and America's culture of violence. Dobson admitted that he was not a theologian or a minister: "I just don't have any training in theology. . . . I was a professor of pediatrics." As a childcare expert and a psychologist, however, he had plenty of advice to offer. Lax morals on television and in the movies were corrupting young people; Americans were becoming more sinful and less family-friendly with each passing year; teens and adults had bought a safe-sex lie from the media that condoms reduced the dangers associated with sex.[1]

Despite Dobson's confident assertions, the medical and psychiatric community had long rejected his arguments. More than a decade earlier the Centers for Disease Control and Prevention (CDC) had reported studies showing that condom users experienced significantly fewer cases of sexually transmitted diseases than non-users. In 2002 the CDC reiterated that condoms were "necessary to ensure optimal patient care" and to prevent sexually transmitted diseases.[2] A 2001 study in the *Journal of the American Medical Association* agreed. Critics argued that it was grossly misleading to make blanket statements about condoms being ineffective.[3]

Along with challenging the medical establishment's consensus on safe sex, Dobson, like many evangelicals, worried that pluralism and lazy sexual tolerance were destroying America's families. "Can a gay couple be a family?" King asked. No, said Dobson. Scientific research, he assured King with professional credibility, *proved* that children did best with a mother and a father. American culture was at war with the family, Dobson wrote in his 2002 bestseller *Bringing Up Boys*.[4] Dangerous, morally reprehensible messages barraged boys on a daily basis. The rock music industry, television, and "advocates of so-called safe-sex ideology" lured impressionable young men down roads of perdition; "homosexual activists" drew young people off the right path. Parents, wrote Dobson, were fittingly asking themselves how they could safeguard their children from "negative influences that confront them on every side."[5]

Homosexuality was especially sinister, Dobson warned. Gay activists wanted to do away with the traditional roles of mother and father and eliminate designations like "husband," "wife," "son," and "daughter," which had anchored familial roles throughout history. Homosexuality was a destructive disorder and could not be normalized, regardless of the misleading messages of the entertainment industry or the professional psychiatric community.[6] History revealed that widespread acceptance of homosexuality would tear the moral fabric of society, Dobson told King: "There have been cultures where homosexuality was rampant." Greece, Rome, Sodom and Gomorrah. Gone, said Dobson. King asked if homosexuality could be genetic. "It can't," Dobson assured him. It usually had to do with early childhood experiences. But there was still time for American homosexuals to redeem themselves and bring the country back from the edge. Gay Americans should—and could—change their sexual orientation.[7]

In the 1990s journalists began to note the appeal of Dobson's advice on homosexuality, family relations, and childcare. Dobson's organization was producing books, films, ten radio shows, and eleven magazines. "James Dobson speaks for a 'parallel culture' Washington has ignored," observed a reporter in 1995. Yet that parallel culture seldom made its way into the *New York Times.* It rarely appeared on the nightly news or even in sitcoms like *Seinfeld* or *Frasier.* Nonetheless, it shaped the worldview of millions of evangelicals, and it contained a world of products, experts, ministers, musicians, churches, and parachurch groups, united by shared values and basic assumptions about society, God, and the family.[8]

Since the 1960s, best-selling evangelical experts on child-rearing, family psychology, and therapy have shaped the views of their followers on sexuality, family life and dynamics, and human nature. Christian book and gift shops are well stocked with their advice manuals and psychologically informed guidebooks, announcing their broad appeal on their covers: "#1 Bestseller," "National Bestseller," "Over One Million in Print."[9] High-profile authors, speakers, and radio personalities tell audiences how to raise children in a corrupt, sinful world. They explain how parents can keep their children from wetting the bed, throwing tantrums, or becoming homosexual. They offer up wisdom on marital relations, sex, and dating. Many of them counter more formal expertise with biblical truths and common sense, often challenging secular and professional expertise. In the marketplace of evangelical ideas, they wield great authority.

Sympathetic readers of James Dobson's parenting guides—and those who buy the books of similar experts—suspect that the medical and psychological establishments hold an inherently secular bias that menaces spirituality. The professional community cannot be fully trusted. As one critic complained in the late 1970s, the American Psychological Association (APA) had embraced a "secular and humanistic psychology" that led members to support both abortion and "the removal of homosexuality from any official list of pathologies." These were not people who valued Christian morals and righteous living.[10]

Skepticism of psychology had once dominated conservative Christian thinking. Through much of the twentieth century fundamentalists rejected Sigmund Freud, Erich Fromm, Erik Erikson, Carl Jung, Carl Rogers, and the relatively new field of psychotherapy. The therapeutic culture that helped Americans focus less on sin and salvation and more on mental illness and well-being seemed alien to conservative believers from the 1920s to the 1950s. Fundamentalist critics considered modern men and women overly concerned with the pursuit of happiness and self-fulfillment.[11] The salvation of souls, not self-improvement, was what mattered to Christians, and sin, not neurosis, stood in its way. In 1929, the pastor of Boston's influential Park Street Church delivered a sermon titled "Modern Psychology: The Foe of Truth." As believers doubted evolutionary biology, they also suspected that the science of psychology harbored a dangerous materialism that sapped faith.[12] Tracts published by the fundamentalist Moody Press, along with editorials in the popular *Sunday School Times,* called psychologists cranks and charlatans and railed against the nonsense of talk therapy and the psychoanalytic craze.[13]

But psychology was not a fad or a short-lived pseudo-science, destined to join phrenology and hydropathy in the dustbin of history. Popular interest in the science of mind rose with each decade. Tests of mental fitness became *de rigueur* by World War II, and fears of brainwashing and instability gripped the nation during the Korean War. The unconscious mind, once perceived as a canard of radical theorists, was taken for granted by mid-century professionals. By 1952, a third of the country's corporations employed personality tests to evaluate potential managers. The APA grew tremendously in size and influence during the

Eisenhower years, and America became a leader in psychoanalysis. Mid-century literary critic and public intellectual Alfred Kazin lamented: "No one can count the number of people who now think of any crisis as a personal failure, and who turn to a psychoanalyst or to psychoanalytical literature for an explanation of their suffering where once they would have turned to the Bible for consolation."[14]

Partly because of psychology's widespread acceptance in popular literature and culture, evangelical animosity diminished through the 1940s and 1950s. Leaders discovered that professional psychologists were not consistently anti-Christian, or raging libertines, and that their counsel could be very helpful. They warmed to ideas of "wholeness"—the undivided personality—and mental health. Believers who dabbled in self-help and therapy engaged psychological theories with caution, discarding the Oedipus Complex and views of a collective unconscious as incompatible with the biblical view of the person. Yet soon Christian counselors emerged and fashioned a psychology that reinforced Christian ideas of soul rather than challenged them.

Christian popularizers like Clyde M. Narramore were, nonetheless, heavily influenced by the counseling theories of Carl Rogers, who articulated a client-oriented, nondirective psychotherapy. Narramore, with an Ed.D. from Columbia University, based his views on scripture and psychology, emphasizing self-esteem. Evangelical leaders in California convinced him to target a broader audience, and in the 1950s he taped his popular radio show, *Psychology for Living,* from his Pasadena home. He later established a foundation and a graduate school that moved to the campus of the Bible Institute of Los Angeles—now Biola—one of the more conservative Christian colleges in the country, the academic center of the intelligent design movement, and an institution that had spearheaded the production of *The Fundamentals* pamphlets.[15]

God was interested in individuals, Narramore wrote in a 1960 counseling text. Though fundamentalists had harbored grave suspicions of psychology, Narramore assured his listeners that counseling was Christian. Jesus engaged men and women on a personal level and spoke to them about their innermost secrets. "God wants people to be born anew spiritually," said Narramore. "He would have His creatures find the happiness He has planned for them." But there were complications. Satan, he warned, "lies in wait to sabotage this therapeutic power."[16]

Influenced by Narramore and others, Fuller Theological Seminary established a School of Psychology in 1965; outside the academy practitioners created organizations of evangelical psychologists. Progressive evangelical voices called for an end to the long war on psychology. Some popular counselors, of course, rejected the social science emphasis of the field; Satan, they warned, lurked behind every psychiatrist's couch, ready to sabotage the so-called science. One critic even wrote in a widely read 1970 book that his conclusions were "not based upon scientific findings" but on "the inerrant Bible as the Standard of all faith and practice." Other evangelical practitioners shunned such anti-intellectualism and emphasized the importance of research and keeping up with trends in the field.[17]

Christians seeking practical biblical advice and guidance on family matters through the 1970s and 1980s created a vast audience for newly minted experts like Dobson. They asked simple questions: Can the Bible save my marriage? What does God's Word have to say about family life? How can I best use scripture to raise righteous children? Does my daughter dress too provocatively? What should I do if my son is gay? Such questions seemed urgent after the alarming 1960s assault on traditional values.

Believers, fearing secular responses to such intimate problems, wanted answers from scripture, and advisors happily obliged. J. Richard Fugate, for example, claimed that the Bible could answer all of a parent's questions. Claiming "no formal education," he nonetheless adopted the mantle of childcare expert and homeschooling leader in the late 1970s, satisfied with his calling from God.[18] Ignoring psychology and theology, Fugate studied scripture in the original languages, looking directly to those ancient texts for divine wisdom on raising children and ordering one's family. Fugate proudly ignored "existing systematic Theologies or Bible commentaries; preferring to perform . . . exegesis and word studies to develop doctrines that are substantiated by Scripture alone."[19] Unverified information about raising righteous kids was all too common, and most of it was not based on the Bible, wrote Fugate in *What the Bible Says . . . about Child Training* (1980). The book—endorsed by Tim LaHaye and Jerry Falwell—had sold over 200,000 copies by the late 1990s.[20] "The author takes no personal credit for the information presented in this book," wrote Fugate in a familiar caveat. "May God alone be glorified through this presentation of His Word."[21]

Conservatives praised Fugate's manual for its use of scripture. "I have read and reread *What the Bible Says about Child Training*," a grateful woman wrote to the author. "Your book helped me understand God's philosophy for raising children and gave me the methods to apply in everyday life." Fugate quoted the King James Bible on every imaginable social and familial issue: "And he who killeth any man shall surely be put to death" (Leviticus 24:17); "Fathers, provoke not your children to anger, lest they be discouraged" (Colossians 3:21); "He that spareth his rod hateth his son; but he that loveth him chasteneth him early" (Proverbs 13:24).[22] Children, he warned, were corrupt and filled with sin: "Every sweet, innocent cuddly baby possesses within his flesh the constant temptation to fulfill the strong desire of sin . . . I'd rather spank a 2-year-old once a day than deal with a 16-year-old dealing in drugs."[23] Women might be squeamish about administering such harsh justice, but Fugate assured his readers that it was part of God's plan. After all, as another expert mused, God created children with spankable buttocks.[24]

Controversy erupted in the mid-1980s over the use of Fugate's book at several churches and at a Christian school in Sacramento, California.

A state senator thought the advocacy of physical punishment sanctioned child abuse. Another was amazed by the book's appeal. "With all the attention that has been paid to child abuse by the media, the Legislature, and child protection professionals," she remarked, "it is astonishing to find a book that actually tells parents it's OK to beat their child, and to cloak it in pseudo-legitimacy by claiming the Bible condones this."[25]

Fugate was unfazed by the fuss. He comforted his readers by quoting familiar biblical passages: "Do not marvel, my brethren, if the world hates you." His followers should ignore critics of his biblical approach: "They are of the world. Therefore they speak as of the world, and the world hears them. We are of God. He who knows God hears us; he who is not of God does not hear us."[26]

Most Christian childcare authors advise parents to exercise strong authority over their children, including corporal punishment and spanking. Their sinful sons and daughters need to be shaped by a firm hand, as well as by rewards and encouragement.[27] Research in the 1990s revealed that 90 percent of parents in the United States used corporal punishment. Secular experts like Benjamin Spock had said little on the matter, although twenty-first-century childcare professionals would unanimously oppose hitting children.[28] In 1998 the American Academy of Pediatrics (AAP) officially condemned spanking, advising that "parents be encouraged and assisted in the development of methods other than spanking for managing undesired behavior." AAP officials explained that spanking modeled aggressive behavior to children and damaged the parent-child relationship.[29] Conservative evangelicals looked the other way, however, sticking with familiar Old Testament passages and the advice of people like Fugate.

Evangelicals in the postwar era generally believed that God had ordained the traditional family as the basic building block of society. Tinkering with this time-honored, hierarchical, divinely created institution courted disaster. Experts like Fugate rose to prominence amid changing notions of authority and the family.[30] Evangelicals worried that the culture wars of the 1960s had redrawn the battle lines between men and women and between children and parents. They were shocked by alternative visions of society as described in a 1966 credo of the National Organization for Women (NOW): "We believe that a true partnership between the sexes demands a different concept of marriage, an equitable sharing of home and children and of the economic burdens of their support."[31] For postwar evangelicals, "family" rested on a more traditional, male-dominated, middle-class ideal that "sentimentalized childhood and motherhood, and, at the same time, celebrated domestic life as a utopian retreat from the harsh realities of industrial society," as one sociologist put it.[32] Critics found this vision of Christian domesticity hopelessly flawed—a "surrealistic blend of Horace Bushnell, John Dewey, and an emasculated Freud," in the words of one cynic.[33]

Conservatives ignored such critics. The home should be a safe haven, a retreat uncontaminated by the foul stench of sin. The sentimental Bill Gaither hymn "The Family of God" became an anthem in the 1970s, circling the evangelical station wagons against encroaching secularism: "When one has a heartache we all share the tears / And rejoice in each victory in this family so dear."[34] The traditional family ideal faced grave challenges in the 1960s. Madness stalked America's streets, wrote an editor of *Christianity Today* in 1968. The church had become politicized, even radicalized. Even ministers were caught up in the revolutionary fervor of the times. The antiauthority ideals of the new generation were troubling. "The Bible teaches," warned the relatively calm Billy Graham, "that there will be more and more false teachers, preachers" as the end of the world draws near.[35]

Though evangelicals were registering fears about the family toward the end of the 1960s, it was not until the 1970s, with the rise of the Christian Right, that defense of the family took center stage. Conservative Christians hoped to change America from Sodom to Jerusalem.

"Are you unhappy about the increasing 'anything goes' morality of television programming?" asked a 1973 petition in the *Christian Herald.* Readers could register their outrage over racy shows like *All in the Family, The Jeffersons,* or *The Sonny and Cher Comedy Hour,* with their new visions of family life. Concerned evangelicals perceived television as obsessed with antifamily themes—violence, teenage promiscuity, lewdness, and homosexuality.[36]

By the middle of the 1970s evangelical stalwarts zeroed in on abortion, feminism, and homosexuality as the chief enemies of the traditional family. Concerns about abortion linked the Christian Right to prolife Catholics. Antifeminism fed into arguments against the Equal Rights Amendment (ERA), a proposal many viewed as antifamily.[37] Falwell wrote his 1980 clarion call, *Listen, America!,* to awaken citizens to the unholy dangers surrounding them, and to warn of feminists like Gloria Steinem and Betty Friedan, who disparaged traditional religion and marriage. Falwell set his sights on the ERA, the embodiment of the post-1960s culture that fundamentalists despised. The leader of the Moral Majority painted an apocalyptic picture of a country defined by the ERA. All schools would be coed. There could be no Boy Scouts, Girl Scouts, or YMCA. An intrusive government would force Americans to accept abortion, homosexuality, and liberal divorce laws. Falwell saw the problem clearly: "Many women have never accepted their God-given roles," he judged. "They live in disobedience to God's laws and have promoted their godless philosophy throughout our society." Feminist arguments that gender differences were psychological and socially constructed shocked Christians convinced that the Bible taught that God created man and woman separately and gave them distinct roles.[38]

A pastor of Trinity Lutheran Church in San Pedro, California, published what would become the manual for conservative Christian families. Larry Christenson, a leader in the Lutheran charismatic movement, feared that America was losing its biblical grounding. *The Chris-*

tian Family—published in 1970 and filled with advice on securing male authority, wifely submission, and obedient children—sold over two million copies. Ruth Graham, listed on the back cover as "Mrs. Billy Graham," gave it high praise, as did other leaders.[39]

Christenson conceived the book after interacting with fellow parents who had tried unsuccessfully to apply the wisdom of Benjamin Spock, Ann Landers, and the new child psychology. While he claimed no academic expertise in family dynamics—he graduated with a Bachelor of Arts degree from St. Olaf College in 1952 and a Bachelor of Divinity degree from Luther Theological Seminary in 1959—that did not stop him from weighing in on the matter. He decided to write about ordering family life according to God's word, basing his book "unashamedly on certain passages and principles written down in the Bible"—enduring patriarchal principles that were as true in 1970 as they were in A.D. 70. Americans had mindlessly neglected scripture, fretted Christenson, leading to permissive parenting, unruly, protesting teenagers, and loose morals.[40]

For Christenson, Christ headed the family hierarchy, followed by the husband, the wife, and finally the children. Though the National Organization for Women promoted gender equality and secular family experts spoke of coparenting, wives should be subject to their husband's authority. Vulnerable women needed protection, he insisted. They were not suited to lead the family. His program harkened back to a simpler, if largely imaginary, time. "A wife's primary responsibility," Christenson counseled, "is to give herself, her time, and her energy to her husband, children, and home." Wives, he exhorted, "rejoice in your husband's authority over you!"[41]

Husbands and wives were responsible for maintaining family unity and morale. Families should sing in the parlor, like the Victorians did; they should set aside time to worship together and memorize scripture. Christenson responded to liberationist demands by upholding staunch disciplinary and authoritarian tactics. The Bible did not call for children to obey parents only when parents were right, he noted. Parental authority was absolute; corporal punishment was a must. "A spanking combines the two aspects of love and fear," Christenson assured his readers, "and in this it is patterned after our relationship with the Heavenly Father." The current generation had exchanged everything right and true for demonic falsehoods, Christenson warned. You could see it everywhere: young men with long hair and tight pants, cavorting with girls in miniskirts; rock groups like the Beatles and the Rolling Stones flaunting their drug use and promiscuity, setting terrible examples for the children of parents who had sacrificed so much during WWII. Christenson issued a welcome, biblically based call for parents to reign supreme within their families.[42]

The deterioration of the traditional family weighed heavily on the hearts of evangelicals, but few were more passionate about the subject than Tim and Beverly LaHaye, who were about to emerge as the chief voices of the evangelical right. "Will your family and the families of those you love survive the closing decades of the twentieth century?" asked Tim LaHaye in 1982. "Probably not, unless you take definite steps to preserve them."[43] Divorce, rebellious children, and wily secular humanists were all conspiring to destroy the most important institution of Christian civilization—the family. Opposition to pluralist, secular values energized the LaHayes' career. Like Christenson, they upheld male dominance and female submission as ordained by God, and advised parents to control their children as a means of defending themselves against the sinfulness of the secular world.

Long before he became America's apocalyptic sage, Tim LaHaye promoted Christian counseling and self-help. Although he was untrained in either counseling or psychology, his 1966 book, *The Spirit-Controlled Temperament,* sold millions. In it, he retreaded truly ancient ground. "With the advance of modern medical science," he noted, "the idea that temperament is determined by body liquid was discarded, but the fourfold names for the classifications are still widely used." The humors of ancient physiology—blood, phlegm, yellow bile, and black bile—might be a thing of the past, he acknowledged, but the related idea of "temperament"—the unseen force that controlled human action—revealed much about individuals. The nature of men and women, children and adults, could be better understood, wrote LaHaye, by knowing which of the four temperaments controlled a person. It was a simplistic outlook that was matched by LaHaye's basic view of melancholia. He identified the causes of depression: lack of the Holy Spirit, hypocrisy, and self-pity. A Christian counselor could diagnose problems of temperament and depression, but his work for a family or a father was in vain if he could not bring his charge to Christ.[44]

IN THE PANTHEON OF leaders dispensing advice, no one came close to James Dobson as an authority on the family and as a counselor for evangelical America. And few were as opposed to the cultural developments of the 1960s. In Dobson's view, the damage done by sexual liberation could be traced directly to that decade. "Many of you remember 1967's infamous 'Summer of Love,'" Dobson wrote in his *Focus on the Family* magazine in 2008. What looked like freedom to America's hippies was little more than a breakdown in traditional morality. The problems Christians faced now, Dobson argued, were rooted in that era's sexual and social hedonism.[45] The opening argument in his 1970 book *Dare to Discipline* laid out the theme he would return to over and over again: "In a day of widespread drug usage, immorality, civil disobedience, vandalism, and violence, we must not depend on hope and luck to fashion the critical attitudes we value in our children. That unstructured technique was applied during the childhood of the generation that is now in college, and the outcome has been quite discouraging. Permissiveness has not just been a failure; it's been a disaster!"[46]

Dobson, born in Louisiana in 1936, came of age in a seemingly ordered world. The sexes had distinct but complementary roles. Children respected their elders and obeyed their parents. Homes were filled with love and domestic bliss. Homosexuality was shameful and always hidden. God established the traditional family, and any deviation from that divine model—whether in the relationship between men and women, the proper roles of children and parents, or the acceptance of homosexuality—would lead to disaster.

Dobson was the only child of a traveling minister in the socially and theologically conservative Church of the Nazarene. He spent his youth moving from town to town in dusty, arid Texas and Oklahoma, under the firm control of his parents. Sin and salvation were omnipresent themes, and he recalls his mother describing heaven and hell in vivid detail. God would separate the sheep from the goats on that great Judgment Day. Those "covered by the blood of Jesus will be separated eternally from those" who were not, a message of cosmic retribution that Dobson felt compelled to share with his friends, who often recoiled in horror. Yet Dobson was glad his mother spared no fiery detail, for he believed it would have kept an eternal truth from him. Other parents, he would emphasize, should educate their kids similarly.[47]

The Dobsons' Church of the Nazarene was part of the American holiness tradition and stressed a higher religious calling and a doctrine called *entire sanctification,* defined as an act of God "by which believers are made free from original sin."[48] In the 1950s Nazarene leaders, in a quest for sin-free environments, cautioned, "it is essential that the most rigid safeguards be observed to keep our homes from becoming secularized and worldly." Television, popular novels, or frivolous entertainment magazines were perceived as Trojan horses filled with wicked ideas. God's people must have nothing to do with secular entertainment. The denomination shielded members from the heresies of modernism, the perils of loose living, the frivolity of pop culture. Nazarenes, as they were known, had clear ideas about sin and how to avoid it: Men and women must not swim together; theater attendance was strictly forbidden; dancing, even folk or ballroom, was off-limits. The plethora of rules led insiders to joke that Nazarenes were not allowed to have sex standing up because it looked too much like dancing.[49]

Nazarenes established liberal arts colleges, strategically located around the country, where their young people could be educated in an insulated environment. Consistent with this commitment, college administrators took seriously their roles as moral guardians and enforcers of a strict holiness decorum. America's campuses in the 1950s, of course, were sedate by the rowdy standards of a decade later, but fraternity parties, panty raids, and juvenile rituals were becoming increasingly common at state and private schools. Wild pranks and bacchanalian revelries were forbidden at the Church of the Nazarene's Pasadena College—Dobson's alma mater—where students lived lives of rigorous, administratively enforced holiness.[50] The California school, not far from Hollywood, required daily chapel attendance and weekly church attendance, both of which were closely monitored. The college prohibited smoking, dancing, movie attendance, and drinking. In the late 1950s the school's strict president, eager to maximize campus holiness, canceled all non-Nazarene chapel speakers, curtailed student involvement in school decisions, and disciplined students for lapses in behavior and breaches of the austere dress code.[51]

Jimmy Dobson entered tiny Pasadena College in 1954. He majored in psychology, became a popular campus leader, played tennis, and honed his talents as a cartoonist. He and his future wife, Shirley, attended a Sunday night church service for their first date; in 1960 they would be married by Dobson's father. The Texas undergrad with the blond brush cut impressed his professors and fellow students. A classmate recalled that many people on campus knew Dobson "would amount to something. It just showed. He had it, and you couldn't miss it."[52]

A psychology professor inspired Dobson to make a career in the field. This mentor held devotionals before class and, in Dobson's words, taught that "God desires persons to be whole—and that psychology was a means to bring about healing even though God was the ultimate source of it." The program offered courses in abnormal psychology, psychology of adolescence, child growth and development, and personality.[53] Dobson thrived. He ventured off campus to meet Clyde Narramore, the local celebrity and pioneer Christian psychologist, who encouraged the young, ambitious pastor's son to pursue behavioral studies.[54]

Dobson enrolled in graduate school at the University of Southern California (USC), earning an M.A. and then a Ph.D. in child development in 1967. James and Shirley had already started their family, which led to financial and social pressures that shaped Dobson's views of marriage and childcare.[55] Young couples, he knew from firsthand experience, needed all the help and advice they could get.

Dobson joined the University of Southern California Medical School in the mid-1960s, where he launched a brief, successful research career. His work appeared in the *New England Journal of Medicine, Pediatrics,* and the *Journal of Pediatrics.* It was the only time in his life that he produced a high level of peer-reviewed research. Dobson authored papers with colleagues on childhood education and mental retardation. He oversaw a five-million-dollar study on a genetic disorder that caused mental retardation. Yet because he was at a medical school without an M.D., he felt limited. Believing he had a higher calling, he turned to God and prayed: "You've got people who are very willing to serve you, but they are not qualified." In contrast, he was credentialed and trained and stood ready to address the trials of the family. How could God use him? he asked.[56]

At USC Dobson encountered the excesses of the sexual revolution; he was shaken by the effects of permissive parenting and preoccupied with child abuse, divorce, and the disintegrating family. Out of that experience, and reacting to what he saw as misguided liberalism, Dobson published *Dare to Discipline* in 1970, his first book for a general audience. He opened it with a vignette about a well-meaning but naïve mother of a defiant three-year-old girl. This woman had been under the impression that her daughter would respond favorably to tolerant, patient parenting. Strict discipline would be unnecessary. Let the child lead, experts told her. "Unfortunately, Mrs. Nichols and her advisors were wrong!" Dobson declared, in the opening salvo of a lifetime battle against secular expertise on parenting and the family. The daughter rejected the authority of her mother. Such anecdotes proved that children needed boundaries and resolute, firm discipline.[57]

The book took America's baby-care expert, Benjamin Spock, to task. His permissive parenting style had dominated for too long, Dobson implied. In his 1946 book *Baby and Child Care,* Spock told parents that they knew more about their children than he did, and that he hoped they would not take his advice too literally. Spock believed children should live fulfilled, happy lives, free of harsh ideological convictions or weighty concerns. He urged parents not to try to control a son or daughter's every move. Children "do the major share in civilizing themselves," Spock assured them. By the time he died in 1998 at the age of ninety-four, his classic manual had been through numerous editions and sold over fifty million copies.[58]

Dobson thought Spock treated children like rational, self-possessed beings, when they were anything but. "Under this setting, the child is his own master," objected Dobson. "He thinks the world revolves around his heady empire, and he often has utter contempt and disrespect for those closest to him."[59]

Dobson was not alone. Others challenged Spock's laissez-faire approach to parenting, linking it to the decadence of the 1960s. Even President Nixon spoke of a "fog of permissiveness" and laid blame for student protests and campus hedonism at the feet of America's foremost pediatrician. Critics said a generation of young people had been "Spocked" when they should have been spanked.[60] Dobson took up the cudgel and responded to Spock's perceived lenience with *Dare to Disci-*

pline, a book that called for beating back permissiveness. Above all else, Dobson argued, children should be taught to respect their parents and be responsible. Children needed firm boundaries and parents must be consistent and unyielding in disciplining their sons and daughters.[61]

Throughout the book, Dobson answered questions, many from concerned parents. He peppered his responses with scripture, social science, and general observations. Some people asked about working mothers. Dobson responded, "Motherhood is a full-time job during the child's first five years." A babysitter or a nanny could never fill that role. "The traditional concept of motherhood, full-time motherhood," he reasoned, "still sounds like a pretty good idea to me." Should religion be taught in public schools? Yes, replied Dobson. The Supreme Court decision banning school prayer was regrettable. Should a child be punished for wetting the bed? No, unless the child had done it intentionally. How was a divorced mother supposed to raise her children? You must demand respect, insisted Dobson, playing the difficult roles of both mother and father.[62] He emphasized firmness and control as essential to managing children.

Like the home, the school was often a moral battleground on which parents would either win or lose control. Parents must monitor an underachieving child's classroom performance and should use a system of rewards and punishments to change his or her behavior. Parents should also be careful about how their children were taught about sex. Preferably, said Dobson, sex education should be left to Christian parents or church groups, and not the public schools. Dobson also wrote about enforcing rules in high schools and halting the tide of juvenile delinquency. Parents and school administrators were responsible for the failures of the educational system. They had been neither firm nor consistent when they should have been both. Authorities turned a blind eye to teenage drug use, Dobson noted, devoting an entire chapter to the topic, listing slang terms for narcotics, giving accounts of burnouts, and offering advice. "There is no more certain destroyer of self-discipline and self-control," he remarked, "than the abusive use of drugs."[63] Supporters encouraged educational leaders to read the book for help addressing drug abuse and other ills plaguing public schools. Dobson's more nuanced view of children and adolescents, based on his own research and education, distinguished his brand of family counseling from those that were fully dependent on biblical injunctions.[64]

In the early 1970s, the National Education Association took an official stance against corporal punishment. Dobson, however, believed that the country's schools, behind parents, were most responsible for the breakdown in authority. While he didn't want teachers and administrators spanking children, he worried about the passive approach to discipline, which contributed to chaos inside and outside the classroom.[65]

Dare to Discipline succeeded in ways that few, even Dobson—who believed it was blessed by God—could have imagined. By 2008 it had sold over 4.5 million copies.[66] He had struck a deep nerve with his emphasis on firm parental control and authority. Evangelicals who were increasingly ill-at-ease with the permissiveness of secular culture thought Dobson was profound in his pronouncements on education, drug abuse, and unruly young people.[67]

After the success of *Dare to Discipline,* Dobson took on additional speaking engagements and wrote an advice column in the Church of the Nazarene's *Herald of Holiness,* assuring parents that if they followed God's plan for families and listened to reasonable advice, their youngsters would mature into upright American citizens. A passage from Exodus 20:12 stated it clearly: "Honour thy father and thy mother: that thy days may be long upon the land which the Lord thy God giveth thee." Dobson used Bible verses to make his case for the biblical family. He pointed to 1 Timothy 3:4–5: "He (the father) must have proper authority in his own household, and be able to control and command the respect of his children. (For if a man cannot rule in his own house how can he look after the Church of God?)" For Dobson, Proverbs

22:15 laid out the specifics of firm discipline: "Foolishness is bound in the heart of a child; but the rod of correction shall drive it far from him."[68]

Young people, said Dobson, should learn Bible stories at an early age. He reacted forcefully when a famous child psychiatrist, in an essay titled "Religion May Be Hazardous to Your Health," warned of the dangers of teaching violent Bible stories to young children. Dobson turned the phrase on its head: "Ungodly Experts May Be Hazardous to Your Children!"[69]

The Bible was not only a useful guide for boys and girls, of course; it also contained much wisdom on the proper relationship of men and women. Wives needed to be loved completely by their husbands. Husbands needed to be respected by their wives. "That understanding is hardly new," he wrote when asked about the proper relationship of wives and husbands, citing Ephesians 5:33 to make his case: "Each one of you [men] must love his wife as he loves himself, and the wife must respect her husband."[70] In 1972 Dobson noted that modern unisex fashions and the shifting boundaries of gender were about as unbiblical as you could get. God specified clear roles for men and women. When asked about women's liberation, Dobson admitted that women had long been oppressed and ill-treated. Yet "these and similar wrongs are now being used to justify an anti-Christian philosophy which threatens to undermine the most basic cornerstone in our society: the family."[71]

Dobson spoke effectively to the millions of Americans alarmed by recent social changes and fearful for their children's future, the future of their families, the future of their communities, and the future of a society sinking into an amoral swamp. He assured them that all would be set right if they returned to God's way. Later in the 1970s his public profile rose. He starred in a seven-part film series, some of which ran on television and was viewed by ten million people. Tom Snyder and Phil Donahue interviewed the up-and-coming counselor on their television programs.[72]

Dobson capitalized on his accomplishments as a speaker, editorialist, family spokesperson, and author by founding Focus on the Family in 1977. He had already left the Southern California School of Medicine in 1976 to become a fulltime public speaker and author. A Christian family-advocacy organization seemed like a logical next step. Focus on the Family would greatly enlarge Dobson's capacity to help newly married couples and veteran parents navigate the choppy waters of relationships, childcare, and family life with thoroughly biblical guidelines. The organization would counter ill-conceived secular childcare and family counseling advice. "We really do believe that Focus on the Family was conceived in the mind of God," reflected Dobson fifteen years after he started the nonprofit. "It was not our plan to build the large organization that now exists; we simply followed the leading of the Lord." It helped that the evangelical Tyndale House Publishers offered Dobson a $35,000 grant to start the enterprise. Focus grew steadily and dramatically into a media empire, with production facilities, magazines, advice books, audiotapes, conferences, and speakers.[73]

By 1979 Dobson was hiring staff to answer the hundreds of letters pouring into the office at Focus on the Family. A decade later the organization had a $34 million annual budget and was receiving 150,000 letters a month. Dobson cofounded the Family Research Council, a conservative Washington, D.C., advocacy group that developed a family-values agenda for the Religious Right. He served on six government panels in the Reagan administration and was ascending rapidly as a national expert of influence. Nevertheless, consistent with his values, he lived modestly and cared genuinely for the welfare of his millions of readers and listeners. For like-minded Christians, he was an inspiring leader, untainted by personal scandal, who helped guide them through the death of a spouse, an abusive relationship, depression, discipline problems in the family, and more.[74]

Readers deeply appreciated the *Focus on the Family* magazine, with its regular articles about balancing busy suburban lives, planning for a child's future, meeting the spiritual needs of sons and daughters, or getting the most out of marriage. Feature stories on homosexuality, abortion, and strict discipline kept them apprised of ongoing concerns. Over the decades of his far-reaching ministry Dobson and his growing army of staffers talked young people out of suicide, advised mothers on dealing with unruly, belligerent kids, grieved with husbands and wives facing divorce, and prayed with individuals over the phone. They counseled against abortion and spoke frankly about the sin of homosexuality. By 2008 Focus on the Family's trained counselors were receiving 1,300 calls a week. They served a substantial population with their particular brand of conservative Christian guidance.[75]

That guidance was increasingly political. The culture wars of the 1990s provided political action for Focus and other Christian organizations. Focus took on the Clinton administration with relish. Shortly before Clinton's inauguration in 1993, an editorial in the Focus magazine declared that "the next four years seem bleak to all those who cherish concepts of sanctity of life, full-time motherhood, innocent childhood, parental authority and heterosexual marriages."[76] Focus criticized the "don't ask, don't tell" policy that allowed homosexuals to serve in the military, challenged Clinton on abortion, and called for his impeachment when his extramarital affair came to light.[77] Tony Campolo, a Clinton confidante and sociology professor at an evangelical college, decried Dobson's adversarial tactics. After the end of the Clinton administration and the defeat of Al Gore, Campolo observed: "a movement can exist without a God but can't exist without a devil, and Focus has lost its devil in Bill Clinton."[78]

The Christian Right has trusted Dobson as a political authority since the 1990s. For far longer, though, he had served the masses as a family expert. His medical credentials, practical counseling, research work, and years of experience at a university hospital gave him an almost unique authority among believers. When parents called in to his radio program or wrote to Focus with difficult questions, the avuncular

Dobson responded with evangelical common sense peppered with social science research. He referenced other childcare authorities and offered assurance with phrases like "most studies show" or "the weight of evidence proves." Despite such tips of the hat to the professional community, however, Dobson was leery of secular professionals, especially those who were not Christian. By the 1980s he had resigned from the APA, an organization with which he no longer identified, and he had little clinical experience as a family counselor in any case. Educational psychology was his forté.

Dobson was a popularizer who focused less on current research than on homey advice for families. Psychologists paid scant attention to his work. When they did, however, their assessment was uniformly negative. In the mid-1980s two child-development experts denounced Dobson's cavalier disregard for research. "Dr. Dobson's teachings negate 30 years of research on punishment and aggression," they complained. His religious dogmatism and selective use of theory, in their words, represented "pop psychology at its worst." Dobson shrugged off such secular criticism. In his view, families needed informed biblical education, and he was providing it.[79]

As the extended family disappeared and the nuclear family took its place, Dobson warned parents against naïvely turning to secular experts for assistance. The secularists' bad advice had been disastrous: Unwanted pregnancies, juvenile delinquency, drug use, alcoholism, mental illness, and even suicide were all on the rise. He did not blame the experts—behavioral scientists, psychologists, pediatricians, and educators—entirely, but he did claim that they had helped create society's problems because they "lacked confidence in the Judeo-Christian ethic and have disregarded the wisdom of this priceless tradition!" Professionals, said Dobson, had ignored 2,000 years of wisdom to the peril of America's families.[80]

As his organization grew and he became a major political force, Dobson's basic child-rearing advice remained the same. Children had not changed, and neither had the guidelines laid out by God in the Bible. "The inspired concepts in scripture have been handed down generation after generation," he wrote, "and are just as valid for the 21st century as they were for our ancestors."[81] Drawing on the Old Testament, Dobson emphasized God's simultaneous compassion and judgment. He pointed out Isaiah 1:18, which promised redemption: "Though your sins are like scarlet, they shall be as white as snow." But four chapters later, God's anger burned against the Israelites: "his hand is raised and he strikes them down" (Isaiah 5:25). That timeless message of love and justice was well suited to parenting, too. "Learning to balance the intersection between these two forces is especially useful to the understanding of children," he said. Dobson insisted that both parents and their children must heed the ancient wisdom of scripture. He quoted Ephesians 6:4, which admonishes: "Fathers, do not exasperate your children, instead bring them up in the training and instruction of the Lord." Dobson also cautioned young people: "Obey your parents in everything, for this pleases the Lord" (Colossians 3:20).[82]

Dobson quoted the scriptures extensively, but he was no Bible scholar. His confidence as a conservative spokesperson and childcare expert gave him an undue sense of authority when it came to the Bible. A writer in *Christianity Today* took Dobson to task for his simplistic, combative, "one response fits all" arguments. Dobson issued strident proclamations on matters he knew little about. In the late 1990s he even denounced Bible translators for using gender-inclusive language.[83]

Dobson was certain that he was right about scripture. Like other, lesser-known experts and family counselors, he claimed that stern discipline was not one choice among many options. His disciplinarian models were taken directly from the Good Book, which clearly called for spanking and resolute firmness. Those following God's directives could punish with confidence. Nothing "brings a parent and child closer together," said Dobson, "than for the mother or father to win decisively after being defiantly challenged."[84] In the battle of wills between child and parent, it was important that the parent was the victor. "Who is going to win? Who has the most courage? Who is in charge here?" asked Dobson.[85]

Dobson's biblical approach to human relations makes selective use of physical and behavioral science. Focus on the Family, consistent with its biblical literalism, rejects evolution, for example. Its bookstore stocks antievolution resources, and critics of Darwin were invited on Dobson's radio program. But ideas from evolutionary psychology inform his views on gender, sexuality, and the family. Many male-female differences and appropriate heterosexual relationships, he argues, are biologically determined and not socially constructed as some in the social sciences argue. To those claiming that gender roles are culturally based, Dobson responds: "I couldn't disagree more. God created two sexes, not one. He built genetic characteristics in males and females that no amount of training in childhood will eliminate."[86]

By the 1990s Focus had outgrown its headquarters in Pomona, California, and moved to Colorado Springs, home to the U.S. Air Force Academy and several conservative Christian organizations. The sprawling new Focus headquarters at the foot of the mountains received so much mail that it got its own zip code.

The headquarters, consistent with the organization's mission, paid special attention to families with children and included a large play center. The campus also housed a studio, a massive mailroom, a 75,000-square-foot warehouse, and a 10,000-square-foot bookstore. The thousands of visitors browsing the store every year could purchase books by evangelical authors like Tim LaHaye, D. James Kennedy, Chuck Colson, and Ken Ham. Authors such as Jerry Jenkins, of *Left Behind* fame, occasionally visited for book signings. A Focus orthodoxy censor vetted the titles. "We carry a variety of opinions on creationism," she remarked in summer 2008, "because committed Christians disagree on that." The same held true of titles on the end of the world. Books by left-of-center evangelical authors like Jim Wallis and Tony

Campolo, though, did not make the cut. Amateur Christian historian David Barton, who often appeared on Dobson's radio program, was featured heavily.[87]

In 1995 Dobson established the Focus on the Family Institute, a one-semester, five-course college program for evangelical undergraduates located in Colorado Springs. The competitive program enrolled over two hundred students, who took classes like "Family, Church and Society Studies," "Family Life Studies," and "Christian Worldview Studies," the last of which empowered students to challenge their anti-Christian peers. A course on marriage and family emphasized the permanence of marriage and the value of children. All classes encouraged young men and women to scrutinize secular culture and to examine their core beliefs. A student who attended the institute in spring 2009 summed up the benefits of the godly training. He came to Focus Institute from a school that was "very secular, very liberal, and very draining for a Christian." At the institute he found "a place where I didn't have to be constantly on my guard against everything I was taught, against the very secular—even hopeless—mindset that pervades my campus." Several evangelical colleges and universities advised students to attend the institute in Colorado Springs, including Liberty University, Biola University, Bryan College, Geneva College, Oral Roberts University, and Azusa Pacific University.[88]

Colorado Springs hummed with evangelical activity and was dubbed "Vatican West." Locals expressed their skepticism with bumper stickers that read: "Focus on Your Own Damn Family." Critics viewed Focus as self-righteous, intolerant, and overconfident—all just white noise to the faithful. Shoppers at the retail and online stores bought DVDs proclaiming America's godly heritage or challenging the theory of evolution. They picked up calendars with scripture verses on them and ordered sentimental Thomas Kinkade prints of cottages in an imaginary English countryside. Prophecy encyclopedias and Bible dictionaries lined the shelves. Parents could purchase books like *Bible Atlas, The*

Baker Encyclopedia of Bible People, Harmony of the Gospels, The Faith of the American Soldier, The Wonder of America, The Focus on the Family Guide to Growing a Healthy Home, A Parent's Guide to Preventing Homosexuality, and *Reparative Therapy of Male Homosexuality.*[89]

Down the road from the Focus campus stood the 11,000-member New Life Church. The pastor, Ted Haggard, became president of the National Association of Evangelicals and a vocal critic of the so-called gay agenda. *Time* magazine named Haggard and Dobson two of the twenty-five most influential evangelicals in America. Haggard, not surprisingly, admired the elder statesman up the road. "I think if Dr. Dobson were alive 225 years ago, he would have been one of the founding fathers," he told a reporter. "He's thoughtful, he's courageous, and he is right. People trust him." Few knew how little they could trust the megachurch pastor and national leader himself.[90] In 1996 Haggard told a reporter that he didn't understand Colorado Springs' Gay Pride festivities. "It would be like having Murderer's Pride Day," he quipped in a failed attempt at humor. Haggard's scandalous secret life, including a sordid affair with a homosexual prostitute, soon came to light, and he was forced to leave town in 2006.[91]

Haggard's drug use and gay affair proved only that those in power needed to be especially wary of the sins of the flesh. One leading figure at Focus commented in 2008: "We believe, as Christians, that we're not perfect and we as individuals aren't always right but we know the principles that we fight for are God's truth." Such messages appeal strongly to middle America. In the early 1990s, Focus conducted a poll of its audience—mainly white women between the ages of thirty and forty-nine. Most were married, and half held college or postgraduate degrees. Those surveyed ranked their concerns: At the top were marital issues, followed by parenting and abortion. Focus kept track of the top twenty-five topics on which callers sought advice. For a typical week in June 2008 "relationships / adult child" ranked number one, followed by marriage conflict. Concerns related to homosexuality came in at a distant twenty-three. Nevertheless, homosexuality was a surprisingly frequent Focus on the Family radio topic and appeared regularly in Focus books and magazines.[92]

As Dobson's star rose in the political firmament through the late 1980s and 1990s, journalists and outside observers took note, wanting to know how he had emerged as the country's most trusted Christian psychologist. "James Dobson still believes in absolutes," remarked a Texas woman and fan of the Focus radio program, in a typical response. Focus enthusiasts like the Texas woman lauded Dobson's unwavering commitment to prolife causes, his emphasis on discipline, his stand against same-sex marriage, and his support for suburban Christian families. Dobson's political activism had even inspired some Christians to greater involvement in local politics. James Talent, a Republican congressman from Missouri who in the late 1990s stated that Dobson led him to Christ, was one of Focus's strongest supporters. The organization was, said Talent, the most important thing that had ever happened to him.[93]

For years after founding Focus in 1977 Dobson avoided politics, concerned that direct political action would betray the trust he had worked so diligently to build with millions of families. He never ran for political office or developed the high political profile of other evangelicals in the limelight, like Jerry Falwell or Tony Perkins. If anything, his forays into politics united supporters. A 2004 poll conducted by PBS and *U.S. News and World Report* was revealing. Evangelicals gave "marginally unfavorable" ratings to two key figures: Pat Robertson (55 out of a possible 100) and Jerry Falwell (44 out of a possible 100). Yet Dobson received 73 out of a possible 100. His avuncular, kindly manner on the radio and the slight drawl in his comforting voice pulled people in. He seemed like a part of his own audience and, despite having a Ph.D., didn't speak down to the callers who phoned in to his radio program. Many could imagine attending church with him or having his family over for a barbecue.[94]

Dobson had become a trusted authority. Readers and listeners took comfort that he weighed research against the word of God. But how could a mother or father, wife or husband, be sure his advice was professionally trustworthy? Dobson answered that question directly in his 1978 book *The Strong-Willed Child:* "How do my writings differ from the unsupported recommendations of those whom I have criticized? The distinction lies in the source of the views being presented. The underlying principles expressed herein are not my own innovative insights which would be forgotten in a brief season or two. Instead, they originated with the inspired biblical writers who gave us the foundation for all relationships in the home."[95]

Dobson was consistent. Answering a *Focus* magazine reader's question on the impact of secular humanism more than a decade later, he made the same point. Liberal secularists wanted to discredit parents, he said. They argued, for instance, that government-commissioned child-development experts knew better how to raise your children. But they were wrong.[96]

Mainstream child-rearing experts diverge sharply from Dobson on parent-child relations. The traditional, hierarchical parenting practices promoted by Fugate, Christenson, the LaHayes, and Dobson emphasize the basic sinfulness of children. Peppered with questions about the nature of children, Dobson points to the "Owner's Manual," meaning the Bible. He references the words of King David from Psalm 51:5: "In sin did my mother *conceive* me." He turns to St. Paul, who spelled out the ubiquity of sin in Romans 3:23: "For all have sinned, and fallen short of the glory of God." The implications of such passages are crystal clear to Dobson and others. "Therefore," he writes, "with or without bad associations children are naturally inclined toward rebellion, selfishness, dishonesty, aggression, exploitation, and greed."[97] Young people, first and foremost, need redemption. In contrast, mainstream professionals urge parents to foster self-respect, mastery, and hopefulness in their children. Empathy and communication skills also rank high. Some encourage mothers and fathers to work as equal partners and model ungendered parenting roles. This was anathema to Dobson and his colleagues.[98]

For conservative authorities the family was no democracy; nor was it a laboratory for gender experimentation. Men and women were different. Ungendered parenting would emasculate men and create unhealthy children. Evangelical family experts did, of course, encourage fathers to be nurturing, but Larry Christenson commented, fairly typically, in 1970 that nothing could be more unnatural and unbiblical than a father as a "part-time nursemaid." Though Dobson offers a gentler reading of parenting roles and the relationship of husbands and wives, he nonetheless insists that mothers are better suited to take the heavier load in raising children and teens. Not only is teenage rebellion stressful, writes Dobson, "but the chauffeuring, supervising, cooking, and cleaning required to support a teenager can be exhausting." Someone in the family had to assume greater responsibility for day-to-day affairs. "Mom is the candidate of choice," he reasons without explanation. Dobson also argues that marriages suffer if a wife is aggressive and angry and a husband is passive and distant. American women, in Dobson's estimation, had become unrealistic about romantic marriage. The dangers of unreal expectations and maternal or passive fathers were common themes in the early 1970s, when Dobson moved into the limelight. One medical doctor expressed, in a widely circulated evangelical magazine, what was to become a persistent, if tragically uninformed, view: "I suspect that many who fight for women's emancipation have a loss of sexual identity; are of the 'gay' world or lesbians."[99]

Dobson spoke confidently and frequently about the biblical measure of good family life, even as social acceptance of alternative family structures grew. The Bible spoke wisely on many modern subjects: "Everything from handling money to sexual attitudes to the discipline of children is discussed in Scripture," he counseled a future husband writing for advice. The Bible was the "ultimate resource." Dobson was profoundly and aggressively traditional on sexual relations. Homosexuality, a pernicious threat to the biblical family, received a surprising amount of attention. Leviticus 18:22, Dobson assured another letter writer, condemned homosexuality in no uncertain terms: "Do not lie with a man as one lies with a woman, that is detestable." Such wicked individuals would not enter paradise, he warned. For him, 1 Corinthians 6:9–10 also needed no updating or nuanced unpacking: "Do you not know that the wicked will not inherit the kingdom of God? Do not be deceived: Neither the sexually immoral nor idolaters nor adulterers nor male prostitutes nor homosexual offenders nor thieves nor the greedy nor drunkards nor slanderers nor swindlers will inherit the kingdom of God." In Dobson's view, Christians should never accept homosexuality as normal or right.[100]

Dobson also believed that accepting homosexuality and same-sex marriage would destroy the institution of the family. The matter was more pressing than the war on terror, he wrote in his 2004 book *Marriage under Fire.* Children of gay parents were the innocent victims of an amoral society. The ancient institution of marriage was being forever altered, he declared. Christians needed to stand up and take action. "There is only one way to get the attention of our leaders in Washington," he pleaded. "We must overwhelm them with calls, e-mails, visits, letters, and publications, and most importantly, we need to support their opponents." He wrote editorials and entire book chapters on homosexuality and addressed the topic often on his radio program. The latter proved impossible in Canada when government authorities prohibited his discussion of the subject on the grounds that it violated laws against hate speech.[101]

The Bible and social science research made clear that children needed both a mother and a father, Dobson insisted in a *Time* editorial in 2006, the year that Dick Cheney's lesbian daughter, Mary, and her partner, Heather Poe, announced their decision to have a baby. In his estimation, social science studies provided *indisputable* evidence on the subject. Most important, though, having children and adoption were "the purview of heterosexual couples." This was God's design, "rooted in biblical truth." Only the dense fog of political correctness prevented commentators from seeing this simple fact.[102]

None of this sat well with the scholars whose research Dobson and Focus often cited to make their case. After the *Time* op-ed appeared, Kyle Pruett of Yale Medical School claimed that Dobson had "cherry-picked" material from his research on male role models and fathers. Exposure to gay or lesbian relationships did *not* harm children, said a riled Pruett, contradicting Dobson's claims in the op-ed. American feminist, ethicist, and psychologist Carol Gilligan alleged that Dobson had misused and oversimplified her research: "Dear Dr. Dobson," she wrote, "I ask that you cease and desist from quoting my research in the future." Gilligan assured Dobson that her "work in no way suggests that same-gender families are harmful to children."[103] It was, in her words, a manipulation of her research for political ends.

Dobson also used the work of Angela Phillips, citing the London-based journalist and professor on the socialization of young men. The "high incidence of homosexuality occurring in Western nations is related, at least in part," Dobson inferred from Phillips, "to the absence of positive male influence when boys are moving through the first crisis of child development." Nothing could be further from the truth, objected Phillips. Her concern was that boys who lacked a strong male presence in their lives could become violent and angry at a later stage. Nowhere did she even hint that those characteristics related to homosexuality. She pleaded unsuccessfully for Focus to publish her letter of clarification on its website.[104] Journalists discovered other researchers whose work had been misrepresented or taken out of context by Dobson. A professor at the University of British Columbia charged that her work on suicide rates among homosexual youths had been hijacked. She did not see how Focus could make such a political case out of her studies. Correlation, she lectured Dobson, was not the same as causation.[105]

Dobson responded to such critics directly: "The benefits of a child being raised by a married mother and a father have been established in the professional literature for decades. It was not even questioned until the gay rights movement succeeded in making that understanding politically incorrect." He further informed readers of the *Rocky Mountain News* that he was, in fact, an expert on the subject, with a Ph.D. in child development and seventeen years on the staff of a large children's hospital. Critics like Pruett, said Dobson, were acting in narrow academic self-interest, reacting more to the defense of traditional marriage than to the issue of evidence. "I've sold 15 million books" dealing with childcare and family matters, Dobson declared, to settle the matter of who was right.[106]

Conflict between Dobson and the academic community grew, as the professional establishment countered the influential Focus organization. The American Medical Association, drawing on emerging studies, supported legislation allowing same-sex couples to adopt children and opposing discrimination against homosexuals.[107] Research tracking the parenting effectiveness of gay and lesbian couples directly contradicted Focus's claim. A longitudinal study in a 2010 issue of *Pediatrics* revealed that "the 17-year-old daughters and sons of lesbian mothers were rated significantly higher in social, school/academic, and total competence and significantly lower in social problems, rule-breaking, aggressive, and externalizing problem behavior than their age-matched counterparts." Earlier studies showed that the children of gay and lesbian parents turned out to be about the same as children of straight parents.[108] The 150,000-member APA declared that sexual orientation most likely resulted from environmental, biological, and cognitive influences, and was certainly not a choice. Homosexuality was not an illness; it did not require treatment, as many evangelicals believed; and there were no therapies to "repair" it.[109] Dobson viewed such pronouncements as baldly political. Brave souls who try to help homosexuals change, he said with alarm, "are subjected to continual harassment and accusations of malpractice."[110]

Focus psychologist William Maier claims the APA shift on homosexuality, from mental disorder to normalcy, was a conspiracy driven by the relentless pressure of gay activists, not science.[111] Dobson agreed. In his view homosexuality emerged early in life. Babies were heterosexual at birth and would stay that way if nothing went wrong. Homosexuality took root, he told a television interviewer, in "early childhood, and this is very controversial, but this is what I believe and many other people believe." The cause was an identity crisis. A boy who failed to form an attachment with his father between eighteen months and five years of age might become gay.[112] Dobson acknowledged the relevance of other factors, but he would not retreat in the face of evidence contradicting his position. Homosexuality is "not chosen, but it is also not genetic," he said on Fox News. He wished someone would make that case, and then admitted, "I guess I just did." His view was widely held in the 1950s but had been transformed by ensuing decades of research and social change.[113]

Focus established a controversial gay conversion ministry in the late 1990s called Love Won Out. The program trained pastors and laypeople to build strong relationships with homosexuals, in the hope that love might win them over. It put a kinder face on evangelical disapproval. The offshoot organization made headlines in 2000 when founder and self-described repentant—and cured—homosexual John Paulk was photographed in a gay bar in Washington, D.C. Focus maintained that Paulk was innocent of any wrongdoing.[114]

In 2006 Love Won Out asked for the advice of Warren Throckmorton, professor of psychology at the conservative evangelical Grove City College. "Dobson says being homosexual is all about looking for Dad," Throckmorton said after the visit. "But there is almost no evidence that all homosexuals come that way." The evangelical Throckmorton disparaged the Focus chief's theories as antiquated. "Most homosexuals had decent dads," he remarked, but Dobson and his followers "can't see that because it compromises their best political tools, that homosexuality is mutable."[115] Love Won Out bled money until shutting down in 2009.

According to an official statement from the APA, "some homosexual or bisexual people may seek to change their sexual orientation through therapy, often coerced by family members or religious groups to try and do so. The reality is that homosexuality is not an illness. It does not require treatment and is not changeable."[116] The APA condemned conversion therapies as harmful in 1997. Ten years later one hundred conservatives and evangelicals across the country sent a letter to the APA. "We consider it a foundational principle that respect be afforded to clients who determine that their religious teachings forbid homosexual conduct and construct their lives accordingly," the signers complained. Dobson and Richard Land, president of the Southern Baptist Convention's Ethics and Religious Liberty Commission, endorsed the missive. Other signers included professors and administrators at Christian colleges, universities, and seminaries along with ministers, heads of nonprofits, and practicing professionals. The letter insisted that psychologists respect the religious values of their clients as much as they respected their clients' sexual orientation.[117] The letter failed to change professional opinion. In a vote of 125 to 4 in 2009, the APA adopted a report rejecting efforts to change sexual orientation. Conversion therapy, the group reiterated, was ineffective and harmful.[118]

Some biblically literalist evangelicals took on Dobson and his like-minded disciplinarians, convinced that his position was not appropriate for Christians. Ross Campbell, a clinical psychiatrist and popular parenting specialist, asserts that unconditional love—not decisive discipline—is the root of good Christian parenting. Campbell, a Baptist, is bothered that fundamentalists cherry-pick Old Testament passages about corporal punishment while ignoring the child's basic need, which is love. He claims that his reading of the Bible, which is literal like Dobson's, is superior. The "rod" in scripture that Dobson invokes to support spanking children is not, in fact, a tool of corporal punishment. The relevant and oft-quoted verse is "He that spareth his rod hateth his son: but he that loveth him chasteneth him betimes" (Proverbs 13:24). Campbell contends that this verse refers to the rod that shepherds used to gently guide their sheep. It was not a bludgeon.[119]

Donald Capps, a professor of pastoral theology at Princeton Theological Seminary, notes a connection between religiosity and child abuse, presumably the result of corporal punishment. Dobson and others, argues Capps, did not call such treatment abuse, referring to it instead as tough love or chastisement. Yet abuse was compounded, Capps says, when it was misrepresented as wholesome and thus encouraged when it should be discouraged.[120]

Most mainline Protestants agree with the APA on the proper approach to homosexuality. But some left-leaning evangelicals also challenge Dobson on homosexuality and gay marriage. Some even argue that there is no strong case that the Bible opposes homosexuality. Evangelicals Concerned (EC), though small compared with Focus, operates a nationwide ministry to lesbian, gay, bisexual, and transgendered Christians. The organization holds Bible studies, support groups, and social events throughout the country. God does not judge men and women on the basis of race, gender, or sexual orientation, leaders of EC state. Their website features resources and answers questions that conservatives ask: How can someone justify homosexuality from the Bible? Is your group political? What do you mean by "evangelical"? Dobson and others, according to an EC document, want to pretend that "gay Christian" is an oxymoron. Using scripture, experience, and recent findings about gender and sexuality, EC offers an alternative view. Psychotherapist Ralph Blair, the group's founder, empathizes with Dobson, believing he has fallen into the trap of stereotyping one's enemies and marginalizing those who are different.[121]

Social psychologist David Myers is the most powerful Christian critic of the Focus view of homosexuality. He earned his Ph.D. from the University of Iowa and went on to become one of the most significant Christian scholars in America. Myers is a popular professor at Hope College, a four-year liberal arts school connected to the Reformed Church in America in Holland, Michigan. Over the years he won several prestigious National Science Foundation grants, served as a consulting editor for the chief journals in the field, authored dozens of articles and book chapters, and lectured at universities across the country. *Psychology,* his introductory textbook, is widely adopted for courses. Another, *Exploring Psychology,* ranked as the best-selling general introduction to the subject and is broadly used at both secular and Christian colleges and universities.[122]

Myers believes that Christians can be faithful to God, the Bible, and their tradition and still believe that homosexuality is morally acceptable. In 2005 he wrote *What God Has Joined Together: The Christian Case for Gay Marriage* with Letha Dawson Scanzoni, a Christian feminist who has published on ethics and social justice. The evidence shows, they argue, that children and adults thrive when and where communities value marriage. Christians should support the aspirations of "gay and lesbian persons . . . not despite, but because of our eagerness to renew marriage." Ostracizing homosexuals and building a wall around marriage is no way to create vibrant communities, they write.[123] In their view commentators across the spectrum agree that being a single parent is difficult and undesirable. But in extending that argument to challenge gay marriage, Myers and Scanzoni observe, Dobson and others go too far. Few studies had compared "children in single-parent or neglectful homes with children adopted or born into families where they are co-parented by two stable partners of the same sex."[124] Needless to say, Myers's views are controversial, but they are also increasingly attractive to younger evangelicals raised among more positive public images of homosexuals.

Conservative guardians of orthodoxy viewed Myers as a liberal sellout, a part of the reason for America's moral crisis. In 2006 Dobson appeared on Fox News and made exactly this point to Bill O'Reilly. In countries embracing same-sex marriage and civil unions, he said, children were increasingly born out of wedlock and marriage had disappeared as a viable institution. Sanctioning gay unions, as Myers advocated, would hurt heterosexual marriages. Dobson admitted that homosexuals should be treated equally under the law, but he thought they were asking for special rights. "Bill, while people have the right to equality under the law," Dobson responded to O'Reilly's prodding, "they do not have the right to define marriage. Redefine marriage. For 5,000 years in every continent on earth, marriage has been the standard between a man and a woman." The changelessness of marriage was an oft-repeated theme on the Focus website, on the air, and in affiliated books and magazines.[125] It bears more careful consideration, however.

The Judeo-Christian tradition that supposedly undergirds Dobson's beliefs does not support the idea of marriage as a changeless institution created by God in the beginning. The Old Testament patriarch Jacob had four wives. King David's eight wives are named in the Bible, though he had many more. The book of I Kings describes the amorous King Solomon, who "loved many strange women, together with the daughter of Pharaoh, women of the Moabites, Ammonites, Edomites, Zidonians, and Hittites." He took seven hundred wives and three hundred concubines. To be sure, these various marital structures were never same-sex, but only in that limited sense do they seem continuous with marriage as understood in the twenty-first century. In contemporary Western culture women are no longer property to be hoarded by kings or jealous tribal chiefs. Fathers do not barter their daughters to advance family fortunes. And nobody has hundreds of wives. Strangely, that historical context and the dramatic changes to marriage that Americans had adopted seemed lost on Focus, which continued to argue that gay marriage amounted to the first radical change in the history of the institution.[126]

Dobson was convinced that marriage and the family were in worse shape now than they had been in ages past. With Barack Obama's campaign thriving in October 2008, Dobson penned a fanciful letter from the year 2012, describing Obama's America as a dystopian wasteland. The letter, which could have ranged widely over a host of social and political issues, from war and climate change to healthcare and racism, seemed strangely obsessed with homosexuality. In Obama's America, gay marriage received federal sanction and government goons banned religious adoption agencies. Homeschooling parents were losing their sacred right to educate their children. Time-honored institutions collapsed under government's iron fist. The country seemed to have lost God's favor, the letter speculated in closing. Critics called it apocalyptic kitsch, vindictive, desperate, and brazenly political. Jim Wallis of *Sojourners* asked Dobson to apologize for a fear-mongering, wildly irresponsible piece of propaganda.[127]

Focus continued to engage in politics and evolve, even when challenged by financial crises, political scandals, and a major shift in leadership. In 2009 officials announced that Dobson would cut ties with Focus in 2010. Dobson continued to write for the newsletter, but he no longer hosted the radio program, which had first aired in 1977.[128] (In 2008 the Radio Hall of Fame inducted Dobson, who beat out shock-jock Howard Stern.)[129]

The tireless and talented Dobson did not go gently into retirement. He launched a new radio program and continued writing and speaking, as he had for decades. Issues related to the family and healthy relationships, increasingly charged by politics, still demanded his attention.

Focus remained aggressively political. A fall 2009 Washington state referendum expanded the legal rights of same-sex couples in civil union. The defeat stung Focus, which had donated $91,000 to kill the proposal. Across the country in Maine they were more successful. Focus gave over $115,000 to a state coalition to repeal a same-sex marriage law. It helped, and the law was revoked by a popular vote of 53 percent to 43 percent. The victory proved, said Focus officials, that Americans still supported traditional marriage.[130] Regular email dispatches to millions of supporters kept same-sex marriage, abortion, and conservative politics front and center. In June 2010 Jim Daly, the organization's new president, called Obama to task for a Father's Day proclamation. Obama stated: "Nurturing families come in many forms, and children may be raised by a father and mother, a single father, two fathers, a step father, a grandfather, or caring guardian." That was one father too many for Daly. "[W]e know," Daly wrote, "that kids need both a mother and a father, and two fathers cannot make up for not having a mother."[131]

But not all Americans knew that. A 2010 Gallup survey registered a major shift in Americans' perception of homosexuality. More than 50 percent thought gay and lesbian relations were morally acceptable. Those who considered such relationships morally wrong dipped to 43 percent, "the lowest in Gallup's decade-long trend." Record high numbers of Americans supported same-sex unions.[132] The changes were no doubt motivated in part by a greater cultural openness to different sexual orientations as well as by the acceptance of homosexuality as a normal sexual expression on the part of the scientific, medical, and psychiatric community. Younger people, feared older leaders like Dobson, were increasingly likely to approve of perverse behavior.

Amid that sea change, evangelicals remained far more conservative than the country as a whole when it came to the family, child-rearing, and sexual orientation. Evangelical parents reported spanking their preschool-age children and toddlers more often than other parents, justifying corporal punishment as approved by an inerrant Bible. At the same time, evangelical fathers—despite the warnings of fundamentalist, antifeminist Cassandras—were more involved with their children than fathers in other faith traditions.[133] Evangelicals are still more conservative on gender relations within the family, but even that has changed in recent years. (One observer calls the new brand of male leadership "soft patriarchy.") A 1996 survey showed that evangelicals were twice as likely as nonevangelicals to agree that preschool children suffer when their mothers work. Still, notions of male domination have declined, more evangelical women are in the workplace now than in the 1960s and 1970s, and ideas of a husband as a "servant leader," not an authoritarian despot, are spreading.[134]

Researchers conducted study after study on same-sex relationships, childcare, and family life. The conclusions countered traditional views held sacred by many Americans, particularly evangelicals. But that did little to alter opinions. A 2008 Pew poll revealed that only 26 percent of evangelicals surveyed agreed that "homosexuality should be accepted by society." By contrast, 56 percent of mainline Protestants agreed with that statement. Sixty-four percent of evangelicals held that "homosexuality should be discouraged by society," compared with only 34 percent of mainliners.[135]

Most evangelicals believe that their traditional views of sexuality and family hierarchy come straight and unambiguously from scripture. They are following God's recommendations, regardless of the latest studies or psychological fads. For decades Bible believers rejected what counted as conventional expertise on these matters, embracing instead the views of counterexperts like James Dobson, J. Richard Fugate, Tim and Beverly LaHaye, and Larry Christenson. A longitudinal study of 10,000 families, an investigation into the outcomes of corporal punishment, or neuroscience research on human sexuality is no match for directives from God. Of course, evangelicals are not typically opposed to using scientific studies to bolster their viewpoint. Yet they do so with caution. Secular experts, Dobson wrote in *Dare to Discipline,* had forever been in conflict with one another. Why? Because experts couldn't even agree on the basics. The sheer magnitude of disagreement on issues such as sexual orientation and child-rearing made this expertise questionable at best. Moreover, good disciplinary strategies could not be discovered by scientific inquiry, claimed Dobson. Sound advice and scripture were better guides.[136] The appeal to biblical truth, the assurances of a trusted evangelical, and the claims of tradition trumped other forms of expertise, in whatever guise.

Evolutionary theories and scientific facts do not team together.

An antievolution cartoon that George McCready Price included in his book *The Predicament of Evolution* (Nashville: Southern Publishing Association, 1925), 96.

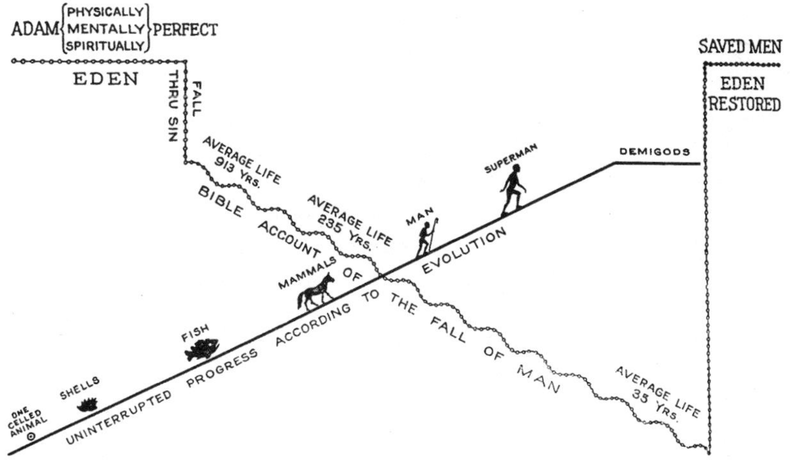

How can it be said that evolution and Christianity agree, when God's history is diametrically opposed to man's?

George McCready Price's timeline of Christian and evolutionary development, 1925. From *The Predicament of Evolution*, 104.

Henry Morris, the father of the modern creationist movement. From *Faithful Messenger* (DVD). Institute for Creation Research, 2006.

A display at the Creation Museum, Petersburg, Kentucky. Photograph by Karl Giberson.

Ken Ham in front of a dinosaur replica, Creation Museum, Petersburg, Kentucky. From *The New Answers* (DVD). Answers in Genesis, 2010.

David Barton as a guest on Glenn Beck's Fox News program. The topic was "Faith in America: Can Faith Restore America?" April 12, 2010.

Peter Marshall lecturing to a crowd. From *Restoring America* (DVD), disc 1. Peter Marshall Ministries, 2006.

D. James Kennedy in Bruton Parish Church in Colonial Williamsburg. From *One Nation under God* (DVD). Coral Ridge Ministries, 2005.

Reenactment of a seventeenth-century historical procession for D. James Kennedy's documentary *What If America Were a Christian Nation Again?* Coral Ridge Ministries, 2004.

J. Richard Fugate speaking to a crowd in the early 1980s. From *What the Bible Says about Child Training* (VHS), tape 1. Aletheia Publishers, Inc., 1981.

Beverly LaHaye leading a seminar titled "Overcoming Fear, Anxiety, and Worry," 1978. From *Spirit-Controlled Family Living* (VHS), part 3. Family Life Distributors, 1978.

James Dobson fielding questions for *Bringing Up Boys* (DVD), disc 3. Focus on the Family, 2002.

The entrance to the Focus on the Family headquarters, with the Rocky Mountains in the background. Photograph by Randall Stephens.

The large Focus on the Family bookstore at the foot of the Rocky Mountains, Colorado Springs, Colorado. Photograph by Randall Stephens.

"Superstition has always ruled the world." A detail of a *Puck* magazine cartoon satirizing the Millerite folly, April 10, 1901. Library of Congress.

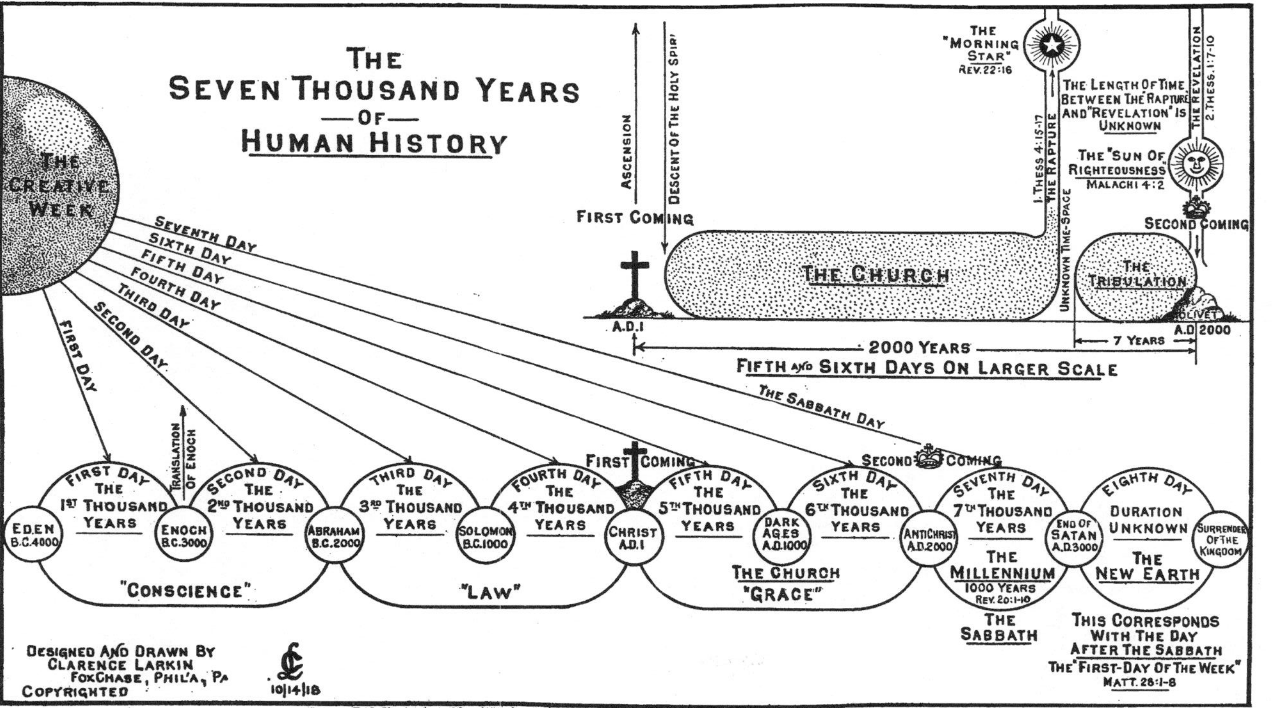

A detailed premillennial dispensationalist chart from the early twentieth century that lays out the sequence of events leading up to the second coming of Jesus. From Clarence Larkin, *Dispensational Truth, or God's Plan and Purpose in the Ages* (Philadelphia, 1918), 16.

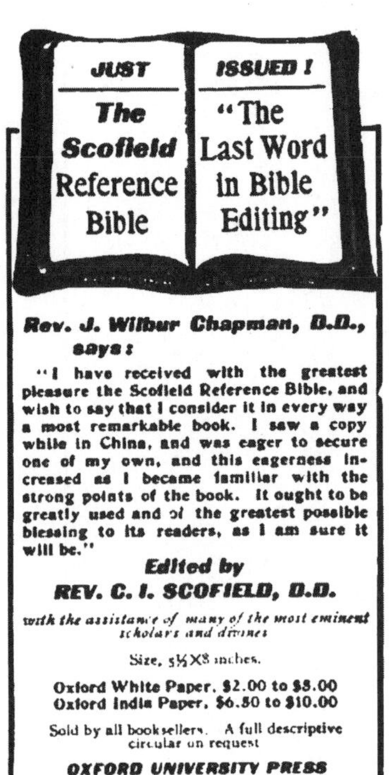

A 1910 advertisement for the *Scofield Reference Bible.* From the *New York Observer,* December 8, 1910, 747.

Hal Lindsey speaking about the Anti-Christ in the 1978 film adaptation of his book *The Late Great Planet Earth.* Trinity Home Entertainment, 2004.

Television prophecy expert Jack Van Impe speaking about the perils of the Soviet Union in the late 1980s. "Russia, World War III, and Armageddon" (VHS). Jack Van Impe Ministries, 1989.

Tim LaHaye describing the tribulation that will take place after the rapture of the saints. From *The End Times: In the Words of Jesus* (DVD). Questar, 2006.

A large Christian bookstore in Olathe, Kansas. Photograph by Randall Stephens.

Alpine sage Francis Schaeffer narrating his 1977 documentary *How Should We Then Live? The Reformation.* Gospel Films Incorporated, 1977.

Adam and Eve display at the Creation Museum, Petersburg, Kentucky. Photograph by Karl Giberson.

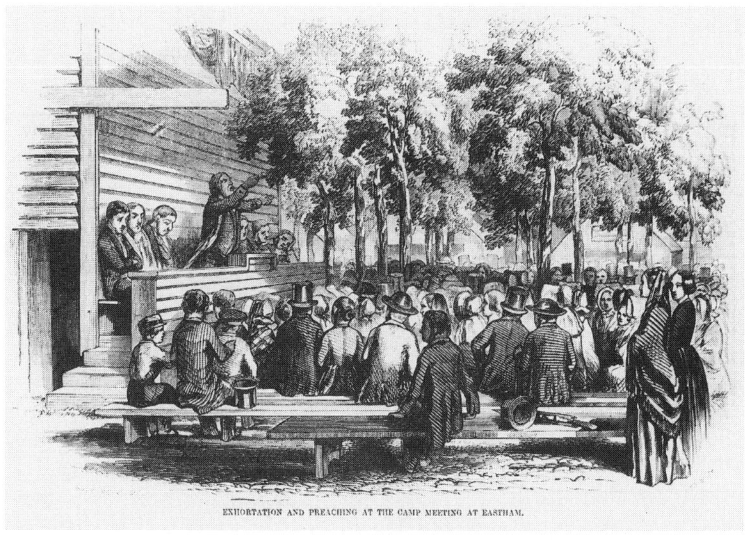

A pre–Civil War camp meeting. At such meetings the charisma and speaking skills of Baptist and Methodist ministers captivated congregants. *Gleason's Pictorial,* September 18, 1852.

America's most popular early twentieth-century preacher, Billy Sunday, posing for the camera. From William T. Ellis, *"Billy" Sunday: The Man and His Message* (Philadelphia: Universal Book and Bible House, 1914).

4 Trust Me, the End Is Near

Ronald Reagan rode a wave of disenchantment to the White House in the 1980 election, cheered on by America's evangelicals. Though his opponent, Jimmy Carter, was an evangelical, most conservative Christians came to view the Georgia native as a weak, ineffective president who had squandered what little remained of the nation's prestige. Reagan pledged to restore faith in America and to rekindle patriotism. An ideological conservative who condemned big government and endorsed deregulation, he was also a social conservative reaching out to evangelicals. In 1980 Reagan told voters that legislation reinstituting school prayer would counter the harmful cultural revolutions of the 1960s. He called for restoration of the traditional family and ratification of an antiabortion human-life amendment, pledges that resonated with the emerging Christian Right.[1]

The Religious Roundtable, an August 1980 gathering of evangelicals in Dallas, invited both Carter and Reagan to address the faithful. Carter declined. Reagan accepted, wowing the fifteen thousand attendees who had made the Dallas pilgrimage to hear speakers like Jerry Falwell, Pat Robertson, D. James Kennedy, and Texas fundamentalist television preacher James Robison. Aware that an outright endorsement might appear partisan, Reagan told the throng of activists, "I know you can't endorse me, but I want you to know that I endorse you and what you are doing." The audience was thrilled to have an ally in the Gipper. It was an "incontrovertible fact," he proclaimed, "that all the complex and horrendous questions confronting us at home and worldwide have their answers in that single book," the Bible.[2]

After his speech, Reagan appeared at a press conference to answer questions about the relationship of biblical faith to public policy. When a reporter asked if the theory of evolution should be taught in public schools, Reagan responded: "Well, it is a scientific theory only, and it has in recent years been challenged in the world of science and is not yet believed in the scientific community to be as infallible as it once was believed. But if it was going to be taught in the schools," he reasoned, "then I think that also the biblical theory of creation, which is not a theory but the biblical story of creation, should also be taught." While running for his second term, Reagan told another gathering of evangelicals in Dallas that "faith and religion play a critical role in the political life of our nation." Yet in his view, since the 1960s that time-honored truth had been threatened by a tide of godless secularism and liberal intolerance. While Reagan's cheery optimism energized most Americans, another side of him—a dark, bleak, pessimistic side—was also shared by millions of evangelicals.[3]

Early into his presidency, and not long after a failed assassination attempt, Reagan faced growing unrest in the Middle East. Career diplomat and Middle East troubleshooter Philip C. Habib advised Reagan on the crisis in Lebanon. Religious factions were squaring off against one another as nations took advantage of social unrest. Habib had been shuttling between Syria, Lebanon, Israel, and Saudi Arabia in search of solutions to the mounting troubles. His news did "not sound good" to the newly elected president. Would escalating hostilities draw Russia into the conflict? Would dire events reignite anti-Americanism in the region? These and other questions loomed large, and Reagan confided to his diary, "Sometimes I wonder if we are destined to witness Armageddon." Described in Revelation, the last book in the Bible, Armageddon was the site where God's angel of vengeance would bring "kings of the earth and of the whole world, to gather them to the battle of that great day of God Almighty." The world's armies would annihilate one another as the drama of the last days unfolded. It would be the final battle of human history, gruesome and bloody beyond imagination. Wicked forces of Earth would clash with the armies of God. With biblical passages weighing on his mind, Reagan worried again about violence elsewhere in the Middle East: "Got word of Israeli bombing of Iraq—nuclear reactor. I swear I believe Armageddon is near."[4]

Reagan kept his apocalyptic speculations largely private, to the relief of his press secretary. But the president finally aired his views concerning humanity's big finale. In October 1983, as the world's attention turned again to Lebanon, Reagan told the executive director of the American-Israeli Public Affairs Committee: "I turn back to your ancient prophets in the Old Testament and the signs foretelling Armageddon, and I find myself wondering if we're the generation that's going to see that come about." He continued, "I don't know if you've noted any of those prophecies lately, but, believe me, they certainly describe the times we're going through." Mainline religious leaders reacted immediately. A group of 110 Protestant, Roman Catholic, and Jewish officials demanded that the president and his Democratic rival, Walter F. Mondale, repudiate the violent, literalist speculations about Armageddon, which they viewed as a perversion of scripture. Whether the president shared his perspective with the Christian Right or was just pandering to them, a spokesperson for the ministers groused, it was a dangerous outlook. Annoyed, Reagan responded that his comments were made "in philosophical discussions with people who are interested in the same things." He was not setting his agenda according to the Armageddon clock.[5]

The matter refused to go away. In fact, Reagan's end-times views received even greater attention in his 1984 campaign. During a televised debate with Walter Mondale, an NBC reporter baited the president: "Do you feel that we are now heading, perhaps, for some kind of nuclear Armageddon?" Reagan replied that he had discussed the matter with friends. But, he said, with his endearing confidence, no one really knew whether "Armageddon is a thousand years away or [the] day after tomorrow." Nancy Reagan breathed, "Oh, no!" to those sitting with her. The president's comment would not play well in San Francisco, New York, or Boston. Reagan had made similar allusions in an interview with Jim Bakker on the PTL network. But the Mondale debate was broadcast to a national audience largely unfamiliar with end-times conjecture. Flummoxed commentators and shocked religious officials responded once again. Over one hundred public radio stations from coast to coast aired a ninety-minute exposé, "Ronald Reagan and the Prophecy of Armageddon." The program blasted the president for his nonchalant reading of destruction and doom: "Ronald Reagan said it as Governor and as President, in his home in the White House, over lunch, over dinner, in the car and over the phone, to religious leaders and lobbyists, to his staff, a Senator and even to *People* magazine. On at least 11 occasions Ronald Reagan has suggested that the end of the world is coming, and it may be coming soon." The president again assured worried Americans that he was not setting policy according to an apocalyptic countdown. As he had noted earlier, he knew that "a great many theologians over a number of years . . . have been struck with the fact that in recent years, as at no other time in history, have most of these prophecies (which foretell Armageddon) been coming together."[6]

That clarification did little to assuage fears. The president's unidentified "great many theologians" did not pass muster with numerous Christians and non-Christians. Roughly one hundred religious leaders signed a well-publicized statement of concern, denouncing Reagan's apocalypticism. The signers were Roman Catholics, evangelicals, mainstream Protestants, and Jews. The head of the Episcopal Diocese of New York fretted over the president's espousing "such fringe religious theologies as Armageddon and the concept of 'rapture,'" God's speeding the saints to heaven before a time of tribulation. "The foreign policy of the most powerful nation on earth cannot be built upon fundamentalist concepts which cannot even be found in the pages of the Bible," the bishop warned. Jim Wallis, the center-left evangelical editor of *Sojourners,* also raised the alarm. Wild theories about nuclear Armageddon were heretical, he said at a press conference flanked by other critics of Reagan's folksy, if terrifying, theology. "The Bible has been used and twisted to justify some of the worst sins in history," Wallis admonished. "Slavery was justified by the Bible. Racism was justified by a misuse of Scriptures. . . . [A]partheid in South Africa, oppression of women. And now nuclear war is being justified from the Bible." Another commentator cautioned Christians against using the Bible as an almanac.[7]

Reagan and his supporters brushed off the critics. Naysayers were "liberal clergymen who have thus far found him invulnerable," Jerry Falwell snapped. According to one source close to the Virginia Baptist leader, Falwell gave Reagan a four-hour lecture on all things prophecy-related before he entered the White House, confirming much of what the future president believed, but providing a more elaborate picture. The condemnations did little to dampen the president's burning interest in eschatology. Current events and natural disasters were portents of doomsday. Like other evangelicals, Reagan read earthquakes, hurricanes, famine, and war as signs of the Second Coming of Christ. And political turmoil in the Middle East and Soviet saber-rattling presaged coming calamity as foretold in the Bible.[8]

Reagan's ideas about judgment day rattled his advisors and others in the Oval Office. Once, while waxing apocalyptic on the record to his official biographer, Edmund Morris, Reagan was interrupted by Chief of Staff Howard Baker: "I tell you, Mr. President, I wish you'd quit talking about that. It upsets me!" Unfazed, Reagan wondered aloud to Morris about who might play the end-times roles of Gog, Meshech, and the Ten Kings. On another occasion the president frightened a visiting South Korean leader with a doomsday warning. Macabre apocalypticism was "kind of scary to be talking about," an advisor confessed to the commander-in-chief. "Yeah, but it's going to happen," Reagan responded matter-of-factly.[9]

The Apocalypse had long captivated the president. His mother's Disciples of Christ church made him receptive to the doctrine as a young man. His later fascination with Armageddon came from conversations with his pastor Donn Moomaw of Bel-Air Presbyterian Church. Governor Reagan conversed with Billy Graham and Pat Boone about the end of history. According to his legal secretary, Reagan "repeatedly discussed" the 1970 last-days bestseller *The Late Great Planet Earth* with acquaintances. Its author, one of Reagan's "great many theologians," Hal Lindsey, depicted horrendous global struggles between Satan's minions and God's righteous saints. In Lindsey's telling the world was set to devolve into panic and holy terror. He creatively assembled Bible verses from Ezekiel, Daniel, Revelation, and Zechariah to claim that Armageddon would obliterate Russia and its Arab allies. A subsequent war between Western forces and the Chinese would conclude with a nuclear holocaust.[10]

Odd though it may seem for the leader of the free world to meditate on eschatology, Americans have been discussing, debating, and writing about the end of history since they landed on the country's shores. One scholar even describes an "Americanization of the apocalyptic tradition." Ethicist, theologian, and historian H. Richard Niebuhr thought that over the ages the "expectation of the coming kingdom . . . became the dominant idea of American Christianity." While the meaning of the millennium would change, the idea of Armageddon was there from the start. Early New England divines like Cotton Mather thought they were living in the last days. The Puritans rushed to America from the heady apocalyptic environment of seventeenth-century England. The powers of hell—namely, Catholics, Anglicans, and almost everyone else—seemed arrayed against them as history was drawing to a close. The Massachusetts Bay Colony governor John Winthrop heralded America as the new millennial kingdom of God. Indeed, apocalyptic thinking resonated with Americans who viewed their new land as divinely set apart for a special purpose. America's first best-selling book was a terrifying poem, *The Day of Doom* (1662), by Michael Wigglesworth. The Puritan minister and master of the Jeremiad brought end-times horrors into sharp relief with descriptions of evildoers scurrying into caves and reprobates casting themselves into the sea. As God meted out judgment there would be "no Peace-maker, no undertaker, to shroud them from God's ire, Ever obtain'd; they must be pain'd with everlasting fire."[11]

Yet for most of the country's history few had such a dark view of the Second Coming as Hal Lindsey and other latter-day prophets espoused. Americans in the colonial era and in the nineteenth century tended to believe that Jesus would return to Earth after the thousand years of peace—the millennium—described in the Bible. That end-times scenario, called postmillennialism, animated the social and cultural movements of the early nineteenth century, showcasing the optimistic spirit of reform. Preachers in the Revolutionary era and abolitionist radicals from the 1850s shared a mostly positive outlook concerning human potential. The flurry of nineteenth-century Protestant missionary activity around the globe, the temperance movement, and various social panaceas were ushering in a brighter future.

The Second Coming also animated Americans outside mainstream Protestantism. Joseph Smith, founder of Mormonism, believed in the imminent return of Christ. With time, though, he cautioned the Latter-Day Saints to temper their end-times zeal. The chief newspaper for the Disciples of Christ, the *Millennial Harbinger,* regularly featured passages from the books of Daniel and Revelation to illuminate contemporary events. The Shakers thought Jesus had returned to Earth as their Mother Ann Lee. Even the mid-nineteenth-century perfectionist free-love libertines at the utopian Oneida, New York, community speculated on the end. Jesus had already returned, they thought, in 70 A.D.[12]

William Miller, a self-taught New York farmer and former army captain who led the largest premillennial movement before the Civil War, embodied the rustic populism and democratic ethos of American evangelicalism. When Miller died in 1849, a prominent Philadelphia journalist called him "uneducated, and not largely read in even the common English commentaries; his views were absurd, and supported but feebly." What he lacked in education, Miller made up for in conviction and charisma. Still, he was largely reviled in his day and for decades to come. A twentieth-century critic called him a "theological leper," whose ostracism set the tone for later premillennial prophets. Unlike postmillennialists, who dominated the nineteenth-century Protestant establishment, premillennialists seldom put their faith in social reform and tended to disparage human endeavors that would bring about God's kingdom on Earth. A fatalistic strain ran through premillennialism. Adherents thought the world grew worse by the day, as described in the Bible when correctly interpreted.[13]

Miller became convinced of the premillennial return of Jesus after harmonizing contradictory passages in the Bible. Enthusiasts, including Isaac Newton, had been figuring the end—using charts, tables, and prophetic math—for decades. By 1818 Miller had spent much time calculating the Second Advent from Daniel and Revelation. The Bible's puzzles begged to be solved.[14]

In the 1830s the farmer-turned-prophet took to the countryside on a whirlwind revival tour, preaching to hundreds of thousands in New York, New Hampshire, Maine, Massachusetts, and Canada. The *New York Tribune* estimated that there were forty thousand "Millerites" at the movement's peak. Later scholars figured they numbered fifty thousand or more. Miller and his followers proclaimed that Jesus was coming very soon. The secular order would burn and doubters would suffer immeasurable pain. Millerites adopted a Methodist hymn that took on a grim new meaning for them: "We, while the stars from heaven shall fall / And mountains are on mountains, hurl'd / Shall stand unmov'd amidst them all / And smile to see a burning world."[15]

When Jesus did not return as expected between March 21, 1843, and March 21, 1844, Miller accepted a new date: October 22, 1844. The ensuing failure become known as the Great Disappointment. "What a set of disappointed fools the Millerites must be today," wrote an angry commentator in a New Hampshire paper. "They have brought their own reason to an end."[16]

The Millerite fiasco dampened premillennial enthusiasm. It was out of step with the heady optimism of nineteenth-century America, and only inspired a handful of groups like the Seventh-day Adventists. Not until after the Civil War did premillennial divines gain a larger hearing, with some inspiration from across the Atlantic.

Since the early nineteenth century, some English churchmen had preached premillennialism in Britain and Europe through journals, books, and prophecy conferences. The English minister John Nelson Darby, founder of the Plymouth Brethren, helped spread the influential theology of dispensationalism. This interpretation divided history into dispensations or eras, all leading to the end of the world. Biblical prophecy played a key role in determining the signs and other details of the last days. Dispensational premillennialism had a bleak historical outlook: "From the time of the exaltation of Jesus to the right hand of God, and the association of the Church with Him, Christ has been ready to judge," Darby thundered in his book *Notes on the Book of Revelations* (1839). "And now in the manifested failure of the Church on earth . . . though the bridegroom might tarry, the Church, knowing His mind, had but one cry, 'Come quickly!' In this position, therefore, the

Church is practically set." The world was in bad shape and nothing could make it better. Anyone who contradicted that terrible truth was in league with the Devil.[17]

Darby popularized the idea of the rapture, an end-times prophecy whereby God would rescue the saints, sparing them the horrific turmoil of the tribulation. Unbelievers, left behind, would suffer grave torments. Darby and other end-times enthusiasts quoted Matthew 24:21: "For then shall be great tribulation, such as was not since the beginning of the world to this time, no, nor ever shall be." The Anti-Christ, a wicked but charismatic world leader, would rule without mercy until the tribulation ended with the epic battle of Armageddon. The Christian church, tied to the state in England, was wrecked. We live, wrote the stern Darby, in an age of apostasy and wickedness.[18]

Premillennialism later had an unlikely scholar-saint in the New World, and its most important early twentieth-century American champion, in C. I. Scofield. Born in 1843, Scofield early made a name for himself as a heavy drinker, a forger, and a political swindler. He fought for the Confederacy during the Civil War and was later admitted to the bar in Kansas, where he served as a state representative and U.S. attorney for the district of Kansas. He left his wife and his career before landing in a St. Louis prison in 1879. Incarcerated, divorced, and distraught, Scofield found Jesus. A local Darbyite minister who had been active in prophecy conferences took the ex-con under his wing. Scofield became a pastor and an editor in Dallas, a close associate of the famous preacher Dwight Moody, and a militant premillennial dispensationalist.

Scofield's legacy rests on his incredibly popular *Scofield Reference Bible.* Published by Oxford University Press in 1909, the heavily annotated Bible clearly laid out the prophetic truths of scripture. "The remarkable results of the modern study of the Prophets," Scofield proclaimed in his introduction, "in recovering to the church not only a clear and coherent harmony of the predictive portions, but also great treasures of ethical truth, are indicated in expository notes." Unfortunately, the details of prophecy had been kept from many Christians through "fanciful and allegorical schemes of interpretation." Abstractions would not do for Scofield, though, who sailed through the scriptures thumbing his nose at scholarship. His common-sense conceit infuriated critics, who typically found his premillennialism crude, primitive, and based on a false view of scripture. Scofield's approach, in the words of one doubter, presumed that his theology was "nothing more than a transcript of what the Bible itself says."[19]

Such criticisms failed to blunt the success of *The Scofield Reference Bible.* It would sell over ten million copies and be translated into French, Spanish, German, Portuguese, and Korean. Its clear, simple notes appealed to laypeople, eager to read that the Bible was without error and as comprehensible as a *McGuffey's Reader.* Anyone, thought Scofield, could understand prophecy and interpret even the most complex passages of scripture. In his populist view, theological training of the sort he did not have was unnecessary. Scofield explained away biblical contradictions by pointing to the dispensations of history. What was justifiable in one age—murdering the infants of enemies, distributing captured virgins to soldiers, or pimping your daughter—was not justifiable in another era. Throughout, Scofield claimed he was merely clarifying the true meaning of scripture.[20]

Armed with a holy almanac, conservative evangelicals in the twentieth century energetically exposed liberal threats and demonic forces. Like most premillennial pundits, Scofield wanted to show Christian liberalism and secularism for what they truly were: satanic. An intense pessimism and militancy suffused this apocalyptic-driven fundamentalism. "After 1800 years of Bibles and Gospel preaching," complained one exponent, "there is not a nation, or a country, or a parish, or a long-established congregation, where the devil has not more subjects than Christ."[21]

The ravages of World Wars I and II raised cynicism and apocalyptic expectations to new levels. Some, like R. A. Torrey, educator and editor of *The Fundamentals,* thrilled as he contemplated global calamities. God would smite all enemies and set things right. "As awful as conditions are across the waters today," Torrey commented as the bloodbath of war raged on in 1917, "and as awful as they may become in our own country, the darker the night gets, the lighter my heart gets."[22]

Such thinking ran utterly counter to the ideals of progressive liberal Protestants, whose numeric strength and influence in this era far surpassed that of their conservative opponents. Theologians like Walter Rauschenbusch described salvation in communal terms and charted the steep moral progress of society. The so-called premillennial menace horrified liberal Protestants. As American troops fought in the trenches on the Western Front during World War I, one leading biblical scholar warned that supposed prophecy experts were dangerous malcontents. He cautioned readers that such modern-day heretics were criminally antisocial. "The American nation is engaged in a gigantic effort to make the world safe for democracy," he pointed out, while unpatriotic premillennialists were indifferent or even triumphant when they looked at catastrophic world events. He groused, "In the name of religion we are told that the world cannot be appreciably improved by human effort. Why not lay down for the Huns?"[23]

Sunny liberal progressivism faced a variety of challenges in the post–World War II years. With Europe in ruins and the looming threat of nuclear holocaust, more and more Americans adopted a secularized version of the once-fringe, end-times views of fundamentalists. When President Harry Truman learned of the first successful detonation of the A-bomb on July 16, 1945, he confided to his diary about the biblical significance of the event. This was the most "terrible bomb in history," and Truman mused that it might lead to "the fire destruction prophesied in the Euphrates Valley Era, after Noah and his fabulous Ark." Even Reinhold Niebuhr, America's foremost mid-century theologian, had doubted the liberal faith in humanity. Liberals had placed far too much confidence in moral progress, a naïve hope that two wars and global nuclear fears had largely wiped away. Horrible weapons of war fired the imaginations of some Christians. Passages in scripture, like 2 Peter 3:10, took on a new, grisly cast: "But the day of the Lord will come as a thief in the night; in which the heavens shall pass away with a great noise, and the elements shall melt with fervent heat, the earth also and the works that are therein shall be burned up."[24]

For all the interest in the devastating potential of nuclear weaponry and how that might connect to last things, Americans in the 1950s and 1960s were not all that interested in theological premillennialism and its latter-day prophets. To many, scientific progress and the postwar economic miracle made eschatology appear strangely out of sync. In 1963 a well-known American Protestant teacher and theologian declared: "Should anyone today make minute predictions about events in world history between now and A.D. 2400, he would not be likely to have an audience." Moreover, such an individual would be labeled a "fanatic." Yet so rapidly did things run downhill in the late 1960s that many evangelicals began thumbing through their Bibles for just such "minute predictions." A new age of anxiety took hold as student radicalism, turmoil, and chaos gripped middle America.[25]

Optimistic millennialism, or postmillennialism, largely faded by the late twentieth century, its once vibrant voice now echoing mainly in remnants animating the civil rights movement and campaigns for Christian social justice. In contrast, millions of Americans had moved to the nightmarish Armageddon camp of President Reagan. Of course, evangelicals and fundamentalists argued endlessly about the details. Would it be possible to convert souls after the rapture? Would the rapture take place before or after the tribulation? Would Catholics be among the saints? Questions continued to animate the faithful. But on some of the basics, Americans were of a surprisingly similar mind. According to a 2006 Pew Research Center poll 79 percent of Christians in the United States believed that Christ would return to Earth someday.

Of those, 20 percent were convinced that he would return in their lifetime and 33 percent thought the Bible revealed the time of the Second Coming. Another Pew poll from 2010 revealed that 41 percent of Americans expected Jesus to return to Earth by the year 2050.[26]

Nobody was more accomplished at inspiring such beliefs, nor more adept at taking advantage of social upheaval, than Hal Lindsey. Playing off everything from the raging culture wars to the threat of terrorism in the late twentieth century, he profoundly influenced millions of evangelicals for decades. Evangelical pastors and authors often identified him as the leading scholar/expert of the Apocalypse.

Once a self-described agnostic with an interest in conspiracy theories, Lindsey tossed about for a career before entering the evangelical fold. He attended the University of Texas business school but dropped out, dissatisfied. During the Korean War, he served in the Coast Guard and later worked as a tugboat captain on the Mississippi. After his first marriage ended in divorce, he fell into a deep depression, even contemplating suicide. He describes his eventual conversion, after reading a Gideon New Testament, as "like taking a dare."[27]

Lindsey remained an uninspired believer until he encountered the thrilling world of Bible prophecy. Before that point, scripture—confusing and contradictory—was a mystery. He was baptized three times as a young man but didn't take the ritual seriously. Religion made him feel guilty, so he "kissed it off." Liberal Christians had also sowed doubt in his mind: The Bible was riddled "with errors, it wasn't historical, and I couldn't believe it." A prophecy expert speaking at a church in the mid-1950s reignited his faith. Looking back years later, Lindsey emphasized the renewing power of eschatology: "Every time I have fallen away, gotten out of fellowship with God, or really gone lax in my Christian experience, prophecy has jerked me back." The exigencies of the last days brought him to life and proved that the Bible was an infallible guide to the past, present, and future.[28]

Rescued from confusion and skepticism, in 1958 Lindsey made his way to Dallas Theological Seminary, a bastion of twentieth-century fundamentalism and cultural conservatism. Women could not earn master's degrees at the institution until 1986. The seminary's founder was a well-known associate of the famed C. I. Scofield. Faculty and students adhered to biblical inerrancy and premillennial dispensationalism. That doctrine, argued one of the seminary's revered professors, was a *sine qua non.* Scripture could not be interpreted consistently without it. Professors championed creationism and biblical literalism against the onslaughts of liberal Protestantism and secular humanism. The seminary's website still announces with pride: "Dallas Seminary stands unequivocally committed to God's inerrant Scriptures. Members of the school's boards and faculty subscribe to the Seminary's Doctrinal Statement, which safeguards the school's unswerving theological stance." A rigorous fundamentalist curriculum has long required courses on the books of the Bible, prophecy, and, for most students, compulsory Greek and Hebrew classes. The seminary was regionally accredited in 1969.[29]

Fresh from Bible training, Lindsey spent the 1960s working with Campus Crusade for Christ, a conservative evangelical ministry to America's colleges and universities. He and his second wife, Jan, witnessed to students in Canada, Mexico, and in California at Berkeley and San Francisco State. Lindsey finally settled on a stable ministry to students at UCLA with a snappy name inspired by San Francisco's trippy psychedelic rock bands: the Jesus Christ Power and Light Company.

Lindsey quickly learned that young adults didn't care for the arcane language and complicated charts of moldy premillennialism. So even though his theology differed little from Scofield's, he updated his message with hip allusions and slangy affectations. Lindsey "had a knack," noted one observer, "for writing like a stoner." The rapture was "the ultimate trip." Psychedelic drugs couldn't match the far-out truths of prophecy. His eager pupils had many labels: Jesus Freaks, Children of

God, Street Christians, the God Squad, or simply Straight People. They joined the swelling ranks of new earthy believers—half-hippie, half-fundamentalist. One of Lindsey's students recalled that he wore a tank top, blue jeans, and leather boots as he confidently walked baby boomers through the Bible. This young disciple also remembered the "sense of excitement, and urgency we felt as Hal linked the Scripture to our world, our dilemmas, our questions." Lindsey's "interest in biblical prophecy fed into the wider apocalyptic fervor of the youth culture and the American culture at large," his pupil recalled.[30]

War, violence, social upheaval, and natural disasters loomed large in the public imagination. Close to home, Lindsey read the signs of the times on campus. In 1969 UCLA erupted in student protest and racial unrest. Drugs and the hippie counterculture were ubiquitous. *Time* reported that LSD use had spread like an epidemic. An estimated 10,000 college students in the California system had dropped acid by March 1966. And trouble brewed elsewhere. Two UCLA campus student groups, the Black Panthers and United Slaves, engaged in a deadly shootout in 1969 over ideological matters. Police squared off with antiwar protesters. Twenty thousand turned out for a UCLA antiwar protest. Governor Reagan avoided University of California campuses for fear that his presence might spark a riot. Not long after taking office in 1969, Richard Nixon chalked up student radicalism and youth-driven hedonism to a decadent, sick society. "It is not too strong a statement to declare that this is the way civilizations begin to die," he lamented. "The process is altogether too familiar to those who would survey the wreckage of history: assault and counterassault, one extreme leading to the opposite extreme, the voices of reason and calm discredited." Lindsey agreed wholeheartedly. But, unlike Nixon, Lindsey believed that decline was an inevitable part of God's plan.[31]

Eschatological revenge fantasies centered on the excesses of the 1960s. Larry Norman, later dubbed the father of Christian rock, moved in some of Lindsey's circles. Norman set 1960s premillennial anxieties to music on his 1969 LP *Upon This Rock.* God would spirit believers into heaven, away from the chaos of the world. On "I Wish We'd All Been Ready" he sang of a husband taken, a wife left. Two would walk together, and one would vanish. "Life was filled with guns and war / And everyone got trampled on the floor," Norman sang in folk tones reminiscent of Neil Young. "There's no time to change your mind / The Son has come and you've been left behind."[32]

A Dallas Theological Seminary professor explained why so many Christians looked to prophecy in uncertain times. Americans saw the "problems of lawlessness, crime and anarchy and realize[d] that no government can handle them." Such calm commentary on the turbulent, godless 1960s would gradually grow into a loud diatribe. The reaction to the ferment of that decade has been so strong that many evangelicals still mark it as the time when things started to go bad. The Assemblies of God denominational magazine published a jeremiad in the wake of 9/11 making this point. Signed by a who's who of the Religious Right—including Bill Bright, James Dobson, and Pat Robertson—the document took aim at America's post-1960s culture: "We need to repent for America's rejection of God's Word. . . . The highest court in our land has forced the Ten Commandments out of our schools and has forbidden little children to pray and read God's Word. America has flooded the world with unimaginable perversion on the Internet and through films and television. We have given legal protection to conduct that God calls an abomination, and we have slaughtered up to 40 million innocent babies in the last three decades."[33]

Looking at a world in ruins, Lindsey struck on an idea in the late 1960s. He would write a popular book based on his end-times talks and compulsive prophecy watching. Aided by journalist Carole C. Carlson, he published *The Late Great Planet Earth* in 1970. Carlson, known for working with Dutch Christian Holocaust survivor Corrie Ten Boom, gave the book a breezy, jocular, conversational style. *The Late Great Planet Earth* rested on a few key arguments. Many prophecies in the

Bible had already come true, Lindsey contended. The establishment of Israel in 1948, for example, was predicted in scripture; the Jewish recovery of Old Jerusalem in 1967 likewise confirmed the end of history. Those developments were "like the key piece[s] of a jigsaw puzzle," Lindsey wrote, implying that scripture was a game to be figured out. Finally, a coming global conflict, pitting Russia and united Arab forces against Israel, would culminate in mass slaughter. The chapter on Armageddon included a map with bold arrows marking the invasion of Israel by a "Russian confederacy." Drama was further increased by a revival of the occult with demonic implications. A European Common Market would aid the Anti-Christ's ascent to power. No speculation was too bizarre. Lindsey wondered about the Anti-Christ's head wound and his eventual recovery described in Revelation 13:14. Imagine what it would have been like if John F. Kennedy had "come to life again!" he asked gleefully. If JFK *had been* the Anti-Christ and if he *had* indeed risen from the dead, it would have shaken the world. This, of course, did not happen. Lindsey consistently fortified his account with passages from scripture, recent studies, news items, and quotes from secular scholars, all bolstering his argument that the Bible accurately forecasted the fast-approaching last days.[34]

Lindsey's followers came from a large group enamored of fringe literature in the "Me Decade." Pop psychology, New Age tracts, pseudo-science, and futurism countered mainstream discourse in more ways than one. In his 1968 bestseller *Chariots of the Gods,* Erich von Däniken claimed that advanced creatures from outer space had built early civilizations. A 1978 poll showed that 57 percent of Americans believed in the existence of UFOs. Some wondered just what the government was hiding in airplane hangars in the Southwest. This was the age of Watergate, and conspiracy theories abounded. References to world governments and sinister secularists filled the pages of *The Late Great Planet Earth* and Lindsey's subsequent books. African nations would unite with Russia against Israel. A European Common Market would become the ten-nation confederacy described in the book of Daniel. Lindsey exploited the fears of the era: war in the Middle East, widespread drug abuse, sexual libertinism, political corruption, terrorism, killer bees. He was not alone. Other prominent authors in the late 1960s and early 1970s warned of horrors on the horizon. Prophet of doom Paul Ehrlich's influential book *The Population Bomb* vividly described the famine and widespread death that would sweep over the world in the 1970s as food and resources ran out. That alarming book counseled Americans that nothing could be done to halt civilization's demise. "Between now and the 21st century," wrote Alvin Toffler in his immensely popular book *Future Shock* (1970), "millions of ordinary, psychologically normal people will face an abrupt collision with the future." Americans were casting about for the latest fad theories to make sense of a rapidly changing world. Even Hollywood cashed in on disastermania, commercializing chaos and destruction in 1970s films like *The Towering Inferno, Earthquake, The Swarm,* and *Airport 1975*.[35]

Yet few could frighten readers like Lindsey could. He was certain of his predictions, for they came from the Bible and the Bible did not lie. In the eyes of readers, his confidence and swagger lent his forecasts an almost scientific air. "I'm not out to scare people, but to wake them up," he told a reporter in 1981. Turning that statement on its head, he said he'd rather "scare hell out of them than have them go there." The former tugboat captain told audiences that even if the world didn't end by 1988, the curtain of history would certainly fall before 2000. One sincere fan of *The Late Great Planet Earth,* an Air Force colonel, approached Lindsey at a speaking engagement and confessed that he was irreligious and hadn't cared much about prophecy before. Then he read the book. "It scared the hell out of me," he confided. "I got on my knees and accepted Jesus." *The Late Great Planet Earth* was a powerful book and an uncommon success.[36]

Lindsey remarked that God had assured him, even before he finished the manuscript, that the book would sell over a million copies.

The *New York Times* named Lindsey's book the number one nonfiction bestseller of the 1970s. It came out at just the right time and quickly became the heart of a growing fascination with the end-times. The number of Christian bookstores in America rose from 725 to 1,850 between 1965 and 1975. At such outlets, Americans bought t-shirts emblazoned with the words, "In Case of Rapture This T-Shirt Will Be Empty," and bumper stickers that read, "If I'm raptured, take the wheel." In the late 1970s an Assemblies of God church in Los Angeles took the matter very seriously, creating bylaws to ensure that when the rapture occurred those who were left behind would dispose of the church's $1.5 million property. The plan trusted that unraptured sinners would be scrupulous.

All this was part of a dramatically growing fundamentalism that was measured by far more than postrapture property stipulations. Sales of Christian books climbed over 112 percent from 1972 to 1977 and made up 15 percent of the book market, or $3.8 billion of sales. In 1976 the *New Scofield Reference Bible* sold a respectable 100,000 copies. In that same year Lindsey had two paperbacks on the Religious Bestseller List.[37]

The twenty-eight million copies of *The Late Great Planet Earth* sold by the early 1990s made Lindsey very rich. In the late 1970s he lectured about 150 times a year, usually drawing a tidy speaker's fee of $3,500, the equivalent of more than $7,000 in 2011. With a taste for sports cars, he wore a Porsche racing jacket and zipped around Los Angeles in his Mercedes 450. His suite of office complexes in posh Santa Monica, where he plotted new ventures, added to his profile. He produced a film version of *The Late Great Planet Earth* in 1978. Narrated by both Lindsey—clad in denim and wearing a large gold Star of David necklace—and an obese, bearded Orson Welles, the movie paraded one disaster scenario after another across the screen and featured various "experts." Reenactments and archival footage gave the movie a documentary edge. The film won a ready audience in churches across the country, although a reviewer in *Christianity Today* said the special effects reminded him of *Godzilla* meets *The Samurai Warrior.* Many a Sunday night gathering or Bible study group previewed it and discussed its startling contents.[38]

Lindsey bristled when asked about his wealth, real estate holdings, and lavish lifestyle. "No one has the right to criticize me just because God favors the work that I was called on to do," he snapped at an inquisitive reporter. Irritated by such questions, he confessed that he'd "come close to punching a few guys for the way they ask about my personal finances." Lindsey hit a rough patch in the late 1970s after his second divorce. But, as always, he bounced back and produced more bestsellers. His 1980 book *The 1980's: Countdown to Armageddon* sold 360,000 copies in its first nine months. Added to that, his prophecy cassette service grossed over $150,000 per month. Lindsey's large Christian audience was not deterred by questions of wealth or marital status, strangely oblivious to Jesus' teachings about both.[39]

Lindsey influenced evangelicals like few others could. *The Late Great Planet Earth* and the avalanche of books he produced taught evangelicals about the sham of world peace in the eleventh hour, the place of Israel among nations, and what to expect as the clock of history ran out. *The Late Great Planet Earth* was "the first book I ever read about last days," recalled a pastor of a 4,000-member Colorado megachurch in 2002. It changed his life. "All of a sudden, I was made aware that wow, there's an order to this thing." Though Lindsey's doomsday scenario inspired fear in many, others found a clearer sense of purpose and vision in it. Lindsey's populist apocalypticism stirred millions, and even brought some into the Christian fold. Michael Shermer, a born-again college student, read *The Late Great Planet Earth* in the 1970s. Long before he became America's premier doubter and founding editor of the popular *Skeptic* magazine, he devoured Lindsey's text. Convinced of immense conspiracies and taking the apocalyptic message to heart—an enthusiasm that would soon pass—Shermer transferred to Pepperdine University to study theology.[40]

Lindsey's calculations and predictions inspired others. In 1980 a former space program employee in Texas wrote his own book on the subject, "with prophetic timetables." Just as Lindsey read the Bible like a roadmap to the future, this author called the Bible "the first computer." "God set up the first computer system and each letter and number to go with it." By his estimation the Lord would return, oddly enough, on April Fool's Day. Scripture's "secret language" captivated this Texas Tech grad and chemical engineer as it did so many others. Though Lindsey may or may not have inspired compulsive numerology and date setting, he cultivated a deep suspicion of secularism, pluralism, and liberalism among readers. Did it matter that many scholars who studied scripture in the original languages and in the context of ancient history disagreed with Lindsey? No, such interpreters were, quite simply, horribly wrong. They did not read scripture literally, as God intended.[41]

Modern scholars of the Bible were not just misguided souls. They were pawns of the Devil, Lindsey wrote in *Satan Is Alive and Well on Planet Earth* (1972), which sold more than two million copies in the six years after its publication. It all began when Western intellectuals started to doubt "medieval superstitions related to demons and devils." Soon liberal German biblical scholars and their American allies questioned the historical integrity of the Bible: "Using subjective literary methods of analysis (not based on hard facts of history or archeology), they dissected the books of Moses and attributed them to a host of different writers." When Lindsey surveyed the secular philosophy that dominated the West in the last two centuries, he came to better understand the meaning of Revelation 2:24, concerning "the depths of Satan."[42]

Liberal theologians and Bible scholars were guilty of more than just bending scripture to suit their secular perspectives. They had stripped the Bible of its authority, Lindsey wrote in his 1973 retooling of earlier works, *There's a New World Coming: An In-Depth Analysis of the Book of Revelation.* Murder rates climbed in the absence of absolute truths and law and order was on the way out. It was no wonder, Lindsey observed, that "men can explode with their passions and then somehow justify to themselves the taking of another's life." A strange anti-intellectual thread ran through such arguments. "Biblically well-taught" Christians, sneered Lindsey, tended to ruin the churches they attended. Yet when approached to debate these vilified biblical and religious studies scholars at a 1984 UCLA conference on Armageddon, Lindsey declined. He agreed to speak at an event related to the conference but stipulated that only students could ask questions. He consistently dismissed rather than engaged scholars. Lindsey even used Bible verses to cut off debate. Premillennialism was the only true interpretation. "We need to be alert," he warned. "When we hear church leaders, teachers, or preachers questioning the visible return of Christ, this is a doctrine of apostasy."[43]

Lindsey was a Jeremiah for the common man and woman, articulating their concerns in blockbuster books. His ardent fans have been oddly untroubled by predictions that have not come true and which, in hindsight, have seemed laughably off the mark. America would become a second-rate power in the years leading up to 1988, he said in the early 1970s. The Soviet Union would take over Iran. Communism would be more dangerous in the 1980s than at any time before. Shifting with the times, Lindsey kept extending his apocalyptic timeline, just as William Miller had in the previous century. The 1970s had looked like the end. So had the 1980s and 1990s. But the millennium posed new threats, and the resourceful Lindsey could always refashion his apocalypticism to accommodate.[44]

Lindsey told Americans, in the wake of 9/11, that they were right to fear and loathe Muslims. In regular columns for the right-wing *WorldNet Daily,* Lindsey made hash of secular elites, liberal policy makers, and advocates of religious pluralism. He joined other notable commentators on that website, including Ann Coulter, David Limbaugh (Rush's evangelical brother), Bill O'Reilly, and action hero turned pundit Chuck Norris. Like them, he defended conservative truth against all liberal adversaries. "So what is this 'great moral failure'" of President Bush, he asked rhetorically in 2006. The president had "dared to disregard the mythical 'wall separating church and state' and prayed for God's guidance regarding the war on Iraq." Lindsey saw a kindred spirit in Bush, for he, too, had been raked over the coals by a "liberal-dominated media."[45]

Capitalizing on growing Islamophobia, Lindsey turned his attention to Muslim threats, large and small. In 2002 he warned that in the last days God's people would suffer all kinds of persecution. Islamic belligerents "who murder Christians will believe they are following God's word and performing a religious duty for Him," he stated. Muslims violated human rights and revered the Koran, a viciously dangerous book. He claimed that when he wrote *The Late Great Planet Earth* Muslim nations were "nothing like the threat they are now." He had slowly changed his mind. Violence was endemic to Arab culture, and Islam was a cruel religion, he said bluntly. That was a view he shared with a range of best-selling conservative authors, some evangelical, some not. Mohammad, said Lindsey, was inspired by the Devil. In an era of growing anti-Islamic sentiment, such claims were not unique to Lindsey, but few marshaled scripture and doomsday scenarios in the service of Islamophobia like he did.[46]

Lindsey's anti-Muslim crusade intensified in 2006. He veered so far to the right that he even ran afoul of the Pentecostal, evangelical Trinity Broadcasting Network (TBN), which pulled his program, *International Intelligence Briefing*. End-times advocates, as well as Lindsey himself, were shocked. TBN featured wooly creationist Carl Baugh, Christian America historian David Barton, Christian Zionist John Hagee, and a range of other vocal conservative evangelicals. Lindsey's ouster revealed that even some of the most conservative Christians in America were squeamish about the American Jeremiah's fierce claims. Paul Crouch, TBN founder and president, worried that Lindsey's anti-Muslim harangues would wreck the network's global outreach. "I am not aware of a single instance where making inflammatory, derogatory anti-Muslim statements has led a single follower of Islam to Christ," Crouch told the press. Worse, foreign governments were monitoring TBN's shows for incendiary material. In the larger scheme of things, though, the brouhaha barely dented Lindsey's influence. He had amassed a fortune over the years and was able to produce his program, airing it on his website. TBN later again picked up *The Hal Lindsey Report,* with Lindsey footing the bill.[47]

Although Lindsey's message alarmed even TBN's administrators, it was largely in step with that of other teleprophets and premillennial experts from the nation's most watched religious network. In 2007 TBN boasted more than 12,500 TV and cable affiliates around the globe. One of its chief end-times authorities, Jack Van Impe, hosted a weekly program that reached millions of homes in the United States and abroad. *Jack Van Impe Presents* was one of the longest-running and most popular programs on the network. Van Impe and his wife, Rexella, breathlessly read news of peace treaties and the growth of the European Union as irrefutable evidence of Christ's Second Coming. Van Impe announced on his website: "Current international events reflect exactly the conditions and happenings predicted throughout the Bible for the last days of this age." Cold War predictions of a Russian-led invasion of Israel dominated the program, but after 2001, the war on terrorism and global conflicts between Muslims and Christians took center stage. The role of Israel was critical for Van Impe and every other premillennialist.[48] "Evangelicals' view of the Bible gives them a proprietary interest in Israel," writes one historian. "It is the Holy Land, the site of God's mighty deeds. In a way, they think the Promised Land belongs to them as much as it does to Israelis."[49]

Another popular TBN celebrity, the San Antonio, Texas, Pentecostal pastor John Hagee, rallied his faithful with intensely political messages of Christian Zionism. According to a survey conducted by a religious pollster, Hagee ranked among the top ten Christian spokesmen for black and white Pentecostal ministers. In that regard he joined James Dobson, best-selling author and television preacher T. D. Jakes, Jerry Falwell, and Billy Graham. His call to arms against Israel's enemies and his message of America's moral failings have also won him avid followers. Christian Zionism, he argues, is a biblical imperative. Israel is "the only nation that God ever created," he told a National Public Radio reporter in 2006. "It's the only nation that Christians are told to pray for, and therefore, because the Bible is the compass of our faith, we do what it says." *Jerusalem Countdown,* his best-selling premillennial jeremiad, sold half a million copies by the summer of 2006.

That same year Hagee planned a mass meeting in the nation's Capitol, the Washington/Israel Summit, demanding that President Bush and American lawmakers pledge greater support for Israel. In attendance were Republican National Committee Chairman Ken Mehlman, Republican Senators Sam Brownback and Rick Santorum, Gary Bauer, and Jerry Falwell. Hagee organized his supporters in a campaign for a preemptive war on Iran, or Persia, in his latter-day political scenario. Hagee justified such a move to thwart Iranian terrorism, while also relishing that the ensuing conflagration would lead to Armageddon. As one journalist noted, "His end-times theology is nothing new." Yet "TBN's relentless fund raising—along with advances in digital and satellite broadcasting technology—has permitted worldwide dissemination of his ominous predictions."[50] In 2006 the San Antonio pastor created Christians United for Israel, a nationwide lobbying organization to support Israel. The group began with over four hundred leaders, and Hagee's national profile rose dramatically. It is not entirely surprising that Republican presidential candidate John McCain publicly accepted Hagee's endorsement in March 2008, a decision he reversed under pressure when he learned that in the 1990s Hagee had proclaimed that Hitler ushered in God's plan to bring Jews back to Israel. "I just think that the statement is crazy and unacceptable," said McCain.[51]

While Hagee and Lindsey continued to polarize evangelicals with their red-hot, headline-grabbing apocalypticism and enrage those outside the fold, another, even more successful, entrepreneurial millennialist emerged as the most popular end-times authority in the world. If Lindsey produced the basic template for the doomsday bestseller, Tim LaHaye brought premillennialism to new, unimaginable heights. He took cues from Lindsey, whose nonfiction blockbuster, wrote LaHaye, "mapped out God's prophetic timetable and described how events seemed to show that the end times are not far off."[52]

Few could match the star power that LaHaye and his wife, Beverly, had gained by the 1980s. Indeed, the LaHayes took part in almost every significant Christian Right campaign of the late twentieth century. In 2005 *Time* magazine named LaHaye one of the twenty-five most influential evangelicals in America. A group of scholars who studied evangelicalism went one step further. The *Evangelical Studies Bulletin* singled out LaHaye as the most influential evangelical of the last quarter of the twentieth century. He was the "driving force" behind the 1970 establishment of Henry Morris's Institute for Creation Research. Evolution, LaHaye complained, was nothing more than an atheistic religion. "Since humanists reject a belief in God, they must next explain man's existence independent of God," he reasoned. Moreover, evolutionary science had nothing to do with the quest for truth. In 1976 he cowrote *The Ark on Ararat* to solve the mystery of Noah's Ark. The discovery of that ancient vessel would open the eyes of doubters and forever seal the fate of evolutionary science.[53]

LaHaye was a pioneer Christian educator, having set up Christian Heritage College in 1970. He and Beverly wrote pop psychology books that developed a new Christian therapeutic genre. And the couple cowrote the 1976 bestseller *The Act of Marriage: The Beauty of Sexual Love,* a sex manual for the born-again. That book, and other popular psychology titles, sold millions. Tim and Beverly, the first family of fundamentalism, exemplified the combative, antisecular wing of evangelicalism. They had devoted their long careers to battling a sinister public school system, a godless scientific establishment, liberal academics, feminists, and more.[54]

LaHaye was from a working-class Detroit family. He served in the Air Force in the 1940s, where the feisty Midwesterner had his share of fistfights. He had a lifelong struggle with rage, he once confessed. His education helped him harness his anger for a greater cause. After the service he enrolled at Bob Jones University (BJU), a fundamentalist stronghold and a training ground for the emerging Christian Right. The school's founder, Bob Jones, Sr., was a staunch absolutist. He had long been leery of traditional college accreditation, which he equated with selling out to atheists, and he would not seek accreditation for BJU. In his view, the Bible not only set out the path to salvation but also laid down timeless rules regarding gender and sanctified racial segregation. Blacks couldn't attend BJU. African Americans, thought the school's founder, might date white coeds and pollute white blood. Equipped with a solid and strident BJU education, LaHaye went on to pastor Baptist churches in Minnesota and San Diego. He received his doctorate in ministry from Western Conservative Baptist Seminary, in Portland, Oregon, and an honorary doctorate of literature from Liberty University.[55]

Though he pastored a large San Diego Baptist church for twenty-five years, LaHaye was restless and often roamed outside the walls of his church. He and thousands of other evangelicals in the 1960s worried that the classroom had become a new battleground, pitting good against evil. When he founded Christian Heritage High School of San Diego in 1965, he, like tens of thousands of other conservatives in the Golden State, had had enough. His school would be a safe haven for decent, clean-cut, godly youths. Though he started his school with only a handful of students, by 1981 he oversaw a school district consisting of 2,500 pupils. LaHaye kept tight hold on his schools and once fired an errant, slightly moderate principal, probably for hiring Catholics. LaHaye's high school survived the ensuing controversy and flourished in the 1980s. Students learned about creation science, providential history, and the horrors of an immoral, sick society that was fleeing from God.[56]

Fiercely antisecular, Tim and Beverly LaHaye focused their rage on humanists, whose pernicious influence made their blood boil. Beverly's massive national organization, Concerned Women for America, called on submissive wives to reject feminism and secularism. The group claimed 150,000 members by the mid-1980s. In her role as a leader, Beverly counseled wifely obedience. A Spirit-filled woman, she said, would want to be "totally submissive to her husband." Regardless of what "Women's Lib" radicals said, submission was God's design for the fairer sex. "When we dwell on the positive and learn to accept things we cannot change," Beverly advised, "we will be one step higher up the ladder of happiness."[57]

Not to be outdone by his wife's crusade against NOW and the ERA, Tim wrote conservative tactical manuals in the early 1980s. *The Battle for the Mind* (1980), *The Battle for the Family* (1982), and *The Battle for the Public Schools* (1983) raised the alarm on threats to America's supposedly beleaguered fundamentalists. He drew on the wisdom of Francis Schaeffer and Bill Bright, fellow Christian warriors. LaHaye dedicated the first *Battle* book to Schaeffer. His conclusions, like those of Schaeffer, were simple and straightforward. "Humanism"—a word that one observer said LaHaye uttered in ominous tones like a seventeenth-century Londoner said the word "plague"—gave the nation nothing but grief. That philosophy led to big government, self-centeredness, situation ethics, the animalization of man, and materialism. Worst of all, humanism had infected the country's schools. When the topic of religion came up in the classroom it was "the religion of the Antichrist during the tribulation period—liberalism, humanism and Eastern religion," or "the Ecumenical Church of Revelation 13 and 17." Teachers were intent on making their pupils into "sex animals." Critics, LaHaye realized, would think his antihumanist rants smacked of conspiracy theory, but he didn't care—this *was* a conspiracy: "Many people, however, maintain that a conspiracy has been operating, first in Europe and presently in our country, in an attempt to destroy traditional Judeo-Christian moral values." Unlike Lindsey, though, LaHaye was satisfied to leave it at "many people." He seldom engaged in particulars, preferring to paint with as broad a brush as possible.[58]

Like a John Bircher ferreting out communists, LaHaye found humanists and their hapless dupes under every rock. (LaHaye was connected to the John Birch Society in the 1960s and 1970s.) He spared few, and even Jimmy Carter received his wrath. When LaHaye helped found the Moral Majority with Jerry Falwell he hoped to counter the influence of Carter, an archliberal appeaser. Carter had "totally ignored us," LaHaye vented in 1980. Then the president "chose to surround himself . . . with committed humanists." Even mild Billy Graham looked like a sellout to the angry fundamentalist leader from San Diego. "Graham has been derelict in his responsibilities," he griped to a reporter in the early 1980s. True enough, Graham had been cautiously distancing himself from separatist fundamentalists for years. More than three decades earlier America's preacher had castigated "so-called 'ultra-Fundamentalism' whose object is not to fight the world, the flesh and the devil, but to fight other Christians whose interpretation is not like theirs." And so LaHaye fought Graham. "He hasn't lifted a finger to stop the mass murder of the unborn," LaHaye grumbled. "What has Billy Graham done to stop pornographic filth from corrupting the minds of children?" He concluded with a rhetorical flourish: "I'd like to ask Billy Graham this—if John the Baptist were alive today, would he be silent in the face of all these homosexuals and pornographers and abortionists?"[59]

Always controversial, the LaHayes were among the most influential, militant fundamentalists in America. In the eyes of the faithful, the evangelical power couple stood for biblical truth. Liberal graduate school professors had humiliated too many former fundamentalist scholars, Tim LaHaye lamented. "Taking the Bible literally was ridiculed," he wrote. Ministers turned their backs on biblical truth. Not LaHaye. A strident literalist, he read scripture as an antisecular, antihumanist playbook for the last days.[60]

Nobody fused eschatology, conservative politics, and antisecularism like Tim LaHaye. His popular premillennial adventure series, *Left Behind,* coauthored with journalist Jerry Jenkins, was an unparalleled success. The two divided the labor of writing. LaHaye offered his prophecy expertise and a general timeline and scope, while Jenkins banged out the story. The volumes sold well, not just in Christian bookstores but also at Walmart, Target, and Kmart. As of 2009 the 16 novels had sold 70,000,000 copies, making the series one of the all-time bestsellers in American publishing history. The ninth installment, *Desecration: Antichrist Takes the Throne,* was the best-selling hardback of 2001, moving a John Grisham thriller to the number-two spot.[61]

Left Behind: A Novel of the Earth's Last Days, the first book, opens with the rapture. The hero of the series, a brawny, handsome pilot named Rayford Steele, flies across the Atlantic in a 747. Though married, he audaciously flirts with the "drop-dead gorgeous" flight attendant. His wife was becoming such a religious bore, he confided, always droning on about the rapture. Steele learns that dozens of his passengers have vanished, leaving behind clothes, jewelry, fillings, and pacemakers in their empty seats. From then on calamity after calamity befalls those who remain. Plagues, war, and natural disasters wreck civilization in the run-up to the Second Coming.[62]

The conservative bent of the series is unmistakable. Prolife, patriarchal, antisecular, and antigovernment messages appear on page after page. A key character, Nicolae Carpathia—sex-symbol demagogue, media darling, and Anti-Christ—pursues aid to Third World countries, as he works for world peace, disarmament, interfaith dialogue, and environmental initiatives.[63] The simplistic, conservative plotlines are utterly implausible, even for an apocalyptic thriller. Carpathia wins the hearts of United Nations delegates by delivering a passionate speech and listing the two hundred member nations, which he has committed to memory. Stunned by his powers of recall, members make him the general secretary of the U.N. In this cartoon version of geopolitics, the world is flat and colorless. Non-American characters seem surprisingly American. The American Midwest serves as center stage. Israel is happily free of Palestinians. A macho cast of technophiles make up the Tom Clancy–style "Tribulation Force." An English wag aptly commented, "When it comes to real problems like poverty, or war, or disputes over natural resources, the subtext of the *Left Behind* series is plain: who gives a toss? Jesus is coming soon for his chosen followers, and everyone else can rot for eternity."[64]

The books offer little insight into serious global issues, but they do reveal the anti-intellectual and antielitist views of the authors. The chattering classes and sophisticates are special targets in the books. In the first installment, Rayford Steele has a heart-to-heart with his daughter, another soul left behind. She's a skeptic and can't believe the simple Bible stories her raptured mother once taught her. Steele wonders to himself if he had been that "pseudosophisticated" when he was his daughter's age. Now the supernatural "came crashing through his academic pretense." In another instance, Steele listens to a fundamentalist sermon on the book of Revelation. He reflects on his former, doubting self: "Not long ago he would have scoffed at such teaching, at such a literal take on so clearly a poetic and metaphorical passage."

Now his eyes are opened to a simple, unmediated truth. Erudition and scholarly charades melt away, like the wax on Icarus's wings.[65]

At other times Jenkins and LaHaye conjure Bible experts to bolster the premillennial cause. The not-so-subtly named Dr. Tsion Ben-Judah appears in the second volume in the series, *Tribulation Force: The Continuing Drama of Those Left Behind.* A master of twenty-two languages—"the world's most astute Bible scholar"—Ben-Judah is commissioned by the Israeli government to study messianic passages in scripture. After exhaustive research, he appears on an international TV broadcast to proclaim, "Jesus Christ is the Messiah!" Angry Jewish protesters rush the studio as technicians cut the television feed. Another Jewish Bible scholar, a one-time humanist, enters the Christian fold once he realizes the error of his ways. "I was not a religious Jew," he confesses, "until God destroyed the Russian Air Force." Like many other liberals, he had once thought prophecy was symbolic. Not anymore. Reasonable Jews, in LaHaye and Jenkins's telling, must accept Jesus and premillennialism when presented with unvarnished evidence.[66]

The authors lampoon Bible scholars who doubt their version of the Second Coming. A character in one novel compares the views of modern interpreters of scripture to those of conspiracy theorists and UFO enthusiasts. Through literary ventriloquism, LaHaye and Jenkins parody doubters of all stripes. The postrapture pope, Peter Mathews, champions bloodless ecumenism through an organization called "Enigma Babylon One World Faith." Uncharitable and narrow, Mathews shuns conservative beliefs. A lead character asks the pontiff about the wrath of God and the doom predicted in the Bible. Such ideas, scoffs Mathews, derive from long-discredited views. "These same preachers, and I dare say many of their parishioners, are the ones who take the creation account—the Adam and Eve myth, if you will—literally," he says. "They believe the entire world was under water at the time of Noah and that only he and his three sons and their wives survived to begin the entire human race as we now know it." Heaven is just a state of mind; the virgin birth, an impossibility. Besides, the world leader remarks, to unite humankind, religion must be inclusive, tolerant. In such ways, the authors imply, all who challenge literalism are hollow, naïve, or ridiculously pretentious. But their fate is sealed. Mathews, of course, gets assassinated.[67]

When the last book in the series rolled off the presses in 2007, LaHaye was evangelicalism's reigning prophecy expert. The Bible was "God's road map to the future. And he wants you and I to get there," he told conservative talk show host Glenn Beck in a one-hour interview on CNN in 2007. Beck peppered his panelists with questions. How will things transpire in Earth's final hour? What will the rapture look like? What role will the Middle East play? LaHaye, along with Jerry Jenkins and up-and-coming prophecy author Joel Rosenberg, fired back answers with the certainty of hard scientists. The Bible is "history written in advance," said LaHaye in an oft-repeated phrase. Beck swooned. "I've read every one of the *Left Behind* books," he gushed. Beck concluded the interview by signing off: "We'll see you again, unless we disappear."[68]

LaHaye ventured again into higher education, capitalizing on the success of the series. In 2001 he and Jerry Falwell planned the establishment of the Tim LaHaye School of Prophecy at Falwell's Liberty University. A one-year academic program, it was to combine "biblical studies on prophecy with a practical internship in evangelism, church growth and discipleship at my Thomas Road Baptist Church," said Falwell. He and LaHaye believed that "we must now provide specialized prophetic training for a multitude of '21st century prophecy scholars.'" From now on, a new generation of prophecy experts, bolstered with scriptural knowledge, could explain the events of the day in light of the book of Revelation or Daniel. Falwell sought heavy subsidies for the first 500 students who enrolled. LaHaye had played a similarly instrumental role in the creation of the Pre-Trib Research Center

(PTRC) in the early 1990s. Based out of Liberty University, the group hoped to convince average Christians that the pretribulation view of the rapture was the only right interpretation of scripture. The PTRC hosted conferences and speakers and produced literature and audiotapes. Most important, it sought to convince pastors and laypeople that prophecy, and "especially the any-moment possibility of the rapture," were basic to Christianity.[69]

In addition to training a new generation of prophecy experts, LaHaye and Jenkins lent their names to countless spin-off projects, stretching their original vision beyond recognition. They published books explaining the theology and background of premillennialism. Their *Authorized Left Behind Handbook* answered questions that kept some fans of the books awake at night. Why is so much of the series set in Chicago? How might atheists and agnostics explain the disappearance of millions of people from the globe? Are we living in the last days? Would pets be raptured along with their Christian owners?[70]

Left Behind readers were typically Southern, white, married females between the ages of twenty-five and fifty-four. Eleven percent were Catholic. Many may have read the series like others read thrillers written by Anne Rice or Stephen King. (Readers of Rice and King books do not tend to believe in vampires or cursed pet cemeteries.) But anecdotal evidence suggests that the perceived biblicism of *Left Behind* was a real draw. Fans could hardly contain their interest in the series: "It was almost a message right out of the Bible," a San Francisco woman told *Time* magazine. She wanted to "talk about it all the time." Another reader told the *Washington Post* that he bought a new *Left Behind* book every payday. "I dropped to my knees after reading the first one and said a prayer. I've been a Christian ever since." Thousands of fans offered similar testimonies online and in print. Plots confirmed what conservatives already thought about big government, liberals, and haughty skeptics. And LaHaye's status as a prophecy guru only added to the presumed authority of the series.[71]

The *Left Behind* novels naturally spawned movies—starring former child star Kirk Cameron and including cameo appearances from premillennial stalwarts Jack and Rexella Van Impe, John Walvoord, and John Hagee. Though the first film was a critical and box office failure, the franchise branched off into comic books, audiotapes, graphic novels, board games, internet fan sites, a *Left Behind* series for children, daily calendars with *Left Behind* quotations, and a controversial videogame that allowed gamers to make their way through a postrapture New York City. Players joined the Tribulation Force and took control of the action, killing or converting the opposition. "Recover ancient scriptures and witness spectacular Angelic and Demonic activity as a direct consequence of your choices," the game's developer enticed buyers. Waxing hyperbolic, LaHaye hailed it as "the greatest invention developed in my lifetime to reach this generation." The game won the endorsement of Focus on the Family, Women of Faith, and Promise Keepers.[72]

Critics—both evangelical and nonevangelical—vented. How could a Christian promote a videogame so at odds with the gospel? One leader of a progressive Christian advocacy group lamented, "This is the first time any Christian religious instructional video has recommended killing all non-Christians who refuse to convert to Christianity." The game's developers and supporters cried foul. A player could lose points for wanton killing, they responded, although those points could be recovered if a player's avatar prayed. Unconvinced, another critic countered, "The idea that you could pray, and the deleterious effects of one's foul deeds would simply be wiped away, is a horrible thing to be teaching Christian young people." Opponents asked Walmart to pull the game from shelves. Shouting matches on CNBC and Fox News followed.[73]

The highly symbolic videogame controversy was just the latest in a string of heated conflicts between premillennialists and their adversaries. Christian critics worried that Lindsey, LaHaye, and televangelists like John Hagee or commentators like Jack Van Impe had utterly misread scripture. Premillennial experts did not just have a mistaken hermeneutic. Their theology was as dangerous as it was inaccurate, as unchristian as it was ahistorical.[74]

Critics of all theological stripes readied their arsenal against premillennial rivals in the 1990s and 2000s. Dozens of books hit the shelves with titles like *Skipping Towards Armageddon; The Rapture Exposed; Who Will Be Left Behind and When?; The Rapture Trap; The Left Behind Deception;* and *Kiss My Left Behind.* Critics came in all forms. Some were evangelicals, others were liberal Protestants or Catholics. They ranged across the liberal to conservative spectrum as well.

As far back as the 1970s, Lindsey had drawn fire from evangelical theologians and Bible scholars. Many lambasted Lindsey—and LaHaye in years to come—for an ahistorical view of prophecy. Scholars had long read the Bible as a historically conditioned series of texts. Lindsey and LaHaye's premillennial futurism and their lack of interest in the original context made no sense to academics. Regardless of how arcane a passage from Ezekiel, Daniel, or Revelation was, premillennial prophets forced it to speak to contemporary world events. "Lindsey has robbed the material with which he deals of any significance for its own time," argued a Lutheran theologian in the 1970s. The presentist hubris of fundamentalist interpreters was particularly galling. For this Lutheran critic, the anti-intellectual, historically ignorant Lindsey was also just plain tacky. "Any moment now," he joked, "I expect to hear that with all his royalties Lindsey has commenced construction of a mini-Holy Land somewhere near Encino, complete with Disney animated prophet-puppets; has prepared a series of television specials with Rodney Dangerfield and John Denver, or has begun laying the forms for a new Hal Lindsey University, complete with an underground library for all the pap he's written so as to be made available for those souls suffering under the reign of the Antichrist."[75]

In 1980 a professor of early Christianity and the New Testament at the University of North Carolina, Wilmington, attacked Lindsey's "apocalyptic pornography" as right-wing and extremist. *The Late Great Planet Earth*, he said, reeked of anti-intellectualism and religious bigotry. Lindsey appeared to denigrate almost every major Western thinker since 1800. "As science fiction or purely imaginative writing his work is tolerable," this observer noted, "but the shame is that it is represented authoritatively as the real meaning of the Bible, with no indication that it is a fringe position foreign to the vast majority of Christian believers throughout time."[76]

A leading Catholic scholar of the New Testament at the Episcopal Divinity School in Cambridge, Massachusetts, spoke for many when she accused Lindsey of yanking scripture out of its context. Worse still, Lindsey's interpretations warped the role of the prophet at a time when "scholarship has long moved away from the concept that apocalyptic prophecy makes any predictions." Prophets delivered messages to the people of their era, she remarked. Prophetic voices spoke to the social and political concerns of another age.[77]

Let the critics bellow, countered Lindsey and LaHaye. Literalists, not their critics, read the Bible correctly. Scripture should be read plainly and logically, without the fuss of allegory and modern glosses, they claimed. Common-sense principles had long guided rationalistic fundamentalists who saw themselves as heirs of the Scottish Enlightenment. Human perceptions revealed the real world directly to believers. Fundamentalist Bible scholar David L. Cooper coined an oft-repeated "Golden Rule of Biblical Interpretation" that guided millions: "When the plain sense of Scripture makes common sense, seek no other sense; therefore, take every word at its primary, ordinary, usual, literal meaning unless the facts of the immediate context, studied in the light of related passages and axiomatic and fundamental truths, indicate clearly otherwise." LaHaye and Lindsey, more than any other popular theologians, had convinced American evangelicals that premillennialism was the most direct, common-sense reading of the

Bible. It helped that both were skilled entrepreneurs and entertainers, which put their many foes at a disadvantage.[78]

The common-sense populist hermeneutic favored by the end-times evangelists spawned a tragic anti-intellectualism that hobbled American evangelicalism. Mark Noll argued this forcefully in a scathing critique of premillennial dispensationalism. Rigid end-times dogmatism shut off debate and stifled creative thinking. With universities and formal learning under suspicion, Noll charged, evangelicals welcomed "the spokesperson who could step forth confidently" as a biblical authority. "If intellectual life involves a certain amount of self-awareness about alternative interpretations," he wrote, "or a certain amount of tentativeness in exploring the connection between evidence and conclusions, it was hard to find any encouragement for the intellectual life in the self-assured dogmatism of fundamentalism." Most troublesome to Noll and others, dispensationalism "promoted a kind of supernaturalism that, for all of its virtues in defending the faith, failed to give proper attention to the world." Another evangelical critic agreed, calling Darby's enthusiastic rapture theology an "ultra-simplistic view of the Bible." A "hard biblical literalism" made evangelicalism especially vulnerable to criticism from scientists and biblical scholars.[79]

Well-known critics who have challenged premillennialism do not have the same sway on conservatives that popularizers do, regardless of their credentials. Conservative Anglican bishop and New Testament scholar N. T. Wright, for example, has authored biting criticism of rapture-ready evangelicalism. The author of dozens of best-selling books, Wright is widely respected by Christians across the spectrum. His work has focused on the life of Jesus within the context of Jewish history, and he has tried to bridge the gap between evangelical and liberal biblical scholarship. Wright is bewildered by the popularity of the *Left Behind* novels. LaHaye's outlook is frighteningly *unbiblical,* claims Wright. Thanks largely to LaHaye, "the American obsession with the second coming of Jesus," he wrote in 2001, "continues unabated."

Popular ideas about the rapture and the tribulation were bizarre and puzzling. LaHaye misunderstood scripture and hawked a theological system based on a mountain of errors.[80]

Eugene Peterson, a widely read pastoral theologian, offered a more subtle rebuke. Peterson—the author of the massively popular contemporary translation of the Bible *The Message* and a variety of essays and books—was raised in a Pentecostal church and thoroughly understood dispensationalism. His expertise in biblical languages, the graduate training he received at Johns Hopkins University, and his long pastoral career endeared him to his target audience of evangelicals. His work on the nature of Christian community and the role of narrative in the church has won him a substantial readership. In 2005 he wrote about growing up with the burden of the rapture on his heart and mind. "We had to make sure we were ready and then hurry and get everybody we knew ready for the end, the rapture, the second coming of Jesus," he recalled. Whatever did not fit into the great commission or the dictates of the last days was discarded. It was an unhealthy habit of mind. Peterson wrote that the book of Revelation had been irresponsibly taken out of context, misread, and misused. Revelation was a work of poetry. He warned that the "inability (or refusal) to deal with St. John, the poet, is responsible for most of the misreading, misinterpretations, and misuse of the book."[81]

LaHaye and Lindsey shunned allegorical, poetic, and all nonliteral perspectives. Such interpretations looked fanciful, even dangerous to them. They assaulted their poetry-loving skeptics. "They are just liberal, socialists, really," LaHaye said in 2007 of those who doubted premillennialism. Premillennialism wasn't *an* interpretation, it was *the* interpretation. Critics, in LaHaye's estimation, "don't believe the Bible." Millions of readers bought the *Left Behind* books, said LaHaye, because they took the Bible literally. And, for all their sneering ivory-tower trumpeting of the Bible as literature, liberals and moderates, ironically, couldn't tell a good story: "What [critics] probably will come up with is a plausible explanation from their liberal standpoint to satisfy their adherents that are reading our series and liked it." But that interpretation "will be inferior," he concluded, "because the story will be inferior."[82]

LaHaye's heated rhetoric was not far off the mark. No other contemporary American Christian authors or ministers shaped the way evangelicals thought about the end quite the way LaHaye and Lindsey did. Anti-intellectual populism and a disengagement with the world of ideas had made evangelicals susceptible to the whims of confident, if misguided and uninformed, prophecy experts. Evangelicals preferred charismatic figures, authoritatively quoting the Bible and never wavering in their commitments. The speculations of Hal Lindsey, put forth with absolute certainty in defiance of almost everything scholars have learned about the Bible, convinced Ronald Reagan that a horrifyingly violent end was near. The leader of the free world spoke of "a great many theologians" eagerly looking for God to soon draw the curtain on history. Lindsey and LaHaye were nothing if not confident. And the president was contented with such expertise. In the end, if authority rests primarily on mass appeal—as it increasingly does in this age of the internet and poll-driven politics—then surely LaHaye and Lindsey have been the leading evangelical authorities on all things eschatological.

5 A Carnival of Christians

Paul Miller, a young man in his twenties, works full time in the admissions department of a liberal arts college on Boston's North Shore. He has never had a secular friend. Yet Miller did not grow up on a hermetically sealed compound; nor were his parents religious fanatics who, afraid for his soul, kept him cloistered with his siblings behind stacks of end-times pamphlets written by doomsayers. Paul was in no sect that shunned outside influences. His parents held "secular" jobs in a world that Paul simply did not encounter as he was growing up. For Paul Miller, the extended evangelical network into which he was born was, simply and unremarkably, his world. His life within this world was atypical, perhaps, only because he experienced more aspects of it than most, not because his immersion in it was unique. He shared the most important, cherished ideals of the movement—the commitment to salvation in Jesus Christ and the absolute authority of the Bible as the word of God—and most evangelicals would identify with much if not most of his experience.[1]

American evangelicalism has developed something of a parallel culture amid the interstices of the secular world. Most of this culture, including the publishing houses, music labels, and colleges, consists simply of message-driven evangelical alternatives to secular offerings. The forms are very similar, which is why they seem invisible. The very evangelical Wheaton College in Illinois appears to resemble the very secular Wheaton College in Massachusetts. Yet the intellectual content of the parallel culture afforded by evangelicalism is single-minded in its biblically based criteria for knowledge, which often leads to the production of in-house versions of natural science, history, social science, and views of the end-times.[2]

Evangelical engagement with this parallel culture ranges from the all-encompassing immersion of Paul Miller to the more modest interactions of children who attend secular schools and have active social and intellectual lives apart from their church communities. Many evangelicals, for example, practice their faith by attending church and Sunday school once a week and have limited engagement on weekdays. The faith commitments of all evangelicals, however, are powered by the same central and universal message—that God has a plan for everything from people's individual lives to the communities in which they live. Evangelicals, to varying degrees, can reject the non-Christian world around them because of the self-sufficiency of their parallel culture. These cultural influences are intended to nurture in young evangelicals a robust Christian worldview, appropriately independent, occasionally suspicious of the outside world but aligned with it in many ways and committed to service. At an intellectual level, however, evangelicalism opposes the predominant secular humanism of the larger society and aims to keep those ideas and values apart from its own teachings. Secular humanists, according to critics, have failed to acknowledge God and even aligned themselves with Satan to destroy all that is good. Tim LaHaye puts it like this: "Humanists have totally rejected God, creation, morality, the fallen state of man, and the free enterprise system. As such, they are the mortal enemy of all pro-moral Americans, and the most serious threat to our nation in its entire history. Unless both

Christian and non-Christian lovers of virtue stand together as upright citizens, humanists will turn this great land into another Sodom and Gomorrah."[3]

This adversarial juxtaposition is more common in the rhetoric of extremist leaders than among rank-and-file evangelicals, no doubt because it plays well politically. Nevertheless, for some it creates an isolationism bordering on xenophobia that makes evangelicals uneasy about participating in the secular world. More sober, moderate evangelicals are dismayed by LaHaye's rhetoric. But the fundamentalist end of the spectrum holds suspicions even about the larger Christian world, with its different expressions of the faith: Protestants fret about Catholics; Pentecostals fret about "high-church" traditions that are not appropriately charismatic; holiness traditions fret about nonholiness traditions; and Baptists fret about everyone, even other Baptists. Fundamentalists tend to see just two boxes—"us" and "them." Great energy is expended keeping heretics out of the "us" box, which contains everyone who believes as they do and thus can be embraced as a part of the "family of God." The "them" box contains everyone else, viewed with suspicion as "liberal," "secular," or "worldly."[4]

Christians born into this bifurcated world, as Paul Miller was, can have their vision so shaped by its paradigms that the secular world rarely intrudes, except to be critiqued. Social, educational, and religious experiences within the community are designed to keep believers firmly on the "straight and narrow," talking mainly to one another, reading approved authors, listening to insider music, and attending to anointed experts. The secular world is kept at bay by demonizing the "other," often to the extent of treating it as Satan's domain. Christians embedded in this parallel culture comprise a well-defined "in-group" who, to varying degrees, carefully observe and protect the boundaries of their world, keeping themselves pure and undefiled. The "out-group," in this worldview, is clearly demarcated.

Evangelicals like Paul are defined by their belief: They have experienced the salvation that leads to eternal life by accepting that Jesus died for their sins and was resurrected. These "born-again" experiences take many forms. For celebrated sinners like convicted Watergate felon Chuck Colson, the transformation was dramatic and inspirational, as when he "found Jesus" in prison after his very public sins on behalf of the Nixon administration.[5] For famous ex-agnostics like C. S. Lewis and Francis Collins, the conversion was provocative and challenging: Both men contemplated largely intellectual arguments and came to faith along an unusually rational road.[6] For most evangelicals, acceptance is a transformative ritual, though it may be just a simple response to a pastor's invitation to come to the altar and "accept Christ as your personal savior." Millions of evangelicals have worn a path to the altar after hearing the oft-repeated lines of a nineteenth-century hymn: "Just as I am, without one plea / but that thy blood was shed for me, / and that thou bidst me come to thee, / O Lamb of God, I come, I come."[7] Many adolescents and even younger children accept Christ *en masse* in annual "summer camp conversions" or church revivals, where they "go forward" in response to eloquent and often lengthy invitations accompanied by spiritually persuasive music. Paul Miller recalls "going down front" to the altar at age five, responding to an invitation at Prince Avenue Baptist Church in Athens, Georgia, that was extended after every service.[8] Six years later, uncertain about the earlier experience, he was "saved again" after a meeting of his youth group and then baptized by immersion a second time. At age seventeen he "went forward" a third time. Multiple conversions are technically (and doctrinally) redundant, but the persuasive setting of the invitation, and the high stakes of conversion, can inspire even the righteous to "go forward" yet again, just to be sure.[9]

Miller's born-again moments are repeated millions of times every year as "seekers" and "reseekers" make their way to altars across the country and kneel, often with a pastor's gentle hand on their shoulder, and pray the "Sinner's Prayer": "Father, I know that I have broken your laws and my sins have separated me from you. I am truly sorry, and now I want to turn away from my past sinful life toward you. Please forgive me, and help me avoid sinning again. I believe that your son, Jesus Christ, died for my sins, was resurrected from the dead, is alive, and hears my prayer. I invite Jesus to become the Lord of my life, to rule and reign in my heart from this day forward. Please send your Holy Spirit to help me obey You, and to do Your will for the rest of my life. In Jesus' name I pray, Amen."[10]

A 2005 Gallup poll revealed that 42 percent of American adults claim to have been "born again," accepting Jesus and embracing the label "evangelical."[11] Another significant fraction would share many of their values but would not identify with the label or the experience of being "born again."[12]

The culture of evangelicalism is vast and dominant in much of the South. Miller's Southern Baptist denomination is the largest religious group not only in Georgia but in Mississippi, Alabama, Oklahoma, Tennessee, Kentucky, South Carolina, Arkansas, North Carolina, and Virginia as well.[13] In many Southern neighborhoods, including Miller's, evangelicalism so pervades the community that it merges seamlessly with mom, apple pie, and all things American.

Miller grew up in Athens, Georgia, a modest-sized university town founded in 1806 and named after the city in Greece where Plato and Aristotle had their schools. Like its historic namesake, Athens is all about education. The University of Georgia is one of the largest employers and owns much of the land in the county. The Georgia Bulldogs football team is the public face of the university. The locals, says Miller, describe Athens as a "drinking town with a football problem."[14]

Born in Athens in 1985, Paul was the youngest of three children. His mother graduated from the University of Georgia and taught for a few years in nearby Blue Ridge public schools until marriage called her back to Athens. His father sold cars on commission at Phil Hughes

Honda, a prosperous Athens dealership. Their middle-class lifestyle contracted when cars were not selling but relaxed once the children were all in school and Paul's mother went back to work.

Their modest 1960s ranch house—his parents' first—was on Tara Way, named for the stately plantation in *Gone with the Wind.* A Southern entrepreneur who loved Margaret Mitchell's classic Civil War romance built their development and called it Forest Heights. The music minister from the Millers' church lived across the street. Everyone went to church, except for the alcoholic down the road, a World War II veteran and former Polish internment camp detainee whom a young Paul found rather "scary."[15]

A few weeks after he was born, Paul experienced the first of several rituals that would gradually transform him into a full-fledged evangelical—he was "dedicated." For evangelicals, the dedication of infants is much like infant baptism for Catholics or Episcopalians—a first experience initiating children into the faith of their parents. Paul's dedication was typical: He and his family were invited to the front of the church, where Brother Bill, the senior pastor, prayed with them and gave them a Bible, symbolizing the parents' commitment to raise baby Paul in the "nurture and admonition of the Lord." The public dedication symbolized the church's commitment to support the Millers as a part of their tightly knit church family. Such commitments are genuine and lead to significant support in times of distress or discouragement.

Paul's mother stayed home to raise her children. She expected the Prince Avenue congregation to help. "Just like in our home as I loved and cared for you, supported and encouraged you—spent time, effort, and energy investing in you, I expected the same from the church," she told Paul. "The folks there who taught you, spent time with you, and cared for you became an extension of our home. By ministering to you and loving you unconditionally at church just as we did at home, we wanted for you to learn to love and minister also. The church was the place where we did this. The church was our extended family—it was the place to be."[16] As for her task, she wanted to be "a godly mom" and "spent time reading, studying, praying and going to seminars and Bible studies to learn how to become one."[17]

The church played its role. Until he was four—old enough for regular Sunday school—Paul spent Sunday mornings in the church nursery, where volunteers doted on the toddlers and taught them Bible stories using flannel boards, videos, and Christian coloring books. This freed his parents to attend adult Sunday school classes and the preaching service. The socially robust programs in churches like Prince Avenue nurture community as people spend time with one another's children, take turns teaching the classes, drink coffee together, and collaborate on running what are often the most substantial social programs in the local community.

Prince Avenue regulars, including Paul, gathered with neighborhood children every summer for week-long "Vacation Bible Schools"—potent mixtures of Christian teaching, music, proselytizing, and activities like sports and crafts. Signs advertising "VBS," often handmade, appear with the dandelions every summer on the byways of heartland America and bring new people—often the socially disenfranchised—into the church. At Christmas, evangelical children across the country energetically gear up to reenact the birth of Jesus and other Christmas stories. From age five to seventeen, Paul participated in a "Living Christmas Tree," a spectacular 300-person choir for which his mother made all the costumes.[18] The annual presentation, with eight shows, outsold every other event at the Classic Center in downtown Athens. It was "the most attended event in Athens that's not an athletic event."[19] Local sponsors included St. Mary's Healthcare, Chick-fil-A, and Wells Fargo.[20]

Most residents of Forest Heights attended one of 174 Baptist churches—about half of the congregations in the area. Weekday playmates squeezed into the back seats of cars every Sunday morning for the 15-minute ride to Prince Avenue, the largest conservative Baptist church in the city, with well over 3,000 members; much of the neighborhood would be reconstituted there at the century-old church, an extension of a close community with shared values, deep social bonds, and a common religion.[21] Paul believes that the strong sense of community in Forest Heights was an extension of the familial character of the church and its nurturing atmosphere.

Not everyone was a part of the Prince Avenue family. Neighbors across the street attended a Methodist church that was so liberal that Paul wasn't entirely sure it was genuinely Christian. Evangelicals emphasize the "born-again" experience, correct theology, and right living as the essential indicators of salvation. A faith community without this holy trinity of markers was suspect and perhaps even taught a false gospel. Sunday worship without altar calls was a red flag, as were liberal (nonliteral) interpretations of the resurrection of Jesus or the virgin birth, and even the beer cans in the weekend trash of the Methodist neighbors. Some theologically marginal local residents attended St. Joseph's Catholic Church, where they got some "strange ideas about Mary."[22] Some conservative Protestants consider the Catholic Church to be a sinister and subversive false Christianity.[23] A 2008 survey revealed that 14 percent of white evangelicals thought Catholics could not go to heaven. Another 11 percent were not sure.[24] Paul happily avoided a church that he believed did not have "Christ at the center of what was going on."[25] Less charitable evangelicals refer to Catholicism as the "Great Whore of Babylon."[26] Paul would meet his first Catholic years later in college.

Prince Avenue Baptists fell on the conservative side of a fissure dividing their denomination. With sixteen million members, the Southern Baptist Convention probably does more than any other denomination to patrol the theological and social boundaries of the evangelical culture that runs parallel to secular culture. The denomination emerged in 1845, splitting from a larger Baptist fellowship over slavery. Southern Baptists, as they came to be known, embraced a racism for which they did not officially repent until 1995. En route to that repentance, however, countless overtures were made to the disadvantaged, including racial minorities. Southern Baptists are now one of the most ethnically diverse religious groups in the country.[27]

Baptists energetically protect the doctrinal purity of their fellowships—an often rancorous enterprise. Their unwavering commitment to the literal truth of the Bible, combined with the belief that anyone and everyone can interpret scripture, provides a natural incubator for conflict. Such discord, amplified by the conviction that "wrong" beliefs are spiritually corrosive and contrary to God's will, constantly drives wedges through religious communities.[28] The most visible result of the conservative-moderate split affecting Prince Avenue was the successful push back of Baylor University—itself a Baptist school—against external control by the Texas Baptist Convention.[29] Jimmy Carter's public break with the Southern Baptists also created headlines.[30] The Georgia Baptist Convention booted Mercer University when their gay-lesbian student group was discovered.[31]

The large First Baptist Church of Athens was on the Baylor/Carter/Mercer side of that divide, having "gone liberal," which meant that the leadership—which actually self-identified as "moderate evangelical"—might not consider the Bible to be the absolute, inerrant-on-all-topics-no-matter-how-minor, word of God. Evolution might even be true and homosexuality might not be an abomination. Not coincidentally, First Baptist was near the University of Georgia, where secular ideas were encouraged. Many Christians became liberal there—or at least moderate—breathing unfamiliar air wafting over from outside their parallel culture. The attentive monitoring of "doctrinal slippage" by evangelicals—especially fundamentalists—keeps a spotlight on the issues, even as all parties continue to embrace the label evangelical.

Paul's parents happily enrolled him in the K–12 Christian school run by their own Prince Avenue Baptist Church. The local schools were "dicey," recalls Paul. Their demographic included many poor and English-as-a-second-language students; many students came from troubled families; and the quality of the education was subpar. These public schools were also secular schools, of course, although that was not a major factor for Paul's parents. Thoroughly Christian in its programming and predominantly Christian in its student body, Prince Avenue was the school for Paul. It resembled thousands of other schools, educating hundreds of thousands of students across America, especially in the Bible Belt.[32]

Of the 55 million students enrolled in America's K–12 schools in 2009, 11 percent attended private schools, almost half being taught at Catholic institutions.[33] Over 651,000 were enrolled in an Association of Christian Schools International institution, and over 2 million attended an institution in the National Catholic Educational Association.[34] Nearly 920,000 students were enrolled in "Conservative Christian" evangelical institutions with over 330,000 of those in explicitly Baptist schools like Prince Avenue. Another 1 million were educated in unaffiliated Christian schools (many of which are still overtly evangelical).[35] Another 1.5 million were homeschooled in 2008, up 74 percent since 1999, and expected to keep growing. More than 80 percent of parents polled said that a top motivation for homeschooling their kids was "a desire to provide religious or moral instruction," and for 36 percent of them it was the primary motivation.[36] While the homeschooling surveys have not asked for religious affiliation, experts believe that about 70 percent of homeschooled children are evangelical.[37] All this suggests that at least 2 million American children are being educated in distinctly evangelical environments. Tony Perkins, the president of the conservative Family Research Council, provides a rationale for this separate education by demonizing the public schools: "The government has eliminated God from the classroom and too often replaced

Him with an anti-life, anti-family curriculum that misses life's deepest meaning."[38] Despite such concerns, 4 out of 5 evangelical children remain in the public schools.

Established in 1978, the Prince Avenue Christian School at which Paul spent 13 years now enrolls over 725 students, placing it in the upper 3 percent of private schools in terms of size.[39] It openly and enthusiastically celebrates its biblical educational philosophy. The entire educational experience, from the study of writing to the rationale for education in the first place, is grounded in the Bible. The largest print on the home page of its website is used for the passage: "Do not conform any longer to the pattern of this world, but be transformed by the renewing of your mind" (Romans 12:2).[40] The biblically based distinction between the "world" and the followers of Jesus is a consistent theme. For most evangelicals, the term "worldly" carries negative connotations in a theological sense.

Students at evangelical schools across the country learn that the Bible speaks constantly to the details of their lives. Referred to as the "Word of God," the Bible comes to be viewed as a timeless message directly from God and of great relevance to all areas of contemporary life. The Bible is not considered a collection of ancient and varied books written by different authors in different languages over centuries. The mission statement for Prince Avenue declares that the school exists "to infuse our school community with a Biblical worldview by effectively sharing the gospel and developing fully devoted followers of Jesus Christ through scripturally based discipleship, academics, fine arts, and athletics."[41] This philosophy extends and deepens what many students learned at home and in their churches. At Prince Avenue, "transformation occurs as students come to know the Truth—Jesus Christ." Truth in any discipline, from math to art, centers on "an understanding of reality as God sees it." And God has provided the Bible so we know how he sees it. "Scripture provides the basis of understanding truth, and is integrated into all areas of our academic curriculum and extracurricular activities," notes the academics page of the website.

A few publishers offer educational materials for Christian schools and home schools of the parallel culture. The leaders are A Beka Books, Bob Jones University Press, and Accelerated Christian Education (ACE). The comprehensive materials, designed for instructors without training in education, eliminate the need for supplementary "secular" texts. They are also strongly biblical. The A Beka catalog, under "Distinctives," introduces its approach in every discipline with a Bible verse: "Blessed is the nation whose God is the Lord: Psalm 33:12 (History); How forcible are right words! Job 6:25 (English); Who hath measured the waters in the hollow of his hand: Isaiah 40:12 (Mathematics); It is the glory of God to conceal a thing: but the honour of kings is to search out a matter: Proverbs 25:2 (Science/Health)." The leading distinctive is the study of the Bible, where the lessons "flow from the Word of God, through the heart of the teacher, to the heart of the student."[42]

Christian faith motivates the study of each discipline. English is important because "God has given us the great commission of communicating his truth to mankind." Students need "the finest tools available to carry out this goal in a reasonable, well-articulated manner." "To study mathematics is to study God's thoughts after Him, for He is the great Engineer and Architect of the universe." "Science is the study of God's order, provision, and reasonableness as revealed in His physical creation." A Beka texts provide a "solid, Scriptural foundation in all areas of science." History texts offer a "truthful portrayal of peoples, lands, religions, ideals, heroes, setbacks and triumphs." Government is "ordained by God for the maintenance of law and order." The all-encompassing message is that God has a plan for the world—socially, politically, economically. Nothing falls outside of the plan he has provided in the Bible.

This comprehensive biblical perspective shapes the *content* of as well as the *motivation* for the courses. Paul practiced penmanship by "copying from the Psalms." In his science classes, he learned that Earth was just thousands of years old and that God created everything in six days. The history curriculum of the popular Accelerated Christian Education (ACE) program informs students that Spain was defeated in North America because of its Catholicism, not its armies. Students learn that a miracle rescued George Washington during the French and Indian war. And all Muslims are "descendants of Isaac's half-brother Ishmael," which explains why they don't get along with Jews, who are descended from Isaac.[43] History is portrayed as the unfolding narrative of God's plan, with God meting out rewards and punishments. American history, in particular, is presented in a theological context. Writers describe the Founding Fathers as near-evangelical, Bible-believing Christians, inspired by God to create a new nation that God blessed with unprecedented prosperity. One site popular with homeschoolers approvingly quotes John Adams, minus the crucial ellipses: "The general principles upon which the Fathers achieved independence [. . .] were the general principles of Christianity."[44] The parallel culture of evangelicalism is rooted in this history and, for believers, is continuous with America's Christian past. Securing a Christian present and working for a Christian future will ensure God's ongoing providential blessing on the nation.

Despite the biblical emphasis, the Christian curriculum is mainly standard educational fare. There is no "biblical" way to spell, solve algebraic equations, or calculate the time for a light beam to travel to the moon and back. The chapter on "Light" in Bob Jones University Press's *Basic Science for Christian Schools* follows this pattern. The presentation is secular, attractive, and well organized. Minor religious digressions occur only twice. Readers are told in a discussion of how the eye works: "Evolution fails completely as a scientific explanation for the eye."[45] A "question to talk over" at the end of the chapter about rainbows starts by explaining: "God placed the rainbow in the clouds as a symbol of His promise that He would never again destroy the entire earth by a flood." The question to "talk over" is, "If the rainbow is caused by refraction of light by water droplets in the air, why was there no rainbow before the Flood?"[46] Presumably the students will conclude that the laws of physics changed at the Flood, making rainbows possible, consistent with creationist claims.[47] But, as the laws have not changed since then, rainbows continue to be a reliable and interesting case study in refraction, as students learn in this chapter. The critique of evolution in the context of real science is an effective strategy to convince students that there is indeed a scientific foundation for their biblical worldview. The pedagogical strategy works—uncontroversial and well-established ideas like refraction and mechanics are interwoven with the rejection of evolution, the Big Bang, and the great age of Earth.

Such materials compromise the educational process. To the degree that students master the material, they will have some confusion about God's plans and nature's laws. But like their counterparts in secular schools, students in Christian schools are often not fully engaged with the material and graduate with just a vague general recollection of the details. However, those in Christian schools rarely question the larger Christian context of such details. Public "doubters" in Christian communities often pay a high social price of isolation and disapproval. But this is not likely to be an issue, for most students using these materials are in safe, nurturing environments with strong family support. They study hard. Many graduates of home and Christian schools—like Paul Miller—are well prepared for college or university work, even if some of what they learned is suspect. Their performance on standardized tests may even be better than that of their counterparts in the public schools, but it is clear that the Christian educational focus allows for little distraction or dissent, and students are nurtured into a comprehensive worldview with the Bible at its heart. Genuine intellectual exploration is encouraged only within well-defined boundaries.[48]

The office of Executive Quality Control for ACE lists schools that have accepted students educated in programs using their materials. God's Bible College in Ohio, Arkansas Bible School, and, of course, Bob Jones University are on the list. But so are Harvard University and the University of Pennsylvania.[49] Patrick Henry College, a selective fundamentalist school launched in 2000, markets itself to homeschooled students, who constitute 80 percent of its student body.[50] Known as "God's Harvard," Patrick Henry boasts SAT scores similar to those at the elite Rice University.[51] The best schools of the parallel culture compare favorably with their secular counterparts. And there are many successful evangelical students at elite secular colleges and universities.

However, children like Paul Miller who grow up in nurturing Christian homes attentive to teaching values are predisposed to stick with those who share their Christian ideals. For them, sexual ethics, personal responsibility, and the reality of right and wrong are features of God's creation, no less real than the laws of gravity and electromagnetism. Informal "extracurricular" materials enable this part of the educational process. Interested youths receive evangelically oriented books, DVDs, and magazines for Christmas and birthdays. Churches maintain lending libraries with books by C. S. Lewis, Francis Schaeffer, Josh McDowell, Frank Peretti, Tim LaHaye, and many other evangelical authors.

Quasi-educational/advocacy enterprises support evangelicalism by producing media for every age group. This Christian "curriculum" supplements the more formal education of evangelical youths. Several organizations, including Worldview Weekend, Focus on the Family, Answers in Genesis, and WallBuilders, churn out endless materials for all age groups, promoting the Christian worldview. This curriculum resonates with that of schools like Prince Avenue Baptist, but, more significantly, it functions as the *de facto* Christian curriculum for evangelicals in the public schools. The materials articulate a biblical approach to the disciplines, countering secular influences and critiquing public schools for distorting the truth. They accuse the public schools of removing materials related to the importance of the Bible and Christianity in American history; or embracing false ideas such as biological evolution and the Big Bang; or ignoring basic morality in their presentation of topics like reproduction and homosexuality. Perceiving the Christian worldview as under attack, these organizations are aggressive and assertive. Brannon Howse, the leader of Worldview Weekend, warns his readers that they are losing their children to secularism in the public schools: "Only 11 percent of those who have left the Church did so during the college years," he wrote in a *Worldview Times* essay titled "We Must Reclaim the Church Before We Can Even Begin to Reclaim the Culture." "Almost 90 percent of them were lost in middle school and high school. By the time they got to college they were already gone! About 40 percent are leaving the Church during elementary and middle school years!"[52] For Howse, the data reveal a dire threat from secular education. And this concern is not entirely without foundation, despite Howse's hyperbolic alarmism. A 2007 Pew Foundation study reported a widespread decline in American religious practice. A particular concern related to children: "the number of people who say they are unaffiliated with any particular faith today (16.1%) is more than double the number who say they were not affiliated with any particular religion as children."[53] Such defections, while statistically small, are lamented as evidence that Christians are going in the wrong direction.

The curriculum of the evangelical culture that parallels the secular culture aims to reverse these trends. Assessing the impact of such efforts is difficult, and no systematic study exists. But one important indicator of its influence is revealed in the rejection of evolution by evangelicals who were educated in the public schools. Of the fifty-five million students enrolled in America's schools, less than 10 percent attend Christian schools where biblical creation would be taught. Although there is evidence that America's public schools are not teaching evolution effectively and that some teachers violate the law by teaching creationism, the majority of schools certainly teach evolution as the legitimate scientific explanation of origins.[54] America's remarkable and widespread rejection of evolution testifies clearly to the power of the alternative science curriculum of the parallel culture.[55] Polls also indicate that many Americans, particularly evangelicals, hold different ideas about homosexuality than are taught in the public schools, with most rejecting the "gay lifestyle" despite programs promoting tolerance.[56] The same is true for the belief that America is a "Christian nation."[57] Evangelicals reject, *en masse,* ideas that challenge their biblical worldview, despite the best efforts of the public schools.

Multidenominational parachurch organizations also provide alternative visions to reinforce the authentic Christian worldview. The most significant such organization is James Dobson's Focus on the Family. Paul Miller recalls that the radio in the family car was regularly tuned to the local Christian station—sponsored by his church—that broadcast Dobson's programs. Books from Focus on the Family lined the Millers' bookshelves, alongside worn copies of the family's many Bibles. Paul listened to the radio drama/comedy program *Adventures in Odyssey* so many evenings before going to bed that now, years later, he "can still tell you the mailing address that was listed at the end of every program." Paul's sister read the popular *Brio* magazine, targeted at teenage girls. His brother read *Breakaway,* a publication for boys.[58] In high school Paul read Focus's *Plugged In* magazine—"Shining a Light on the World of Popular Entertainment"—still available online.[59]

Focus on the Family provides helpful guidance for families like the Millers, with materials for both parents and their children at each stage of development. It was, and still is, a powerful and beloved enterprise that reaches deep into the hearts of American evangelicals. Like all parents, the Millers wrestled with boundaries for their children—boundaries related to entertainment, dating, clothing, misbehavior, friendships, and so on. They appreciated Dobson's homey biblical advice, dispensed within the framework of their Christian faith.

Other parachurch organizations produce curricula related to origins. Answers in Genesis is the largest, but there is also the more "scholarly" Institute for Creation Research, as well as a collection of well-funded fellow creationists who run their own idiosyncratic projects, like Kent Hovind and Carl Baugh.[60] Hugh Ross operates Reasons to Believe, promoting an antievolutionary variant known as old earth creationism, with the same roster of media as Answers in Genesis. The Center for Science and Culture at the Seattle-based Discovery Institute is a multimillion-dollar project that champions antievolutionary intelligent design through a website, publications, and other media.[61]

Answers in Genesis reinterprets the natural sciences, much as Focus on the Family does the social sciences, with materials for every age group. Children's books teach youngsters that Earth is a few thousand years old, and that dinosaurs and humans lived happily together in the Garden of Eden.[62] Older children move on to more advanced materials, ranging from the magazine *Kids Answers*, which "highlights the wonders of God's creation with kid-friendly information, images and games," to the popular *Answers* magazine to the *Answers Research Journal*, a "professional, peer-reviewed technical journal." In middle school Paul's enthusiasm for science led him to the *Answers in Genesis* newsletter (the precursor to *Answers* magazine). He embraced young earth creationism, which he saw as an important Christian belief that should be shared wherever possible: "I remember telling this woman who was cutting my hair about the real age of the earth and the faultiness of carbon dating," he recalled. "I thought I was 'witnessing.'"[63]

For students in schools like Prince Avenue, the curriculum often aligns with the young earth creationism of leaders like Ham. In some cases Ham's materials would even be used. For students in the public schools, the creationist material serves as a defense against a godless secular curriculum. Ham, for example, instructs students, when told by their high school teachers that something—say, the extinction of dinosaurs or the Cambrian explosion—happened millions of years ago, to politely raise their hand and ask their teacher, "Were you there?"[64]

Groups like American Vision and David Barton's WallBuilders organization provide an alternative Christianized political science curriculum. Paul watched Barton's videos at Prince Avenue, "intrigued by his novel insights on America's Christian History." Although he and his classmates "mocked the low production value," they were fully engaged with Barton's presentation: "He had a way of bringing things together and citing things that were familiar enough but with new insights that were compelling—like *National Treasure*," the blockbuster film that fuses history with fanciful, bizarre scenarios.[65]

Many evangelicals, like Barton, worry about the public schools. The group Concerned Women for America, founded thirty years ago by Beverly LaHaye, sees America's public schools as sinister purveyors of immorality: "Forty million of our nation's children are returning this fall to a system that is broken. They are entering into a culture that has been stripped of all notion of right and wrong. They are sitting down in classrooms designed to educate in math, science and English, and instead are being taught about 'alternative' lifestyles and lessons that promote sex to our youngsters. So how can any of us be shocked when they engage in outrageous sexual behavior? The schools all but endorse it!"[66]

Concerned Women for America, of course, does not speak for all evangelicals. Their membership, according to some estimates, numbers half a million, and many evangelicals consider them extreme. And they certainly do not represent evangelicals like Paul's mother, who supported the public schools. Paul, in fact, would have been enrolled at the secular school where his mother taught if he was not having so much fun with his siblings at Prince Avenue.

The alarmist rhetoric of groups like WallBuilders and Concerned Women for America proclaims a conspiracy in the public square to exclude God. Secularists, says Barton, rewrite American history as if God played no meaningful role. The real truth—their truth—is that God has been active in history, rewarding faithful nations with prosperity. The message resembles that of the creationists, who argue that science has been hijacked by anti-God secularists and distorted to suggest that God is no longer relevant to the scientifically informed. Focus on the Family similarly claims modern psychology assaults biblical principles. These ideas are often couched in terms of worldview, and evangelicals are encouraged to think through what it means to have a Christian/biblical worldview and how that differs from its secular analog.

Paul Miller encountered the biblical worldview in all its intellectual glory—and Barton in person—the summer after his junior year in high school when he attended two events targeting young people, one sponsored by Worldview Weekend, and the other by Summit Ministries.[67] The experience inaugurated a serious and enduring commitment to thinking carefully about what it meant to be a Christian living in a secular culture that did not share his values.

The discussion of the Christian worldview by thoughtful evangelicals is often remarkably sophisticated and lacks a secular counterpart; many young people never have an opportunity to reflect on their deepest beliefs and how they should shape their attitudes toward the issues of the day. Paul says the process was an "intellectual awakening":

> I remember sitting around with my friends at the Summit program at Bryan College, the summer before my senior year and thinking that I was talking about things that mattered. In my youth group, I was encouraged to read my Bible and do devotions; in my school, I was taught the Bible and about creation science. Yet, Summit gave me a cohesive worldview, a rather

> comprehensive system of thought, and a mission to learn to "unpack my faith," as they say. The students that I met at Summit were some of the most dynamic and interesting people I had met. In the talent show, there was a student who had written his own piano pieces, students who sang and juggled and did dance. There were these indie kids running around, the intense bible drillers, the odd homeschooled girls. It was a carnival of Christians for a kid who had only known good southern Baptists.[68]

Such reflections clarify the intellectual content of the evangelical culture and the need to protect it even as it works to transform the larger secular culture. The agenda proceeds outward from key biblical and theological commitments: belief in the reality of God, judgment, morality, the sanctity of marriage, universal human dignity. Those commitments illuminate the issues of the day, as evangelicals see them. "We sat around at lunch and talked about predestination and freewill, nudity in art, environmentalism, feminism, rap music. Everything was on the table, needing to be examined, thought about, and considered for its merits and consistency with a Biblical worldview," said Paul.[69]

Summit was important to Paul: "I am the person I am today because of Summit," he reflects, looking back. "Summit took me—an intellectually curious kid, bored with church and the lameness of Christian school—and gave me something that challenged me." Paul did research for Summit after his freshman year at Bryan College, developing resources regarding gender roles and environmentalism—hot topics for evangelicals.[70]

In awakening him to the richness of a comprehensive Christian worldview, the Summit experience ultimately led Miller to reject the biblical fundamentalism of his youth: "In the end," he recalls, "I found that it was a broken system." His focus had shifted from a simple literalist reading of the Bible and the teaching of his local church to the "broader world of Christian books, conferences, and discussions." He soon discovered that he was no longer at home in the comfortable theological neighborhood of his youth, and he began to embrace a more eclectic understanding of Christianity—one without the tidy boundaries that partitioned, secured, and defined the world of his childhood. But coming as he did from the end of the conservative spectrum, Paul had plenty of room to change intellectually and move theologically before he would even approach the liberal borders of evangelicalism.[71]

If the conservative evangelical worldview looks inward to the Bible and grounds all social and moral problems in its ancient wisdom, it also looks outward to the threat of the more modern forces of secular humanism, an amorphous grab-basket of ideas opposed to Christianity: "All it takes for secular humanism to triumph is for good Christians to do nothing," proclaims a pop-up advertisement on the Worldview Weekend website.[72] Similar rhetoric pervades the Summit Ministries website, where socialism, universal healthcare, the Democratic party, and all things Left are gathered into a worldview competing with the faith.[73] Summit's radio show, the *Christian Worldview,* suggests that all Christians, with appropriate reflection, will ultimately join them.[74]

Programs like those sponsored by Worldview Weekend, Summit Ministries, and other, similar organizations do not just inform—they *inspire.* They bring together important, well-known, charismatic evangelical thinkers and artists who put on impressive shows, sometimes to packed stadiums, making everyone feel a part of something vast, significant, and world changing. Young evangelicals from unsung tracts of America's heartland, fearful that their faith has consigned them to some cultural backwater, return from such events invigorated and confident.[75] "People came from all over the place—pretty dynamic people," Paul reminisces. "They were, in some ways, the brightest, most engaged people I've ever bumped into. They were really committed to their faith, but they were also committed to success in their music, and studies, and athletics. . . . I'd never met people like that before."[76]

The students who engaged Paul were mainly evangelicals raised in churches more or less like his. Their ideas came from interlinked sources, including their homes, where family devotions, Christian DVDs, and general discussion laid important foundations; their Sunday schools and churches, where a general biblical and theological literacy was acquired; their own reading of the Bible and associated religious texts; and their church-sponsored youth activities, where, in addition to church teaching, Christian behaviors were encouraged and strategies developed to resist "worldly" temptations like premarital sex, alcohol, and drugs. Most young evangelicals in America have similar experiences. That minority of evangelical students like Paul, who attend Christian schools, have their values strengthened considerably with additional teaching but, more important, with their near total immersion—spiritual, intellectual, artistic, social, and even athletic—in the evangelical world.

An oft-quoted verse from the New Testament captures the sense that evangelicals, at least in theory, prefer their own separate culture: "Love not the world; neither the things that are in the world. If any man love the world, the love of the father is not in him."[77] California radio preacher and best-selling author John MacArthur expands on this passage: "Do you reject the world and its false religions, damning ideologies, and godless pursuits? Instead, do you love God, His truth, His Kingdom, and all that He stands for? If you reject the world and its devilish desires, that is a strong indication you have a new life in Christ."[78]

Although flamboyant televangelists often flaunt flashy suits and private planes and preach prosperity, an authentic evangelical worldview is often interpreted to demand rejection of the "world," however that is construed. This perspective is reflected in the words of a popular gospel song:

> This world is not my home, I'm just passing through.
> My treasures are laid up somewhere beyond the blue.
> The angels beckon me from Heaven's open door
> And I can't feel at home in this world anymore.[79]

Conservative evangelicals like Paul Miller grow up with a negative perception of the word "worldly." The traditional meaning of the word—to understand and be involved in the affairs of the world, through reading, travel, acquaintances, and so on—acquires a negative connotation: to allow one's values to be inappropriately shaped by cultural forces outside of one's faith.[80] A profoundly wholesome core sits at the center of this concern, namely, that spiritual and moral values should be more important than the pursuit of a materialistic agenda. One should serve God and not mammon. And many evangelicals generously sacrifice their time and money in response to this concern. In practice, however, the avoidance of being "worldly" often amounts to little more than church leaders' baptizing their own preferences and concluding that the new things they don't like are inappropriate. Rock music, rap music, movie theaters, pool halls, bowling alleys, artistic nudity, miniskirts, tight pants, visible midriffs or cleavage, coed swimming, long hair on men, short hair on women, make-up, tattoos, and even pierced ears have all been condemned at various times as "worldly."[81]

Paul's brother was scolded for drinking IBC root beer because it came in a brown bottle that resembled a regular beer bottle: "It always made my dad—a teetotaler—really angry that my brother would drink IBC root beer because if he was in downtown Athens and one of the deacons drove by and saw 'Olan Miller's son drinking IBC root beer'—the appearance of evil—they might have thought something was going on." Such concerns lead to dilemmas like the one Paul posed to his friends at youth group: "If you broke down on the side of the road and needed to use the phone, and the only place available was the bar, would you go into the bar to use the phone?"[82] The message was that the appearance of wrongdoing is also wrong. Evangelicals have been known to wait until midnight Sunday to start playing ping-pong, honoring their commitment to keep the Sabbath holy. Snowmobiling to church is not allowed since it might seem like joyriding on Sunday.

The separation that evangelicals strive to maintain from the "world" can often seem a "separation for separation's sake," a desire to simply be "apart." This, not surprisingly, creates a "parallel market" for Christian alternatives to all those worldly delights. Journalist Daniel Radosh, a secular Jew, took an extended romp through both the fringes and the heartland of this world and reported his finding in *Rapture Ready: Adventures in the Parallel Universe of Christian Pop Culture.* By his estimates, this parallel market is a growing $7 billion industry and increasingly moving into the mainstream. He noted, for example, that Walmart has over "1,200 religious book titles, and 550 inspirational albums, which regularly crack the mainstream bestseller lists and pop charts."[83]

Throughout the 1980s religious media proliferated. Christian radio stations broadcast countless talk shows and every imaginable genre of music, including heavy metal and rap. Today some 1,400 Christian broadcasting companies in the United States serve an estimated 69 million adult listeners—and consumers.[84] Thirty million people, comparable to the listening population of Canada, tune in to Christian radio every day.[85] "The love affair between conservative religion and the mass electronic media," said Harvard religion professor Harvey Cox, "is the most significant recent religious event in the United States."[86]

As a teenager Paul was a fan of the Christian rap group DC Talk. He heard them as the warm-up band for a Billy Graham crusade, singing a song about sex called "I Don't Want It." "It was very strange standing there with my mom," Paul recalled, "while the band sang about why you should wait until you were married to have sex":

Yo, s-e-x is a test when I'm pressed
So back off with less of that zest
Impress this brother with a life of virtue
The innocence that's spent is gonna hurt you
Safe is the way they say to play
But then again safe ain't safe at all today
So just wait for the mate that's straight from God
Don't give it up 'til you tie the knot.[87]

Contemporary Christian Music (CCM) aptly illustrates the evangelical appropriation of secular culture. Its ancestral rock form was condemned in the 1960s as "the Devil's Diversion" by popular speaker, musician, and author Bob Larson.[88] In the 1980s, after Christian rock had gained some acceptance, it was rap that was denounced as Satanic.[89] CCM has come of age and is now a billion-dollar industry.[90] Nevertheless, it remains controversial in some circles because of its obvious similarities to conventional popular music that, with its provocative women, crotch-grabbing men, and gutter lyrics, has even secular parents wringing their hands. A youth worker at Prince Avenue used to listen to Christian rock at low volume because he feared people would think he was listening to secular rock music and "misperceive his Christian faith."[91]

Christian music supports the values and beliefs of the parallel culture. Like most people their age, evangelical teens spend hours every day listening to music with its various messages. Their CDs, however, do not carry warnings about "sexually explicit lyrics" on their cases. Nor do they celebrate one-night stands, homosexuality, masturbation, rape, violence, or drug use. Many encourage sexual abstinence before marriage, respect for parents, or belief in creation. Themes like the return of Jesus, the power of prayer, or the closeness of Jesus remind listeners of their cherished values. Performers are often role models, with exemplary personal lives and inspirational testimonies. CCM is now a bigger niche in the overall music market than jazz and classical combined, and 64 percent of CCM albums are now sold through mainstream media outlets rather than through Christian bookstores, which used to be the sole source.[92]

A widely shared Christian soundtrack plays for the entire life of an evangelical. Paul learned Christian songs with clapping and motions as a toddler, choruses throughout elementary and middle school, and then graduated to Christian rock music in high school. Church musical fare combines traditional hymns sung by virtually all evangelicals—classics like "Amazing Grace" and "A Mighty Fortress Is Our God"—and praise choruses preferred by the younger generation. The latter combine catchy melodies with rudimentary lyrics and have been dubbed "7-11" music—seven words are sung eleven times. Many evangelicals have experienced the powerful bonding that comes through singing such choruses with thousands of their fellow Christians, eyes closed, hands in the air, and swaying gently back and forth.

Christian music, like its secular counterpart, is a mixed bag. *Rolling Stone* reviewed 30 Christian rock songs and concluded, apparently to the magazine's surprise, that they were "no more insipid or derivative than thirty songs randomly selected from the Billboard Hot 100."[93] Most critics, though, consider Christian music less artistic and more formulaic because it must be inoffensive, theologically orthodox, and focused on spiritual topics. By age fifteen Paul found it "lame," and he and his friends moved on to secular music. "Why do we need an alternative Christian music?" he asks, looking back.[94]

The aversion many evangelicals have for the purely "secular" is displayed clearly in the work of the band ApologetiX, which takes popular rock songs and rewrites the lyrics. Even such tame material as the

Beach Boys' "Barbara Ann" is reworked into "Baa, Baa We're Lambs," enabling a Christian rock group to play a popular tune in church, as long as the lyrics have been sanitized: "Baa Baa Baa Baa Baa we're lambs."[95] ApologetiX markets itself as a "parody band" in the style of Weird Al Yankovic, but its retooled lyrics suggest that members are really just baptizing pop tunes so they can be played in church. By high school Paul was long past being impressed, calling their project the "epitome of lameness."

Despite occasional "lameness," the Christian music industry has produced genuine superstars, including Amy Grant, DC Talk, Jars of Clay, Michael W. Smith, Stryper, and the legendary guitarist Phil Keaggy. Grammy Award–winning producer Michael Omartian has worked with top secular acts and coproduced the megahit "We Are the World." Openly Christian country stars like Johnny Cash, Randy Travis, Charlie Daniels, and Ricky Skaggs have had considerable commercial success.

Paul bought Christian music, books, and other paraphernalia at the Carpenter's Shop, owned by a deacon at his church. The website for the store, which is still in operation, invites customers to "see our divine gifts."[96] "From a very young age," Paul remembers, "I was going to the Carpenter Shop and getting toys and books and music." As a teenager he visited the store regularly to check out the new releases.[97] The Carpenter's Shop is one of several thousand Christian bookstores in the country. Twenty-one hundred such outlets belong to the Christian Booksellers Association, and estimates place the total number of members as high as 10,000.[98] All are part of a significant network serving the 100 million Americans who shop in Christian stores.[99]

The vast Christian book market has produced runaway blockbusters that sell tens of millions of copies, like Hal Lindsey's *Late Great Planet Earth,* or the *Left Behind* series. Paul started reading the sprawling *Left Behind* books as a teenager but soon gave up, put off by the stilted dialog and corny plots: "I didn't want to finish them because the quality was so poor." Baptist ethicist and *Christianity Today* columnist David Gushee had a similar reaction, calling the *Left Behind* premise "a distressing aspect of one branch of conservative evangelical Christianity."[100]

Christian stores like the Carpenter's Shop certainly push products like *Left Behind* paraphernalia, often before mainstream outlets do. Most of their products, as befits their mission focus, relate to education; books, magazines, and music are the main items. But a host of other goods are also available: There are message T-shirts proclaiming, "God is Totally Awesome!" or "Got Jesus?" Slogans appealing to youth declare, "God is my DJ," "I'm like totally saved." Advertisements picture young children wearing shirts proclaiming, "My guardian angel is so cool."[101] One interesting message often stretched across the chests of Christian girls proclaims, "Modest is Hottest."[102] You can get a shirt for your dog featuring a picture of a bloody hand with a spike through it and the caption: "His Pain, Your Gain."[103] Political catchphrases are also popular, promoting any number of right-wing agenda items, from antiabortion, to antievolution, to anti-Obama. These messages can be had on pins and bumper stickers as well.

There are Christian breath mints with Bible verses on them called "Testamints"; a rival company, Scripture Candy, is trying to buy their clever name. Scripture Candy makes special jelly beans for Easter, "Try God" hearts for Valentine's Day, and "Faith Pops" to hand out to trick-or-treaters on Halloween. Top-Flite makes "Gospel Golf Balls" imprinted with Bible verses: "Now when you lose a golf ball you will be sharing the Good News of Jesus Christ!" goes the pitch.[104] Coffee mugs can be found with "God First" on one side and "Coffee Second" on the other.[105]

The surging popularity of franchises like Spider-Man and Batman has spawned religious superheroes like "Mr. Christian," "Bibleman," and "Desertwind," a "super-speedster who must make some tough choices about his life and faith."[106] A poster of the hero "Armorbearer," wielding a large sword and shield emblazoned with crosses, features a Bible verse prominently at the top—"Put on the full armor of God that you may be able to stand against the schemes of the devil"—and some space at the bottom for a "prayer list."[107] The website comicbookreligion.com provides an encyclopedic overview of the many evangelical superheroes and villains.[108]

Evangelicals even have their own board games. One—described by Daniel Radosh as "so heavy-handed and tragically uncool that the only people I could imagine enjoying [it] were [*The Simpsons* characters] Rod and Tod Flanders"—is called Salvation Challenge, played as follows: "The players get saved by landing on Calvary and making the salvation call, 'Jesus save me.' After getting saved the players enter a race to see who will be the first to advance God's Kingdom. The winner of the game is the first player to get saved and then give all of his or her cash to missions."[109]

The game is recommended for players from age 10 to 100 and is, as of this writing, ranked 377,000 in toys and games on Amazon. Its secular alter ego celebrating the acquisition of money—Monopoly—is ranked 120.[110]

Evangelical children experience this world of goods and services to varying degrees. All of them would attend Sunday school, where they would learn stories and songs; most would listen to Contemporary Christian Music and read Christian books and magazines. Some, like Paul, would attend Christian schools and intellectual events like Worldview Weekend and Summit. A few would play games like Salvation Challenge. Like any subculture, levels of commitment and participation vary as children first absorb values from their parents, then from their peers and teachers, and finally work through things on their own.

Evangelicals are strongly encouraged to internalize their faith—to "make it their own," so to speak. This rather sophisticated philosophical project has no obvious secular analog. Paul's transformative experience at Summit, between high school and college, was all about "unpacking your faith," understanding its nature and implications for daily life.[111] Programs like Summit help young-adult Christians, of a certain political persuasion, to discover for themselves the reasons for their beliefs and to place an intellectually defensible foundation under the things they have been taught. They have been raised to believe that the Bible is God's word, produced by inspired men. What is the evidence for that claim? They have learned that seeking God's will for their lives is all-important. But how do they do that? Despite their sometime isolation from the secular world, they have been encouraged, through the influence of Francis Schaeffer and others, to engage that world and to share their faith with people they meet. But what does that mean? Summit offers young conservative evangelicals a chance to think through these issues with other Christians at similar points in their spiritual journeys: "As Christian youth," writes Kira on the Summit website, "we stand and fall not so much by our convictions as by our ability to explain, defend, and consistently live out those convictions."[112]

Paul began "unpacking" his worldview the year before Summit. A Worldview Team from Bryan College in Dayton, Tennessee, visited his church and offered a stimulating philosophical challenge, pushing the audience to think hard about the "images, realities, and consequences (both good and bad) representative of the various worldviews" and how to evaluate those worldviews from a "a biblically informed critical perspective." The conclusion, of course, was that "Christianity is the best and only true worldview."[113]

The Bryan College team aimed to reinforce and deepen the faith of young people, like those at Prince Avenue. But for Paul the Bryan team pulled back a curtain and a new world began to appear—the vast secular continent he had only dimly perceived beyond the tidy horizons of Prince Avenue. The Bryan team "pushed me," he recalls, "to own my paradigm." His search led him to move ecclesiastically and geographically upscale, and he began attending a downtown Presbyterian church with a more intellectual orientation than Prince Avenue. His parents supported his decision.

Not surprisingly, Paul enrolled in Bryan College, established shortly after the Scopes trial to honor William Jennings Bryan, who prosecuted John Scopes and died something of a martyr shortly after the verdict. Bryan College was a natural choice. The "Worldview Team" had made a positive impression. Paul's sister had gone there, and the conservative Southern evangelical character of the place was theologically and culturally aligned with Prince Avenue.

Bryan College is part of a network of Christian colleges, universities, seminaries, and Bible schools that play a critical role in the intellectual life of the parallel culture of American evangelicalism. Depending on how widely the net is cast, this network has anywhere from 100 to almost 1,000 schools. Of the over 4,000 degree-granting institutions of higher education in the United States, 1,600 are private, and 900 or so have a religious affiliation. Over 200 are Catholic, but most of those would not endorse an evangelical expression of Christianity.[114]

Religious affiliation is ambiguous and often difficult to assess. Many—if not most—schools in the United States have strong religious roots but have secularized over time. What roots that remain are invisible except on the occasional statue around campus, and on founding documents in the archives. Cornell University, established in 1865, was one of America's first prominent universities without ties to a religious denomination, a controversial concept at the time. Harvard was established in 1636 to "advance Learning and perpetuate it to Posterity; dreading to leave an illiterate Ministry to the Churches."[115]

Education, however, liberalizes and secularizes, and in the evangelical world there is widespread discussion of Christian students abandoning their religious traditions in college and university.[116] Analogously, colleges, regardless of their historical or present religious identities, experience informal pressures to become less sectarian and more liberal.[117] Religious traditions tend to be more conservative than the colleges and universities they sponsor and are perpetually lamenting that "their" institutions are migrating away from them. Catholic schools, for example, hire non-Catholics and even non-Christians; conservative evangelical schools, in their search for qualified faculty who will work for low salaries, often hire instructors with a degree of "liberalism" that has to be "hidden" from various constituencies. Most religiously affiliated colleges and universities are more liberal, sometimes considerably more so, than their "public face" or affiliation would indicate.[118]

Despite these qualifications, evangelical institutions remain faithful to the central and defining characteristics of Christianity, as they understand them. The Council for Christian Colleges and Universities (CCCU) recognizes 108 institutions in the United States, including Bryan College, which they describe as "intentionally Christ-centered."

Most CCCU schools are small, with liberal arts emphases. Some, like Wheaton College in Illinois, with almost 3,000 students, are academically elite, maintain high admissions standards, and have an enviable record of sending their students on to the best graduate and medical schools.[119] In 2000 Alan Wolfe noted in the *Atlantic Monthly* that "Wheaton's rejection rate last year was higher than the University of Chicago's. Its class of 2003 includes sixty-one National Merit Scholars. The average SAT score of last year's entering class was 1310, putting Wheaton in the same range as Oberlin College and the University of Virginia."[120] CCCU schools are certainly not academic backwaters.

Bryan College has 1,150 students with above-average ACT scores. One-third attended public school, one-third were homeschooled, and one-third went to private schools not unlike Prince Avenue. Bryan is fully accredited, with 40 programs of study; 80 percent of its faculty hold doctorates. It was born in 1930 out of the tumultuous fundamentalist movement "for the higher education of men and women under auspices distinctly Christian and spiritual." The college partners with Summit ministries and features their conferences prominently on Bryan's home page. The Bryan-Summit collaboration promises to address a growing concern of the parallel culture that "50% of Christian students walk away from their faith by the time they graduate from many secular and liberal Christian colleges."[121] To prepare students to meet the challenges of secularism, Summit promises to ready students so that they

> Are equipped with the ability to understand dominant non-Biblical worldviews.
>
> Are taught to offer a reasoned answer for biblical Christianity which is often attacked in secular academic settings.
>
> Will learn why they believe what they believe.
>
> Will develop leadership strategies that will help them make a difference in the world around them.[122]

Bryan is also unusual among accredited Christian colleges in being a leader in the young-earth creationist movement. Kurt Wise, a promising young earth creationist educated at Harvard, served on the faculty until 2006, when he moved to Southwestern Baptist Theological Seminary. Wise, whom Richard Dawkins called "creationism's most highly qualified and most intelligent scientist," ran Bryan's Center for Origins Research, or CORE, program since its inception in 1989.[123] CORE, chartered to "develop a creationist model of biology," continues, under the leadership of other faculty, to promote young earth creationism through projects like an origins studies minor, a scholarly monograph series, and conferences.[124] Nevertheless, despite Bryan's leadership within young earth creationism, faculty are not required to hold that view, as long as they can affirm that God did create the world as described in Genesis, more or less. In fact—and perhaps contrary to expectations—the majority of faculty at Christian colleges reject young earth creationism. At many such colleges, moreover, there is considerable hostility toward such views.

Bryan provides a perfect environment for conservative evangelical Christians seeking to develop a strong and rationally defensible foundation—known as an *apologetic*—for their faith. As with most schools near the fundamentalist end of the spectrum, Bryan's guiding paradigm centers on an inerrant Bible, and this is far more than a decaying mission statement from a conservative past. Bryan's entire academic culture was organized to reinforce that belief.

Bryan's programs—its curriculum, CORE's research agenda, the Summit workshops—are all based on a particular biblical paradigm shared by most but not all evangelicals, namely, that the authority of the Bible has a *universal* applicability. The college's statement of faith affirms "that the holy Bible, composed of the Old and New Testaments, is of final and supreme authority in faith and life, and, being inspired by God, is inerrant."[125] The Bible thus trumps knowledge in every other field. This strong stance demands that scripture address questions that the biblical authors could not possibly have anticipated: global warming, gay marriage, abortion, the origin of species, cloning, nuclear weapons. Of course, the limitations of the biblical authors are of no real significance since, in this view, God is the author of the scriptures, and the so-called human authors were little more than secretaries. Wise's belief that God had communicated the young age of Earth in the Bible, if true, certainly provided adequate warrant to reject contrary conclusions based on geology, radioactivity, or astronomy. After all, God should know when he created Earth.

Maintaining the confident assertions of Bryan's brand of conservative evangelicalism is difficult. It is one thing to claim that sacred texts like the Bible originate with humans reflecting on and wrestling with a real spiritual dimension of reality. It is quite another to claim that God actually wrote those texts and encoded them with insights into social and scientific problems that would not emerge for millennia.

Paul Miller was far from a naïve fundamentalist, and he had trouble making sense of all this. The intellectual momentum that carried him, as a high school senior, from Prince Avenue Baptist to a socially oriented and somewhat more liberal Presbyterian church was inadvertently boosted at the Summit conference he attended. The carefully constructed curriculum at Bryan and 1,000 new evangelical peers were comforting, but he began to have doubts. The Southern Christianity that had nurtured him was a comfortable but puzzling blend of culture and faith, and he started to wonder where one stopped and the other began. Unsure exactly what was wrong, he told his advisor he wanted to go to Gordon College in New England because "I could drink alcohol there." His advisor, understandably, was not impressed with this motivation. For Paul, though, it was a symbolic reaction to Bryan's melding of Christianity and Southern culture; a school that let you drink beer would probably also let you think more broadly about your faith, reasoned Paul.[126]

The tightly packaged conservatism of Bryan, Summit, Prince Avenue, and Worldview Weekend can easily come apart. Many of the assumptions anchoring the fundamentalist wing of the parallel culture simply cannot withstand much scrutiny. Earth, for example, is definitely not 10,000 years old, and it doesn't take too much college-level science to make that clear. Even some of the faculty at Bryan did not hold that viewpoint. Fundamentalist churches across America have many empty seats vacated by Christians who once held tightly to biblical inerrancy and cultural conservatism. Evangelicals often abandon their childhood faith when they become free to explore issues on their own. The story is common, and there are many celebrity "deconversions," like those of E. O. Wilson and Michael Shermer.[127] Often the study of science is the catalyst. But a great many evangelicals—like Paul Miller—do not abandon their faith. They simply find another place within evangelicalism where they can reside more comfortably. The informal mission of many Christian colleges is to help young people make this sort of transition within the broad framework of their faith.

Most Christians—Paul Miller included—treasure their childhood faith as a valuable part of their identity. Few find faith to be a set of uncomfortable intellectual blinders or a moral strait jacket. If their faith begins to crumble, they find the loss to be just that—a loss. Even Charles Darwin considered the slippage of his faith demoralizing and imagined ways to prevent it. In *Dover Beach* Matthew Arnold immortalized the angst that attended Victorian England's recognition that the "Sea of Faith" that had once been "full, and round earth's shore" was now just a "melancholy, long withdrawing roar."[128]

Not all born-again Christians lose their faith in such crises, of course. Many simply find a new articulation and a new place in the parallel culture of evangelicalism where they are more comfortable and where they can live more faithfully. The spectrum of evangelical belief runs from a rigid, judgmental, sometimes harsh fundamentalism on one end to more liberal and culturally plural expressions on the other. Often an evangelical "crisis of faith" is resolved with a simple liberalizing, whereby specific beliefs—biblical literalism, young earth creationism, homosexuality as perversion, eternal torment of the damned in a literal hell, the sinfulness of abortion—are abandoned and other beliefs—the Bible as literature, concern for the environment, racial and cultural equality for oppressed groups, universality of salvation, an emphasis on social justice, tolerance of diversity—move to the center as animating ethical and theological concerns. The evangelical spectrum encompasses both of these camps.

Paul's faith crisis came after two unsatisfying years at Bryan College, as he grew increasingly uncomfortable with the way his approach to his faith made him "stick out." Not sure what he believed, but certainly not hostile to his faith tradition or even eager to discard it, he migrated from fundamentalist Christian to agnostic "seeker." The logical destination for such a seeker, who had already experienced thirteen years of Christian schooling, Summit, and Worldview Weekend, and who had half a degree from a fundamentalist college: Francis Schaeffer's L'Abri.

Schaeffer was a fixture on the evangelical scene from the 1960s until his death in 1984. With his many books and videos that were used widely in Christian colleges and universities, he was a ubiquitous mover within evangelicalism. Many consider him the intellectual architect of the Religious Right, which emerged as a powerful political force during the 1980s. This movement brought questions about politics and social issues into focus for evangelicals who had previously defaulted to isolationism. Biblical, theological, philosophical, historical, and even scientific insights were creatively synthesized to develop "Christian" positions on everything from gay marriage and working women to tax rates and the United Nations.[129]

Developing a "Christian worldview" became an important stage in the intellectual maturation of evangelicals. The word "worldview" began to appear everywhere as countless lesser sages picked it up and ran with it. Young men needed to understand that God intended for them to lead their families—to model Christ's headship of the Church. Young women needed to know God wanted them to be submissive to their husbands, dress modestly, and focus their attention on their families rather than on careers. Everyone should rally against gay marriage, higher taxes, pornography, the United Nations, abortion, and above all, secular humanism.

An odd confluence of factors turned Schaeffer into the "guru" of the worldview movement. At Westminster Theological Seminary he studied under Cornelius Van Til and J. Gresham Machen, two of fundamentalism's brightest intellectual lights. He pastored for a while before he and his wife, Edith, moved to Switzerland in 1948 as missionaries. In 1955 they named their home "L'Abri" (French for "the shelter") and turned it into a retreat community.

L'Abri morphed into a beacon for Christian seekers. Running it was Schaeffer's primary project until he became a political activist. In the words of one observer, it was "a place where thoughtful young Christians went to breathe the fortifying alpine air and to sit at the feet of their goateed guru."[130] Just as the Beatles would make much-publicized pilgrimages to India to seek enlightenment from the Maharishi, so Christians who could afford overseas travel sought enlightenment from Schaeffer, a Pennsylvania pastor turned alpine sage.

Schaeffer took to his new role. He adopted the local dress style with pants that came just below the knees and coordinated leggings. His white goatee and pulled-back shock of hair—worn rather long for a middle-aged Christian male at the time—made him look like Heidi's grandfather. In photos he appeared lost in thought, never looking at the camera, pondering something important with the Swiss Alps as a backdrop.

In retrospect, Schaeffer was not an intellectual heavyweight. Little of his prodigious output of popular philosophy and theology has stood the test of time.[131] But he embodied a confident openness to the challenges of belief and was deeply committed to dialog with secular culture. Even the apostle of LSD Timothy Leary made two trips to L'Abri, which certainly contributed to the mystique of the place.

And so when Paul Miller found himself overtaken with doubts that were eating away at his faith, he decided to travel that well-worn path to a L'Abri center in England. (There are now eleven L'Abri locations in Europe, Asia, and America.)[132] Christians with doubts generally feel unwelcome in their communities. Doubts about the truth of the Bible might be regarded as sinful, an indicator that one is not "right with God": "I will pray for you" is the most common—and unhelpful—response of worried fellow Christians. The same response would be forthcoming if the issue was a diagnosis of terminal cancer. Doubters rarely feel comfortable speaking openly about what they are thinking, and many simply keep their concerns private.

Paul's pilgrimage was liberating: "Questions were OK at L'Abri. The Christians were cool: they listened to vulgar rap music and they liked modern art." He could talk openly about his doubts: "I don't believe in God any more," he said one day, while scraping paint with a L'Abri employee. ("Pilgrims" did chores as a part of their program.)[133]

By 2004, when Paul would visit L'Abri in England, Schaeffer had been dead for two decades. A younger generation of Christians, turned off by the Religious Right's negative public face, viewed Schaeffer with suspicion. The questions and the music and the movies were different. But the spirit of Schaeffer's original commitment to taking questions seriously and not trivializing doubt or marginalizing doubters survived the passing of L'Abri's bearded guru. Central to the success of L'Abri was its provision of a path for troubled Christians to find new ground within the parallel culture of their faith.[134]

Paul was looking for a way back to faith, but he needed something different from the rigid Southern fundamentalism of his childhood. That particular form of Christianity lay in tatters on the manicured campus at Bryan College. L'Abri came through for him. He encountered the more liberal Anglican expression of Christianity and became intrigued with its robust sense of tradition, the "richness of its symbols, the appreciation for beauty and music and art." His Anglican counselor at L'Abri recommended that he get out of the South, where Christianity was so entwined with the culture that it was hard to see what life it had on its own.[135]

Finding a school to finish his degree was hard for Paul, a wayward fundamentalist looking for a new Christianity: "I was looking at Catholic universities. I looked into Wheaton and Calvin as evangelical schools. I looked into St. Louis University . . . De Paul University. I had no idea what I was looking for." In the end his choice was Gordon College on Boston's North Shore: "I ended up driving up to Gordon for my admissions interview. I visited Christ Church, which was a local evangelical Episcopal Church. I felt a strong sense of home in that church community, and also at Gordon."[136]

Gordon College had awarded Francis Schaeffer an honorary doctorate in 1971 and remained a favorite of the larger L'Abri organization. One of Paul's counselors at L'Abri suggested he would find soulmates at Gordon, fellow travelers who had abandoned their childhood fundamentalism in search of something with a richer sense of mystery, tradition, and symbol. During his admissions interview, Paul spent over an hour talking about books, and Madeleine L'Engle, and L'Abri, and New England. No one spoke of Ken Ham, David Barton, or Tim LaHaye—figures who Paul soon discovered were of no interest to Gordon faculty.

The Christian identity of evangelical colleges is surprisingly diverse, populating the parallel culture with a host of real choices. Schools with similar mission statements, in fact, often have very different intellectual and theological climates. Some, but not all, schools forbid alcohol. Some require chapel. Some accept only Christians. Some require extensive Bible courses. All such schools, though, employ various strategies to maintain their evangelical identities and prevent the slippage into secularism that compromised the original mission, for example, of Harvard—a history that is often referenced. But these strategies play out rather differently in practice.[137]

Evangelical colleges, almost without exception, hire only Christian faculty, and many require their faculty to sign a "statement of faith" affirming a particular set of Christian beliefs. Such statements anchor the institution at a particular location on the theological landscape of the parallel culture. Wheaton College in Illinois expects its faculty to agree to a roster of traditional beliefs, including the following: "We believe that God directly created Adam and Eve, the historical parents of the entire human race; and that they were created in His own image, distinct from all other living creatures, and in a state of original righteousness."[138]

But even carefully worded and conservative prescriptions offer few guarantees that everyone is "affirming" such beliefs in the same way. Theological language is highly symbolic and notoriously slippery. When theologians, for example, say that they "believe" something, it can take some effort to find out exactly what they mean.

The written mission statements of evangelical colleges—even those signed annually by faculty—often function as *de facto* public relations documents designed to keep conservative constituencies contented and at bay. This is not to say that they have no meaning, of course, but merely that they do not keep the associated institutions on the short theological leash that an outsider might presume.[139]

Individual evangelical colleges can thus develop quite different cultures, even as they work within the framework of similar mission statements. Bryan College and Gordon College, for example, have remarkably similar mission statements. Both affirm the centrality and inerrancy of the Bible. Both claim to be nondenominational. Both require their faculty and students to be practicing Christians. But, as Paul found to his great satisfaction, they are profoundly different institutions.

Gordon College is better defined by its motto, "Freedom within a framework of faith," than by its mission statement. Gordon faculty, unlike their Bryan counterparts, are engaged with the rich complexity of the secular world. Gordon science faculty publish in mainstream scientific journals like *Applied Physics Letters, Journal of Immunology Methods, Journal of Cell Biology, Journal of Physical Chemistry, Physical Review, Virology,* and *Proceedings of the National Academy of Sciences,* rather than in the creationist journals in which Bryan science faculty publish. In fact, Gordon science faculty work carefully and diplomatically to *undermine* ideas like those promoted by Bryan's CORE project, helping their students embrace contemporary science rather than providing arguments to reject it. When publicly challenged on this point by the parents of students, Gordon's then president, Jud Carlberg, defended the approach of his institution. Gordon College "isn't in the business of indoctrination," he said.[140] A creationist like Kurt Wise, despite his Harvard pedigree, could never have gotten a job interview at Gordon, much less have been invited to set up a research center there.

Among America's hundreds of evangelical colleges, Bryan is far from the most conservative, and Gordon is not the most liberal. But the space between them is surprisingly vast, regardless of how it is measured.

The differences between Bryan and Gordon provide a window into the tensions within American evangelicalism. The parallel culture in which many believers live accommodates a wide range of beliefs and values, with varying degrees of separation from and engagement with the larger secular culture. The roster of fundamentalists who visit Bryan for their annual summer Summits would be strangely out of place at Gordon. The rabbis and imams who speak occasionally in Gordon's chapel would never be invited to Bryan. The secular scholarship produced by Gordon faculty has little or no counterpart at Bryan. And yet both colleges are solidly evangelical, with unambiguous Christian commitments across the board, from belief in the reality of miracles and the resurrection of Jesus to the importance of serving the poor. Both consider themselves valuable alternatives to secular schools.

It is not a coincidence, of course, that Bryan is in the red state of Tennessee and Gordon is in deep-blue Massachusetts. Were the two institutions to uproot and change places, Bryan would experience a complex of subtle and not-so-subtle pressures to become more liberal, while Gordon would find itself growing ever more conservative. This, of course, drives home the point that the powerful forces at work within the parallel culture of evangelicalism are largely independent of its central faith commitments. The intellectual disengagement from the larger academic community of Bryan College, with its center promoting young earth creationism and its institutionalized biblical fundamentalism, is sustained by the supporting culture of Southern evangelicalism and its implicit distrust of secular learning, especially if it originates above the Mason-Dixon Line.

Despite the confident claims of the culture warriors of the Worldview Weekends, evangelicals—as Paul happily discovered—need not reject contemporary science in favor of creationism, conventional history in favor of David Barton's "Christian History," or mainstream psychology in favor of James Dobson's biblical alternative. And they most certainly do not have to embrace the far-fetched apocalyptic speculations of Hal Lindsey and Tim LaHaye.

As for Paul Miller, he enjoys New England, where his faith fits with that of the people around him—adventurous, not obsessed with doctrine, wrestling with a vast "horizon of concern." He reads literature and enjoys art and worships every Sunday with like-minded fellow Christians in an Episcopal church that is probably about as liberal as one can get under the evangelical umbrella. But as with so many young people from nurturing families, his roots call him home. Culturally, the reflective boy from Athens, Georgia, who loved poetry is a long way from his Southern tribe.

Paul still does not have a secular friend, however, but when asked if he thought that he would some day, he quickly responded: "God, I hope so."

6 Made in America

Three highly visible evangelical leaders—Jerry Falwell, Pat Robertson, and Oral Roberts—made names for themselves over the past half-century as irascible, controversial religious celebrities. Ridiculed by comedians, unsympathetically dissected by scholars, and critiqued to the point of excoriation by the media, the three men nonetheless embodied holy boldness, righteousness, and right thinking to millions of stalwarts. They had, in their own words, the "anointing."

In 2001 Jerry Falwell proclaimed on national television that the September 11 terrorist attacks were God's judgment on the country. With the help of the American Civil Liberties Union (ACLU), People for the American Way, and other forces working to "secularize America," the United States—after basking in the security of God's favor for two centuries—had gone far enough to "make God mad." "You helped this happen," he said, blaming the 9/11 tragedy on the "pagans, and the abortionists, and the feminists, and the gays and the lesbians." He later backpedaled, but he still maintained that God's shield of protection no longer safeguarded America.[1]

Falwell was the son of an agnostic Virginia bootlegger. In 1956 he received a degree from the then-unaccredited Baptist Bible College in Virginia. Ironically, he was later awarded three honorary doctoral degrees, a Doctor of Divinity from Tennessee Temple Theological Seminary, a Doctor of Letters from California Graduate School of Theology, and a Doctor of Laws from Central University in Seoul, South Korea. He was often called, with his approval, "Dr. Falwell."[2] He went on to cofound the Moral Majority, one of the most powerful political organizations in the country. He helped put the Religious Right on the front page and was credited with delivering two-thirds of the white, evangelical vote to Ronald Reagan in the 1980 presidential election.[3]

Pat Robertson, on whose television show Falwell made his provocative 9/11 remarks, offered a similar explanation for the 2010 earthquake in Haiti that took as many as 230,000 lives and left more than a million people homeless. "Something happened a long time ago in Haiti," he stated with grave authority on his popular television program, the *700 Club*, "and people might not want to talk about it." The Haitians, struggling to get out from "under the heel of the French," had been looking for help. So "they got together and swore a pact to the Devil. They said, we will serve you if you'll get us free from the French. True story. And so, the Devil said, okay it's a deal." In Robertson's retelling, the Devil is a two-bit hustler, cutting deals. Robertson, known for such "explanations," had previously said that a stroke suffered by Israeli Prime Minister Ariel Sharon was God's punishment for withdrawing from the Gaza Strip.[4]

Unlike Falwell, Robertson had a substantial pedigree. His father was a United States senator, and Robertson was well educated, with a Bachelor of Law degree from Yale University Law School in 1955. He failed the bar exam, however, and went on to earn a Master of Divinity from New York Theological Seminary, where he engaged with a hard-right biblical literalism. He would eventually found a variety of conservative organizations, the most influential of which was CBN, the Christian Broadcasting Network. He ran unsuccessfully for president in 1988, but did come out ahead of George Bush, Sr., in the Iowa caucuses. Robertson's Christian Coalition rallied the Christian Right in late twentieth-century America.[5]

Oral Roberts's unique and extraordinary claims, however, deserve special consideration. The charismatic minister, healer, televangelist, and educator studied the Bible after high school but never completed a college degree. Born into poverty in Oklahoma, he pioneered television ministry and was a leading figure in what has been called the *prosperity gospel,* or the belief that God financially blesses those who exercise their faith appropriately. One leading scholar of evangelicalism notes that Roberts's influence has been second only to that of Billy Graham among conservative Protestants. Roberts did not presume merely to speak for God but believed and proclaimed that he was personally performing divine miracles and playing a major role in an end-times drama.[6]

Addressing an audience of five thousand at a Charismatic Bible Ministries conference, Roberts told about the time a member of his audience had died. To restore order, he said, "I had to stop and go back in the crowd and raise the dead person so I could go ahead with the service." There were many such miracles. Roberts told his audience that God had given him a vision that he would indeed die but that he would "be coming back." And, of course, he "would be coming to Tulsa." Roberts captivated his audience, saying, "I'm looking to the world to come because I'm not going to stay over there." He would come back from beyond the veil. "And I'm going to help bring that world to come with me and put it right on top of this world right here that's been persecuting me," he assured his listeners. "And I'm going to get my rightful place. I'm going to rule and I'm going to reign. You look at Oral Roberts University [ORU], what happens to it when I get back from the other side."[7] Quotes from Oral Roberts adorn the walls of ORU lecture halls, just as quotes from Lincoln and Jefferson are engraved on walls of secular universities.

Roberts built a sprawling multimillion-dollar empire, including a university with 2,500 students, and a $250 million medical center. In 1987 he told television viewers that he needed to raise millions to bail out the medical school, which was losing $30 to $40 million a year. If the funds were not forthcoming, Roberts said, God would call him "home," prompting some Tulsans to buy bumper stickers that read: "Send Oral to Heaven in 87." Concerned supporters made pledges to keep Roberts alive, and the fund-raising target was exceeded. All to no avail, however, as the ambitious City of Faith medical center, inspired by Roberts's vision to join faith healing with modern medicine, closed in 1989.[8]

Roberts, Falwell, and Robertson embody the star-making power of the evangelical community. They ascended to positions of enormous national influence, overcoming all manner of obstacles, including humble beginnings and public gaffs of the sort that destroy the careers of most political figures. They were routinely held up to ridicule in the media and mocked mercilessly. Ronald Dworkin offered up a typical criticism of Falwell that could have applied to Robertson as well. "Reverend Jerry Falwell, and other politicians who claim to speak for some 'moral majority,' want to enforce their own personal morality with the steel of the criminal law," Dworkin vented in 1983. Falwell and New Right evangelicals were meddlesome zealots. "They know what kind of sex is bad, which books are fit for public libraries, what place religion should have in education and family life, when human life begins . . . and that abortion is capital sin."[9] Another critic labeled fundamentalist leaders like Falwell "apostles of ignorance" and "basically anti-intellectual." Falwell's college celebrated unenlightened thinking. Falwell and other fundamentalists, ranted the critics, "are not merely opposed to secularism or secular humanism, but to the realities of the modern world."[10]

If Falwell's hard-right views and fundamentalist dogmatism made the critics snarl, then Oral Roberts's made them laugh. Roberts harkened from the Pentecostal wing of evangelicalism, which emphasizes dramatic faith healing and "speaking in tongues"—a highly emotional, ecstatic experience, usually in a worship service, that involves being taken over by the Holy Spirit and literally speaking in unknown languages. The Pentecostal emphasis on faith healing and speaking in tongues is rejected by most other fundamentalist groups. Roberts's public pronouncements and revival antics were, for satirists, gifts that kept on giving. He would instruct television audiences to put their hands on their televisions to receive healing; he got messages directly from God, often while on camera; he was visited by a 900-foot apparition of Jesus, who told him to build a medical center. Journalists in Tulsa had a field day. One critic speculated that the minister's elevator shoes must make him amazingly tall so as to meet the 900-foot Christ face-to-face. Even conservative evangelical ministers chastised Roberts. But the prophet from Tulsa had been scandalizing doubters for ages. He often placed his hands on people during healing services and flung them across the stage. He made a vast fortune telling people that their gifts to him were "seed-faith" offerings and that God would return their "investment" many times over. Born into rural poverty, Roberts led the way in what would become a widespread message linking faith and wealth.[11] He embodied a strange contradiction—using the gospel of Jesus as a vehicle to move money from the poor to meet the extravagant needs of his ministry and his growing empire. Upon his death in 2009, one Christian watchdog organization made plain its views in an obituary: "Oral died stinking filthy rich and he did so at the expense of the poor, widows, and people on fixed incomes." Another journal, making no effort to hide its contempt, ran his obituary under the headline, "Oral Roberts: Insane or Con Artist?"[12]

Falwell, Roberts, and Robertson towered over American evangelicalism. Adored by many, reviled by many more, they shaped America in the latter half of the twentieth century. Their influence even reached beyond the United States. In the 1980s Nigerian entrepreneurs sold videotapes of preachers like Falwell, Jimmy Swaggart, and Roberts to young African ministers, who borrowed heavily from their American brethren's repertoire.[13] The stature of Roberts, Falwell, and Robertson as revered leaders was such that their public remarks, no matter how extreme and polarizing, were accepted with equanimity by many followers. Their statements occasionally tested the limits of what most Americans could endure, and yet they were never rejected *en masse* by their millions of followers. In one extreme example in 2003, Robertson told viewers of his *700 Club* that it was wrong for the United States government to challenge the authority of Charles Taylor, the dictatorial president of Liberia whom an international court had indicted for crimes against humanity. "So we're undermining a Christian, Baptist president to bring in Muslim rebels to take over the country," objected Robertson. "And how dare the president of the United States say to the duly elected president of another country, 'You've got to step down?'" Robertson was less forthcoming about his $8 million investment in a gold-mining operation, secured under Taylor's government and threatened by his possible ouster. Some leading conservative evangelicals thought Robertson had gone too far with this self-serving assessment. Richard Land, head of the Southern Baptist Convention's public policy wing, came out in opposition to Robertson. Others remained loyal. An employee at Robertson's Christian Broadcasting Network charged that the media had repeatedly mischaracterized Robertson's relationship with the brutal African leader. Robertson, he claimed, cared first and foremost for the people of Liberia.[14]

The allegiance of the most dedicated followers seemed unassailable. Indeed, Robertson, Falwell, and Roberts were carried to exalted heights of leadership and influence on mysterious spiritual updrafts produced by the gently waving hands of constituents. With few relevant secular achievements, they conjured success under a dark cloud of constant ridicule from the media. And they did it on their own, starting their ministries in small and unpromising patches of soil that others had neglected to till.

Although these three men of the cloth polarized Americans, many evangelical Christians accepted their messages as legitimate communications from anointed men of God. When Oral Roberts told his television audience that he would die if he could not raise millions, critics penned editorials denouncing the healing evangelist as a fraud. An editorialist in the *Boston Globe* called it a stunt, like a fake "religious ransom note." Shortly after, Roberts told TV viewers that the Devil had skulked into his room at night: "I felt those hands on my throat, and he was choking the life out of me. I yelled to my wife." She came, rebuked Satan, and rescued him. Through it all, students, staff, and faculty at the ORU campus—many with doctorates from respected research universities—were largely unfazed. The editor of the school's student newspaper remarked, "Almost everything that happens around here is at some level supernatural." For this student, like many others, what was surprising was the controversy stirred by Roberts's comments. "I'm not thinking about Brother Roberts dying," said a university employee, "I'm thinking about what kind of wonderful things will be done by his healing team."[15]

Interestingly, Roberts, Falwell, and Robertson, despite never having made a significant contribution to the life of the mind—and often openly hostile to mainstream scholarship—founded universities that became important evangelical centers of learning. They made names for themselves as bold, charismatic ministers and then parlayed their spiritual credibility into educational endeavors that provided genuine intellectual leadership for millions of America's evangelicals.

Falwell's Liberty University is now the largest evangelical university in the world, with an undergraduate enrollment of over 21,000, with 11,500 on-campus students. Its debate team has won national recognition, and the school hosts a robust honors program. Since Falwell's death in 2007 the school has boosted its numbers and grown institutionally under the watchful eyes of Falwell's sons. Oral Roberts University enrolls over 2,500 traditional undergraduates and has been ranked "Best of the West" by the prestigious Princeton Review. Its endowment has climbed to $34 million.[16] Robertson's Regent University has 1,500 undergraduates and a host of graduate and professional students. As of 2010 its endowment was almost $300 million, a staggering amount for an evangelical college. Regent also educated many of the lawyers in the Bush administration's Justice Department and boasted, at one point, that "approximately one out of every six Regent alumni is employed in some form of government work."[17]

These three schools also garnered a measure of academic credibility, at least in the eyes of the faithful. ORU, with some difficulty, gained accreditation from the North Central Association of Colleges and Secondary Schools in 1971. Roberts recalled visiting professors, on campus to judge the school's merit, coming to his office. He got the impression they thought he was a "dumb faith healer," incapable of heading up a university.[18] On the heels of televangelism success, Pat Robertson launched his school in 1978 as Christian Broadcasting Network University. It later changed its name to Regent University and gained accreditation in 1984 from the Southern Association of Colleges and Schools.[19] Like the fundamentalist Bob Jones University, Liberty University receives its accreditation from the specious Transnational Association of Christian Colleges and Schools, which the U.S. Department of Education recognizes as a national accrediting body, despite its requirement that schools be creationist. Liberty has had setbacks in gaining legitimacy. It sought state accreditation for its biology program in the early 1980s, but the ACLU opposed the effort, noting that a required science course, "History of Life," taught creationism. Liberty moved the class into the humanities department and won state accreditation for its biology program.[20]

Within much of the parallel culture of evangelicalism, academic credibility has very little to do with the ability to create and even run universities. Nor are academic credibility and academic credentials very closely related. Leaders like Falwell, Roberts, and Robertson—effective preachers with an impressive surface grasp of the Bible—would be considered solid teachers, even scholars, by many of their followers. The three appeared to fully understand theology and religion. "The Bible in the hands of the common person," wrote George Marsden in his penetrating analysis of fundamentalism, "was of greater value than any amount of education." In that spirit Falwell produced his *Liberty Bible Commentary* series, for which he served as executive editor, in the late 1970s and early 1980s.[21] Evangelical fans of these leaders often praised them for their serious biblical knowledge. Writing in an evangelical magazine in 2005, a Pentecostal minister reflected on the legacy of Oral Roberts. That giant of the faith "preached the Word of God . . . with a strong development of the text of the scriptures (not merely a few clever ideas or a superficial glossing of a passage)."[22]

Throughout the post-1960s era Falwell, Roberts, and Robertson were public symbols of the capacity of the parallel culture of American evangelicalism to anoint leaders using criteria internal to that culture—fidelity to the Bible, inspirational preaching, confident assertions of a special relationship to God. Their ability to make a television plea and raise millions of dollars was unmatched, as anyone can attest who has watched PBS struggle heroically over an entire "pledge week" to raise a few thousand dollars.

America is home to tens of millions of evangelicals, loosely bound together by shared beliefs and common values. The bonds are informal. Unlike in Roman Catholicism, no pope presides over an organized hierarchy of leaders reaching from exalted chambers in Rome, Italy, all the way down into the pews in Rome, Wisconsin. (Groups like the National Association of Evangelicals exist but are largely irrelevant, and the typical person in the pew would not even be aware of them.) The parallel culture of evangelicalism is like a country without monarchs or politicians. It must produce its own leaders, which it does, through informal processes. These leaders, both great and small, build constituencies more or less skillfully, but they generally employ similar strategies—finding themes around which to rally their followers, playing on common fears, identifying out-groups to demonize, and projecting confidence.

The homegrown organizational structure that does exist within evangelicalism is a loosely configured network of overlapping leaders, with new ones appearing regularly to fill vacancies created when elderly leaders die, or when younger leaders are defrocked and run off in scandal, or when a new generation simply wants something different. An incomprehensible "star-making" power is at work, and the audition bar can seem very low. In one extreme case, a child-preaching prodigy named Marjoe Goertner launched a lucrative preaching career that made *Ripley's Believe It or Not.* Ordained at age four, Marjoe crisscrossed the country delivering sermons to large crowds convinced that God had anointed him for this unique ministry.

Teen preachers compete in tournaments around the country, and some Pentecostal and charismatic groups encourage youngsters to preach, open to the possibility that God may have selected one of their children for a special role. Child evangelists like Uldine Utley and, more recently, Terry Durham, who was ordained at age six, have preached to enormous crowds. Not surprisingly, most evangelicals don't support child preachers and toddler revivalists.[23] But the fact that even a small segment within that community thinks that God might call to ministry a five-year-old boy or a six-year-old girl is startling. Francis Schaeffer's wayward son Frank, who rose up the evangelical ranks at a young age, noted in his biography, *Crazy for God,* that God's "anointing" seemed to be something that could be passed on to one's children. He called it the "proudly nepotistic American protestant tradition." In his words, "The Holy Spirit always seems to lead the offspring and spouses of evangelical superstars to 'follow the call.'"[24]

Fascinating mechanisms enable such divine appointments, whether it be children as preachers, or poorly educated preachers as university presidents, or marginally educated leaders functioning as academics. What confluence of factors empowers amateurs like Ken Ham and David Barton, or professional outsiders like James Dobson, or idiosyncratic Bible teachers like Tim LaHaye and Hal Lindsey to rise to national prominence until they wield intellectual authority over tens of millions of people? What winds carry them so comfortably past their credentialed and mainstream evangelical colleagues? Why do their books line the shelves of Christian bookstores, rather than the works of their fellow, well-credentialed evangelicals Francis Collins, Mark Noll, David Myers, and N. T. Wright? What draws followers—often well educated, sometimes with doctorates, employed in mainstream professions, raising wholesome families—to them?

No simple, one-size-fits-all explanation answers these questions, and each case is unique. But provocative similarities suggest that we can find partial explanations for the remarkable ascendency of people like Ham, Henry Morris, Barton, Dobson, Lindsey, and LaHaye.

The anointing phenomenon is deeply rooted in good old-fashioned American anti-intellectualism. It is supported by some specifically evangelical characteristics. And it is completed with the charisma and ingenuity of the individual leader. The phenomenon exploits these energies, combining them synergistically to make the whole more than the sum of its parts.

The widespread American enthusiasm for common sense shades smoothly and imperceptibly into anti-intellectualism. Many Americans have long objected to overly cerebral leaders who claim privileged expertise based on education and affiliation. Both the United States and England share a strain of populist anti-intellectualism that has been especially healthy within American religion. But unlike Britain, America has an open religious marketplace. The absence of a state religion encourages a robust culture of religious entrepreneurship and a never-ending supply of practitioners, with Oral Roberts being a classic example. Churches and individuals have vied for supporters, and some churches and religious leaders have done so by appealing to the lowest common denominator.[25]

Effective leaders unite individuals by creating well-defined in-groups with shared values and goals, and then find—or create—threatening out-groups. This strategy, of course, is not limited to religion: it is constantly on display in the United States as the country lurches from one election to the next. We have seen undocumented immigrants, Wall Street bankers, civil rights preachers, promoters of social justice or universal healthcare, supporters of any and all things European variously employed as politically useful out-groups to both create and empower in-groups.

In addition, in the evangelical world—in contrast to politics or the media—the supernatural plays a variety of roles: leaders can speak "for God" and claim that God speaks to them; outsiders can be *literally* demonized by suggesting that they are following Satan or are aligned with sinister forces of evil; a divinely inspired Bible can be selectively "interpreted" to provide authoritative sanction for the agenda; and urgency can be forced by exploiting widespread belief that "the end is near." In some cases leaders claim that God is bestowing special blessings or powers on them, which accounts for their success.[26] Christians self-identified as evangelicals, however, run along a broad spectrum on all these issues. Many evangelicals don't believe in Satan or demons, despise biblical "proof-texting," and have no interest whatsoever in dire apocalyptic forecasts. But many do believe their faith is besieged by secular, satanic forces, and this belief moves them to look to their anointed leaders for help in understanding what is going on and what they can do about it.

Anti-intellectualism, populism, a religious free market, in- and out-group dynamics, endorsement by God, and threats from Satan all combine to create a potent recipe for inspired leadership among American evangelicals. This recipe, which has long shaped American culture, bears further consideration.

"The mind of this country, taught to aim at low objects, eats upon itself," wrote Ralph Waldo Emerson in 1834, expressing a sentiment that others would echo into the present. Cynical Europeans and disaffected American intellectuals scoffed that the United States produced bankers, lawyers, and tailors but not scholars or poets. In the early twentieth century the French avant-garde artist Marcel Duchamp complained, with tongue in cheek, that "the only works of art America has given are her plumbing and her bridges."[27]

Historian Richard Hofstadter's classic work *Anti-Intellectualism in American Life* provides background for understanding the rise of evangelical leaders, and intellectual authorities, in particular. The book won the 1964 Pulitzer Prize for its trenchant analysis of America's "national disrespect for the mind." The Columbia University historian identified several factors, many dating back to the nineteenth century, that have contributed to America's interesting and troubled relationship with intellectuals. The factors that Hofstadter identifies are broader than religion, of course, but religion in America has long been deeply interwoven with the broader culture. Mutual interaction, both constructive and destructive, is ubiquitous. Hofstadter's list of anti-intellectual influences—which are not necessarily problems, in and of themselves—includes the *democratic impulse:* the polling booth certainly levels the playing field, placing equal weight on the votes of the Harvard professor and the janitor who cleans his office. If their opinions are equally valued in politics, then why should they not be similarly valued on questions of evolution or global warming? Every day, news reports of polls tell how many Americans think that the tax rate should be changed, or that intelligent design should be taught in schools, or that immigration policies should be tightened up. These reports appear to assume that such questions can be reasonably addressed by lay people on Main Street with no particular expertise. Every night on Fox News, for example, Sean Hannity chats with his "Great, Great American Panel" about the issues of the day. Typical panel members include country singers, football coaches, and former beauty queens. Rarely does more than one of the three panelists have any expertise related to the topic.

An emphasis on the practical knowledge of ordinary people in a new nation needing to build itself often trumped purely intellectual pursuits. The development of the railroad, for example, is a great national story immortalized in classic films and adventure tales; the discovery of the laws of thermodynamics that enabled the steam engine to pull cars behind it was the achievement of a forgotten scholar. Hofstadter laid blame on American public education, which, at least in principle, has been provided similarly for everyone, without the "tracking" that contributes to the creation of classes—and the emergence of genuine experts—in many countries.[28] Young Americans grow up believing they can do anything.

A half-century after Hofstadter wrote his book, populist leaders with varying religious affinities have moved to the center of American public life. Armed with simple explanations of the world, winsomely affirming that common people can think for themselves, they are often preferred to experts. Former Republican vice presidential candidate Sarah Palin expressed exactly this widespread disdain for intellectuals when she chided President Barack Obama for mishandling the war on terrorism: "We need a commander-in-chief, not a professor of law standing at the lectern," said Palin to hundreds gathered at a national Tea Party conference in early 2010.[29]

The identity politics that emerges in populist settings like the Tea Party movement—whether religious or not, though religion often plays a major role—creates the basis for well-defined in-groups, as people begin to think of themselves as part of a *movement,* inspired by a leader. After Palin resigned as governor of Alaska she devoted considerable time to building a conservative antiestablishment movement. She set her sights on East Coast elites and effete experts, long the focus of populist suspicion. Middle-class white evangelicals who followed her on Twitter embraced her in-group message of common-sense conservatism, even as she began to attract widespread criticism for her persistent public gaffs. In a review of Palin's memoir *Going Rogue,* Jonathan Raban summarized the appeal:

> Commonsense Conservatism hinges on the not-so-tacit assumption that the average, hardworking churchgoer . . . equipped with the fundamental, God-given ability to distinguish right from wrong, is in a better position to judge, on "principle," the merits of an economic policy or the deployment of American troops abroad than "the 'experts'"—a term here unfailingly placed between derisive quotation marks. Desiccated expertise, of the kind possessed by economists, environmental scientists, and overinformed reporters from the lamestream media, clouds good judgment; Palin's life, by contrast, is presented as one of passion, sincerity, and principle. *Going Rogue,* in other words, is a four-hundred-page paean to virtuous ignorance.[30]

A large portion of Palin's appeal—perhaps most of it—comes from religion, highlighted by Hofstadter as one of the chief culprits in his indictment of American anti-intellectualism. He describes religion, somewhat inadequately perhaps, as an "affair of the heart," not the mind. Rational faculties, while certainly not irrelevant to religion—think theology and hermeneutics—are nevertheless suspect, and sometimes even in competition with the intuitions of the "heart."[31] Certainly Oral Roberts's claim to have spoken with a 900-foot Jesus was a message of the "heart" and not the "head."

Because it began without state control, American religion has always had populist appeal, encouraging broad participation at the leadership level. In the early nineteenth century Methodists and Baptists welcomed unlettered ministers to the pulpit. A mid-century traveler through the Alleghenies commented on the Methodists and Baptists he met: "The people are ignorant, so far as book-learning is concerned," he observed, "but they are well supplied with common sense, and are industrious enough to deserve better success than the most of them enjoy."[32]

Evangelicalism in America owes much of its vitality to large-scale, highly emotional revivals, often called Awakenings. These were populist outpourings of religious fervor, which sometimes lasted decades: 1720s–1740s, 1795–1835, and 1850s–1900. (Some scholars label the evangelical surge in the late twentieth century a Fourth Great Awakening.)[33] All were affairs of the heart, as the spirit moved the faithful. Religious leaders in such movements often arose because they could draw a crowd, rather than because they held a place in an established hierarchy or were credentialed in some way. A booming, confident voice quoting the Bible and reciting platitudes was far more effective than quiet and informed commentary. Revivals thus undercut the time-honored authority of denominations by essentially truncating whatever intellectual content had been accumulated over the centuries. Mass revivals rarely whetted an appetite for book learning.[34]

To Hofstadter, the early twentieth-century fundamentalist preacher Billy Sunday embodied the dangerous and preposterous aspect of conservative Christianity. Sunday's denunciations of an educated clergy and biblical scholarship marked a new low, placing an exclamation mark on a conversation that was already embarrassingly uninformed. But even more broadly, Hofstadter worried about the crippling effects of sentimental Christianity on the larger world of ideas: "One begins with the hardly contestable proposition that religious faith is not, in the main, propagated by logic or learning. One moves on from this to the idea that it is best propagated . . . by men who have been unlearned and ignorant. . . . In fact, learning and cultivation appear to be handicaps in the propagation of faith."[35] Hofstadter pointed out a sobering 1914 poll of the readers of *American Magazine* on the question, "Who is the greatest man in the United States?" The poll revealed that the famous baseball player turned fundamentalist preacher Billy Sunday ranked eighth, tied with Andrew Carnegie.[36]

Hofstadter's work was the product of McCarthy-era concerns and, as it appeared in the early 1960s, is silent on the tumultuous social upheaval of that decade and the resurgence of the Religious Right that followed. No doubt Hofstadter would have had much to say if he had witnessed the transformation of rock musicians like Jim Morrison and John Lennon into guru-like leaders of a generation of young people. American anti-intellectualism persists into the present, of course, and continues to fascinate authors and readers alike. Books like Susan Jacoby's *Age of American Unreason* (2008) and Al Gore's *Assault on Reason* (2007) have risen up the bestseller list. In 2008 E. L. Doctorow penned a scathing essay on "unreason" in the *Nation.* "Two things must be said about knowledge deniers," he warned. "Their rationale is always political. And more often than not, they hold in their hand a sacred text for certification."[37] And there is no more authentic embodiment of this concern than Ken Ham, waving a Bible as he exhorts his listeners to reject much of modern science.

Taking his cue from Hofstadter and others, the respected historian Mark Noll analyzed evangelicalism's tortured relationship with modern science, disinterest in classic liberal arts education, and focus on the life of the spirit to the detriment of the life of the mind.[38] His 1994 book *The Scandal of the Evangelical Mind* cogently critiqued the intellectual poverty of evangelicalism and called for vigilance on the part of those concerned about the pervasive ignorance of their movement. Yet this was no sweeping dismissal of evangelicalism as a barren wasteland populated by quiet simpletons and loud charlatans, as Hofstadter portrayed it in *Anti-Intellectualism.* Unlike Hofstadter, Noll was a well-informed evangelical. In fact, he wrote *The Scandal of the Evangelical Mind* as "a wounded lover." "As one who is in love with the life of the mind, but who has also been drawn to faith in Christ through the love of evangelical Protestants," Noll remarked, "I find myself in a situation where wounding is commonplace." His book was equal parts heartfelt lament and stinging critique. He wondered, for instance, "whether evangelicalism as it has taken shape in North America contributes anything to the life of the mind."[39]

Whereas Hofstadter and other secularists painted with broad strokes, Noll looked closely to see just what had actually halted intellectual engagement. Evangelicals boasted of their seminaries, colleges, and Bible schools—some of which were outstanding—yet they sponsored no research universities. Stalwarts pointed with pride to their television and radio stations as well as to their successful parachurch organizations, yet most, in Noll's estimation, had "neglected sober analysis of nature, human society, and the arts."[40] Believers were utilitarians, who used knowledge as a means to an end. Millennialists studied the Middle East to better understand what might transpire in the last days. Missionaries in training at Bible schools read anthropology primarily to reach the heathen. Historians looked at America's founding to prove their righteous, presentist cause. Creationists learned the science of origins to refute it.

In the context of the development of Western civilization, with its long history of universities and printing presses started by Christians, all this pragmatic anti-intellectualism seemed counterintuitive. Christians had sponsored the intellectual revolutions of ages past. Christian themes had inspired the greatest art and literature produced in the premodern era. Many of the most renowned scientists—Copernicus, Galileo, Kepler, Newton—had been deeply committed Christians. Something had run off the rails somewhere.

The nineteenth- and twentieth-century American context, Noll reasoned, altered Christianity's course. He laid heavy blame on "the intellectual disaster of fundamentalism." That conservative movement's reaction to the academy and to nineteenth-century scholarship—higher criticism of the Bible and evolutionary biology being the most significant—squelched critical thinking for generations. The acute intellects within the movement—B. B. Warfield, Charles Hodge, R. A. Torrey—expended their energies defending biblical literalism against scholarly challenges. Under the sway of fundamentalism the evangelical community, in Noll's estimation, "gave birth to virtually no insights into how, under God, the natural world proceeded, how human societies worked, why human nature acted the way it did, or what constituted the blessings or perils of culture." Biblical literalism and a preoccupation with apocalyptic theology also shut out much light from other traditions. Fundamentalism, and related movements like holiness and Pentecostalism, bound up believers in an intellectual straitjacket.[41] Most important, Noll's book explained the origins of a religious movement in which a creationist, an apocalyptic theologian, or an amateur Christian historian—all out of touch with their putative fields and even the history of Christianity—could have so much influence.[42]

Years after the publication of Noll's insider's critique, Alan Wolfe took a sympathetic outsider's look at the "evangelical mind" in a wide-ranging essay in the *Atlantic Monthly.* While acknowledging that world-class evangelical scholars were appearing—Noll, Alvin Plantinga, Nicholas Wolterstorff—he noted that the best instincts of American evangelicalism worked against the kind of meritocratic structures that produced powerful intellects by advancing them ahead of lesser minds: "Wanting to ensure that everyone succeeds, [evangelicals] spawn a multiplicity of journals and publishing houses so that anyone can publish anything. They are as insistent on multicultural diversity as any good leftist. Evangelicals have created institutions as sensitive and caring as any in America. The downside of all this is that evangelicals sometimes find themselves with no adequate way of distinguishing between ideas that are pathbreaking and those that are gibberish."[43]

Wolfe concluded that the lamps of learning were perhaps starting to glow, but their future was uncertain because of inhospitable winds threatening to snuff them out. Even in the best-case scenario, evangelicalism, of all the religious traditions in America, observed Wolfe, "ranks dead last in intellectual stature."[44] Or as Noll had put it earlier, "The scandal of the evangelical mind is that there is not much of an evangelical mind."[45]

The fundamentalist end of the evangelical spectrum contains a culture that does indeed seem unable to distinguish between meaningful scholarship and what Wolfe has called "gibberish." Ken Ham places a dinosaur looking over Eve's shoulder in the Garden of Eden exhibit at his museum. Tourists pay to look at it and leave the Creation Museum believing that what they just saw is both scientific and biblical. Tim LaHaye inserts the emergence of a common European currency into the book of Revelation; David Barton converts Ben Franklin into a Bible-believing Christian; James Dobson claims that the institution of marriage has not changed for five thousand years. Absent a more vigorous intellectual mind, such ideas take root and flourish. And their spokespersons can function as authority figures.

This explanation is incomplete, however. It explains why intellectual authority can be obtained so cheaply in America, especially in the religious hinterland far from the ivory towers of secular academia. But it does not explain why particular individuals rise and others do not. It makes no distinction between the energy that feeds Ham's popularity and that which feeds equally uninformed but even more popular public figures like Sarah Palin, Glenn Beck, and Sean Hannity, or for more secular consumers, Oprah Winfrey and Judge Judy.[46] The supporters of Ham and Palin, to make a simple comparison, identify in important ways with them and their message. Ham and Palin speak for some group of followers—with considerable overlap—who hear in their messages something that rings true. The strength of the bond between them and their followers depends on several factors that reinforce and build on one another. In particular, such leaders project a charismatic trustworthiness that makes them *sound* like they know what they're talking about.

The perceived trustworthiness of the messenger greatly influences the acceptance of the message. Research at Yale University's Cultural Cognition Project looked at this phenomenon by studying how people respond to arguments. Arguments, of course, rarely arrive in disembodied form, as syllogisms dropped from the sky. They are, instead, delivered by people who may or may not be known to their audience; they are rhetorically packaged; they may or may not be "logical"; they provide certain motivations for their acceptance but not others; they assume background knowledge; and so on.

Dan Kahan of Yale University Law School explored the question of why so many people chose not to vaccinate their children when the evidence was so clear that doing so was the prudent course of action. Bogus counterarguments, he noted, were persuading many parents to reject the consensus of the medical community and follow marginal, uninformed "experts" from outside the medical establishment. Kahan's group found "that individuals' assessments of the substance of the arguments is highly influenced by the fit between individuals' cultural values and the perceived values of the experts making the arguments." People, not surprisingly, more readily follow experts they know or perceive as being like them, even if their expertise is marginal or even suspect.[47] We seek various "cultural cues" that connect us to the expert as a shortcut for determining veracity. Someone just like us is more likely to tell us the truth, we intuit, than is a famous egghead from a far-off university with whom we have nothing in common.

"To figure out what sorts of factual information we can reasonably rely on," Kahan explains, "we make use of all manner of cultural cues, many of which relate to the authority and trustworthiness of others, including people who hold themselves forth as experts." If the mantle of "expertise" is flexible enough that anyone can wear it, then authority can be had by simply making the right connections with one's audience.[48]

These assessment techniques are not without value; nor are they employed primarily by religious people. It makes sense to ask Uncle Joe, an amateur mechanic, for advice on your car, or your sister for insight into your romantic entanglements, for you can be sure that they have your best interests at heart. They share your background and values and thus think, more or less, as you would about such things. And they know you. "The cues we have settled upon really work," says Kahan. "If they didn't, we'd not have amassed as much scientific knowledge as we have as a species (indeed, if we weren't all experts ourselves on using cultural heuristics to figure out what and [whom] to believe, we'd all be dead)."[49]

This "cue-based epistemology" creates a dilemma. In a sense it simply shifts the argument from competing *facts* to competing *criteria* for authoritative cues. Kahan explains:

> These networks of crisscrossing cultural cues can indeed put culturally diverse citizens at cross purposes with one another. When that happens, the debates are usually pretty ugly. We are, in one sense, only arguing about "facts"—Is the earth heating up or not? Does allowing individuals to carry handguns in public increase crime or protect us from it?—but in another sense, we are arguing over something much more basic: whose cultural cues are valid, whose cultural authorities know what they are talking about, whose group is competent and entitled to respect and deference and whose is out of touch and contemptible.[50]

Other researchers have noted that misguided or incorrect ideas are stubborn, like deeply rooted weeds that keep coming back no matter how carefully you remove them. Political scientists have discovered that people resist abandoning cherished political beliefs, even when they are shown to be demonstrably false. Meaningful political participation may depend on an informed citizenry, but citizens are shaped by all sorts of ideas and values. Facts are just one among many variables. Some social scientists call this the "I know I'm right" syndrome.

If people feel insecure or threatened by new information—a standard evangelical reaction to learning about evolution—they are less likely to amend their views. A series of studies implied "not only that most people will resist correcting their factual beliefs," observed a University of Illinois political scientist, "but also that the very people who most need to correct them will be least likely to do so."[51] Michael Shermer treats this phenomenon at length in his fascinating book *Why People Believe Weird Things*.[52]

Evangelical experts "cue up" their argument by making it clear that they are presenting a biblical, overtly Christian, perspective. Ken Ham ably uses that rhetorical device to great effect. "Science is a wonderful tool that God has given us," he remarked in 2008. Yet, he convincingly stated, "science is imperfect, and changing, and because different scientists disagree on what the evidence really means, science cannot serve as an ultimate, infallible standard. . . . But science is not the limit of possibility, and thus is not in a position to judge the Bible upon which it depends."[53]

Ham's argument here is widely employed by evangelical intellectual leaders. Because all fields of study—history, psychology, natural science—are steadily *advancing,* they are constantly *changing.* This means that the science of today may very well be replaced by the science of tomorrow, just as the science of yesterday was replaced. It follows that we need not embrace the science of today.

Al Mohler, the president of Southern Baptist Theological Seminary, made this point most effectively in a 2010 address on the importance of young earth creationism. Mohler, whom *Time* called the "reigning intellectual of the evangelical movement in the U.S.," believes that the Bible is inerrant and must be interpreted literally, although his forays into speculative end-times prophecy might lead one to conclude otherwise.[54] Science, or "general revelation," must not be allowed to "trump special revelation" (the Bible). Mohler speaks with a calm and warm assurance. He is articulate, well educated, and the president of one of the largest seminaries in the world. His Christian credentials are impeccable. He projects a confident assurance that forces his audience to take him seriously, whether or not he is speaking, to use Wolfe's term, "gibberish":

> Our only means of intellectual rescue, brothers and sisters, is the speaking God, who speaks to us in scripture, in special revelation. And it is the scripture, the inerrant and infallible word of God that trumps renderings of general revelation, and it must be so. Otherwise we will face destruction of the entire gospel in intellectual terms. When general revelation is used to trump special revelation, disaster ensues. And not just on this score. It's not just on the question of the age of the earth. What about other questions? The assured results of modern science. There is so much that is packed in that mental category, that intellectual claim. Just remember first of all that science has changed and has gone through many transformations. The assured results of modern science today may very well not be the assured results of modern science tomorrow. And, I can promise you, are not the assured results of science yesterday.[55]

Mohler's bold claims would require some expertise to address effectively. How, for example, would a Christian medical doctor know how to respond to the claim that science changes, and that while the "assured result of modern science" today is that Earth is billions of years old, perhaps that will change tomorrow? After all, her field of medicine is constantly changing. How could she possibly evaluate the staying power of the current geological consensus, or the likelihood that quantum mechanics would be replaced by a better theory? How would a Christian engineer know what to make of the claim that "when general revelation is used to trump special revelation, disaster ensues," when that claim is made by an important theologian? The situation gets even more complex given that well-credentialed experts stand behind the positions promoted by people like Mohler. Were Mohler challenged by the scientific absurdity of an earth 100,000 times younger than the scientific consensus, he could invoke Dr. Kurt Wise, a young earth creationist who earned his Ph.D. at Harvard studying under Stephen Jay Gould. Or Dr. Paul Nelson, with a Ph.D. from the University of Chicago. Or Dr. John Marks Reynolds, with a Ph.D. from the University of Rochester. In a real controversy over the age of Earth, it would come down to which experts seemed the most trustworthy.

Christian audiences, understandably bewildered by competing claims about the age of Earth, human origins, the nature of homosexuality, the religion of the Founding Fathers, genetic engineering, or raising children, often hear two very different arguments. One argument comes from an unknown but well-credentialed scientist who works at a famous but very liberal university that used to be a Christian institution. This case is made with no consideration of how this new information fits within the larger framework of Christian theology and whether the new facts challenge other deeply held beliefs. The other argument comes from a fellow believer and is couched in specifically biblical terms; the more academic argument is critiqued as both uncertain and incompatible with Christian beliefs. The credentials and affiliations might not be as impressive, and the science/history/psychology might even be a bit thin, though that would be challenging to determine. But all the relevant cues indicate that the argument is trustworthy, largely because of who is making it.

By effectively exploiting cultural cues, evangelical leaders resonate with their audiences and quickly become insiders—members of the tribe. In the passage above Mohler calls his audience "brothers and sisters." The faithful who identify with each other as a well-defined in-group empower leaders to tap into this identity with the right message and assume the role of spokesperson for the group, a far more powerful position than simply being an expert instructor speaking from outside. Evangelicals see one another, in commonly used language right out of the Bible, as "brothers and sisters in Christ." They share the most important experience available to humans—salvation. A public figure—politician, educator, minister—who shares that experience and can witness to it with clarity is embraced wholeheartedly. Antony Flew immediately went from despicable atheist to religious hero when he started believing in God. The faithful forgave decades of aggressive criticism of their religious beliefs.[56]

The cultural cues that Kahan and others have identified are a fundamental part of our human nature—our need to belong to each other, to have a group identity, and to embrace leaders we can trust. These needs are deeply rooted in our genes, although they function at the emotional and cognitive level. They are a much deeper part of our human nature than the education we acquire over the course of our lives. Secular critics of evangelical "gibberish" generally fail to understand the "cue-based epistemology" that is so often preferred to conventional expertise.

Kahan's research is illuminated and largely explained by our evolutionary history. Humans originated in Africa in tribes that were essentially extended families, which meant they shared many genes. Such environments favored the evolution of genetically based altruism toward the members of one's tribe. Tribes whose members looked out for each other—sharing food and shelter, protecting the helpless, standing guard in the face of danger—would be more successful than tribes in which members might be perfectly content to let their kin starve, even though they had extra food.[57]

Analysis of gene frequencies in tribal-sized populations shows that genes for altruism can flourish and spread if there is a high probability that the organisms benefiting from the altruism are related. In helping your neighbor flourish and eventually reproduce, you are helping a relative who, by definition, has many of the same genes as you. You are, quite literally, contributing to the welfare of your extended family's gene pool. The great evolutionary biologist J. B. S. Haldane, to illustrate the way that sacrificing one's own life can actually rescue one's genes, once quipped, "I would lay down my life for two brothers or eight cousins."[58]

Genetically based altruism, however, functions *indirectly.* Parents passionately love the children handed to them by the doctors at the hospital. The newborns' genomes are not written on their foreheads or tagged on their toes, so there is, technically, nothing more than a "belief" that this baby is one's biological offspring. Babies switched at birth are loved by their "wrong" parents just as much as they would have been loved by their biological parents. Adopted children are similarly loved by their parents, with few exceptions. Moving out from immediate relatives, altruism naturally extends to an increasing circle of less closely related people, although it weakens with genetic distance. (You tend to love your first cousin more than your second cousin.)

This genetically based altruism is indiscriminate and often misfires to the good of society. Humans are hard-wired—genetically programmed—to build extended family-type relationships with people who may biologically be nonrelations. Because we evolved in a tribal setting, there was a rough equation between "people we encounter regularly" and "people to whom we are related." In the modern world this equation is much less accurate, which is why it is so easy to build meaningful and familial-like relationships with people as long as they seem to be a member of our "tribe." These conclusions are part of an active and cutting-edge exploration of the implications of evolutionary theory and are not without controversy. But it is unlikely that such effects can be fully explained in any other way.[59]

Novelist Stephen Crane's short story "The Open Boat," based on actual events, illustrates this phenomenon powerfully and provides a wonderful microexample of how group identity is generated. Crane shared a dinghy with strangers from a ship that sank in a storm. The threatening situation created strong bonds as the castaways took turns rowing and navigating the craft to safety, united physically and emotionally against the elements. Reflecting on the event later he said, "It would be difficult to describe the subtle brotherhood of men that was here established on the seas."[60]

Philosopher of biology Elliott Sober and evolutionary biologist David Sloan Wilson suggest that Crane's story, written decades before evolutionary psychology would begin to explain such powerful experiences, shows a great deal about how the mind works. "Situations of this sort," they write, "in which the members of a group are bound together by the prospect of a common fate—have been encountered throughout human evolution, with important fitness consequences, so it is reasonable to expect that we are psychologically adapted to cope with them."[61]

Because altruistic team-building is flexible, humans easily form familial bonds with any group with whom they share the right kind of experiences—an athletic team, passengers stranded in an airport, classmates in college, childhood friends who might even be of another race and speak a different language. Psychologist Michael Gazzaniga notes that such coalitions are widespread among all the social mammals—chimpanzees, dolphins, and humans: "They are endemic among humans, who organize themselves spontaneously into mutually exclusive groups. There are the sugar people and the salt people, farmers and herders, dog lovers and cat lovers." Evidence even exists for a "specialized [brain] module that codes for coalition recognition."[62]

Closely knit groups, in which the altruistic impulse is strongest, by definition cannot grow arbitrarily large. In *The Tipping Point,* Malcolm Gladwell notes several lines of research suggesting that 150 serves as an upper bound on the number of people who can meaningfully participate in a tightly knit group where the members would all know one another and be excited about shared ideas. "If we want groups to serve as incubators for contagious messages," he writes, "we have to keep the groups below the 150 Tipping Point."[63] This, of course, is an average with the possibility of variation.

Many social organizations in the modern world unconsciously draw on the power of our tribal instincts. But it would be hard to locate a more natural tribal organization than that which emerges at so many levels within religious communities. By way of reference, the median Protestant congregation in the United States has seventy-five members, comfortably within the limits of tribal instincts.[64] And megachurches with ten thousand members invariably create special programs to ensure that their members are well connected to smaller groups, as well as to the larger congregation. Ken Ham and David Barton speak frequently to church congregations.

In the parallel culture of evangelicalism a believer might take part in several small groups. Typical examples include a Sunday school class, a weeknight Bible study, a mothers' group where a church employee might look after children so their mothers can socialize with other members, various church committees, and the congregation as a whole. Members of a particular congregation understand that they are part of a larger denomination that includes many sister congregations—sibling tribes. When evangelicals travel, they often seek out a church of their own denomination, anticipating that they will be at home there. They sing familiar songs, read accustomed passages from the Bible, and hear a recognizable sermon while sitting among strangers they consider their "brothers and sisters in Christ." Often they will be invited to lunch by people they just met. Believers also understand that their denominations are joined by like-minded denominations, but only up to a point.[65]

Evangelicals, for the most part, are not overly ecumenical by nature.

The entrepreneurial world of American Protestantism encourages everyone with a "new and better Christianity" to split off into another group. The constant splintering of denominations since the early nineteenth century—mini-reformations—attests to that phenomenon. The tribal instincts that bind groups bifurcate them when subgroups become convinced that something is wrong.

Prominent evangelical leaders thus need strategies to unite disparate groups that might be distrustful of one another. The best way to do this is to create a hostile "out-group," which can transform rivals into what Francis Schaeffer called co-belligerents. "A co-belligerent," wrote Schaeffer in his influential 1980 book *Plan for Action,* "is a person with whom I do not agree on all sorts of vital issues, but who, for whatever reasons of their own, is on the same side in a fight for some specific issue of public justice."[66] In-group solidarity is strengthened by the presence of well-defined out-groups that function as a common enemy.

This effect is powerful. If a class of children is divided and made to compete with one another in basketball, considerable aggression and even hostility toward friends can almost immediately be summoned. More significantly, a genuinely threatening out-group can create real enduring hostility that doesn't go away when the game is over. According to a prominent American psychologist, "the perception that an out-group constitutes a threat to in-group interests or survival creates a circumstance in which identification and interdependence with the in-group is directly associated with fear and hostility toward the threatening out-group and vice versa."[67] This is true regardless of the religious affiliations involved. In fact, religion often increases the tensions.

A 2010 study revealed provocative—and disturbing—connections between religiosity and racism. The study sought to uncover subtle connections that operate subconsciously. Few Christians—or people in general—will admit to being racist, of course, and many take offense at the suggestion of any link between their faith and racism. But researchers have found that when white evangelical college students were "religiously primed" by focusing on issues of faith, "their covert racism did increase" and they "were more likely to agree that they dislike blacks." The researchers inferred that "religious thoughts seem to trigger racist thoughts." Their explanation was based entirely on group identity: "religion tends to increase benevolence toward co-religionists, but can increase hostility toward outsiders."[68]

A 1999 study of college students in Canada, generally considered a bastion of tolerance, found that "prejudice against religious out-group members is pervasive." The findings also suggested that "fundamentalism is particularly predictive of out-group derogation."[69] As of this writing, widespread demonization of Muslims is being used to promote solidarity among conservative white Americans. Such tactics are overtly political, but they are enhanced because religious identity is so powerful.

In the 1990s evangelicals set aside their considerable historic quarrels with Catholicism and joined forces with Catholics to battle social evils like abortion and homosexuality. They did not make peace out of common cause, celebrating their joint commitment to Christianity and reverence for the 1,500 years when Catholicism carried Western European Christianity. This was but rhetorical veneer glossed on a commitment to fight a common enemy. A book written by two of the leaders of this historic rapprochement asked, "Can evangelicals and Roman Catholics be allies in the culture wars now being waged against Christian beliefs and values?" In their response they spoke of a "united front against the onslaught of publicly sanctioned unbelief in the land," and the need to seek enough common ground "to engage the larger enemy of skepticism that threatens the country's foundations."[70]

A common enemy capable of bridging the vast gap between Protestants and Catholics can certainly unite swaths of bickering Protestants. It is thus no surprise that evangelical leaders define themselves and their agenda in partially and even largely negative terms, defending the

Christian faith against threats—real and imaginary—from outside. James Dobson and Focus on the Family have energetically sought to defend traditional marriage by rallying forces to oppose gay marriage. One of the first pages from David Barton's WallBuilders website calls for restoring the "foundation on which America was built: a foundation which, in recent years, has been seriously attacked and undermined."[71] Ken Ham's rhetoric is loaded with military metaphors. A popular poster produced by Answers in Genesis shows two castles with Christian soldiers shooting cannons at secular soldiers. One is built on the foundation of "Evolution: Man Decides Truth," and the other on "Creation: God's Word is Truth." Countless other teaching materials use similar military themes and are available for download at the Answers in Genesis website. But few could be more committed to fighting the enemies of faith than Tim LaHaye, whose *Left Behind* series chronicles literal—and incredibly violent—battles between Christians and their secular foes.[72]

This conflict model is part of the cultural DNA of evangelicalism—and of all human groups for that matter—but it gets its power from actual DNA, developed over eons of evolution to deal with more serious threats. Much of the movement's history and theology have been defined in opposition to the Protestant mainstream, Catholicism, or secularism. Chief religious figures throughout the twentieth century warned believers of menacing forces outside the gates: Higher Criticism, Rum, Romanism, Evolution, Mormonism, Modernism, Communism, and Socialism. Two prominent mid-twentieth-century evangelical leaders, Harold Ockenga and Carl Henry, spoke in grave tones of the satanic threats encircling the faithful. "Darkness has engulfed our age," wrote Ockenga in typical fashion in 1947. "Sin, fear, hate, doubt, distrust, and despair characterize the dominant mood of this day." Evangelicals, to varying degrees, sense that a boundary divides them from a menacing secular world. The fiery jeremiad, rather than splintering or devastating the movement with incredulity, has often unified it. So when Ockenga thundered that "all nations including the United States have abandoned the Christian principles of civilization," the truly devout heard it as a call to arms.[73]

Evangelical leaders have similar notions of the enemy their followers are summoned to fight. The foe can be an apostate, compromising, or otherwise dangerous religion, but it is often simply secularism. In the calculus of the righteous, one is either a force for good or a force for evil. "You are either for Christ or against him," Ham tells his audiences.[74] There is no middle ground.

Secularism, instead of being a place where the religious and antireligious might find common ground, is typically a euphemism for "anti-God." After all, it was secularists who lobbied to remove prayer from schools and secularists who are trying to get "In God We Trust" off United States currency. Whether these agitators are viewed as antireligious or simply nonreligious depends very much on one's perspective. Secularists object to the Ten Commandments being displayed in courthouses or nativity scenes appearing on public property at Christmas. Indeed, in 2006 Judge Roy Moore looked back on his recent career with clarity of vision. "As the former chief justice of the Supreme Court of Alabama," Moore recalled, "I lost my position because I chose to follow God and the United States Constitution, our rule of law, instead of a federal judge's unlawful order commanding me to remove a Ten Commandments monument from the rotunda of the Alabama state judicial building." Moore was certain that "*the* most important issue facing our country is whether we will choose to acknowledge God and His sovereignty or continue down the path of destruction paved by secular humanism."[75]

Millions of evangelicals are frustrated that the country and many of its institutions are no longer led by people like them. Secularists, especially, in influential arenas like the Supreme Court, seem to be in charge now and are ruling in ways that evangelicals find alienating and even hostile. To varying degrees, depending on local conditions, this concern is understandable. The spot near city hall where the nativity scene appeared faithfully and without controversy for generations now sits empty, or perhaps is occupied by Santa's sleigh and reindeer. Over decades and centuries major universities have abandoned their erstwhile Christian missions. Some of them have become known as redoubts of intolerance for evangelicals. When the agnostic Steven Pinker, one of America's leading and most antireligious public intellectuals, walks to his office through the main entrance at Harvard, he passes the Johnson Gate. The former mission of America's greatest university, composed by Puritans, is inscribed there: "After God had carried us safe to New England, and wee had builded our houses, provided necessaries for our livelihood, rear'd convenient places for Gods worship, and setled the Civill Government: One of the next things we longed for, and looked after was to advance Learning and perpetuate it to Posterity; dreading to leave an illiterate Ministery to the Churches, when our present Ministers shall lie in the Dust."

These words, written in the seventeenth century as Harvard College was being conceived, are in marked contrast to the decision of that university, four centuries later, to reject a proposal for a general education requirement in "Reason and Faith." Pinker led faculty opposition to the proposal on the grounds that it implied that both reason and faith were paths to truth. "[R]eason and faith are not yin and yang," he told *Newsweek.* "Faith is a phenomenon. Reason is what the university should be in the business of fostering."[76]

Outside the ivory towers even clearer demonstrations of America's steady secularization are in evidence. Prayer, mandatory chapel attendance, Bible reading, and other symbols of the Christian faith are gone from the public schools; evolution is pressed as the only legitimate account of origins; and discussion of a role for God in evolution is not even allowed. Abortion, homosexuality, and sex-change operations are all part of public discourse now and are starting to lose their cultural stigma. Promiscuous, pot-smoking rock stars sneer at traditional sexual mores. Playboy bunnies have primetime reality shows. Celebrities leak personal sex tapes to advance their careers.

In Judge Moore's words, the enemy responsible for so much that had ruined the country could be summed up in one phrase: *secular humanism.* This vague, catchall description has become a monolithic worldview in the eyes of evangelical culture warriors, who are enlisted to challenge it. "Most people today do not realize what humanism really is, and how it is destroying our culture, families, country—and, one day, the entire world," LaHaye wrote in *Battle for the Mind* in 1980, using language Francis Schaeffer had brought into common usage. "Most of the evils in the world today can be traced to humanism, which has taken over our government, the UN, education, TV, and most of the other influential things in life."[77]

Ham said the same thing in his 2010 "State of the Nation" address. After repeatedly telling his audience that there was no "neutral position" between a Christian view based on a literal reading of the Bible and a view he describes as the "religion of atheism," and taking Christians to task for agreeing with the atheists that evolution is true, he laid out the familiar paradigm of biblical Christianity versus secular humanism: "Atheists won't compromise with the Christians but they love the Christians compromising with them, and they use them for their own agenda—to do what? To change the foundation in this nation—to change it from one built on God's word to one built on man's word—from a Christian worldview to a secular worldview. It's an incredible spiritual battle in this nation between Christianity and secular humanism, and unfortunately the church, by and large, is on the side of secular humanism."[78]

Ham blames secular humanism for gay marriage, abortion, and other social evils. There is no gray area in this worldview, no common territory, no spectrum of positions shading from biblical literalism through more moderate expressions of Christianity and friendly secularism to hostile atheism. "Christians," even evangelicals like Francis

Collins, whose public faith raised the ire of the secularists when President Obama appointed him head of the National Institutes of Health in 2009, fall under his sweeping indictment for being "compromisers" and are, ultimately, on the side of the secular humanists.[79]

Secular humanism is an important enemy for those who wield intellectual authority within evangelicalism. It is complex, in need of special attention. It is sinister, demanding a response. It is immediately present, generating clear-cut social and moral problems, from rampant promiscuity to ethical relativism. It has visible and highly symbolic villains, like the notorious and antireligious atheists Bertrand Russell, Madalyn Murray O'Hair, Christopher Hitchens, and Richard Dawkins. Anyone can wage war against pornography or liquor licenses, but it takes a real sage to reveal the widespread threat posed by the secular humanism conspiracy. Ironically, secular humanism *per se* is a tiny, insignificant movement. In 2006, the American Humanist Association claimed only three thousand members. The group's *Humanist Magazine* has a very modest circulation.[80]

The shadowy and tenuous character of secular humanism is not an argument against its reality or efficacy, however. It is an argument for its *subtlety.* A clandestine invisible power, without apparent resources, dedicated armies, or physical structures, working against God, is almost a definition of Satan for many evangelicals. In some of the more extreme views, Satan, and demons in particular, have an overt physical presence, manifested as demon possession, as hallucinations, or in other dramatic ways. More typically Satan is viewed as a quiet tempter who persuades people in certain directions without seeming to do so. A nudge in the direction of pornography or unfaithfulness, a rationalization of white lies, withholding support for the church, or self-promoting pride would all be evidence for the subtle persuasive presence of Satan. Such influences would be largely countered, for Christians, by the presence of God. For unbelievers, however, who don't believe in Satan, the story is very different. They are under the influence of a powerful, subtle, and highly persuasive personality encouraging them to wage political, economic, cultural, and even conventional war against God's faithful followers.

Astute evangelical leaders, though they almost all believe in Satan, avoid public comments about that belief and almost never provide an extended discussion of how Satan is working against them. Getting specific about Satan invites ridicule in the media in ways that talking about God's action does not. When leading fundamentalist theologian Norman Geisler, for example, admitted on the stand in the 1981–1982 Arkansas creationism trial that UFOs were "a satanic manifestation in the world for the purpose of deception," he received an onslaught of media derision, and his effectiveness as an expert witness was effectively demolished.[81]

The most remarkable exposition on the subtle workings of Satan by a leading evangelical intellectual would have to be Henry Morris's book *The Long War against God.* In this substantial work, published by a major evangelical publishing house and endorsed by many fundamentalist leaders, Morris unfolded an elaborate thesis that Satan has worked with great subtlety for thousands of years to build support for evolution. "Satan," he wrote, "is a very real being and one of his deceptive devices is to persuade a certain class of intellectuals that the natural world is all there is."[82] One intellectual influenced by Satan was Alfred Wallace, whose codiscovery of natural selection prompted the reluctant Darwin to finally publish his more developed theory. Morris made much of the fact that evolution came to Wallace in a "moment of strange radiance" while he was in "the throes of a two hour malarial fit." Wallace's thoughts, speculated Morris, "were being directed by some intelligent entity or entities outside himself."[83]

Belief in Satan is widespread but far from universal among evangelicals, and there is great ambiguity in the results. A 2007 Reuters poll found that 62 percent of Americans as a whole believed in hell and the Devil.[84] Presumably this percentage would be higher for evangelicals. A

2004 Gallup poll showed that 70 percent of Americans believed in hell, which is closely associated with belief in Satan. A similar poll revealed that 55 percent believed in the Devil in 1990. By 2004 that number had climbed to 70 percent. Other data from the Pew Forum on Religion and Public Life showed that belief in hell dipped from 2001 to 2008. Of 35,000 Americans surveyed in 2008, 59 percent claimed to believe in a hell "where people who have led bad lives, and die without being sorry, are eternally punished." Of those who were evangelicals, though, 82 percent agreed with that statement.[85]

Ken Ham, James Dobson, Tim and Beverly LaHaye, Peter Marshall, Hal Lindsey, and other like-minded evangelical leaders believe they are engaged in a spiritual war with Satan. The late Peter Marshall wrote on his blog in 2010 that "Satan hates all things Christian, and seeks to destroy Christians altogether instead of being satisfied to make them merely less influential." In fact the Devil, claimed Marshall, would "not allow an increasingly secular society to leave Christians alone to mind their own business."[86] Dobson, too, expressed alarm at the workings of Satan, whom he blamed for sex scandals involving Focus on the Family employees. One such incident involved an "ex-gay" who had been "cured" of his homosexuality but reverted back, a particularly embarrassing revelation when it became public. Dobson told his employees in a recorded message that "Satan has thrown just about everything in his arsenal at us in the last several weeks as you know."[87] Ham is quite frank about Satan's strategy. "Satan knows," he said on one of his podcasts, "that if people doubt the book of Genesis and they start questioning what God said at the very beginning, then this will eventually lead to them not believing the rest of the Bible."[88] It was a theme he had emphasized for decades.[89]

Easy, natural invocations of Satan are rhetorically powerful. The audiences for key evangelical leaders, for the most part, grew up believing that Satan is real. Many of them would believe they had seen Satan at work, or at least heard compelling stories from fellow Christians who had. Missionaries regularly visit Nazarene, Wesleyan, Assemblies of God, and Southern Baptist Convention churches, telling stories of far-off lands and battles between forces of light and darkness. Evangelical novelist Frank Peretti scored major hits with his books *This Present Darkness* (1986) and *Piercing the Darkness* (1988). The latter had sold 1.4 million copies by the mid-1990s. Described by some as a fundamentalist Stephen King, Peretti regaled his readers with tales of violent spiritual warfare in small-town America. Human characters acted out the divine dramas of the invisible world. Angels and demons fought hand-to-hand combat in his novels, powered by the prayer of believers or the wickedness of sinners. The novels' arch-villains include New Age gurus, public school educators, psychologists, and academics. All were under the influence of Satan.[90] These novels confirmed and brought to life what millions of evangelicals believed about God, the Devil, and the supernatural. Such believers grow up reading miracle stories in the book of Acts or divine punishments meted out in the book of Genesis. Peretti put a modern spin on these timeless biblical truths, and, though his novels were works of fiction, many readers shared the view of spiritual warfare on which they were based.[91]

Whatever the realities of satanic opposition, they are no match for the power of God. In traditional Christian theology, Satan is on a short leash controlled by God. The Devil is ambiguously empowered to work his nefarious will. God's will, by contrast, is outlined in the Bible. Fundamentalists, and the majority of evangelicals, believe that the Bible contains the literal words of God. Some even believe that God "dictated" scripture to divine scribes in such a way that it would remain forever true and relevant, whether the topic was physics, history, or ethics.

In a debate on beliefnet.com, Ham presented this view with clarity: "I do believe God's Word is the absolute authority," he said. The Bible "is the foundational starting point for my worldview philosophy." The alternative, what he called "the majority opinion of secular scientists," is simply not acceptable: "My position is that the Bible is the ultimate authority providing the general framework by which all claims and evidences should be evaluated . . . apart from the foundation of the Bible, we couldn't really know anything for certain."[92] Ham's Answers in Genesis website contains countless articles elaborating on this starting point, explaining how every biblical reference to the natural world is completely consistent with contemporary science, as Ham and his followers understand it.

A 2008 Pew survey showed that 59 percent of evangelicals polled have exactly the same view as Ham and consider the Bible the "Word of God" to be taken "literally word for word." That contrasted with those in mainline churches, only 22 percent of whom agreed with the statement. And only 23 percent of Catholics held that belief.[93]

Whenever conservative evangelical leaders can link their cause to the Bible, the stronger their arguments become. When David Barton proclaims that evangelicals must take back their country and get out, register, and vote, he fits a Bible verse into the injunction. Barton notes that Jesus says, "Go be salt. Go be light."[94] In a powerful and compelling presentation titled "Is America a Christian Nation?" Barton speaks eloquently and without notes while standing in front of an enormous American flag. His audience—a Baptist congregation—listens in rapt wonder, laughing on cue, nodding their heads or murmuring approval wherever appropriate. Barton shows engaging slides of the Founding Fathers; he holds up the first English Bible printed in America "by congress." He calls for Americans to think about the Christian foundations of their nation. "Blessed is that nation whose God is the lord," he quotes from Psalm 33:12. The first Americans, he says with conviction, tried harder than any other nation to "apply biblical principles" and "God blessed that. He responded to that." But the nation has lost its way. "If the foundations be destroyed, what shall the righteous do?" he asks, rhetorically, quoting Psalm 11:3, the same Bible verse that Ham uses on a popular poster of the war between Creation and evolution. Barton reminds his audience that they are the "righteous."[95] His message weaves into a biblical message; his listeners are the people of God; his agenda is God's agenda; he is God's man of the hour. "Go be salt. Go be light."

By connecting their objectives to the Bible, leaders draw the faithful into a larger story—the grandest story of all time. If God has promised to bless nations that honor him, and if the United States is running downhill now because its leaders have abandoned God, then what an opportunity to join the cause of recovering God's favor! Juxtaposing Bible verses and key agenda items powerfully amplifies those items needing attention—creationism and prayer in the schools, Christian faith as the foundation of the country, biblical morality in both public and private life, unwavering support for Israel, vouchers for Christian schools.

The Bible also promises that God will bless those who do his will. Direct approval from God, of course, legitimates any agenda. Evidence of miracles and a focus on the direct workings of God are powerful. Evangelicals as a group—and this would be close to universal—accept the reality of God's intervention in some form in the course of events, though such intervention is not always understood as supernatural.[96] The internationally popular Pentecostal faith healer Benny Hinn claims to have spoken to a billion people and has drawn millions to his healing rallies all over the world.[97] Hinn, who embodies the extreme end of the spectrum, performs healings on television, and through the power of God claims to cure cancer, dissolve tumors, restore sight, and eliminate diabetes on camera, in prime time, in front of huge audiences. More mainstream evangelicals like Francis Collins, N. T. Wright, or Mark Noll would think of God's intervention as more subtle—helping along the healing process, motivating donors to be generous for a good cause, encouraging certain social outcomes. Such phenomena are less spectacular and certainly not compelling evidence for the presence of God in the same way as instantaneous healings. Any kind of miracle, of course, is an unqualified endorsement from God. A credible claim to have received such a miracle is thus a powerful invitation to get involved in whatever project God has decided to bless.

When Ham was raising money to build the Creation Museum, he wrote, in language familiar to any evangelical: "It will take many months of planning and securing the necessary building permits, but my hope is that God will lead His people to support the museum." The implication was clear: If you support his project, you are one of God's people.[98]

Evangelicals are committed to the reality of divine miracles because the Bible is filled with miracles.[99] And though more liberal evangelicals might deny the historicity of some biblical miracles—God's stopping the sun in the sky at Joshua's request or causing an axe head to float on water—miracles like the resurrection of Jesus are simply not up for debate, except at the extreme liberal end of the evangelical spectrum, where it begins to shade over into more mainline understandings of Christianity. It would be fair to say that one could not be a true evangelical and deny the *possibility* of miracles, even though many evangelicals have never experienced anything they would call a supernatural miracle in their own lives. More analytical evangelicals would hasten to point out that a "miracle" does not entail breaking the laws of nature. A miracle is simply an act of God that can be accomplished by working *through* rather than *against* the natural order.

The confidence that God has endorsed a project or a person is, understandably, a powerful incentive to embrace that cause. Who wouldn't respond positively if the creator of the universe reached out to them? If God and Ken Ham are building a museum together, then don't we all want to get involved? If David Barton's research into American history truly reveals that "God's fingerprints are evident throughout," then of course we will want to find out about that history.[100] By glossing their work with God's favor, evangelical leaders project the ultimate credibility.

Closely related is the belief that God "calls" Christians to their vocations. Such a call is the ultimate "credential," trumping more conventional qualifications like education, peer recognition, or even common sense. Speaking at Patrick Henry College about America's need for Christian leaders, James Dobson asked: "The question is will the younger generation heed the call?" And this was no generic motivational speech. "I pray that the Lord will anoint a new generation," he went on, "some of the best and the brightest of whom are in this room." These leaders, he said, must be "willing to die if necessary for what they believe."[101]

Claims that God has called a person to a particular position are ubiquitous among evangelicals. It is common—and almost universal—for evangelical leaders to announce to their communities that God has called them to their job or career. Almost every evangelical pastor believes that God has called them to their current assignment. The same is true for administrators at Christian colleges. Sometimes, after years of poor performance and growing concerns about their competence, they will announce that God has "called" them to some other position.[102]

Successful Christian leaders wield a constellation of strategies masterfully—in their public presentations, on their radio shows, in their writings. Most believe in the authenticity of their mission, as near as can be determined. Little evidence suggests insincerity or manipulation. In-group rhetoric unites them to their audience; out-group rhetoric tightens the ties that bind the in-group and enlarges it when necessary; carefully chosen biblical passages make them and their project God's will; God's blessing on their ministry and Satan's role in opposing it create a real tension, legitimizing a call to arms. And, often for good measure, a belief that the end is near creates urgency.

Provocative recent studies provide insight into the power that charismatic religious leaders wield over their audiences. A brain-imaging study looked at Pentecostal Christians while they were listening to prayers from different leaders, who were described as "a non-Christian, an ordinary Christian, and a Christian known for his healing powers." In reality they were all ordinary Christians, and the only difference was what the listener was told about them. Not surprisingly, the subjects "rated the one they were told was a healer as the most charismatic, and the person they thought was nonreligious as much less charismatic."[103]

Subjects reported that they did not sense God's presence in prayers said by what they thought were non-Christians. The researchers discovered that specific regions of the subjects' brains became "deactivated" when they listened to the person they believed was most charismatic. The "deactivated" regions were all associated with the part of the mind that evaluates and makes decisions. The researchers inferred that subjects who listened to trustworthy individuals deactivated their critical faculties. By contrast, when the subjects observed a presumed non-Christian, their critical faculties showed far more activity. The researchers also noted that the reaction bears some similarity to hypnotism.[104] These studies apply only to literal physical presentations, of course, but they illustrate the role played by trust in the communication of information.

The strategies outlined above are not specific to a handful of evangelical leaders. In fact, they would apply generally to great preachers and even charismatic secular leaders. Many of the most persuasive politicians are remarkably similar to great preachers, and some—Jesse Jackson comes to mind—are both. Great speeches and great sermons have much in common.

The ability of evangelical leaders to combine the persuasive powers of a great preacher with the credibility of an academic generates enormous intellectual authority. As purveyors of ideas, they are thus more powerful than either preachers or academics. In particular, this unique combination makes them much more effective than their more academic evangelical counterparts. When Francis Collins was launching his modest "on-line museum" at biologos.org, he made no grand assertions that God was helping with the project, despite his confidence that he was indeed doing God's will. He described the BioLogos project as "just initial efforts to help catalyze a community devoted to seeking harmony in science and faith."[105] This contrasted with the approach of Ham, who waxed eloquent about God's role in getting his museum finished, describing a fortuitous purchase of some exhibits as "one of many miracles in the history of this museum project."[106] Whereas Collins would tentatively hope—and pray—that his project was in line with the will of God, Ham would state with great confidence that his project was right on the bull's-eye of God's will.

The anointed leaders of American evangelicalism achieve their success precisely because of their ability to don the mantle of the academic while employing the communication strategies of the preacher. Whereas David Myers would deliver an engaging *lecture* on sexual orientation, James Dobson would deliver an engaging *sermon.* Ham shows pictures of natural phenomena—fossils or strands of DNA—while quoting Bible verses and warning about the dangers of unbelief. It is not an accident that Ham, Barton, Dobson, LaHaye, and others like them are all compelling public speakers—witty, comfortable, and articulate. Nor is it an accident that they are all active as public speakers—in churches, on the radio, on television talk shows, and in other venues. They present a consistent package of ideas—with "academic" notions confidently interwoven with the faith commitments of the target audience and without complicating nuances—that makes for a forceful and persuasive message.

Christians have long been called "People of the Book." The label is especially appropriate for evangelicals. But the Book is thousands of years old, written in obscure languages, from a mysterious and incomprehensible time and place. The vitality of such a religious tradition depends on the ability of leaders—prophets, preachers, sages—to bring the Book to life so that it engages the worldview of each new generation. "Preachers," writes anthropologist Susan Harding, "convert the ancient recorded speech of the Bible once again into spoken language, translating it into local theological and cultural idioms and placing present events inside the sequence of Biblical stories." Thus renewed, the ancient text remains alive, speaking to a new generation, addressing issues and problems that are often far from those that motivated the original authors. "Church people, in their turn, borrow, customize, and reproduce the Bible based speech of their preachers and other leaders in their daily lives," writes Harding.[107]

The DNA of the parallel culture of evangelism is wound from two very different strands—an ancient religious tradition and a secular world increasingly dominated by science and influenced by forces outside of conservative Christianity. The countless points of contact create complex and bewildering problems for believers, problems that have been with Christianity since its inception. When Jesus said, "Render to Caesar the things that are Caesar's and to God the things that are God's," he was acknowledging this tension—the same tension that led Augustine to write *The City of God* four centuries later and inspired Aquinas's *Summa Theologica* in the thirteenth century. This tension is not one that will be resolved by the clever syntheses of facile televangelists nor put to rest with an intellectual treaty. The timeless ancient Book will be forever asked to speak to a constantly changing world, and prophets will of necessity arise to be anointed and make that happen. Those leaders most skilled in appropriating both the spiritual authority of the Christian tradition and the secular authority of the present culture—whatever its changing epistemological priorities—will provide that intellectual authority and be anointed to lead.

Notes
Acknowledgments
Index

Notes

Introduction

1. See recording of speech "SBOE Chair Don McLeroy Expounds on His View of Evolution," youtube.com, March 27, 2009. Steve Mirsky, "Texas Messes with History," *Scientific American,* March 15, 2010. Laura Beil, "Opponents of Evolution Adopting a New Strategy," *New York Times,* June 4, 2008.

2. Kenneth Miller, quoted in Laura Heinauer, "McLeroy Is Point Man in Fight over Texas' Science Curriculum," *American-Statesman* (Austin, TX), March 8, 2009.

3. Don McLeroy, quoted in Russell Shorto, "How Christian Were the Founders?" *New York Times,* February 11, 2010.

4. Shorto, "How Christian Were the Founders?" Stephanie Simon, "The Culture Wars' New Front: U.S. History Classes in Texas," *Wall Street Journal,* July 14, 2009. Terrence Stutz, "Conservatives Say Texas Social Studies Classes Give Too Much Credit to Civil Rights Leaders," *Dallas Morning News,* July 9, 2009.

5. Cynthia Dunbar, quoted in Shorto, "How Christian Were the Founders?"

6. Associated Press, "Texas Approves Textbook Changes," *New York Times,* May 22, 2010. Shorto, "How Christian Were the Founders?"

7. "SBOE Chair Don McLeroy Expounds on His View of Evolution."

8. Kirk Watson, quoted in Lee Nichols, "McLeroy Gets a Dressing Down," *Austin Chronicle,* May 1, 2009.

9. John Gehring, "Texas School Board: The 'Common Good' as Liberal Conspiracy," *Sojourners,* June 7, 2010, available at http://blog.sojo.net/2010/06/07/

texas-school-board-the-%E2%80%9Ccommon-good%E2%80%9D-as-liberal-conspiracy/#. Bobby Ross, Jr., "Darwin Divides: Christian College Professors Split on Texas Science Standards," *Christianity Today,* March 3, 2010. John Fea, "Don't Taint Teaching of History in Texas," *Houston Chronicle,* July 25, 2009.

10. Michael Luo, "Evangelicals Debate the Meaning of 'Evangelical,'" *New York Times,* April 16, 2006.

11. For an estimate of the strength of American evangelicalism, see Mark A. Noll, "Understanding American Evangelicals," lecture at the Ethics and Public Policy Center, December 22, 2003, available at http://www.eppc.org/publications/pubid.1943/pub_detail.asp; and Pew Forum on Religion and Public Life, U.S. Religious Landscape Survey, Report, February 2008, 5, 10, available at http://religions.pewforum.org/pdf/report-religious-landscape-study-full.pdf.

12. Nathan O. Hatch, *The Democratization of American Christianity* (New Haven: Yale University Press, 1989), 73–81, 179–189, 210–219. Walt Holcomb, ed., *Popular Lectures of Sam P. Jones* (New York: Fleming H. Revell, 1909), 25.

13. Michael Luo and Laurie Goodstein, "Emphasis Shifts for New Breed of Evangelicals," *New York Times,* May 21, 2007. Krista Tippet, "Rick and Kay Warren at Saddleback," interview, Speaking of Faith, American Public Media, August 21, 2008, available at http://being.publicradio.org/programs/2008/warren/.

14. Michael Ruse, "A Black Mark for Calvin College," *Chronicle of Higher Education,* September 26, 2010.

15. D. Michael Lindsay, *Faith in the Halls of Power: How Evangelicals Joined the American Elite* (New York: Oxford University Press, 2007), 107–113. See also Pew Forum on Religion and Public Life, "American Evangelicalism: New Leaders, New Faces, New Issues," June 30, 2008, Pew Research Center Publications, available at http://pewresearch.org/pubs/883/american-evangelicalism; and John Gravois, "Timing of Faculty Firings Spurs Investigation at Ohio College," *Chronicle of Higher Education,* March 21, 2008.

16. Alan Wolfe, "The Opening of the Evangelical Mind," *Atlantic,* October 2000. "Best Colleges of 2009: Liberal Arts Rankings," colleges.usnews.rankingsandreviews.com. Mark A. Noll, *The Scandal of the Evangelical Mind* (Grand Rapids, MI: William B. Eerdmans, 1995).

17. Data from "Science in America: Religious Belief and Public Attitudes," pewforum.org, August 30, 2005. See also Pew Forum on Religion and Public Life, "Public Divided on Origins of Life," August 30, 2005, available at http://pewforum.org/Politics-and-Elections/Public-Divided-on-Origins-of-Life.aspx;

and Pew Forum on Religion and Public Life, "Public Opinion on Religion and Science in the United States," November 5, 2009, available at http://pewforum.org/Science-and-Bioethics/Public-Opinion-on-Religion-and-Science-in-the-United-States.aspx.

18. Hanna Rosin, "Rock of Ages, Ages of Rock," *New York Times,* November 25, 2007. Ronald L. Numbers, *The Creationists: From Scientific Creationism to Intelligent Design* (Cambridge, MA: Harvard University Press, 2006).

19. On Barton, see Mark A. Chancey, "Lesson Plans: The Bible in the Classroom," *Christian Century,* August 23, 2005; and Kurt W. Peterson, "American Idol: David Barton's Dream of a Christian Nation," *Christian Century,* October 31, 2006, 20. On religion and the founding, see Mark Lilla, "Church Meets State," *New York Times,* May 15, 2005; Garry Wills, *Head and Heart: American Christianities* (New York: Penguin Press, 2007); Frank Lambert, *The Founding Fathers and the Place of Religion in America* (Princeton: Princeton University Press, 2006); David Lynn, *The Faiths of the Founding Fathers* (New York: Oxford University Press, 2006); and Mark Noll, Nathan O. Hatch, and George M. Marsden, *The Search for Christian America* (Westchester, IL: Crossway Books, 1984).

20. David Barton, *Original Intent: The Courts, the Constitution, and Religion* (Aledo, TX: WallBuilder Press, 2005). Arlen Specter, "Defending the Wall: Maintaining Church/State Separation in America," *Harvard Journal of Law and Public Policy* 18 (Spring 1995): 582–583.

21. Henry Morris, *The Long War against God: The History and Impact of the Creation/Evolution Conflict* (Grand Rapids, MI: Baker Books, 1989).

22. John F. Harris, "God Gave U.S. 'What We Deserve,' Falwell Says," *Washington Post,* September 14, 2001. Peter Marshall, "Israel and Hezbollah—This Is Not the Prelude to Armageddon!" August 10, 2006, available at http://petermarshallministries.com/commentary.cfm?commentary=69. Pew Research Center for the People and the Press, "23% See AIDs as God's Punishment for Immorality," n.d., available at http://pewresearch.org/databank/dailynumber/?NumberID=311 (accessed January 1, 2009).

23. A 2004 PBS poll found that 73 percent of evangelicals had a favorable view of Dobson. (By contrast, Jerry Falwell received only a 44 percent favorability rating and Pat Robertson a 55 percent favorability rating.) Dobson's conservative-values organization Focus on the Family received 10,000 calls, emails, and letters each day. His radio broadcast averaged 7 to 9 million listeners a week. Thirteen/WNET New York, "Poll: America's Evangelicals More and More Mainstream but Insecure: Diversity, Differences Mark Their Views on Society,

Culture, Politics," *Religion and Ethics Newsweekly,* April 13, 2004, available at http://www.pbs.org/wnet/religionandethics/week733/release.html. Stephanie Simon, "A Voice That Carries: Millions of People Hang on the Advice of Evangelical Psychologist James C. Dobson," *Los Angeles Times,* October 7, 2005.

24. Focus on the Family, "Sexual Purity and Sola Scriptura," citizenlink.org (accessed January 1, 2009).

25. Sandra G. Boodman, "Vowing to Set the World Straight," *Washington Post,* August 16, 2005. John P. Bartkowski and Christopher G. Ellison, "Divergent Models of Childrearing in Popular Manuals: Conservative Protestants vs. the Mainstream Experts," *Sociology of Religion* 56 (Spring 1995): 21–34. Focus on the Family, "Sexual Purity and Sola Scriptura."

26. Ken Ham, *The Lie: Evolution* (Green Forest, AR: Master Books, 1987).

27. David Barton, "War on God in America," WallBuilders, September 25, 2008, video available at http://www.wallbuilders.com/LIBissuesArticles.asp?id=14242. David Barton, "God: Missing in Action from American History," WallBuilders, June 2005, available at http://www.wallbuilders.com/LIBissuesArticles.asp?id=100. James Dobson, quoted in Diana Hochstedt Butler, "Fundamentalists Attack 'Feminist Agenda,'" *Baltimore Sun,* September 6, 1995. See also Americans United for Separation of Church and State, "FOF's Dobson Says Ministry under Attack by Satanic Forces," *Church and State* (December 2000): 16.

28. David Barton, "Lessons from the September Terrorist Attacks," WallBuilders, January 2002, available at http://www.wallbuilders.com/LIBissuesArticles.asp?id=144. Peter Marshall, "The Signs of the Times—Part One," March 9, 2006, available at http://petermarshallministries.com/commentary.cfm?commentary=45. Peter Marshall, "The Signs of the Times—Part Two," March 16, 2006, available at http://petermarshallministries.com/commentary.cfm?commentary=47.

29. Paul Boyer, *When Time Shall Be No More: Prophecy Belief in American Culture* (Cambridge: Harvard University Press, 1992), 207–208, 214–218. barackobamaantichrist.blogspot.com.

30. Tim LaHaye, quoted in Brian Braiker, "Are These the End Times?" *Newsweek,* msnbc.com, July 28, 2006 (accessed March 8, 2007).

31. N. T. Wright, "Farewell to the Rapture," *Bible Review* (August 2001): 8. John Dart, "'Beam Me Up' Theology: The Debate Over 'Left Behind,'" *Christian Century,* September 25, 2002, 8–9.

1. The Answer Man

1. Creation Museum, Petersburg, KY, "Worldview," *Museum Souvenir Guide,* n.d., 8.

2. Creation Museum, "Corruption," *Museum Souvenir Guide,* 16.

3. Creation Museum, "Corruption."

4. David S. MacMillan, "Evolution Is Now an Excuse," Answers in Genesis, June 25, 2007, available at http://www.answersingenesis.org/articles/2007/06/25/evolution-is-now-an-excuse.

5. Henry M. Morris, *The Genesis Record: A Scientific and Devotional Commentary on the Book of Beginnings* (Grand Rapids, MI: Baker Books, 1976), 113.

6. Henry M. Morris, *Genesis Record,* 173.

7. Andrew A. Snelling, "The World's a Graveyard: Flood Evidence Number Two," Answers in Genesis, February 12, 2008, available at http://www.answersingenesis.org/articles/am/v3/n2/world-graveyard.

8. Snelling, "The World's a Graveyard."

9. Patrick Marsh, interview with Answers in Genesis, May 17, 2002, available at http://www.answersingenesis.org/docs2002/0517patrick_marsh.asp.

10. Ken Ham, "Museum Opens Eyes to Need for Christ," Answers in Genesis, February 29, 2008, available at http://blogs.answersingenesis.org/blogs/ken-ham/2008/02/29/museum-opens-eyes-to-need-for-christ/. Quote taken from anonymous feedback sent in by an attendee of the Creation Museum.

11. Ken Ham, *The Lie: Evolution* (Green Forest, AR: Master Books, 1987), 129.

12. Creation Museum, "Letter from Ken Ham," *Museum Souvenir Guide,* 3.

13. Gordy Slack, "Inside the Creation Museum," *Salon,* May 31, 2007, available at http://www.salon.com/news/feature/2007/05/31/creation_museum.

14. William Jennings Bryan, *In His Image* (New York: Fleming H. Revell, 1922), 93.

15. George McCready Price, *The New Geology* (Mountain View, CA: Pacific Press, 1923), 676–677.

16. Ronald L. Numbers, *The Creationists: From Scientific Creationism to Intelligent Design* (Cambridge, MA: Harvard University Press, 2006), 111–116.

17. Edward Larson, *Trial and Error* (New York: Oxford University Press, 2003), 87. National Center for Science Education, "McLeroy Booted in Texas," March 3, 2010, available at http://ncse.com/news/2010/03/mcleroy-booted-texas-005354.

18. Larson, *Trial and Error,* 91.

19. Karl W. Giberson and Donald A. Yerxa, *Species of Origins: America's Search for a Creation Story* (Lanham, MD: Rowman and Littlefield, 2002), 68.

20. Henry M. Morris and John D. Morris, *The Modern Creation Trilogy,* vol. 1: *Scripture and Creation* (Green Forest, AR: Master Books, 1996), 13–14.

21. Ronald Numbers, "The Creationists," in *God and Nature: Historical Essays on the Encounter between Christianity and Science,* ed. David C. Lindberg and Ronald L. Numbers (Berkeley, CA: University of California Press, 1986), 415.

22. John C. Whitcomb and Henry M. Morris, *The Genesis Flood: The Biblical Record and Its Scientific Implications* (Phillipsburg, NJ: Presbyterian and Reformed Publishing, 1961).

23. Kurt P. Wise and Sheila A. Richardson, *Something from Nothing: Understanding What You Believe about Creation and Why* (Nashville, TN: Broadman and Holman, 2004), 162.

24. Henry M. Morris, *Scientific Creationism* (Green Forest, AR: Master Books, 1985), 115–120.

25. Whitcomb and Morris, *Genesis Flood.*

26. Whitcomb and Morris, *Genesis Flood,* 212.

27. Glen J. Kuban, "A Matter of Degree: Carl Baugh's Alleged Credentials," *National Center for Science Education Reports* 9:6 (November–December 1989), available at http://www.talkorigins.org/faqs/paluxy/degrees.html.

28. Trinity Broadcast Network, "Creation in the 21st Century," available at http://www.tbn.org/watch-us/our-programs/creation-in-the-21st-century-hosted-by-dr-carl-baugh.

29. Kuban, "A Matter of Degree."

30. Carl Baugh, *Panorama of Creation* (Oklahoma City: Southwest Radio Church, 1989), 84.

31. Baugh, *Panorama of Creation,* 53.

32. Mark O'Brien, "Hard to Believe a Man with a Ph.D. Didn't Know of a Basic Tax Law," *Pensacola News Journal,* November 3, 2006, C1.

33. For Hovind's status as a federal prisoner, see U.S. Department of Justice, Federal Bureau of Prisons, Inmate Locator, available at http://www.bop.gov/iloc2/LocateInmate.jsp.

34. Karen Bartelt, "The Dissertation Kent Hovind Doesn't Want You to Read," n.d. [2004], No Answers in Genesis, available at http://www.noanswersingenesis.org.au/bartelt_dissertation_on_hovind_thesis.htm.

35. Numbers, *Creationists,* 289.

36. Creationist journals with technical content include *Creation Research Society*

Quarterly, the official journal of the Creation Research Society, available at http://www.creationresearch.org. The Geoscience Research Institute publishes *Origins.* Creation Ministries International publishes *Journal of Creation,* which they describe as "in-depth, peer-reviewed comment, reviews and the latest research findings that relate to origins and the biblical account of Creation, the Flood and the Fall," available at http://www.aboutus.org/CreationOnTheWeb.org#. In 2007 Answers in Genesis launched a "professional, peer-reviewed technical journal for the publication of interdisciplinary scientific and other relevant research from the perspective of the recent Creation and the global Flood within a biblical framework," available at http://www.answersingenesis.org/. It is also of note that, in 2004, Stephen Meyer published a controversial paper, "The Origin of Biological Information and the Higher Taxonomic Categories," in the peer-reviewed scientific journal *Proceedings of the Biological Society of Washington* 117:2 (2005): 213–239. The publisher later withdrew the paper. The then-editor of *Proceedings,* a known supporter of intelligent design, was accused of going outside the usual review procedures in order to get Meyer's paper published. In any case, Meyer was not advocating flood geology; he is, in fact, a philosopher, not a scientist.

37. For Dawkins's praise of Wise, see Richard Dawkins, "Sadly, An Honest Creationist," February 13, 2004, Council for Secular Humanism, available at http://www.secularhumanism.org/library/fi/dawkins_21_4.html.

38. Paul Nelson and John Mark Reynolds, "Young Earth Creationism," in *Three Views on Creation and Evolution,* ed. J. P. Moreland, John Mark Reynolds, et al. (Grand Rapids, MI: Zondervan, 1999), 49.

39. See Larson, *Trial and Error.*

40. Langdon Gilkey, *Creationism on Trial: Evolution and God at Little Rock* (1985; rpt. Charlottesville, VA: University Press of Virginia, 1998), 155–156. See also Judge William R. Overton's official judgment, reprinted in *But Is It Science: The Philosophical Question in the Creation/Evolution Controversy,* ed. Michael Ruse (Amherst, NY: Prometheus Books, 1996), 307–331.

41. National Center for Science Education, "CBS News Poll on Evolution," November 24, 2004, available at http://ncse.com/news/2004/11/cbs-news-poll-evolution-00522.

42. George W. Bush, quoted in Rob Boston, "God, Country, and the Electorate," *Church and State* (October 1988): 8.

43. Henry M. Morris and John D. Morris, *The Modern Creation Trilogy,* vol. 3: *Society and Creation* (Green Forest, AR: Master Books, 1996), 9.

44. Ham, *The Lie,* 83.

45. Ken Ham and A. Charles Ware, *Darwin's Plantation* (Green Forest, AR: Master Books, 2007), 9.

46. Robert H. Bork, *Slouching toward Gomorrah: Modern Liberalism and American Decline* (San Francisco: Harper Perennial, 2003).

47. Henry M. Morris, *The Long War against God: The History and Impact of the Creation/Evolution Conflict* (Grand Rapids, MI: Baker, 1989), 132.

48. Paul Nelson, Robert C. Newman, and Howard Van Till, *Three Views on Creation and Evolution* (Grand Rapids, MI: Zondervan, 1999), 49–50.

49. Kenneth A. Kitchen, *On the Reliability of the Old Testament* (Grand Rapids, MI: Eerdmans, 2003). See also Iain W. Provan, V. Philips Long, and Tremper Longhman, III, *A Biblical History of Israel* (Louisville, KY: Westminster John Knox Press, 2003).

50. Answers in Genesis, Mission Statement, available at http://www.answersingenesis.org/about/mission.

51. *Institute for Creation Research Graduate School v. Texas Higher Education Coordinating Board,* Case No. A-09-CA-382-SS (Texas, 2009).

52. Ken Ham, "Happy Birthday, Mum," Answers in Genesis, February 18, 2008, available at http://blogs.answersingenesis.org/blogs/ken-ham/2008/02/18/happy-birthday-mum/.

53. British Centre for Science Education, "Margaret Buchanan and John Mackay," March 29, 2007, available at http://www.bcseweb.org.uk/index.php/Main/MargaretBuchanan.

54. British Centre for Science Education, "Margaret Buchanan and John Mackay."

55. Creation Ministries International, About Us, http://creation.com/about-us.

56. Margaret Buchanan, *Salem Revisited: The Tragedy of Modern Witch-Hunting—A True Story* (Brisbane, Australia: Buchanan, 1990). The publication is now hosted at *Creation on the Web,* http://creation.com/article/6399.

57. British Centre for Science Education, "Margaret Buchanan and John Mackay."

58. Creation Research, "Richard Dawkins Interviews Mackay," November 27, 2007, available at http://www.creationresearch.net/items%20subjects/Richard-Dawkins-Iinterviews-Mackay.htm.

59. Duane Gish, quoted in Bill Thwaites, "Toe to Toe with Young-Earth Cre-

ationists," National Center for Science Education, January 20, 2003, available at http://ncse.com/creationism/general/toe-to-toe-with-young-earth-creationists.

60. Ham, *The Lie,* 97.

61. Ham, *The Lie,* 45.

62. Thwaites, "Toe to Toe with Young-Earth Creationists."

63. Jerry Falwell, "If the Foundations Be Destroyed," *Falwell Confidential,* February 19, 2004, available at http://www.answersingenesis.org/docs2004/0302foundations.asp.

64. Jonathan Falwell, "Explaining the Foundations of the Universe," *Falwell Confidential,* June 1, 2007, available at http://www.democraticunderground.com/discuss/duboard.php?az=view_all&address=389x1026233.

65. H. Morris and J. Morris, *Society and Creation,* 129.

66. Falwell, "If the Foundations Be Destroyed."

67. Falwell, "If the Foundations Be Destroyed."

68. BioLogos Forum, "Answers in Genesis," n.d., available at http://biologos.org/resources/answers-in-genesis/ (accessed October 1, 2010).

69. Numbers, *Creationists,* 53.

70. Numbers, *Creationists,* 53.

71. Jon H. Roberts, "Darwinism, American Protestant Thinkers, and the Puzzle of Motivation," in *Disseminating Darwinism: The Role of Place, Race, Religion, and Gender,* ed. Ronald L. Numbers and John Stenhouse (Cambridge: Cambridge University Press, 1999), 146.

72. Numbers, *Creationists,* 181.

73. Henry Morris, *A History of Modern Creationism* (San Diego, CA: Master Books, 1984), 130–144; Ham, *The Lie,* 116.

74. Morris, *History of Modern Creationism,* 141.

75. James Moore, "Geologists and Interpreters of Genesis," in *God and Nature: Historical Essays on the Encounter between Christianity and Science,* ed. David C. Lindberg and Ronald L. Numbers (Berkeley, CA: University of California Press, 1986), 329.

76. David N. Livingstone, *Darwin's Forgotten Defenders: The Encounter between Evangelical Theology and Evolutionary Thought* (Grand Rapids, MI: Eerdmans, 1987), 100–145.

77. *Nova: Evolution: What about God?* Part 7, directed by Bill Jersey and Mark Page (Boston: WGBH Boston Video, 2001).

78. Darrel R. Falk, *Coming to Peace with Science: Bridging the Worlds between Faith and Biology* (Downers Grove, IL: InterVarsity Press, 2004).

79. Owen Gingerich, *God's Universe* (Cambridge, MA: Harvard University Press, 2006).

80. E. S. Lander, L. M. Linton, B. Birren, et al., "Initial Sequencing and Analysis of the Human Genome," *Nature* 409 (February 15, 2001): 860–921.

81. Examples include Richard T. Wright, *Biology through the Eyes of Faith* (San Francisco: HarperCollins, 1989); Falk, *Coming to Peace with Science;* Karl Giberson, *Worlds Apart: The Unholy War between Religion and Science* (Kansas City, MO: Beacon Hill Press, 1993); and Charles Hummel, *The Galileo Connection: Resolving Conflicts between Science and the Bible* (Downers Grove, IL: InterVarsity Press, 1986).

82. Francis Collins, *The Language of God: A Scientist Presents Evidence for Belief* (New York: Free Press, 2006), 225.

83. Collins, *Language of God,* 67.

84. Collins, *Language of God,* 78.

85. Collins, *Language of God,* 107.

86. "Bob Abernethy's Interview with Dr. Francis Collins, Director of the Human Genome Project at the National Institutes of Health," *Religion and Ethics Newsweekly,* PBS, November 7, 2008, transcript available at http://www.pbs.org/wnet/religionandethics/transcripts/collins.html.

87. Collins, *Language of God,* 243.

88. Sam Harris, "The Language of Ignorance," Truthdig, August 15, 2006, available at http://www.truthdig.com/report/item/20060815_sam_harris_language_ignorance/.

89. See, for example, Francis Collins, interviewed by Karl Giberson, "Evolution, the Bible, and the Book of Nature," *Books and Culture: A Christian Review* (July–August 2009), available at http://www.booksandculture.com/articles/2009/julaug/evolutionthebibleandthebookofnature.html.

90. *Christianity Today,* Book Awards 2007, May 23, 2007, available at http://www.ctlibrary.com/ct/2007/june/8.36.html.

91. Francis Collins, interviewed by John Horgan, "Francis Collins: The Scientist as Believer," *National Geographic,* February 2007, available at http://ngm.nationalgeographic.com/ngm/0702/voices.html.

92. Francis Collins, interviewed by Steve Paulson, "The Believer," Salon, August 7, 2006, available at http://www.salon.com/books/int/2006/08/07/collins.

93. Collins, *Language of God,* 146.

94. Francis Collins, interviewed by Karl Giberson, "Evolution, the Bible, and the Book of Nature," 20.

95. Francis Collins, interview with Karl Giberson, April 11, 2008, Asuza, California.

96. Joseph Kezele, "Book Review: *The Language of God* by Francis Collins," Answers in Genesis, October 30, 2006, available at http://www.answersingenesis.org/docs2006/1030collins.asp.

97. Kezele, "Book Review: *The Language of God* by Francis Collins."

98. Kezele, "Book Review: *The Language of God* by Francis Collins."

99. Doug Huntington, "Creation Museum Founder Thanks Protestors, Critics," *Christian Post,* May 29, 2007, available at http://www.christianpost.com/news/creation-museum-founder-thanks-protesters-critics-27670/.

100. Mark Isaak, *The Counter-Creationism Handbook* (Berkeley, CA: University of California Press, 2007).

101. "The Monkey Suit," *The Simpsons,* Fox, May 14, 2006; "The Untitled Griffin Family History," *Family Guy,* Fox, May 14, 2006. On *Saturday Night Live,* NBC, October 29, 2005, Tina Fey read the following "news" item: "The latest Gallup poll found that 66 percent of Americans think President Bush is doing a poor job in Iraq. The remaining 34 percent believe that Adam and Eve rode to church on dinosaurs."

102. David Klinghoffer, "The Human Factor," *Weekly Standard* 11:45 (August 14, 2006): 34–36.

103. Buddy Davis, quoted in Frans B. M. de Waal, "Sing the Song of Evolution," *Natural History* 110:8 (October 2001): 77.

2. *The Amateur Christian Historian*

1. J. Randy Forbes, "The Stripping of Purpose," September 15, 2006, available at http://forbes.house.gov/News/DocumentSingle.aspx?DocumentID=5458.

2. "Randy Forbes," On the Issues, n.d., available at http://www.issues2000.org/VA/Randy_Forbes.htm (accessed March 24, 2011). Congressional Prayer Caucus, "About the Congressional Prayer Caucus," n.d., available at http://forbes.house.gov/PrayerCaucus/About.aspx (accessed December 8, 2008). 2 Chronicles 7:14 (ASV). Americans United for Separation of Church and State, "House Members Urge Americans to Pray, Say Jesus Is Answer," *Church and State* 5 (May 2007): 14.

3. David Waters, "God Bless America," December 5, 2008, available at http://newsweek.washingtonpost.com/onfaith/undergod/2008/12/godbless_america.html.

4. Lisa Kindervatter, "Reader's Opinions: 'Angry' Evangelicals Grew in Re-

sponse to Scorn," October 10, 2008, http://blogs.usatoday.com (accessed December 11, 2008).

5. David Barton and Rick Green, "Guest: Congressman Randy Forbes," WallBuilders Live, November 27, 2006, podcast available at http://www.wallbuilderslive.com/archives.asp?d=200611. J. Randy Forbes, "Point of View," *Capitol Monitor,* March 6, 2004, available at http://www.house.gov/forbes/newsroom/enewsletter/2004/03062004.html. "Randy Forbes," On the Issues.

6. Rep. J. Randy Forbes [VA-4], H.R. 888, "Affirming the rich spiritual and religious history of our Nation's founding and subsequent history and expressing support for designation of the first week in May as 'American Religious History Week' for the appreciation of and education on America's history of religious faith." *Congressional Record,* December 18, 2007, available at http://thomas.loc.gov/cgi-bin/query/z?c110:H.RES.888:.

7. David Barton, founder and President of WallBuilders, telephone interview with Randall J. Stephens, August 25, 2008. According to Barton, the WallBuilders collection contains over 100,000 pre-1812 documents.

8. Secular Coalition for America, "Congress Aims to Dumb Down History, Pushes Fiction of Christian Nation in Public Schools," January 15, 2008, available at http://www.commondreams.org/news2008/0115-05.htm. Chris Hedges, "Christianizing US History," *Nation,* January 10, 2008. Bruce Wilson, "Stop House Resolution 888!" Daily Kos, January 4, 2008, available at http://www.dailykos.com/story/2008/01/04/430331/-updated-w-action-item-STOP-HOUSE-RESOLUTION-888-!.

9. Richard G. Lee, *The American Patriot's Bible* (Nashville: Thomas Nelson, 2009), I–45 to I–47. Gregory A. Boyd, "Book Review: *The Patriot's Bible* (part 1)," *Christianity Today,* Out of Ur, May 22, 2009, available at http://www.outofur.com/archives/2009/05/book_review_the.html.

10. Peter Marshall, quoted in Dale Hurd, "Planting a Lasting Covenant," Christian World News, Christian Broadcasting Network, November 26, 2009, available at http://www.cbn.com/cbnnews/shows/cwn/2009/November/Planting-a-Lasting-Covenant-/.

11. Richard Hughes, *Myths America Lives By* (Urbana: University of Illinois Press, 2003), 66, 85–89. Gordon Wood, "Evangelical America and Early Mormonism," *New York History* 61 (1980), 359. Gordon Wood, "Praying with the Founders," *New York Review of Books,* May 1, 2008. See also Gordon S. Wood, *The Radicalism of the American Revolution* (New York: Knopf, 1992), 330.

12. Martin E. Marty, "Religion and the Constitution: The Triumph of Practical Politics," *Christian Century,* March 3, 1994.

13. Thomas S. Kidd, *God of Liberty: A Religious History of the American Revolution* (New York: Basic Books, 2010), 6–10, 253–254.

14. David L. Holmes, *The Faiths of the Founding Fathers* (New York: Oxford University Press, 2006), 134–135, 141. Alf J. Mapp, Jr., *The Faiths of Our Fathers: What America's Founders Really Believed* (New York: Barnes and Noble, 2006), 7.

15. Georg G. Iggers and James M. Powell, *Leopold Von Ranke and the Shaping of the Historical Discipline* (Syracuse: Syracuse University Press, 1990), xiv. Leopold von Ranke, quoted in Peter Novick, *That Noble Dream: The "Objectivity Question" and the American Historical Profession* (Cambridge: Cambridge University Press, 1988), 27.

16. George Bancroft, *The History of the United States of America from the Discovery of the Continent,* ed. Russel B. Nye (Chicago: University of Chicago Press, 1966), 5. Bert James Loewenberg, *American History in American Thought: Christopher Columbus to Henry Adams* (New York: Simon and Schuster, 1972), 329.

17. Emma Willard, *Abridged History of United States* (Philadelphia: A. S. Barnes, 1844), 15–16.

18. George H. Callcott, *History in the United States, 1800–1860: Its Practice and Purpose* (Baltimore: Johns Hopkins University Press, 1970), 163, 183. George Bancroft, *Literary and Historical Miscellanies* (New York: Harper and Brothers, 1855), 484.

19. Albert Bushnell Hart, "Imagination in History," *American Historical Review* 15 (January 1910): 232. Novick, *That Noble Dream,* 30–38.

20. Washington Gladden, *Who Wrote the Bible? A Book for the People* (Boston: Houghton Mifflin, 1891), 351–352. Charles A. Beard, *An Economic Interpretation of the Constitution of the United States* (New York: Macmillan, 1914).

21. Billy Sunday, quoted in Martin E. Marty, *Modern American Religion: The Irony of It All, 1893–1919* (Chicago: University of Chicago Press, 1997), 217. George M. Marsden, *Fundamentalism and American Culture: The Shaping of Twentieth Century Evangelicalism, 1870–1925* (New York: Oxford University Press, 1980), 206–207.

22. J. G. Machen, *Christianity and Liberalism* (New York: Macmillan, 1923), 6–8.

23. Paul Boyer, "The Evangelical Resurgence in 1970s American Protestantism," in *Rightward Bound: Making America Conservative in the 1970s,* ed. Bruce J. Schulman and Julian E. Zelizer (Cambridge, MA: Harvard University Press, 2008), 31–33.

24. Billy James Hargis, *Why I Fight for a Christian America* (Nashville: Thomas Nelson, 1974), 152.

25. Billy James Hargis, *Communist America—Must It Be?* (Tulsa: Christian Crusade, 1960), VII, quotes pp. 31 and 37.

26. William C. Martin, *With God on Our Side: The Rise of the Religious Right in America* (New York: Broadway Books, 2005), 33–34. Anticommunism and Christian patriotism sparked the imaginations of Bob Jones University administrators, students, and faculty. The school became a bastion of Christian Americanism in the stormy 1960s. Mark Taylor Dalhouse, *An Island in a Lake of Fire: Bob Jones University, Fundamentalism, and the Separatist Movement* (Athens: University of Georgia Press, 1996), 105–106.

27. Billy Graham, "America's Hope," in *The Early Billy Graham: Sermon and Revival Accounts,* ed. Joel Carpenter (New York: Garland, 1988), 12, 13–15, 17, 19. The authors are indebted to John G. Turner for pointing them to this source.

28. Billy Graham, quoted in William Martin, *A Prophet with Honor: The Billy Graham Story* (New York: W. Morrow, 1991), 286. Jerry Falwell, *Strength for the Journey: An Autobiography* (New York: Simon and Schuster, 1987), 276.

29. John Ashcroft, quoted in Dan Betzer, *Destiny: The Story of John Ashcroft* (Springfield, MO: Revivaltime Media Ministries, 1988), 15.

30. Carl F. H. Henry, "Ours Is the Generation," *Christianity Today,* October 13, 1967, 28. Paul M. Weyrich, "Blue Collar or Blue Blood? The New Right Compared with the Old," in *The New Right Papers,* ed. Robert W. Whitaker (New York: St. Martin's Press, 1982), 52.

31. Falwell, *Strength for the Journey,* 319–321. Ralph Reed, *Active Faith: How Christians Are Changing the Soul of American Politics* (New York: Free Press, 1996), 105. Randall Herbert Balmer, *Thy Kingdom Come: How the Religious Right Distorts the Faith and Threatens America, an Evangelical's Lament* (New York: Basic Books, 2006), 14–17.

32. Philip W. Ziegler, "My Country under God," *Christian Life* (July 1971): 48. Donald S. Metz, *MidAmerica Nazarene College: The Pioneer Years, 1966–1991* (Kansas City, MO: Nazarene Publishing House, 1991), 38–41, 255. *MidAmerica Nazarene College Conestoga* (Olathe, KS: MANC, 1976), 4–16. Mark A. Noll, Nathan O. Hatch, and George M. Marsden, *The Search for Christian America* (Westchester, IL: Crossway Books, 1983), 14. *Newsweek,* October 26, 1976.

33. James McGraw, "The Spirit of 76," *Preacher's Magazine* 51 (July 1976): 1–2. Pat Brooks, "After 200 Years—Freedom Still the Issue," *Christian Life* 38 (July 1976): 20; quotes pp. 21, 57. Carl F. H. Henry, "Of Bicentennial Concerns and Patriotic Symbols," *Christianity Today,* July 2, 1976, 14; quote p. 16.

34. Peter Marshall, "A Generation Later, Part Two," July 10, 2008, available at http://www.petermarshallministries.com/commentary.cfm?commentary=172.

Peter Marshall and David Manuel, *The Light and the Glory* (Grand Rapids, MI: Fleming H. Revell, 1977), 17–18; quote p. 16.

35. Francis Jennings, *The Invasion of America: Indians, Colonialism, and the Cant of Conquest* (New York: W. W. Norton, 1976), 34, 302; quote p. vii.

36. Marshall and Manuel, *Light and the Glory,* 14–15. Marshall, "A Generation Later, Part Two." Peter Marshall, "A Generation Later, Part One," June 26, 2008, available at http://petermarshallministries.com/commentary.cfm?commentary=167.

37. John Fea, "Thirty Years of Light and Glory," *Touchstone,* July/August 2008, available at http://www.touchstonemag.com/archives/article.php?id=21-06-027-f. Marshall and Manuel, *Light and the Glory,* 193–195, 200–201, 235–238.

38. Marshall, "A Generation Later, Part One."

39. Peter Marshall, interview in *One Nation Under God: A Journey of Discovery to Find the Truth about America's Founding,* directed by John Quarquesso (Fort Lauderdale, FL: Coral Ridge Ministries, 2005).

40. Peter Marshall, "Signs of the Times, Part One," March 9, 2006, available athttp://www.petermarshallministries.com/commentary.cfm?commentary=45; "Virginia Tech: Reaping What We Have Sowed," April 26, 2007, available at http://www.petermarshallministries.com/commentary.cfm?commentary=106; "California Burning: The Fire of God?" October 25, 2007, available at http://www.petermarshallministries.com/commentary.cfm?commentary=131; and "The Verdict Is In," November 5, 2008, available at http://www.petermarshallministries.com/commentary.cfm?commentary=188.

41. Jennifer Jill Schwirzer, "Theocracy Now?" libertymagazine.org, August 29, 2002 (accessed August 15, 2008).

42. Francis A. Schaeffer, *How Should We Then Live: The Decline of Western Thought and Culture* (Westchester, IL: Crossway Books, 1976), 163–165, 205, 258. Frank Schaeffer, *Crazy for God: How I Grew Up as One of the Elect, Helped Found the Religious Right, and Lived to Take All (or Almost All) of It Back* (New York: Carroll and Graf, 2007), 211, 260.

43. Kenneth L. Woodward, "Guru of Fundamentalism," *Newsweek,* November 1, 1982, 88. Francis A. Schaeffer, *A Christian Manifesto* (Westchester, IL: Crossway Books, 1981), 39; quote p. 32. Florida Baptist Witness, "Katherine Harris," August 22, 2006, available at http://www.gofbw.com/news.asp?ID=6298.

44. Barry Hankins, *Francis Schaeffer and the Shaping of Evangelical America* (Grand Rapids, MI: Eerdmans, 2008), 193–194. William Edgar, "The Passing of R. J. Rushdoony," First Things, August/September 2001, available at http://www.

firstthings.com/article/2007/01/the-passing-of-r-j-rushdoony-40. Sara Diamond, *Roads to Dominion: Right Wing Movements and Political Power in the United States* (New York: Guilford Press, 1995), 248. Rousas John Rushdoony, "The Politics of Babel: Utopia Revisited," *Vital Speeches of the Day,* May 1, 1973, 423. Paul Nelson, "An Unapologetic Middle Ground," *Christian Century,* October 4, 1989, 881. Rousas John Rushdoony, *This Independent Republic: Studies in the Nature and Meaning of American History* (Nutley, NJ: Craig Press, 1964), 6–7. See also Rushdoony's connections to creationism in Ronald L. Numbers, *The Creationists: From Scientific Creationism to Intelligent Design* (Cambridge, MA: Harvard University Press, 2006), 382.

45. Rushdoony, *This Independent Republic,* 116, 49.

46. Keyword search for "Rushdoony," christianitytoday.com (accessed September 16, 2008).

47. Sarah Pulliam, "Empire Builder D. James Kennedy Dies at 76," *Christianity Today,* September 6, 2007, available at http://www.christianitytoday.com/ct/2007/septemberweb-only/136-42.0.html.

48. George Barna, "Pastors Reveal Major Influencers on Churches," January 14, 2005, available at http://www.barna.org/barna-update/article/5-barna-update/187-pastors-reveal-major-influencers-on-churches.

49. D. James Kennedy, "The Man Who Founded America," *Impact* (July 2007): 6.

50. D. James Kennedy and Jerry Newcombe, *What If America Were a Christian Nation Again?* (Nashville: Thomas Nelson, 2003), 5, 9–17; quote p. 18.

51. Gustav Niebuhr, "To Mobilize the Faithful: A Christian Civics Class," *New York Times,* March 3, 1996, 12.

52. Bob Moser, "The Crusaders: Christian Evangelicals Are Plotting to Remake America in Their Own Image," *Rolling Stone,* April 7, 2005, available at http://www.blueguitar.org/new/misc/political/rs_crusaders.pdf. Florida Baptist Witness, "Katherine Harris."

53. Terry Gross, "Closing the Gap between Church and State," Fresh Air, National Public Radio, May 18, 2005, available at http://www.npr.org/templates/story/story.php?storyId=4656600.

54. Nate Blakeslee, "King of the Christocrats," *Texas Monthly,* September 1, 2006.

55. Quotes from Mark Preston, "Judicial Critic to Lead Frist Tour; Activist Favors Impeachment," *Roll Call,* April 7, 2005; and Americans United for Separa-

tion of Church and State, "Senate Majority Leader Invites 'Christian Nation' Advocate to Lead Tour," *Church and State* (May 2005): 16–17.

56. Kent Willis, director of ACLU Virginia, quoted in Donald P. Baker, "School Prayer Activist to Address Allen Spiritual Event," *Washington Post*, January 15, 1994, A12.

57. On religion in textbooks, see Jon Butler, "Jack-in-the-Box Faith: The Religion Problem in Modern American History," *Journal of American History* 90:4 (March 2004): 1357–1378. Rob Boston, "David Barton's 'Christian Nation' Myth Factory: Admits Its Products Have Been Defective," *Church and State* 49:7 (July/August 1996): 11–13. David Barton, "Unconfirmed Quotations," WallBuilders, January 2000, available at http://www.wallbuilders.com/LIBissuesArticles.asp?id=126.

58. Robert S. Alley, "Public Education and the Public Good," *William and Mary Bill of Rights Journal* (Summer 1995), 316–317; quote p. 315.

59. David Barton, *Original Intent: The Courts, the Constitution, and Religion* (Aledo, TX: WallBuilder Press, 2005), 17–19; quote p. 158.

60. David Barton, "The Separation of Church and State," WallBuilders, January 2001, available at http://www.wallbuilders.com/LIBissuesArticles.asp?id=123. David Barton, "God: Missing in Action from American History," WallBuilders, June 2005, available at http://www.wallbuilders.com/LIBissuesArticles.asp?id=100. Barton, *Original Intent*, 43–48. David Barton, "Taking On the Critics," WallBuilders, October 2003, available at http://www.wallbuilders.com/LIBissuesArticles.asp?id=115. Barton, telephone interview, August 25, 2008. Glenn Beck, quoted in Thomas Frank, "Glenn Beck and Our 'Stolen' History," *Wall Street Journal*, August 4, 2010.

61. "Issues and Articles," wallbuilders.com (accessed September 18, 2008). David Barton, "Treaty of Tripoli," WallBuilders, January 2000, available at http://www.wallbuilders.com/LIBissuesArticles.asp?id=125. WallBuilders Customer Service, email, September 18, 2008. Blakeslee, "King of the Christocrats."

62. Jennifer Schuessler, "Hayek for Dummies," *New York Times* blog, July 9, 2010, available at http://artsbeat.blogs.nytimes.com/2010/07/09/hayek-for-dummies/.

63. Reuters, "Oprah Reigns, Beck Follows in TV Personality Poll," January 25, 2010, available at http://www.reuters.com/article/2010/01/25/us-beck-idUSTRE60O5RJ20100125. Glenn Beck, quoted in "Glenn Interviews David Barton," April 29, 2010, available at http://www.reuters.com/arti-

cle/2010/01/25/us-beck-idUSTRE60O5RJ20100125. "Announcing Beck University," July 6, 2010, available at http://www.glennbeck.com/content/articles/article/198/42502/#. "Glenn Beck: Palin's Big Announcement . . . ," May 26, 2010, available at http://www.glennbeck.com/content/articles/article/198/41148/#.

64. U.S. Senate, Committee on Environment and Public Works, hearing on "An Examination of the Views of Religious Organizations Regarding Global Warming," June 7, 2007, available at http://epw.senate.gov/public/index.cfm?FuseAction=Hearings.Hearing&Hearing_ID=e39940af-802a-23ad-4371-252edd78194f.

65. Elizabeth Ridenour, National Council on Bible Curriculum in Public Schools, "It's Coming Back . . . and It's Our Constitutional Right!" National Council on Bible Curriculum in Public Schools, n.d., available at http://www.bibleinschools.net (accessed September 21, 2010).

66. Mark A. Chancey, "Lesson Plans: The Bible in the Classroom," *Christian Century,* August 23, 2005, 18–21. Mark A. Chancey, "Sectarian Elements in Public School Bible Courses: Lessons from the Lone Star State," *Journal of Church and State* 49 (Autumn 2007): 719–742. Mark A. Chancey, "A Textbook Example of the Christian Right: The National Council on Bible Curriculum in Public Schools," *Journal of the American Academy of Religion* 75 (September 2007), quote p. 555.

67. bibleinschools.net/. Chancey, "Textbook Example of the Christian Right," 563, 569, 573.

68. See Texas Education Agency, "Social Studies Expert Reviewers," September 10, 2009, available at http://www.tea.state.tx.us/index2.aspx?id=6184. Texas Education Agency, "Text of Proposed Revisions to 19 TAC. Chapter 113. Texas Essential Knowledge and Skills for Social Studies. Subchapter C. High School," April 14, 2010, available at www.tea.state.tx.us/WorkArea/linkit.aspx?LinkIdentifier=id&ItemID.

69. David Barton, quoted by Mariah Blake, "Revisionaries: How a Group of Texas Conservatives Is Rewriting Your Kids' Textbooks," *Washington Monthly,* January/February 2010. John Fea, "Don't Taint Teaching of History in Texas," *Houston Chronicle,* July 25, 2009. Mavis Knight, quoted in Terrence Stutz, "More Conservative Textbook Curriculum OK'd," *Dallas Morning News,* May 22, 2010.

70. American Historical Association, "To the Members, Current and Elected, of the Texas State Board of Education," May 18, 2010, available at http://www.

historians.org/perspectives/issues/2010/1009/1009new4.cfm. See also the National Council of History Education's call for the Texas State Board of Education to maintain "ideological neutrality," Fritz Fischer, Chair, National Council for History Education, "Distinguished Members of the Texas State Board of Education," nche.net, n.d. (accessed August 3, 2010). See also "History in the Making: Will the Texas Social Studies Curriculum Get Stuck in the 1700s?" *Houston Chronicle,* July 23, 2009, B8.

71. "The 25 Most Influential Evangelicals in America," *Time,* January 30, 2005.

72. Benjamin Schwarz, "*America's God* by Mark A. Noll," *Atlantic,* December 2002.

73. Mark Lilla, "Church Meets State," *New York Times,* May 15, 2005. See also Kidd, *God of Liberty,* 253–254.

74. David D. Kirkpatrick, "Putting God Back Into American History," *New York Times,* February 27, 2005. Mark Noll, Francis A. McAnaney Professor of History at the University of Notre Dame, telephone interview with Randall J. Stephens, June 26, 2008. Texas Freedom Network Education Fund, "The Anatomy of Power: Texas and the Religious Right in 2006," n.d., 19, available at http://www.tfn.org/site/DocServer/SORR_06_ReportWEB.pdf?docID=222 (accessed September 20, 2008).

75. Mark Noll, quoted in Tim Stafford, "Whatever Happened to Christian History?" *Christianity Today,* April 2, 2001, 45–46.

76. Mark Noll, *One Nation under God? Christian Faith and Political Action in America* (San Francisco: Harper and Row, 1988), 9. Gordon S. Wood, "American Religion: The Great Retreat," *New York Review of Books,* June 8, 2006.

77. Noll, *One Nation under God?* 10.

78. Mark Noll, telephone interview, June 26, 2008.

79. Noll, Hatch, and Marsden, *Search for Christian America,* 17. Barton, telephone interview, August 25, 2008. Noll, Hatch, and Marsden, *Search for Christian America,* 161. Fea, "Thirty Years of Light and Glory."

80. "'I'm Just Making a Point': Francis Schaeffer and the Irony of Faithful Christian Scholarship," *Fides et Historia* 39 (Winter/Spring), 24–26, 30. Richard V. Pierard, "Standing the Founding Fathers on Their Heads," *Christian Century,* April 20, 1983, 372. Franky Schaeffer, *Bad News for Modern Man: An Agenda for Christian Activism* (Westchester, IL: Crossway Books, 1984), 84.

81. Noll, Hatch, and Marsden, *Search for Christian America,* 161. Fea, "Thirty Years of Light and Glory." Randall Balmer, *Mine Eyes Have Seen the Glory: A Jour-*

ney into the Evangelical Subculture in America (New York: Oxford University Press, 1989), 122.

82. Texas Freedom Network, "The Anatomy of Power," 19. Barton, "Taking On the Critics."

83. "'I'm Just Making a Point,'" 30. Pierard, "Standing the Founding Fathers on Their Heads," 372. Franky Schaeffer, *Bad News for Modern Man,* 84.

84. First Amendment Center, "'07 Survey Shows Americans' Views Mixed on Basic Freedoms," September 24, 2007, available at http://www.firstamendmentcenter.org/news.aspx?id=19031. Pew Research Center for People and the Press, "Many Americans Uneasy with Mix of Religion and Politics," August 24, 2006, available at http://people-press.org/2006/018/24/many-americans-uneasy-with-mix-of-religion-and-politics/.

85. Affirming the Rich . . . , H.R. 397, 111th Cong. (2009–2010), List of cosponsors, available at http://thomas.loc.gov/cgi-bin/bdquery/z?d111:HE00397:@@@P. Tom Minnery, "A Special Alert from Focus on the Family," Focus on the Family email, May 15, 2009. Representative Steve Austria (R-OH 7th), "House Resolution 397," congress.org, June 11, 2009.

3. The Family of God

1. James Dobson interviewed by Larry King, "Interview with Dr. James Dobson," March 7, 2002, available at http://transcripts.cnn.com/TRANSCRIPTS/0203/07/lkl.00.html. On June 22, 2010, Dobson's *Bringing Up Girls: Practical Advice and Encouragement for Those Shaping the Next Generation of Women* (Carol Stream, IL: Tyndale House, 2010) ranked at number four on christianbook.com's "Bestselling Christian Resources." In addition to books, that list contained DVDs, CDs, and gift items. "Bestselling Christian Resources," christianbook.com (accessed June 22, 2010). That same day, *Bringing Up Girls* charted at 261 for all books sold by Amazon. James C. Dobson, *The New Dare to Discipline* (Wheaton, IL: Tyndale House Publishers, 1996), came in at 3,873 on amazon.com (accessed June 22, 2010). On condoms and STDs, see also "Dr. Dobson Answers Your Questions," *Focus on the Family* (October 1993): 5. Dobson is listed as a "licensed psychologist in the state of California" on the Focus on the Family website. "About Us: Dr. James Dobson," focusonthefamily.com (accessed August 25, 2010).

2. Centers for Disease Control, "Perspectives in Disease Prevention and Health Promotion Condoms for Prevention of Sexually Transmitted Diseases,"

Morbidity and Mortality Weekly Report (March 11, 1988), 133–137. Centers for Disease Control, "Program Operations Guidelines for STD Prevention: Leadership and Program Management," www.cdc.gov/std/program/Leadership.pdf, L-7 (accessed July 23, 2002).

3. Anna Wald, Andria G. M. Langenberg, Katherine Link, et al., "Effect of Condoms on Reducing the Transmission of Herpes Simplex Virus Type 2 from Men to Women," *Journal of the American Medical Association* 285 (2001): 3100–3106. See also Centers for Disease Control, "Sexually Transmitted Diseases, Research by Year: 2002," http://www.cdc.gov/std/research/2002.htm. Chris Mooney, *The Republican War on Science* (New York: Basic Books, 2005), 9, 225.

4. Sales of James Dobson, *Bringing Up Boys* (Wheaton, IL: Tyndale House, 2001) in 2002 alone topped 600,000. Dave Bogart, ed., *The Bowker Annual: Library and Book Trade Almanac* (Medford, NJ: Information Today, 2003), 579.

5. Dobson, *Bringing Up Boys,* 6.

6. Dobson, *Bringing Up Boys,* 17, 115.

7. James Dobson interviewed by Larry King, March 7, 2002.

8. Steven V. Roberts and Dorian Friedman, "The Heavy Hitter," *U.S. News and World Report,* April 24, 1995, 39.

9. Michael Lienesch, *Redeeming America: Piety and Politics in the New Christian Right* (Chapel Hill: University of North Carolina Press, 1993), 53.

10. Paul C. Vitz, *Psychology as Religion: The Cult of Self-Worship* (1977; reprint, Grand Rapids: William B. Eerdmans and Paternoster Press, 1994), 143. See also Martin Bobgan and Deidre Bobgan, *The Psychological Way/The Spiritual Way* (Minneapolis: Bethany House Publishers, 1979).

11. David Harrington Watt, *A Transforming Faith: Explorations of Twentieth-Century American Evangelicalism* (New Brunswick, NJ: Rutgers University Press, 1991), 137–138.

12. Watt, *A Transforming Faith,* 139.

13. Watt, *A Transforming Faith,* 139, 140. See also David Arthur Powlison, "Competent to Counsel? The History of a Conservative Protestant Anti-Psychiatry Movement" (Ph.D. diss., University of Pennsylvania, 1996).

14. E. Brooks Holifield, *A History of Pastoral Care in America: From Salvation to Self-Realization* (Nashville: Abingdon Press, 1983), 261–263. Alfred Kazin, "The Freudian Revolution Analyzed," *New York Times,* May 6, 1956, 22.

15. Watt, *A Transforming Faith,* 143–151. "Narramore, Clyde Maurice," in *Religious Leaders of America,* ed. J. Gordon Melton (Detroit: Gale Group, 1999), 407.

16. Clyde M. Narramore, *The Psychology of Counseling: Professional Techniques for Pastors, Teachers, Youth Leaders and All Who Are Engaged in the Incomparable Art of Counseling* (Grand Rapids, MI: Zondervan, 1960), 12, 13; quote p. 119.

17. Susan E. Myers-Shirk, *Helping the Good Shepherd: Pastoral Counseling in a Psychotherapeutic Culture, 1925–1975* (Baltimore: Johns Hopkins University Press, 2009), 210–211, 214. Jay Edward Adams, *Competent to Counsel: Introduction to Nouthetic Counseling* (1970; repr., Grand Rapids, MI: Zondervan, 1986), xxi. On the change in attitudes about psychology, see also Russell Chandler, "Psychology, Theology: Two Old Enemies Forming Alliance," *Los Angeles Times,* September 2, 1975, C1.

18. "History," foundationforbiblicalresearch.org (accessed May 26, 2010).

19. "History," foundationforbiblicalresearch.org (accessed May 26, 2010).

20. J. Richard Fugate, *What the Bible Says about Child Training,* 2nd ed. (Elkton, MD: Holly Hall, 1998).

21. Fugate, *What the Bible Says about Child Training,* iii.

22. Fugate, *What the Bible Says about Child Training,* 131, 180, 208.

23. J. Richard Fugate, quoted in Diane Divoky, "Theory on Whipping Children Stirs Debate," *Sacramento Bee,* March 26, 1986, B1.

24. Fugate, *What the Bible Says about Child Training,* 141. Larry Tomczak, *God, the Rod, and Your Child's Bod: The Art of Loving Correction for Christian Parents* (Old Tappan, NJ: Power Publications, 1982), 118. Diane Watson, quoted in Diane Divoky, "Theory on Whipping Children Stirs Debate." Philip Greven, *Spare the Child: The Religious Roots of Punishment and the Psychological Impact of Physical Abuse* (New York: Vintage Books, 1992), 55–81.

25. Diane Watson, quoted in Diane Divoky, "Theory on Whipping Children Stirs Debate."

26. "Testimonials/Endorsements," Foundation for Biblical Research, available at http://www.foundationforbiblicalresearch.org/ss/live/index.php?action=getpage&pid=2216 (accessed June 9, 2010).

27. George Lakoff, *Moral Politics: How Liberals and Conservatives Think* (Chicago: University of Chicago Press, 2002), 341–342.

28. Murray A. Straus with Denise A. Donnelly, *Beating the Devil Out of Them: Corporal Punishment in American Families and Its Effects on Children* (New Brunswick, NJ: Transaction, 2001), 13–14.

29. Committee on Psychosocial Aspects of Child and Family Health, "Guidance for Effective Discipline," *Pediatrics* 101:4 (1998): 726; quote p. 723. According to the AAP, "A statement of reaffirmation for this policy was published on October 1, 2004." "AAP Policy," aappolicy.aappublications.org (accessed May

27, 2010). See also American Academy of Pediatrics, *Caring for Your Baby and Young Child: Birth to Age 5*, rev. ed. (New York: Bantam, 2004), 260; Nancy Shute, "A Good Parent's Dilemma: Is It Bad to Spank?" *U.S. News and World Report*, June 23, 2008, 60–61; Nancy Shute, "More on Spanking: The Side Effects," *U.S. News and World Report* blog, June 16, 2008, http://health.usnews.com/health-news/blogs/on-parenting/2008/06/16/more-on-spanking-the-side-effects.

30. James Davidson Hunter, *Culture Wars: The Struggle to Define America* (New York: Basic Books, 1991), 181–182.

31. "The Time Has Come for a New Movement toward True Equality: The National Organization for Women (NOW)," in *The Columbia Documentary History of American Women since 1941*, ed. Harriet Sigerman (New York: Columbia University Press, 2003), 206.

32. Hunter, *Culture Wars*, 180.

33. Peter Berger, quoted in Margaret L. Bendroth, *Growing Up Protestant: Parents, Children and Mainline Churches* (New Brunswick, NJ: Rutgers University Press, 2002), 104; quote p. 108.

34. "The Family of God," quoted in Robert M. McManus, "Southern Gospel Music vs. Contemporary Christian Music: Competing for the Soul of Evangelicalism," in *More than Precious Memories: The Rhetoric of Southern Gospel Music*, ed. Michael P. Graves and David Fillingim (Mercer, GA: Mercer University Press, 2004), 67.

35. "Where Is America Going," *Christianity Today*, June 21, 1968, 23. "The Ugly Spirit of Mobbism," *Christianity Today*, May 24, 1968, 26. Billy Graham, "False Prophets in the Church," *Christianity Today*, January 19, 1968, 3. See also Robert Booth Fowler, *A New Engagement: Evangelical Political Thought, 1966–1976* (Grand Rapids, MI: William B. Eerdmans, 1982), 25–30, 191–211.

36. "Television and Prime Time Morals," *Christian Herald* (June 1973): 24–25.

37. Seth Dowland, "'Family Values' and the Formation of the Christian Right Agenda," *Church History* 78:3 (September 2009): 606–608.

38. Dowland, "'Family Values,' 623. Jerry Falwell, *Listen, America!* (Garden City, NY: Doubleday, 1980), 153–154, 156, 157; quote p. 150.

39. Larry Christenson, *The Christian Family* (1970; repr., Minneapolis: Bethany House, 1980), back cover.

40. Christenson, *The Christian Family*, 3, 106. For biographical information, see H. V. Synan, "Christenson, Laurence Donald ('Larry')," in *The New International Dictionary of Pentecostal and Charismatic Movements*, ed. Stanley M. Burgess and Eduard M. Van Der Maas (Grand Rapids, MI: Zondervan, 2002), 522–523; and Jerry

L. Sandidge, *Roman Catholic/Pentecostal Dialogue (1977–1982): A Study in Developing Ecumenism,* vol. 1 (New York: Peter Lang, 1987), 159.

41. Christenson, *The Christian Family,* 33, 35, quotes pp. 47, 54.

42. Christenson, *The Christian Family,* 167, 168, 79, 57; quote p. 100.

43. Tim LaHaye, *The Battle for the Family* (Old Tappan, NJ: Fleming H. Revell, 1982), 13.

44. Tim LaHaye, *Spirit-Controlled Temperament* (1966; repr., Wheaton, IL: Tyndale House, 1994), 152, 175–179; quote p. 11. Myers-Shirk, *Helping the Good Shepherd,* 227–228, 231. R. Marie Griffith, *God's Daughters: Evangelical Women and the Power of Submission* (Berkeley: University of California Press, 1997), 150–153.

45. James C. Dobson, "Fallout from the Summer of Love," *Focus on the Family* (July 2008): 5.

46. James C. Dobson, *Dare to Discipline,* 3 (1970; repr., New York: Bantam Books, 1982).

47. James C. Dobson, *Parenting Isn't for Cowards: Dealing Confidently with the Frustrations of Child-Rearing* (Dallas: Word, 1987), 107–108. See also James Dobson, "God in the Nursery," *Herald of Holiness,* August 30, 1972, 9.

48. *Manual of the Church of the Nazarene* (Kansas City, MO: Nazarene Publishing House, 1956), 31.

49. *Manual of the Church of the Nazarene,* 325; quote p. 324. On a slightly later era, see John A. Knight, "Separated Living," *Herald of Holiness,* April 29, 1970, 9. The Nazarene Church also shared with the Salvation Army a concern for the poor and downtrodden. Nazarenes often had an uneasy relationship with fundamentalism. Although many members gravitated toward fundamentalism, quite a few church leaders tried to distance the church from fundamentalist doctrine and political stridency. *Manual of the Church of the Nazarene,* 321–322.

50. Beth Bailey, "From Panty Raids to Revolution: Youth and Authority, 1950–1970," in *Generations of Youth: Youth Cultures and History in Twentieth-Century America,* ed. Joe Austin and Michael Willard (New York: New York University Press, 1998), 188, 193–194.

51. *Pasadena College Catalog, 1955–1956* (Pasadena: Pasadena College, 1955), 41. Ronald Kirkemo, *For Zion's Sake: A History of Pasadena/Point Loma College* (San Diego: Point Loma Press, 2008), 115–127, 291–293.

52. Dan Gilgoff, *The Jesus Machine* (New York: St. Martin's Press, 2007), 20, 21. Sandee Foster, quoted in Dale Buss, *Family Man: The Biography of Dr. James Dobson* (Wheaton, IL: Tyndale House, 2005), 27.

53. James C. Dobson, quoted in Buss, *Family Man,* 31. *Pasadena College Catalog, 1955–1956,* 121, 122.

54. Buss, *Family Man,* 30.

55. Buss, *Family Man,* 34–35.

56. James C. Dobson and Kenneth D. Hopkins, "The Reliability and Predictive Validity of the Lee-Clark Reading Readiness Test," *Journal of Developmental Reading* 6:4 (1963): 278–281. Buss, *Family Man,* 36, 37; James Dobson quote p. 39.

57. Dobson, *Dare to Discipline,* 2.

58. Benjamin Spock, *Baby and Child Care* (1946, 1968; repr., New York: Pocket Books, 1976), xv, 11, 12, 37, 41, 372, 371, 374. Eric Pace, "Benjamin Spock, World's Pediatrician, Dies at 94," *New York Times,* March 17, 1998, A1.

59. Dobson, *Dare to Discipline,* 33.

60. Thomas Maier, *Dr. Spock: An American Life* (New York: Basic Books, 1998), 322–324.

61. Dobson, *Dare to Discipline,* 5–12, 30–31.

62. Dobson, *Dare to Discipline,* 42, 159; quote pp. 39–40.

63. Dobson, *Dare to Discipline,* 47, 127–129, 150, 166.

64. Ione Quinby Griggs, "Book Offers Parents Roads to Discipline," *Milwaukee Journal,* September 20, 1974, 4. Davieann Witt, "Dear Editor," *Anchorage Daily News,* May 8, 1976, 4.

65. "Discipline Problems 'Sticky,'" *Cape Girardeau Southeast Missourian,* August 15, 1974, 16.

66. Ellen Goodman, "The Lords of Discipline in the Era of 'Supernanny,' Understand the Appeal of James Dobson," *Pittsburgh Post Gazette,* May 18, 2005, B7. On sales, see Barry Hankins, *American Evangelicals: A Contemporary History of a Mainstream Religious Movement* (Lanham, MD: Rowman and Littlefield, 2008), 156.

67. Charles Millhuff, *You Asked For It* (Kansas City, MO: Pedestal Press, 1970), 14, 38–39, 41–42, 43–44, 48; p. 37.

68. Scripture quoted in Dobson, *Dare to Discipline,* 195, 197.

69. James Dobson, "God in the Nursery."

70. James Dobson, *Solid Answers: America's Foremost Family Counselor Responds to Tough Questions Facing Today's Families* (Wheaton, IL: Tyndale House, 1997), 395.

71. James Dobson, "Insights: The Psychologist's Page," *Herald of Holiness,* March 1, 1972, 15. See also Esther J. Uerkvitz, "Snakes, Margaret Mead and Marijuana," *Herald of Holiness,* April 8, 1970, 5.

72. Charles W. Phillips, "Focus on the Family," *Saturday Evening Post,* April 1982, 34.

73. James Dobson, quoted in "Focus at 15," *Focus on the Family* (March 1992), 10; quote p. 13.

74. Gilgoff, *The Jesus Machine,* 10, 24, 25, 27.

75. Wilford D. Wooten, interview with Randall Stephens, July 24, 2008, Colorado Springs, CO. For a summary of Focus on the Family's mission, see "Focus on the Family: Who We Are and What We Stand For," *Focus on the Family* (August 1993): 10–13. "Social Issues: Talking Point (Abortion)," focusonthefamily.com (accessed August 28, 2010).

76. Rolf Zettersten, "In Focus: A Strategy for the Next Four Years," *Focus on the Family* (February 1993): 14.

77. William J. Bennett, "Where Have We Gone Wrong? (And How to Make Things Right)," *Focus on the Family* (January 1999): 11. Gilgoff, *The Jesus Machine,* 97, 111, 118.

78. Steve Rabey, "For Giant Evangelical Ministry, Midlife Crisis at 25," *New York Times,* July 27, 2002, B6.

79. Tim Stafford, "His Father's Son: The Drive behind James Dobson, Jr.," *Christianity Today,* April 22, 1988, 17. Amy K. Mishkin and Irwin A. Hyman, review of *Dare to Discipline* by James Dobson, *Aggressive Behavior* 11:3 (1985): 261–262.

80. James Dobson, *The Strong-Willed Child: Birth through Adolescence* (Wheaton, IL: Tyndale House, 1978), 232; quote p. 233.

81. James Dobson, "Dare to Discipline in the '90s," *Focus on the Family* (September 1992): 2. See also James Dobson, interview with Sarah Pulliam Bailey, "Focus on the Females: James Dobson Explains His Ideas for Raising Daughters, and Life after Focus," *Christianity Today,* July 1, 2010, 31.

82. Dobson, *Bringing Up Boys,* 236.

83. Wendy Murray Zoba, "Daring to Discipline America," *Christianity Today,* March 1, 1999, 36.

84. James C. Dobson, *The New Dare to Discipline,* rev. ed. (Carol Stream, IL: Tyndale House, 1992), 34.

85. Dobson, *The New Dare to Discipline,* 21.

86. Focus on the Family, "Defending the Faith: Resources to Help Defend the Christian Faith," focusonthefamily.com (accessed June 17, 2010). Eithne Johnson, "Dr. Dobson's Advice to Christian Women: The Story of Strategic Motherhood," *Social Text* 57 (Winter 1998): 64–66. James Dobson, *Complete Marriage and Family Home Reference Guide* (Carol Stream, IL: Tyndale House, 2000), quote pp. 73–74. See also Focus on the Family, "Answers: Could you list the physical

characteristics unique to males and females?" http://family.custhelp.com (accessed June 17, 2010).

87. Diane Pasno, interview with Randall Stephens, August 24, 2008, Colorado Springs, CO.

88. Randall Stephens, notes from a visit to Focus on the Family store, July 2008, Colorado Springs, CO. Gilgoff, *The Jesus Machine,* 57. "Elijah Tice, Spring 2009," focusleadership.org (accessed August 29, 2010). "Liaison Form," focusleadership.org (accessed August 29, 2010).

89. Randall Stephens, notes from a visit to Focus on the Family store, July 2008. Gilgoff, *The Jesus Machine,* 44, 45, 46.

90. Ted Haggard, quoted in Michael Lewis, "Crucifixation," *New Republic,* July 8, 1996, 23. "The 25 Most Influential Evangelicals in America," *Time,* January 30, 2005.

91. Paul Asay, "Dobson's Impact Widely Felt," *Gazette* (Colorado Springs, CO), January 18, 2005.

92. Gary Schneeberger, interview with Randall Stephens, *Gazette* (Colorado Springs, CO), July 24, 2008. Gustav Niebuhr, "Advice for Parents, and for Politicians," *New York Times,* May 30, 1995, A12. "Focus on the Family Counseling Department: Top 25 Topics," June 2008.

93. Ann Horton and Ken Eckstrom, quoted in Roberts and Friedman, "The Heavy Hitter," 39. See also Johnson, "Dr. Dobson's Advice to Christian Women," 55–82. James Talent, quoted in William F. Buckley, "Coalescing Confrontation," *National Review,* June 1, 1998, 63.

94. "Poll: America's Evangelicals More and More Mainstream but Insecure," April 13, 2004, pbs.org (accessed June 14, 2010). Gilgoff, *The Jesus Machine,* 40.

95. Dobson, *The Strong-Willed Child,* 234. For a later iteration of that skeptical view of secular experts, see Dobson, *Bringing Up Boys,* 66.

96. "Dr. Dobson Answers Your Questions," *Focus on the Family* (July 1992): 7. "Interview: Dobson's New Dare," *Christianity Today,* February 8, 1993, 69–70.

97. Dobson, *Solid Answers,* 29; quote p. 13.

98. John P. Bartkowski and Christopher G. Ellison, "Divergent Models of Childrearing in Popular Manuals: Conservative Protestants vs. the Mainstream Experts," *Sociology of Religion* 56:1 (1995), 22, 25, 28, 31. On mainstream views see, for example, Lawrence Balter with Anita Shreve, *Who's in Control? Dr. Balter's Guide to Discipline without Combat* (New York: Poseidon Press, 1989); Eda LeShan, *When Your Child Drives You Crazy* (New York: St. Martin's Press, 1985); and T. Berry

Brazelton and Joshua D. Sparrow, *Touchpoints, Birth to Three: Your Child's Emotional and Behavioral Development* (Cambridge, MA: Da Capo, 2006). Mishkin and Hyman, review of *Dare to Discipline,* by James Dobson.

99. Christenson, *The Christian Family,* 44. Focus on the Family, "Is It Important for Mothers to Stay Home during the Teen Years?" family.custhelp.com (accessed August 29, 2010). James Dobson, *Love Must Be Tough* (Dallas: Word, 1983), 179. A. D. Dennison, "Wanted: More Manpower," *Christian Life* (October 1970): 45.

100. Dobson, *Solid Answers,* 397, 514–515.

101. James C. Dobson, quoted in Michael Foust, "New Book by James Dobson Tackles Same-Sex 'Marriage,'" June 14, 2004, available at http://sbcbaptistpress.org/bpnews.asp?id=18465.

102. James Dobson, "Two Mommies Is One Too Many," *Time,* December 12, 2006. See also James Dobson interviewed by Larry King, "Interview with James Dobson," http://transcripts.cnn.com/TRANSCRIPTS/0309/05/lkl.00.html (accessed May 25, 2010); and Jennifer Chrisler, "Two Mommies and Two Daddies Will Do Fine, Thanks," *Time,* December 14, 2006.

103. Mary E. O'Leary, "Yale Expert Says Group Misused His Words," *New Haven Register,* February 12, 2007, 11. Interview with Carol Gilligan, "James Dobson Distorts Research . . . Again!" youtube.com (accessed May 26, 2010).

104. See Dobson's use of an array of experts to bolster his child-rearing arguments in Dobson, *Bringing Up Boys,* 43, 54–55, 57–58. Paul D. Thacker, "Fighting a Distortion of Research," http://www.insidehighereducation.com/news/2006/12/19/Gilligan.

105. Thacker, "Fighting a Distortion of Research."

106. James C. Dobson, "Criticism Aside, Fathers Matter," *Rocky Mountain News,* February 28, 2007, 36.

107. American Medical Association, "AMA Policy Regarding Sexual Orientation," available at http://www.ama-assn.org/ama/pub/about-ama/our-people/member-groups-sections/glbt-advisory-committee/ama-policy-regarding-sexual-orientation.shtml (accessed June 1, 2010).

108. Nanette Gartrell and Henny Bos, "US National Longitudinal Lesbian Family Study: Psychological Adjustment of 17-Year-Old Adolescents," *Pediatrics* 126 (2010): 28–33. Mackenzie Carpenter, "What Happens to Kids Raised by Gay Parents?" *Pittsburgh Post-Gazette,* June 10, 2007.

109. American Psychological Association, "Sexual Orientation and Homosexu-

ality," available at http://www.apa.org/helpcenter/sexual-orientation.aspx (accessed August 30, 2010).

110. Dobson, *Bringing Up Boys,* 115.

111. Glenn T. Stanton and Bill Maier, *Marriage on Trial: The Case against Same-Sex Marriage and Parenting* (Downers Grove, IL: Intervarsity Press, 2004), 144–146. William Maier, interview with Randall J. Stephens, July 24, 2008, Colorado Springs, CO.

112. James Dobson, interviewed by Larry King, "Interview with Dr. James Dobson," November 22, 2006, http://transcripts.cnn.com/TRANSCRIPTS/0611/22/lkl.01.html.

113. James Dobson, interview with Sean Hannity and Alan Colmes, "Religion, Morality, and the Supreme Court," October 15, 2004, available at http://www.foxnews.com/story/0,2933,135600,00.html. See also Jeff Johnston, "What *Does* the Research Show about Homosexuality?" June 17, 2010, available at http://www.citizenlink.com/2010/06/what-does-the-research-show-about-homosexuality/. Henry L. Minton, *Departing from Deviance: A History of Homosexual Rights and Emancipatory Science in America* (Chicago: University of Chicago Press, 2002), 259–260. Vernon A. Rosario, *Homosexuality and Science: A Guide to the Debates* (Santa Barbara, CA: ABC-CLIO, 2002), 117–118.

114. Gilgoff, *The Jesus Machine,* 55–57.

115. Warren Throckmorton, quoted in Mark Barna, "Love Won Out Auditor: Dobson's Gay Theories 'Pretty Ancient Stuff,'" *Gazette* (Colorado Springs, CO), February 25, 2010. See also Mark Barna, "Focus: Psychologist Oversimplifies Dobson's Gay Views," *Gazette* (Colorado Springs, CO), March 2, 2010.

116. American Psychological Association, "Sexual Orientation and Homosexuality."

117. "To the Board of Directors of the American Psychological Association," http://www.citizenlink.org/pdfs/apa_letter.pdf, June 29, 2007.

118. American Psychological Association, "Sexual Orientation and Homosexuality." David G. Myers, "Bridging the Gay-Evangelical Divide," *Wall Street Journal,* August 28, 2009.

119. John Bartkowski, "Beyond Biblical Literalism and Inerrancy: Conservative Protestants and the Hermeneutic Interpretation of Scripture," *Sociology of Religion* 57:3 (1996), 268. Ross Campbell, *Relational Parenting: Going Beyond Your Child's Behavior to Meet Their Deepest Needs* (Chicago: Moody Press, 2000), 33–34, 67–69.

120. Donald Capps, *The Child's Song: The Religious Abuse of Children* (Louisville: Westminster John Knox Press, 1995), ix–xi, 156.

121. "News Release: 25th Anniversary of Conferences," June 7, 2004, ecwr.org. "EC FAQ," ecwr.org (accessed June 30, 2010). Ralph Blair, "Empathways," ecwr.org (accessed June 30, 2010). See also Soulforce, soulforce.org (accessed June 30, 2010).

122. *Psychology* and *Exploring Psychology,* worthpublishers.com (accessed June 24, 2010).

123. David G. Myers and Letha Dawson Scanzoni, *What God Has Joined Together: The Christian Case for Gay Marriage* (San Francisco: HarperCollins, 2005), 4. See also Mel White, *Stranger at the Gate: To Be Gay and Christian in America* (New York: Simon and Schuster, 1994); and Jack Rogers, *Jesus, the Bible, and Homosexuality: Explode the Myths, Heal the Church* (Louisville: Westminster John Knox, 2006).

124. Myers and Scanzoni, *What God Has Joined Together,* 36.

125. James Dobson, interviewed by Bill O'Reilly, "Dr. James Dobson Talks with Bill O'Reilly," The O'Reilly Factor, foxnews.com, February 16, 2006.

126. 1 Kings 11:1 (KJV).

127. Jim Wallis, "James Dobson's 'Letter from 2012 in Obama's America,'" huffingtonpost.com, October 30, 2008.

128. Mark Barna, "Evangelical Leader Dobson Leaving Radio Show," *Gazette* (Colorado Springs, CO), October 30, 2009.

129. Barry Noreen, "Carving Up Community Property at Focus," *Gazette* (Colorado Springs, CO), January 2, 2010. Mark Barna, "Dobson Starting New Nonprofit and Radio Show," *Gazette* (Colorado Springs, CO), December 31, 2009.

130. Mark Barna, "Maine Vote on Gay Marriage Validates Dobson's Message, Focus Officials Say," *Gazette* (Colorado Springs, CO), November 4, 2009.

131. Jim Daly, "One Father Too Many," focusonlinecommunities.com, June 23, 2010. The White House, Office of the Press Secretary, June 18, 2010, "Presidential Proclamation—Father's Day," whitehouse.gov.

132. Lydia Saad, "Americans' Acceptance of Gay Relations Crosses 50% Threshold," gallup.com, May 25, 2010.

133. John P. Bartkowski and Christopher G. Ellison, "Conservative Protestants on Children and Parenting," in *Children and Childhood in American Religions,* ed. Don S. Browning and Bonnie J. Miller-McLemore (New Brunswick, NJ: Rutgers University Press, 2009), 49, 50.

134. W. Bradford Wilcox, "Conservative Protestants and the Family: Resisting, Engaging, or Accommodating Modernity?" in *A Public Faith: Evangelicals and Civic Engagement,* ed. Michael Cromartie (Oxford: Rowman and Littlefield, 2003), 59,

60. See also the president of Southern Baptist Seminary on resisting changes in public opinion: R. Albert Mohler, "Against an Immoral Tide: Southern Baptists Have No Desire to Modernize," *New York Times,* June 19, 2000, A23. For a dissenting view from a decade later, see Anne Eggebroten, "The Persistence of Patriarchy: Hard to Believe, but Some Churches Are Still Talking about Male Headship," sojo.net, July 2010.

135. "Portraits: Social and Political Views," in *U.S. Religious Landscape Survey,* http://religions.pewforum.org, February 2008. See also a 2010 Pew survey on related issues: "Few Say Religion Shapes Immigration, Environment Views," pewforum.org, September 17, 2010. For the official views of some of the larger white evangelical denominations, see Fellows of the Research Institute, "Homosexuality: Your Questions Answered," sbc.net, June 15, 2005; "AG Position Papers and Other Statements: Homosexuality," http://ag.org, 2001; "Administrative Committee: Presbyterian Church in America. General Assembly Meeting, June 20–23, 2000, Tampa Convention Center, Tampa, Florida," pcanet.org; "Homosexuality: Q. What Is the Missouri Synod's Response to Homosexuality?" lcms.org (accessed July 9, 2010); J. K. Warrick, Kansas City, Missouri, Secretary, Board of General Superintendents, Church of the Nazarene, to pastors, September 2, 2008; and "Further Clarification Concerning the Document 'A Pastoral Perspective on Homosexuality,'" nazarene.org, October 23, 2008.

136. Dobson, *Dare to Discipline,* 13–14, 195–197.

4. Trust Me, the End Is Near

1. Donald T. Critchlow, *The Conservative Ascendancy: How the GOP Right Made Political History* (Cambridge, MA: Harvard University Press, 2007), 172–180.

2. "Reagan Backs Evangelicals in Their Political Activities," *New York Times,* August 23, 1980, 8.

3. Constance Holden, "Republican Candidate Picks Fight with Darwin," *Science* 209 (1980): 1214. Phil Gailey, "Reagan, at Prayer Breakfast, Calls Politics and Religion Inseparable," *New York Times,* August 24, 1984, A1.

4. Ronald Reagan, *The Reagan Diaries,* ed. Douglas Brinkley (New York: HarperCollins, 2007), 19, 24. David K. Shipler, "Israel and Syria Are at 'the Edge of a Precipice,'" *New York Times,* May 17, 1981, E1. Revelation 16:14 (KJV).

5. John Herbers, "Armageddon View Prompts a Debate," *New York Times,* October 24, 1984, A1, A25. "Reagan Had Wondered: Is Armageddon Near?" *Boston Globe,* October 28, 1983, 1. "Clerics Oppose Armageddon Theory," *Boston Globe,* October 24, 1984, 19.

6. Walter Goodman, "Religious Debate Fueled by Politics," *New York Times,* October 28, 1984, 31; "On the Record: 3 Views of Armageddon," *New York Times,* October 24, 1984, A25. *Ronald Reagan and the Prophecy of Armageddon,* quoted in John Herbers, "Religious Leaders Tell of Worry on Armageddon View Ascribed to Reagan," *New York Times,* October 21, 1984, 32. Reagan's 1983 remark quoted in "President Has No Plans for Day of Judgment," *Wall Street Journal,* February 8, 1985, 1. See also Richard N. Ostling, Michael P. Harris, and James Castelli, "Armageddon and the End Times," *Time,* November 5, 1984.

7. Kenneth A. Briggs, "Bishop Criticizes Mixing of Church and State," *New York Times,* November 4, 1984, A59. Jim Wallis, quoted in Marjorie Hyer, "Armageddon: Group of Church Leaders Asks Candidates to Repudiate Nuclear Doomsday Theory," *Washington Post,* October 24, 1984, 6. Bryan Johnson, "The Prophets of Armageddon," *Globe and Mail* (Toronto), January 12, 1985, 10.

8. Jerry Falwell, quoted in Ostling, Harris, and Castelli, "Armageddon and the End Times," 73.

9. Howard Baker, quoted in Edmund Morris, *Dutch: A Memoir of Ronald Reagan* (New York: Random House, 1999), 633; quote p. 632. Paul Kengor, *God and Ronald Reagan: A Spiritual Life* (New York: HarperCollins, 2004), 194. Daniel Shorr, "Reagan Recants His Path from Armageddon to Detente," *Los Angeles Times,* January 3, 1988, 5. Stuart Spencer and Ronald Reagan, quoted in Michael R. Beschloss, *Presidential Courage: Brave Leaders and How They Changed America, 1789–1989* (New York: Simon and Schuster, 2007), 285.

10. Stephen D. O'Leary, *Arguing the Apocalypse: A Theory of Millennial Rhetoric* (New York: Oxford University Press, 1994), 182. Walter Goodman, "Religious Debate Fueled by Politics," *New York Times,* October 28, 1984, A31. For further insight into Reagan's relationship with Moomaw, see William Rose, "The Reagans and Their Pastor," *Christian Life* (May 1968): 47.

11. Stephen J. Stein, "Transatlantic Extensions: Apocalyptic in Early New England," in *The Apocalypse in English Renaissance Thought and Literature: Patterns, Antecedents, and Repercussions,* ed. C. A. Patrides and Joseph Anthony Wittreich (Ithaca: Cornell University Press, 1984), 276. H. Richard Niebuhr, *The Kingdom of God in America* (New York: Harper and Brothers, 1959), 127–163; quote p. 150. Michael Wigglesworth, *The Day of Doom: Or, a Poetical Description of the Great and Last Judgment with Other Poems* (1662; New York: American News Company, 1867), 31.

12. Ernest R. Sandeen, *The Roots of Fundamentalism: British and American Millenarianism, 1800–1930* (Chicago: University of Chicago Press, 1970), 42–49.

13. "Obituary, December 20th 1849," *The American Quarterly Register and Magazine* 3:2 (December 1849): 498. Sandeen, *The Roots of Fundamentalism,* 42.

14. Daniel 8:14 (KJV). William Miller, *Evidence from Scripture and History of the Second Coming of Christ about the Year 1843; Exhibited in a Course of Lectures* (Boston: Joshua V. Himes, 1842), 51.

15. Everett N. Dick, "The Millerite Movement, 1830–1845," in *Adventism in America: A History,* ed. Gary Land (Grand Rapids, MI: William B. Eerdmans, 1986), 2–5, 8, 34. William Miller, *Miller's Reply to Stuart's "Hints on the Interpretation of Prophecy," in Three Letters, Addressed to Joshua V. Himes* (Boston: Joshua V. Himes, 1842), 10. On the number of adherents, see David L. Rowe, "Millerites: A Shadow Portrait," in *The Disappointed: Millerism and Millenarianism in the Nineteenth Century,* ed. Ronald L. Numbers and Jonathan M. Butler, 2nd ed. (Knoxville: University of Tennessee Press, 1993), 7. "Hymn 315" in *The Methodist Pockett Hymn-Book* (New York: J. Soule and T. Mason, 1817), 260.

16. "Guy Fawkes, Millerism, Second-Advent, Scripture," *The Farmer's Cabinet,* October 31, 1844, 1.

17. John Nelson Darby, *Notes on the Book of Revelations: To Assist Inquirers in Searching into that Book* (London: Central Tract Depôt, 1839), 169–171.

18. Darby, *Notes on the Book of Revelations,* 41. John Nelson Darby, quoted in "The Plymouth Brethren," in *The Church Quarterly Review for April 1879; July 1879, Volume VIII* (London: Spottiswoode, 1879), 201. Matthew 24:21 (KJV).

19. C. I. Scofield, "Introduction," in *The Scofield Reference Bible* (1909; repr., New York: Oxford University Press, 1945), iv. Harris Franklin Rall, "Premillennialism: II. Premillennialism and the Bible," *Biblical World* 53:5 (1919): 459.

20. Paul Boyer, *When Time Shall Be No More: Prophecy Belief in Modern American Culture* (Cambridge, MA: Harvard University Press, 1992), 97–99. Larry V. Crutchfield, "C. I. Scofield," in *Twentieth-Century Shapers of American Popular Religion,* ed. Charles H. Lippy (New York: Greenwood Press, 1989), 371–379.

21. J. C. Ryle, *Coming Events and Present Duties: Being Miscellaneous Sermons on Prophetical Subjects* (1879; repr., Whitefish, MT: Kessinger, 2007), 54.

22. R. A. Torrey, quoted in Harris Franklin Rall, "Premillennialism: I. The Issue," *Biblical World* 53:4 (1919): 341.

23. Shirley Jackson Case, "The Premillennial Menace," *Biblical World* 52:1 (1918), 16, 17, 19, 21.

24. Robert H. Ferrell, *Off the Record: The Private Papers of Harry S. Truman* (Columbia: University of Missouri Press, 1997), 55. Reinhold Niebuhr, *Moral Man and*

Immoral Society (1931; repr., New York: Charles Scribner's Sons, 1960), ix, xxiii–xxiv. 2 Peter 3:10 (KJV).

25. Thomas S. Kepler, quoted in Lloyd J. Averill, "Is the End Near?" *Christian Century,* January 19, 1983, 45.

26. Pew Forum on Religion and Public Life, "Many Americans Uneasy with Mix of Religion and Politics," August 24, 2006, available at http://pewforum.org/Politics-and-Elections/Many-Americans-Uneasy-with-Mix-of-Religion-and-Politics.aspx. Pew Research Center for the People and the Press, "Life in 2050: Amazing Science, Familiar Threats," June 22, 2010, available at http://people-press.org/report/625/. See also Nancy Gibbs, "Apocalypse Now," *Time,* June 23, 2002.

27. Stephen R. Graham, "Hal Lindsey," in *Twentieth-Century Shapers,* 247.

28. Jonathan Kirsch, "Hal Lindsey," *Publishers Weekly,* March 14, 1977, 30. Stephen Clark, "The Last Days According to Hal Lindsey," *Christian Life* (February 1982): 44.

29. Charles C. Ryrie, "What Is Dispensationalism?" (1980; repr., Dallas: Dallas Theological Seminary, 1986), 5. "Dallas Theological Seminary," in *Encyclopedia of Evangelicalism,* ed. Randall Balmer (Waco, TX: Baylor University Press, 2004), 202–203. Randall Balmer, *Mine Eyes Have Seen the Glory: A Journey into the Evangelical Subculture in America* (New York: Oxford University Press, 1989), 31–45. Dallas Theological Seminary, "About DTS," available at http://www.dts.edu/about/ (accessed July 21, 2009).

30. Nicholas Guyatt, *Have a Nice Doomsday: Why Millions of Americans Are Looking Forward to the End of the World* (New York: Harper Perennial, 2007), 130. Chris Hall, "What Hal Lindsey Taught Me about the Second Coming," *Christianity Today,* October 25, 1999, 83.

31. "An Epidemic of 'Acid Heads,'" *Time,* March 11, 1966. "At War with War," *Time,* May 18, 1970, 6–8. R. Jeffrey Lustig, "The War at Home: California's Struggle to Stop the Vietnam War," in *What's Going On? California and the Vietnam Era,* ed. Marcia A. Eymann and Charles Wollenberg (Berkeley: University of California Press, 2004), 75. Richard Nixon, "123-Statement on Campus Disorders, March 22, 1969," from John T. Woolley and Gerhard Peters, *The American Presidency Project* [online], Santa Barbara, CA: University of California (hosted), Gerhard Peters (database), available at http://www.presidency.ucsb.edu/ws/?pid=1968 (accessed July 10, 2009).

32. Larry Norman, "I Wish We'd All Been Ready," from *Upon This Rock* (Hollywood: Capitol, 1969).

33. Dwight J. Pentecost, quoted in Edward B. Fiske, "There Are Those Who Think It Is Imminent," *New York Times,* October 8, 1972, E8. Assemblies of God, "A Biblical Response to America's Emergency," ag.org/pentecostal-evangel (accessed April 27, 2008).

34. Hal Lindsey with C. C. Carlson, *The Late Great Planet Earth* (Grand Rapids, MI: Zondervan, 1970), 19–26, 42–58, 59–71, 146–168; quotes pp. 58, 108.

35. On belief in UFOs in the 1970s, see Michael Barkun, *A Culture of Conspiracy: Apocalyptic Visions in Contemporary America* (Berkeley: University of California Press, 2003), 80. On doomsday scenarios and conspiracy theories in the 1970s, see Thomas Hine, *The Great Funk: Falling Apart and Coming Together (on a Shag Rug) in the Seventies* (New York: Farrar, Straus, and Giroux, 2007), 44–52. Alvin Toffler, *Future Shock* (New York: Random House, 1970), 9. See also "The Deluge of Disastermania," *Time,* March 5, 1979, 84.

36. Hal Lindsey, quoted in "Author Hal Lindsey: 'Prophecy is Happening Right Before Our Eyes,'" *St. Petersburg Independent,* June 13, 1981, 9-A. Bohdan Hodiak, "End of the World Predicted by Author-Cleric Here," *Pittsburgh Post-Gazette,* November 7, 1977, 3. Air Force colonel, quoted in "When Is Christ Coming," *Christian Life* (January 1973): 40.

37. Aarlie J. Hull, "A Christian Woman's World: Jesus Is Coming," *Herald of Holiness,* July 19, 1972, 15. Hal Lindsey, *The 1980's: Countdown to Armageddon* (New York: Bantam Books, 1981), 4, 11. Ray Walters, "Ten Years of Best Sellers," *New York Times,* December 30, 1979, BR3. See also the Zondervan website for the book, zondervan.com (accessed August 17, 2009). Daniel Wojcik, *The End of the World as We Know It: Faith, Fatalism and Apocalypse in America* (New York: New York University Press, 1997), 38.

38. Hodiak, "End of the World Predicted by Author-Cleric Here," 3. Kirsch, "Hal Lindsey," 30–31. On the Assemblies of God Church in Los Angeles, see James Robison, "The Doomsday Boom: Prophets Wait Impatiently for 'End,'" *Chicago Tribune,* June 26, 1977, 8. Gary Wilburn, "The Doomsday Chic," *Christianity Today,* January 27, 1978, 22.

39. Hal Lindsey, quoted in Jonathan Kirsch, "Hal Lindsey," 32.

40. George Morrison, quoted in Nancy Gibbs, "Apocalypse Now." Gordon Story, "My Journey: The Portions I Felt Led to Share," bereanwatchmen.com/my-journey/my-journey/pdf.html, December 8, 2007. Michael Shermer, *How We Believe: Science, Skepticism, and the Search for God,* 2nd ed. (New York: Henry Holt, 2000), 3–4. Russell Chandler, "It's Heyday for Prophets of Doomsday," *Los Angeles Times,* April 8, 1981, 26. On Lindsey and Israel, see Melani McAlister, *Epic*

Encounters: Culture, Media, and U.S. Interests in the Middle East since 1945 (Berkeley: University of California Press, 2005), 165–167.

41. Willie Day Smith, quoted in George W. Cornell, "The Countdown Begins for Tuesday," *Spokesman-Review* (Spokane, WA), March 29, 1980, 14. See also Nicholas Guyatt, *Have a Nice Doomsday: Why Millions of Americans Are Looking Forward to the End of the World* (New York: Harper Perennial, 2007), 146.

42. John F. Walvoord, one of Lindsey's mentors at Dallas Theological Seminary, rejected "liberal" scholarship—historical, literary, and critical views of scripture—in his premillennial tome *Every Prophecy of the Bible: Clear Explanations for Uncertain Times by One of Today's Premier Prophecy Scholars* (Colorado Springs: David C. Cook, 1999), 17, 164, 223, 237–238, 250, 256, 263–264, 381, 520. Ray Walters, "Paperback Talk," *New York Times Book Review*, March 12, 1978, BR12. Hal Lindsey with C. C. Carlson, *Satan Is Alive and Well on Planet Earth* (Grand Rapids, MI: Zondervan, 1972), 43; quotes pp. 42, 97.

43. Lindsey, *The Late Great Planet Earth*, 129. Hal Lindsey, *There's a New World Coming: An In-Depth Analysis of the Book of Revelation* (1973; repr., Eugene, OR: Harvest House, 1984), 33, 130. Maxine Negri, "Why Biblical Criticism by Scholars Is Imperative," *Humanist* (May/June 1984): 27–28.

44. "When Is Christ Coming," *Christian Life* (January 1973): 40. Stephen Clark, "The Last Days According to Hal Lindsey," *Christian Life* (February 1982): 45. Lindsey, *There's a New World Coming*, 134–135.

45. Hal Lindsey, "Agnostic Arrogance of the 'Liberal Elite,'" April 22, 2004, available at http://www.wnd.com/news/article.asp?ARTICLE_ID=38161.

46. Hal Lindsey, "Killing for God," March 6, 2002, available at http://www.wnd.com/news/article.asp?ARTICLE_ID=26715. Hal Lindsey, "Islam a Violent Religion," January 11, 2006, available at http://www.wnd.com/?pageId=34293. Hal Lindsey, *The Everlasting Hatred—The Roots of Jihad* (Murrieta, CA: Oracle House, 2002), 87, 90, 104; quote p. 231.

47. Paul Crouch, quoted in Roy Rivenburg, "Author Lindsey, Christian Network Reconcile," *Los Angeles Times*, February 10, 2007, B2.

48. Jack Van Impe, "Bible Prophecy and You," n.d., available at http://www.jvim.com/about_bpay.htm (accessed May 2, 2008). Robert Glenn Howard, "Apocalypse in Your In-Box: End-Times Communication on the Internet," *Western Folklore* 56:3/4 (1997): 304, 306, 307.

49. Timothy P. Weber, "How Evangelicals Became Israel's Best Friend," *Christianity Today*, October 5, 1998, 38.

50. Barna Group, "Pastors Reveal Major Influencers on Churches," January 14,

2005, available at http://www.barna.org/barna-update/article/5-barna-update/187-pastors-reveal-major-influencers-on-churches. Julia Duin, "Christian Group to Advocate More Support for Israel," *Washington Times,* July 13, 2006. Guy Raz, "Pro-Israel Christians Lobby in Washington," July 17, 2006, available at http://www.npr.org/templates/story/story.php?storyId=5554303. Sarah Posner, "Pastor Strangelove," *American Prospect,* May 21, 2006. On the lasting appeal of premillennialism among conservative Protestants, see Timothy P. Weber, *Living in the Shadow of the Second Coming: American Premillennialism, 1875–1925* (Chicago: University of Chicago Press, 1987), 231–244. The Pew Forum's 2006 study (Pew Forum, "Many Americans Uneasy with Mix of Religion and Politics") showed that 60 percent of Pentecostals surveyed sympathized with "Israel rather than with Palestinians." Only 40 percent of non-Pentecostal Christians surveyed said the same. *Spirit and Power: A 10-Country Survey of Pentecostals* (Washington, D.C.: The Pew Forum on Religion and Public Life), 61, available at http://pewforum.org/uploadedfiles/Orphan_Migrated_Content/pentecostals-08.pdf (accessed September 15, 2009).

51. Conn Hallinan, "The Religion of Divide and Conquer," *Foreign Policy in Focus,* October 3, 2007. Peggy Fletcher Stack, "McCain Accepts a Controversial Endorsement," *Salt Lake Tribune,* March 7, 2008. John McCain, quoted in Maeve Reston and Stuart Silverstein, "McCain Disavows Pastors," *Los Angeles Times,* May 23, 2008.

52. Tim LaHaye and Jerry B. Jenkins with Norman B. Rohrer, *These Will Not Be Left Behind: True Stories of Changed Lives* (Wheaton, IL: Tyndale House, 2003), xi.

53. David Van Biema et al., "The 25 Most Influential Evangelicals in America," *Time,* January 30, 2005. Larry Eskridge, "And, the Most Influential American Evangelical of the Last 25 Years Is . . ." *Evangelical Studies Bulletin* 17:4 (2001): 1–4. Tim LaHaye, *The Battle for the Mind* (Old Tappan, NJ: Fleming H. Revell, 1980), 60.

54. "Beverly LaHaye (1930–)," in Glenn H. Utter and John W. Storey, *The Religious Right: A Reference Handbook,* 3rd ed. (Millerton, NY: Grey House, 2007), 99–100.

55. Nancy Skelton, "Tim LaHaye—Waging War Against Humanism," *Los Angeles Times,* February 22, 1981, 10. Mark Taylor Dalhouse, *An Island in the Lake of Fire: Bob Jones University, Fundamentalism, and the Separatist Movement* (Athens: University of Georgia Press, 1996), 8, 155. David Garrison, "Tim and Beverly LaHaye," in *Twentieth-Century Shapers of American Popular Religion,* 233–235.

56. Ted Vollmer, "Christian Schools Expanding Rapidly," *Los Angeles Times,* May

17, 1981, A1. Ted Vollmer, "Principal's Firing, Bias Charges Shake Christian High," *Los Angeles Times,* April 30, 1981, A1.

57. Betty Cuniberti, "Other Voices Crying Out Against the Feminists," *Los Angeles Times,* October 2, 1985, D1. Beverly LaHaye, *The Spirit Controlled Woman* (Irvine, CA: Harvest House, 1976), 71, 84.

58. Tim LaHaye, *The Battle for the Family* (Old Tappan, NJ: Fleming H. Revell, 1982), 39. Tim LaHaye, quoted in Martin E. Marty, "The Humanist 'Conspiracy,'" *Christian Century,* January 26, 1983, 79. Tim LaHaye, *The Battle for the Public Schools* (Old Tappan, NJ: Fleming H. Revell, 1983), 46.

59. Tim LaHaye, quoted in Joan Sweeney, "Evangelicals Seeking to Establish Political Force," *Los Angeles Times,* May 19, 1980, 20. Skelton, "Tim LaHaye—Waging War against Humanism." Joel Carpenter, ed., *The Early Billy Graham: Sermon and Revival Accounts* (New York: Garland, 1988), 23. Jason C. Bivins, *Religion of Fear: The Politics of Horror in Conservative Evangelicalism* (New York: Oxford University Press, 2008), 179.

60. Tim LaHaye and Jerry B. Jenkins, *Are We Living in the End Times? Current Events Foretold in Scripture . . . And What They Mean* (Wheaton, IL: Tyndale House, 1999), 4.

61. Jerry B. Jenkins, "Biography," n.d., http://www.jerryjenkins.com/about-2/biography/ (accessed August 13, 2009). Melani McAlister, "Prophecy, Politics, and the Popular: The *Left Behind* Series and Christian Fundamentalism's New World Order," *South Atlantic Quarterly* 102:4 (2003): 773.

62. Tim LaHaye and Jerry B. Jenkins, *Left Behind: A Novel of the Earth's Last Days* (Wheaton, IL: Tyndale House, 1995), 2. Andrew Gumbel, "The Profits of Doom," *Independent,* November 12, 2000, 7. Tim LaHaye and Jerry B. Jenkins, *Armageddon: The Cosmic Battle of the Ages* (Wheaton, IL: Tyndale House, 2003), the eleventh book in the series, sold 1,620,480 in the year it was published. Dave Bogart, ed., *The Bowker Annual: Library and Book Trade Almanac* (Medford, NJ: Information Today, 2004), 575.

63. Jane Lampman, "The End of the World," *Christian Science Monitor,* February 18, 2004. "A Half-Century of Evangelical Influence in U.S.," *Hartford Courant,* July 30, 2006, 5. Ann Banks, "In a Nervous World, a Series of Apocalyptic Thrillers Continues to Dominate Bestseller Lists," *Washington Post,* October 17, 2004, T10. Amy Johnson Frykholm, *Rapture Culture: Left Behind in Evangelical America* (New York: Oxford University Press, 2004), 3–4, 178. See also the interview in the Assemblies of God denomination's magazine, "Conversation with Tim LaHaye: Prophecy-based Fiction," *Pentecostal Evangel,* n.d., available at http://www.

ag.org/pentecostal-evangel/articles/conversations/4490_LaHaye.cfm (accessed April 2, 2008).

64. LaHaye and Jenkins, *Left Behind,* 245–246. Gumbel, "The Profits of Doom," 9.

65. LaHaye and Jenkins, *Left Behind,* 172. Tim LaHaye and Jerry B. Jenkins, *Tribulation Force: The Continuing Drama of Those Left Behind* (Wheaton, IL: Tyndale House, 1996), 66; quote p. 65.

66. LaHaye and Jenkins, *Tribulation Force,* 318, 319; quotes pp. 107 and 396. Tim LaHaye and Jerry B. Jenkins, *Assassins: Assignment: Jerusalem, Target: Antichrist* (Wheaton, IL: Tyndale House, 2000), 25.

67. Tim LaHaye and Jerry B. Jenkins, *Soul Harvest: The World Takes Sides* (Wheaton IL: Tyndale House, 1998), 172. Tim LaHaye and Jerry B. Jenkins, *Nicolae: The Rise of Antichrist* (Wheaton, IL: Tyndale House, 1998), 359–360.

68. Tim LaHaye, Jerry Jenkins, and Joel Rosenberg interviewed by Glenn Beck, "Honest Questions about the End of Days," March 30, 2007, available at transcripts.cnn.com/TRANSCRIPTS/0703/30/gb.01.html.

69. Jerry Falwell, "Don't Be Left Behind!" July 21, 2001, available at http://www.wnd.com/index.php?pageId=10121. "What the Pre-Trib Research Center Is About," pre-trib.org/about (accessed August 14, 2009).

70. Tim LaHaye, Jerry B. Jenkins, and Sandi L. Swanson, *The Authorized Left Behind Handbook* (Wheaton, IL: Tyndale House, 2005), 14, 18, 21, 78–79. McAlister, "Prophecy, Politics, and the Popular," 784.

71. Nancy Gibbs, "Apocalypse Now." Linton Weeks, "The End, To Be Continued," *Washington Post,* July 23, 2002, C1.

72. "Features: Gameplay," available at http://www.eternalforces.com/features.aspx (accessed August 24, 2009). "Christian Coalition Applauds Impact of New Left Behind Video Game," *Electronic News Publishing Newswire,* January 10, 2007.

73. Quotes from William Fisher, "Christians Clash over Rapture-Themed Videogame," *Inter Press Service,* December 14, 2006.

74. Andrea Hopkins, "Moderate Christians Fight Rapture with Sunday School," *Reuters News,* March 13, 2007.

75. John Dart, "Armageddon—Threat or Bunk? Academicians Debate Fundamentalist View of the World," *Los Angeles Times,* March 3, 1984, C6. Roy A. Harrisville, "Tomorrow with Hal Lindsey," *Dialog* 13:4 (1974): 294, 296.

76. James J. Megivern, "A Decade of Doomsday," *Wilmington Morning Star,* May 31, 1980, 6-A.

77. Elizabeth Schussler, quoted in Adon Taft, "'Prophets' of Doom Misguided Worried Biblical Scholars Say," *Toronto Star,* August 24, 1985, L8.

78. David L. Cooper, *The World's Greatest Library: Graphically Illustrated* (Los Angeles: Biblical Research Society, 1970), 11. Mark Noll, "Common Sense Traditions and American Evangelical Thought," *American Quarterly* 37:2 (1985): 220, 224, 230.

79. Mark Noll, *The Scandal of the Evangelical Mind* (Grand Rapids, MI: William B. Eerdmans, 1994), 125–126, 132. D. N. Hempton, "Evangelicalism and Eschatology," *Journal of Ecclesiastical History* 31 (1980): 187, 194.

80. N. T. Wright, "Farewell to the Rapture," *Bible Review,* August 2001, available at http://www.ntwrightpage.com/Wright_BR_Farewell_Rapture.htm.

81. Eugene Peterson, *Christ Plays in Ten Thousand Places: A Conversation in Spiritual Theology* (Grand Rapids, MI: William B. Eerdmans, 2005), 65. Eugene Peterson, *Reversed Thunder: The Revelation of John and the Praying Imagination* (New York: HarperCollins, 1991), 5. Eugene H. Peterson, "Apocalypse: The Medium Is the Message," *Theology Today* 26:2 (1969): 133–141.

82. Tim LaHaye, quoted in Hopkins, "Moderate Christians Fight Rapture with Sunday School."

5. A Carnival of Christians

1. Stephen Phillip Broughman and Kathleen W. Pugh, *Characteristics of Private Schools in the United States: Results from the 2003–2004 Private School Survey* (Jessup, MD: U.S. Department of Education, 2006), C-24, D-3–D-8.

2. Randall Balmer, *The Making of Evangelicalism: From Revivalism to Politics and Beyond* (Waco, TX: Baylor University Press, 2010), 43–54. Colleen McDannell, *Material Christianity: Religion and Popular Culture in America* (New Haven: Yale University Press, 1995), 222–266.

3. Tim LaHaye, *The Battle for the Mind* (Old Tappan, NJ: Fleming H. Revell, 1980), 187–188.

4. Nancy T. Ammerman, *Baptist Battles: Social Change and Religious Conflict in the Southern Baptist Convention* (New Brunswick, NJ: Rutgers University Press, 1990). Kenneth D. Wald and Allison Calhoun-Brown, *Religion and Politics in the United States* (Lanham, MD: Rowman and Littlefield, 2007), 236–239. George M. Marsden, *Fundamentalism and American Culture* (New York: Oxford University Press, 2006), 94.

5. Charles W. Colson, *Born Again* (Grand Rapids, MI: Chosen, 1976).

6. C. S. Lewis, *Surprised by Joy: The Shape of My Early Life* (Orlando: Harcourt Brace, 1955).

7. Charlotte Elliott, "Just as I Am," from *Covenant Hymns: A Collection of Psalms, Hymns, and Spiritual Songs* (London: City Press, 1849), 207.

8. Paul Miller, interview with Karl Giberson and Randall Stephens, December 6, 2008, Boston, MA.

9. James Craig Holte, *The Conversion Experience in America: A Sourcebook on Religious Conversion Autobiography* (Westport, CT: Greenwood Press, 1992), ix–xiv. Barry Hankins, *American Evangelicals: A Contemporary History of a Mainstream Religious Movement* (Lanham, MD: Rowman and Littlefield, 2008), 2–3.

10. "Sinner's Prayer," sinner-prayer.com (accessed March 31, 2010).

11. Frank Newport, "Who Are the Evangelicals?" June 24, 2005, available at http://www.gallup.com/poll/17041/who-evangelicals.aspx.

12. "ARIS 2008 Report," available at http://www.americanreligionsurvey-aris.org/reports/ARIS_Report_2008.pdf.

13. Pew Forum on Religion and Public Life, "About One-in-Six Americans Are Baptist," June 18, 2009, available at http://pewforum.org/About-One-in-Six-Americans-Are-Baptist.aspx; and map: percentage of U.S. adults who are affiliated with: Evangelical Protestant Tradition, available at http://religions.pewforum.org/maps.

14. Paul Miller, interview, December 6, 2008.

15. Paul Miller, interview, December 6, 2008.

16. Paul Miller, interview, December 6, 2008.

17. Paul Miller, interview, December 6, 2008.

18. Paul Miller, interview, December 6, 2008.

19. Rebecca Rudolph, "Singing Tree Lights Tradition Continues," *Red and Black* (University of Georgia student newspaper), December 10, 2004.

20. Paul Miller, interview, December 6, 2008.

21. Athens, Georgia, church directory, available at http://www.usachurch.com/georgia/athens/home.htm (accessed March 31, 2010).

22. Paul Miller, email communication with Karl Giberson, June 22, 2010.

23. Paul Miller, interview, December 6, 2008.

24. Pew Forum on Religion and Public Life, "Many Americans Say Other Faiths Can Lead to Eternal Life: Most Christians Say Non-Christian Faiths Can Lead to Salvation," December 18, 2008, available at http://pewforum.org/Many-Americans-Say-Other-Faiths-Can-Lead-to-Eternal-Life.aspx. Phillip Jen-

kins, *The New Anti-Catholicism: The Last Acceptable Prejudice* (New York: Oxford University Press, 2003). T. A. McMahon, "*Christianity Today*'s Anti-Christianity Today," worldviewweekend.com, August 2, 2010.

25. Paul Miller, email communication with Karl Giberson, June 22, 2010.

26. "Catholic League: Hagee Goes Off the Rails, McCain Must Act," March 5, 2008, available at http://www.catholic.org/national/national_story.php?id=27068.

27. Robert J. Priest and Alvaro L. Nieves, eds., *This Side of Heaven: Race, Ethnicity, and Christian Faith* (Oxford: Oxford University Press, 2007), 275, 339.

28. Barry Hankins, *Uneasy in Babylon: Southern Baptist Conservatives and American Culture* (Tuscaloosa: University of Alabama Press, 2002), 224–225. Ammerman, *Baptist Battles,* 104–105.

29. Rose French, "Southern Baptist Colleges Seek Greater Independence," *Victoria Advocate,* December 2, 2006.

30. Jimmy Carter, *Our Endangered Values: America's Moral Crisis* (New York: Simon and Schuster, 2005), 42.

31. Gerald Harris, "Georgia Baptists Vote to End Relationship with Mercer University after 172 years," November 24, 2005, available at http://www.christianindex.org/1759.article.

32. Patrick Allitt, *Religion in America since 1945: A History* (New York: Columbia University Press, 2003), 185–186.

33. Center for Education Reform, "K–12 Facts," n.d., available at http://www.edreform.com/Fast_Facts/K12_Facts/ (accessed September 17, 2010).

34. National Center for Education Statistics, U.S. Department of Education, Private School Universe Survey (PSS), Table 14, "Number of private schools, students and teachers . . . , 2007–08," available at http://nces.ed.gov/surveys/pss/tables/table_2008_14.asp; and National Catholic Education Association, "Catholic School Data," n.d., available at http://www.ncea.org/news/CatholicSchoolData.asp (accessed September 17, 2010).

35. Council for American Private Education, "Facts and Studies," n.d. (data from 2007–08, 2009), available at http://www.capenet.org/facts.html (accessed September 17, 2010).

36. National Center for Education Statistics, "Homeschooled Students," n.d. (data from 1999, 2003, 2007), available at http://nces.ed.gov/programs/coe/2009/section1/indicator06.asp (accessed September 17, 2010); and Dan Gilgoff, "As Home Schooling Surges, the Evangelical Share Drops," *U.S. News and World Report,* January 9, 2009.

37. Gilgoff, "As Home Schooling Surges."

38. Gilgoff, "As Home Schooling Surges."

39. Prince Avenue Christian School, "Who We Are," April 22, 2011, princeave.org; and National Center for Education Statistics, Private School Universe Survey, Table 1, "Number and Percentage Distribution of Private Schools, Students, and . . . Teacher . . . 2007–08," available at http://nces.ed.gov/surveys/pss/tables/table_2008_01.asp (accessed September 17, 2010).

40. Prince Avenue Christian School, "Academics," n.d., princeave.org (accessed April 12, 2010).

41. Prince Avenue Christian School, "Mission Statement," n.d., available at http://princeave.org/spiritual-emphasis/mission-statement (accessed April 12, 2010).

42. A Beka Book, Home School Catalog, http://www.abeka.com/Interactive-PDF/HomeSchoolCatalog/pageflip.html (accessed June 12, 2009).

43. "God's Own Scholars: Alternative Education: The Growing Number of Fundamentalist Christian Schools," *Economist,* June 6, 1998, 30.

44. David Barton, "The Founding Fathers on Jesus, Christianity, and the Bible," May 2008, available at http://www.wallbuilders.com/LIBissuesArticles.asp?id=8755.

45. John E. Jenkins and George Mulfinger, Jr., *Basic Science for Christian Schools* (Greenville, SC: Bob Jones University Press, 1983), 505.

46. Jenkins and Mulfinger, *Basic Science for Christian Schools,* 513.

47. Wayne Anderson, "A World Without Rainbows?" *Free Inquiry* 21:3 (2001), available at http://www.secularhumanism.org/index.php?section=library&page=anderson_21_3.

48. Brian D. Ray, "Research Facts on Homeschooling," January 11, 2011, National Home Education Research Institute, available at http://www.nheri.org/Research-Facts-on-Homeschooling.html (accessed April 26, 2011).

49. Accelerated Christian Education, "A Partial List of Colleges and Universities That Have Accepted Graduates of Accelerated Christian Education Curriculum and Programs," 2008 revision, available at https://aceweb.schooloftomorrow.com/aboutus/09-2008-CollegeUniv-web.pdf.

50. Patrick Henry College, "Statement of Faith," n.d., available at http://www.phc.edu/statement_2.php (accessed September 2, 2010).

51. Hanna Rosin, *God's Harvard: A Christian College on a Mission to Save America* (Orlando: Harcourt, 2007), 46.

52. Brannon Howse, "We Must Reclaim the Church before We Can Even

Begin to Reclaim the Culture," August 17, 2009, available at http://www.worldviewweekend.com/worldview-times/article.php?articleid=5294.

53. Pew Forum on Religion and Public Life, "U.S. Religious Landscape Survey," n.d., available at http://religions.pewforum.org/reports (accessed September 2, 2010).

54. National Center for Education Statistics, Private School Universe Survey (PSS), Table 14, "Number of private schools, students and teacher . . . , 2007–08." Ronald L. Numbers, *The Creationists: From Scientific Creationism to Intelligent Design* (Cambridge, MA: Harvard University Press, 2006), 330–331. Alan Peshkin, *God's Choice: The Total World of a Fundamentalist Christian School* (Chicago: University of Chicago Press, 1988), 26.

55. Karl W. Giberson and Donald A. Yerxa, *Species of Origins: America's Search for a Creation Story* (Lanham, MD: Rowman and Littlefield, 2002). Lee Weeks, "Unraveling the Myth of Evolution: Classroom Victory in the Battle for Truth," *SBC Life,* October 1999, available at http://www.sbclife.net/Articles/1999/10/sla10.asp. Pew Forum on Religion and Public Life, "Religious Differences on the Question of Evolution," February 4, 2009, available at http://stage.pewforum.org/Science-and-Bioethics/Religious-Differences-on-the-Question-of-Evolution.aspx.

56. Jeffrey M. Jones, "Majority of Americans Continue to Oppose Gay Marriage," May 27, 2009, available at http://www.gallup.com/poll/118378/majority-americans-continue-oppose-gay-marriage.aspx.

57. First Amendment Center, "'07 Survey Shows Americans' Views Mixed on Basic Freedoms," September 24, 2007, available at http://www.firstamendmentcenter.org/news.aspx?id=19031. Pew Forum on Religion and Public Life, "Many Americans Uneasy with Mix of Religion and Politics," August 24, 2006, available at http://pewforum.org/Politics-and-Elections/Many-Americans-Uneasy-with-Mix-of-Religion-and-Politics.aspx.

58. "Dr. Dobson Offers Encouragement to Parents of Teens," focusonthefamily.com (accessed June 12, 2009).

59. "Focus on the Family's Plugged in Online," pluggedinonline.com (accessed June 12, 2009).

60. answersingenesis.org, drdino.com, creationevidence.org.

61. reasons.org, IntelligentDesign.org, EvolutionNews.org, IDTheFuture.com, DissentFromDarwin.org, DarwinAndDesign.com, DarwinismandID.com, IconsofEvolution.com, DarwinToHitler.com, PriviledgedPlanet.com, DarwinDayInAmerica.com, JudgingPBS.com.

62. Ken Ham, "D is for Dinosaur" (video), n.d., available at http://www.answersingenesis.org/media/video/kids/d-is-for-dinosaur/d-dinosaur (accessed July 15, 2009). "Kids Answers," answersingenesis.org (accessed June 12, 2009). John MacArthur, "What's Your Worldview?," May 2, 2006, available at http://www.answersingenesis.org/articles/am/v1/n1/whats-your-worldview. "Building the Creation Model," answersingenesis.org (accessed June 12, 2009).

63. Paul Miller, interview with Karl Giberson, June 8, 2009, Boston, MA.

64. *Nova: Evolution: What about God?* Part 7, directed by Bill Jersey and Mark Page (Boston: WGBH Boston Video, 2001).

65. Paul Miller, interview, June 8, 2009.

66. Quoted in Joseph L. Conn, "Public School Calumny: LaHaye Launches Vicious Attack on Public School System," Wall of Separation, August 12, 2008, available at http://blog.au.org/2008/08/12/public-school-calumny-lahaye-launches-vicious-attack-on-public-school-system/.

67. Worldviewweekend.org, summit.org.

68. Paul Miller, interview, June 8, 2009.

69. Paul Miller, interview, June 8, 2009. Rick Freed, "What Is Your Business Worldview?" October 4, 2004, available at http://www.christianitytoday.com/workplace/articles/whatbusinessworldview.html. Clem Boyd, "The Good, the Bad, and the Filter: Seven Ways to Help Screen Culture's Impurities from Your Children's Minds," *Christian Parenting Today,* 2005, available at http://www.kyria.com/topics/marriagefamily/parenting/kidsculture/19.40.html?start=1.

70. Paul Miller, interview, June 8, 2009.

71. Paul Miller, interview, June 8, 2009.

72. "Think and Live Like a Christian," worldviewweekend.com (accessed July 17, 2009).

73. "Summit Ministries," http://www.summit.org/ (accessed July 17, 2009).

74. The Christian Worldview (radio program), available at thechristianworldview.com (accessed July 17, 2009).

75. "Worldview Weekend Coming to Grace Community Church," *Osage County Chronicle,* January 18, 2007, 1. "Midwestern Partners with Worldview Weekend Conferences," sbcbaptistpress.org (accessed August 24, 2010). "Worldview Weekend Recap," *Gettysburg Times,* April 20, 2005, B8. St. Gail Hollenbeck, "Is Your Worldview Schizophrenic?" *St. Petersburg Times,* October 9, 2004, 10.

76. Paul Miller, interview, June 8, 2009.

77. I John 2:15 (KJV).

78. John MacArthur, *Strength for Today* (Wheaton, IL: Crossway Books, 1997), 13.

79. Quoted in Joe Beam and Lee Wilson, *The Real Heaven: It's Not What You Think* (Webb City, MO: Covenant, 2006), 65.

80. See Randall Balmer's description of "worldliness" in Balmer, *Encyclopedia of Evangelicalism* (Waco, TX: Baylor University Press, 2004), 642.

81. Restored Church of God, "Worldliness: What Is It?" 2008, available at http://www.thercg.org/articles/wwii.html#c. Balmer, *The Making of Evangelicalism*, 82–83. Grant Wacker, *Heaven Below: Early Pentecostals and American Culture* (Cambridge, MA: Harvard University Press, 2001), 128–130.

82. Paul Miller, interview, June 8, 2009.

83. Daniel Radosh, *Rapture Ready! Adventures in the Parallel Universe of Christian Pop Culture* (New York: Scribner, 2008), 3.

84. National Religious Broadcasters, "Who Are We?" http://nrb.org/about (accessed July 16, 2009).

85. Josh Kimball, "Survey: Only 3 in 5 Christian Radio Listeners Tune in for Music," *Christian Post*, July 15, 2008, available at http://www.christianpost.com/news/survey-only-3-in-5-christian-radio-listeners-tune-in-for-music-33305/. Robert H. Lochte, *Christian Radio: The Growth of a Mainstream Broadcasting Force* (Jefferson, NC: McFarland, 2006). Robert S. Fortner, "Media," in *The Blackwell Companion to Religion in America*, ed. Philip Goff (Chichester, UK: Blackwell, 2010), 206–213. Paul A. Creasman, "Looking Beyond Radio for Listeners," in *Understanding Evangelical Media: The Changing Face of Christian Communication*, ed. Quentin J. Schultze and Robert Woods (Downers Grove, IL: InterVarsity Press, 2008), 33–45.

86. Harvey Cox, *Religion in the Secular City: Toward a Postmodern Theology* (New York: Simon and Schuster, 1984), 43.

87. DC Talk, "I Don't Want It," from *Free at Last* (Franklin, TN: ForeFront Records, 1992).

88. Bob Larson, *Rock and Roll: The Devil's Diversion* (Creation House, 1967).

89. "Christian Rap Music," ezinearticles.com (accessed July 17, 2009).

90. Mark Allan Powell, "Jesus Climbs the Charts: The Business of Contemporary Christian Music," *Christian Century*, December 18, 2002, 20.

91. Paul Miller, interview, June 8, 2009. Jay R. Howard and John M. Streck, *Apostles of Rock: The Splintered World of Contemporary Christian Music* (Lexington: Uni-

versity Press of Kentucky, 1999). "Third Day Keeps the Faith," *Billboard,* June 7, 2008, 22.

92. Radosh, *Rapture Ready!* 153. Paul Y. Chang and Dale J. Lim, "Renegotiating the Sacred-Secular Binary: IX Saves and Contemporary Christian Music," *Review of Religious Research* 50:4 (2009): 392–412. Howard and Streck, *Apostles of Rock,* 43–44, 192.

93. Radosh, *Rapture Ready!* 160. Quote from *Rolling Stone* in Powell, "Jesus Climbs the Charts," 21.

94. Paul Miller, interview, June 8, 2009. Joshua Langhoff, "Music for the Megachurch: Amy Grant Leads Christian Rock into Promised Land, but It Settles for Bake Sale Normalcy," *Village Voice,* June 28, 2005.

95. ApologetiX, "Discography and Mission," n.d., available at http://www.apologetix.com/music/music.php (accessed September 2, 2010).

96. The Carpenter's Shop, Athens, Georgia, home page available at http://www.logosbookstores.com/joomla/index.php?option=com_content&task=view&id=50&Itemid=116 (accessed June 23, 2009).

97. Paul Miller, interview, June 8, 2009.

98. Radosh, *Rapture Ready!* 89.

99. Radosh, *Rapture Ready!* 9.

100. Peter Chattaway, "What Theology Has Been 'Left Behind' in Best Selling Novel Series?" June 25, 2001, available at http://www.baptiststandard.com/2001/6_25/print/left_behind.html.

101. virtuousplanet.com (accessed September 2, 2010).

102. "Modest Is Hottest" T-shirt, available at http://www.modestishottest.com/category/modest-is-hottest/ (accessed April 26, 2011).

103. "His Pain, Your Gain" T-shirt, available at http://www.all-christian-t-shirts.com/hispain.html (accessed July 17, 2009).

104. Christian Tools of Affirmation, available at ctainc.com (accessed July 17, 2009).

105. Christianbook, Gift and Home, available at http://www.christianbook.com/Christian/Books/easy_find?event=HPT&category=Gift%20%26%20Home&N=1014723&Ne=1000000&Nso=1&Nu=product%2Eendeca%5Frollup&Ns=product%2Enumber%5Fsold (accessed July 17, 2009). On Christian kitsch, see McDannell, *Material Christianity.*

106. "Christian Superheroes: Origins: The Cross and the Glory," christianknight-comics.com (accessed July 20, 2009).

107. Christian Knight Comics, available at christianknightcomics.com (accessed July 20, 2009).

108. Comic Book Religion, available at comicbookreligion.com (accessed July 20, 2009).

109. "Salvation Challenge," biblicalstrategy.com (accessed July 20, 2009).

110. amazon.com (accessed September 16, 2010).

111. Paul Miller, interview, June 8, 2009.

112. "Summit Ministries: Adult Conferences," summit.org (accessed July 1, 2009).

113. "Our Goal, Vision, and Mission," bryan.edu (accessed July 20, 2009). Ravi Zacharias, *Jesus among Other Gods: The Absolute Claims of the Christian Message* (Nashville: Word Publishing, 2000), vii–x.

114. "Impressive Facts about Catholic Colleges," http://www.thehighschool-graduate.com/editorial/catholic-colleges-and-universities.html.

115. Harvard University, "The Harvard Guide," available at http://www.news.harvard.edu/guide/ (accessed September 2, 2010). George M. Marsden, *The Soul of the American University: From Protestant Establishment to Established Nonbelief* (New York: Oxford University Press, 1994), 3–8.

116. Pew Forum on Religion and Public Life, "UCLA Study: Students Become More Spiritual in College," February 14, 2008, available at http://pewforum.org/UCLA-Study-Students-Become-More-Spiritual-in-College.aspx.

117. William C. Ringenberg, *The Christian College: A History of Protestant Higher Education in America* (Grand Rapids, MI: Baker Books, 2006), 113–143.

118. One of the most elite Christian institutions, Wheaton College in Illinois, has an essentially fundamentalist faith statement that often seems at odds with even the publications of its faculty.

119. College Board, "College Search," available at http://collegesearch.college-board.com/search/index.jsp (accessed July 20, 2009).

120. Alan Wolfe, "The Opening of the Evangelical Mind," *Atlantic Monthly* (October 2000).

121. "Higher Education?" facingthechallenge.org (accessed July 20, 2009). Statistics tell us that 50 percent of them will lose their faith during college. That percentage escalates if they are not plugged in to a campus group or local church.

122. Bryan College, "Summit at Bryan College," available at http://www.bryan.edu/summit.html (accessed July 17, 2009).

123. Richard Dawkins, "Sadly, an Honest Creationist," *Free Inquiry* 21:4 (2001), available at http://www.secularhumanism.org/library/fi/dawkins_21_4.html.
124. Center for Origins Research, Bryan College: "Developing and Teaching a Creation Model of Biology," available at http://www.bryancore.org/about.html; "Origin Studies Minor at Bryan College," http://www.bryancore.org/originsminor.html; "*CORE Issues in Creation*," available at http://www.bryancore.org/issues/index.html; and "Center for Origins Research Celebrates 20th Anniversary," available at http://www.bryancore.org/anniversary/events.html (accessed March 16, 2011).
125. Bryan College, "Statement of Belief," available at http://www.bryan.edu/379.html (accessed February 14, 2010).
126. Paul Miller, interview, June 8, 2009. Alan Wolfe, *The Transformation of American Religion: How We Actually Live Our Faith* (Chicago: University of Chicago Press, 2003), 35–36. Hankins, *American Evangelicals*, ix–x. Christian Smith with Michael Emerson, Sally Gallagher, Paul Kennedy, and David Sikkink, *American Evangelicalism: Embattled and Thriving* (Chicago: University of Chicago Press, 1998), 226–231.
127. E. O. Wilson's faith story is recounted in Robert Wright, *Three Scientists and Their Gods: Looking for Meaning in an Age of Information* (New York: HarperCollins, 1989). Michael Shermer "Why I Am an Atheist," June 2005, available at http://www.michaelshermer.com/2005/06/why-i-am-an-atheist/.
128. Matthew Arnold, *Poems by Matthew Arnold* (New York: MacMillan, 1890), 212. A. N. Wilson chronicles the Victorian loss of faith in *God's Funeral: The Decline of Faith in Western Civilization* (New York: W. W. Norton, 1999). David Hempton, *Evangelical Disenchantment: Nine Portraits of Faith and Doubt* (New Haven: Yale University Press, 2008), 3–4, 12–18.
129. Barry Hankins, *Francis Schaeffer and the Shaping of Evangelical America* (Grand Rapids, MI: Eerdmans, 2008), xi.
130. Molly Worthen, "Not Your Father's L'Abri," *Christianity Today*, March 2008, 60.
131. Hankins, *Francis Schaeffer and the Shaping of Evangelical America*, 96–105.
132. L'Abri, "L'Abri Fellowship," available at http://www.labri.org/ (accessed July 20, 2009).
133. Paul Miller, interview, June 8, 2009.
134. Eduardo J. Echeverria, "The Christian Faith as a Way of Life: In Appreciation of Francis Schaeffer (on the Fiftieth Anniversary of L'Abri Fellowship)," *Evangelical Quarterly* 79:3 (2007): 241.

135. Paul Miller, interview, June 8, 2009. Worthen, "Not Your Father's L'Abri," 60.
136. Paul Miller, interview, June 8, 2009.
137. Duane Litfin, *Conceiving the Christian College* (Grand Rapids, MI: Eerdmans, 2004), 13–17, 83–84. Marsden, *The Soul of the American University*, 421–422.
138. Wheaton College, "About Us: Mission," available at http://www.wheaton.edu/welcome/aboutus_mission.html (accessed August 10, 2010).
139. Litfin, *Conceiving the Christian College*, 18–20.
140. Scott Jaschik, "Believing in God and Evolution," Inside Higher Ed, October 14, 2009, available at http://www.insidehighered.com/news/2009/10/14/evolution.

6. *Made in America*

1. Jerry Falwell, quoted in "Loathed by Liberals, Falwell Was Force among Right-Wing," May 15, 2007, available at http://articles.cnn.com/2007-05-15/politics/falwell.politics_1_thomas-road-baptist-church-jerry-falwell-moral-majority?_s=PM:POLITICS. Laurie Goodstein, "After the Attacks: Finding Fault; Falwell's Finger-Pointing Inappropriate, Bush Says," *New York Times*, September 15, 2001.

2. The honorary doctorates were Doctor of Divinity from Tennessee Temple Theological Seminary, Doctor of Letters from California Graduate School of Theology, and Doctor of Laws from Central University in Seoul, South Korea. Liberty University, Executive Biographies: Dr. Jerry Falwell, available at http://www.liberty.edu/index.cfm?PID=6921 (accessed August 11, 2010).

3. On Falwell's background, see Susan Friend Harding, *The Book of Jerry Falwell: Fundamentalist Language and Politics* (Princeton: Princeton University Press, 2000), 88, 90–93. "Falwell's Farewell," *National Review*, July 14, 1989, 19. William Martin, *With God on Our Side: The Rise of the Religious Right in America* (New York: Broadway Books, 2005), 219–220. "Falwell's Group Pushes Vote Drive; Moral Majority Expects to Be Responsible for 8 Million Registrations by 1984," *New York Times*, October 21, 1982, B13.

4. Pat Robertson, quoted in Paul Farhi, "Talking Heads' Comments about Haiti Draw Fire from Both Sides," *Washington Post*, January 15, 2010. Stephanie Condon, "Pat Robertson Haiti Comments Spark Uproar," January 14, 2010, available at http://www.cbsnews.com/8301-503544_162-6096806-503544.html#.

5. David Edwin Harrell, Jr., *Pat Robertson: A Life and Legacy* (Grand Rapids, MI: Eerdmans, 2010), 6–10, 15.

6. David Edwin Harrell, Jr., *Oral Roberts: An American Life* (Bloomington: Indiana University Press, 1985), 26–29. Justin Juozapavicius, "Evangelist Oral Roberts Dies in Calif. at Age 91," *Seattle Times,* December 16, 2009.

7. Oral Roberts, quoted in "Oral Roberts Tells Conference He Has Raised People from the Dead," *New York Times,* June 27, 1987, 12.

8. David Van Biema, "Oral Roberts to the Rescue?" *Time,* October 27, 2007. Elizabeth Greene, "Closing of the Medical School at Oral Roberts U Turns 150-Million Dollar Center into a Ghost Town," *Chronicle of Higher Education,* June 24, 1990, 27, 29. Martin Gardner, "Giving God a Hand," *New York Review of Books,* August 13, 1987.

9. Ronald Dworkin, "What Liberalism Isn't," *New York Review of Books,* January 20, 1983. See also Charles Krauthammer, "Varieties of Apocalyptic Experience: The End of the World," *New Republic,* March 28, 1983, 12–15.

10. Richard Cohen, ". . . And Apostles of Ignorance," *Washington Post,* September 21, 1984, A21.

11. Christopher Reed, "Oral Roberts Obituary," *Guardian* (UK), December 15, 2009. Harrell, *Oral Roberts,* 416–417.

12. Robert Liichow, "Oral Roberts: Dead and Damage Done," Discernment Ministries International, January 2010, available at http://discernmentministriesinternational.wordpress.com/category/william-branham/. Donald B. Ardell, "Oral Roberts: Insane or Con Artist?" December 17, 2009, available at http://www.seekwellness.com/wellness/reports/2009-12-17.htm.

13. Robert Wuthnow, *Boundless Faith: The Global Outreach of American Churches* (Berkeley: University of California Press, 2009), 73.

14. Pat Robertson, quoted in Alan Cooperman, "Robertson Defends Liberia's President; Other Evangelical Leaders Disagree," *Washington Post,* July 10, 2003, A19. Angell Watts, "Concern for Liberia, Not Charles Taylor," *Washington Post,* August 9, 2003, A13. Chuck Fager, "Mining Controversy: Robertson Takes Flak for Gold-Mining Venture," *Christianity Today,* February 4, 2002.

15. Mike Barnicle, "Almighty Dollars," *Boston Globe,* March 27, 1987, 17. Mike Royko, "A Devilish Night for Oral Roberts," *Chicago Tribune,* February 20, 1987. Mike Jeffries and Tom Blankenship, quoted in Peter Applebome, "At Oral Roberts U., Evangelist's Divine Plea Causes No Alarm," *New York Times,* February 16, 1987, 8. Phil Musick, "For Oral Roberts, Donations Are a Life-and-Death Matter," *Pittsburgh Press,* January 13, 1987, A13. See also this letter to the editor praising Falwell's reaching out to homosexuals: Theo Caldwell, "To the Editor," *New York Times,* October 28, 1999, A30.

16. Princeton Review, *Complete Book of Colleges, 2010 Edition* (New York: Princeton Review, 2009), 471–472, 646. John W. Kennedy, "Liberty Unbound: How Jerry Falwell's Ambitious Sons Have Led the Lynchburg University to Financial Success and a Burgeoning Student Body," *Christianity Today*, September 2009, 40–44. *U.S. News and World Report*, College Rankings and Reviews: Oral Roberts University, available at http://colleges.usnews.rankingsandreviews.com/best-colleges/oral-roberts-university-3985; and Liberty University, available at http://colleges.usnews.rankingsandreviews.com/best-colleges/liberty-university-10392 (accessed August 12, 2010).

17. *U.S. News and World Report*, College Rankings and Reviews, Regent University, available at http://colleges.usnews.rankingsandreviews.com/best-colleges/regent-university-30913 (accessed August 12, 2010). A Regent University official, quoted in Dahlia Lithwick, "Who's the Boss? How Pat Robertson's Law School Is Changing America," April 7, 2007, available at http://www.slate.com/id/2163601/. Alan Cooperman, "Bush Loyalist Rose Quickly at Justice," *Washington Post*, March 30, 2007.

18. Harrell, *Oral Roberts*, 230; Roberts quote p. 231.

19. Regent University, "History of Regent," n.d., available at http://www.regent.edu/about_us/overview/history.cfm (accessed September 12, 2010).

20. Transnational Association of Christian Colleges and Schools, "Accreditation Standards," available at http://www.tracs.org/tracs_standards.htm (accessed September 26, 2010). "Accreditation Manual," January 2011, available at http://www.tracs.org/files/AccreditationManual_January_2011.pdf. Randy Moore, Mark Decker, and Sehoya Cotner, *Chronology of the Evolution-Creationism Controversy* (Santa Barbara, CA: Greenwood Press/ABC-CLIO, 2010), 263. Frederick S. Lane, *The Court and the Cross: The Religious Right's Crusade to Reshape the Supreme Court* (Boston: Beacon Press, 2008), 61.

21. George Marsden, *Fundamentalism and American Culture: The Shaping of Twentieth-Century Evangelicalism, 1870–1925* (New York: Oxford University Press, 1980), 212.

22. Jack Hayford, "Time for an 'Oral Review,'" *Ministry Today*, July/August 2005, available at http://www.ministrytodaymag.com/index.php/pastors-heart/11395-time-for-an-oral-review.

23. Roger Ebert, "Interview with Marjoe Gortner," *Chicago Sun-Times*, September 25, 1972. See also Steven S. Gaines, *Marjoe* (San Francisco: Harper and Row, 1973). "Child Preacher: Show Biz or Salvation?" *Nightline*, May 19, 2009, available

at http://abcnews.go.com/video/playerIndex?id=7620566. Alissa Quart, *Hothouse Kids: How the Pressure to Succeed Threatens Childhood* (New York: Penguin, 2006), 169–184.

24. Frank Schaeffer, *Crazy for God: How I Grew Up as One of the Elect, Helped Found the Religious Right, and Lived to Take All (or Almost All) of It Back* (New York: Carroll and Graf, 2007), 1.

25. David Martin, *On Secularization: Towards a Revised General Theory* (Aldershot, UK: Ashgate, 2005), 152.

26. Stephen Worchel and William G. Austin, eds., *Psychology of Intergroup Relations* (Chicago: Nelson-Hall, 1986). Henri Tajfel, ed., *Social Identity and Intergroup Relations* (Cambridge: Cambridge University Press, 1982). John C. Turner, *Rediscovering the Social Group: A Self-Categorization Theory* (Oxford: Blackwell, 1987). James M. Penning, "Americans' Views of Muslims and Mormons: A Social Identity Theory Approach," *Politics and Religion* 2 (2009): 277–302.

27. Ralph Waldo Emerson, *The Complete Works of Ralph Waldo Emerson,* vol. 1 (Boston: Houghton, Mifflin, 1904), 114. Marcel Duchamp, quoted in Michael Leja, *Looking Askance: Skepticism and American Art from Eakins to Duchamp* (Berkeley: University of California Press, 2004), 233.

28. Richard Hofstadter, *Anti-Intellectualism in American Life* (New York: Alfred A. Knopf, 1969), 3, 145–149, 30–31. See also Stephen J. Whitfield, "The Eggheads and the Fatheads," *Change* 10:4 (1978): 64–66; and Kenneth H. Ashworth, "McCarthyism in the Classroom: Anti-Intellectualism at Its Worst," *Change* 17:6 (1985), 10.

29. Sarah Palin, quoted in Robert Costa, "The National Review: The Palin Revolution Re-cap," February 8, 2010, available at http://www.npr.org/templates/story/story.php?storyId=123492972.

30. Jonathan Raban, "Sarah and Her Tribe," *New York Review of Books,* January 14, 2010. See also Mark Lilla, "The Perils of 'Populist Chic,'" *Wall Street Journal,* November 8, 2008; Yuval Levin, "The Meaning of Sarah Palin," *Commentary* (February 2009): 15–19; and Sarah Palin, *Going Rogue: An American Life* (New York: HarperCollins, 2009), 232, 385–387, 395.

31. Hofstadter, *Anti-Intellectualism in American Life,* 47.

32. Nathan O. Hatch, *The Democratization of American Christianity* (New Haven: Yale University Press, 1989), 162–163. Charles Lanman, *Adventures in the Wilds of the United States and British American Provinces,* vol. 1 (Philadelphia: John W. More, 1856), 500.

33. William Gerald McLoughlin, *Revivals, Awakenings, and Reform* (Chicago: University of Chicago Press, 1978). Robert Fogel, *The Fourth Great Awakening and the Future of Egalitarianism* (Chicago: University of Chicago Press, 2002).

34. Mark A. Noll, *The Scandal of the Evangelical Mind* (Grand Rapids, MI: Eerdmans, 1994), 61.

35. Hofstadter, *Anti-Intellectualism in American Life,* 81–116; quote p. 48, note 8.

36. Hofstadter, *Anti-Intellectualism in American Life,* 115.

37. E. L. Doctorow, "Bush's Intelligence," *Nation,* July 14, 2008.

38. Charles Malik, *The Two Tasks* (Westchester, IL: Cornerstone, 1980).

39. Noll, *Scandal of the Evangelical Mind,* ix, 328–329.

40. Noll, *Scandal of the Evangelical Mind,* 3, 4.

41. Noll, *Scandal of the Evangelical Mind,* 137.

42. Peter Steinfels, "An Evangelical Intellectual Finds a Kind of Heresy in Evangelicalism's Neglect of the Mind," *New York Times,* September 10, 1994. Grant Wacker, Keith Pavlischek, J. Daryl Charles, and Robert Wuthnow, "The Scandal of the Evangelical Mind: A Symposium," *First Things,* March 1995, available at http://www.firstthings.com/article/2008/08/003-the-scandal-of-the-evangelical-mind-a-symposium-33. Carl Wieland, "Book Review: *The Scandal of the Evangelical Mind,*" April 1996, available at http://creation.com/book-review-the-scandal-of-the-evangelical-mind.

43. Alan Wolfe, "The Opening of the Evangelical Mind," *Atlantic Monthly* (October 2000).

44. Wolfe, "Opening of the Evangelical Mind."

45. Noll, *Scandal of the Evangelical Mind,* 3.

46. On Oprah Winfrey's hawking of suspect panaceas see Weston Kosova, "Live Your Best Life Ever!" *Newsweek,* May 30, 2009. See also Chris Mooney, *The Republican War on Science* (New York: Basic Books, 2005); Francis Wheen, *How Mumbo-Jumbo Conquered the World: A Short History of Modern Delusions* (New York: PublicAffairs, 2004); Solomon Schimmel, *The Tenacity of Unreasonable Beliefs: Fundamentalism and the Fear of Truth* (New York: Oxford University Press, 2008); and Jonathan B. Imber, *Trusting Doctors: The Decline of Moral Authority in American Medicine* (Princeton: Princeton University Press, 2008).

47. Dan Kahan, "Is the Person Relaying an Argument More Important than the Argument Itself?" scienceandreligiontoday.com, June 14, 2010, in science and religion, June 2010 list, or on Kahan's website. See also Dan M. Kahan and Donald Braman, "Cultural Cognition and Public Policy," *Yale Law and Policy Review* 24:1 (2006), 150, 164, 166; Dan M. Kahan and Donald Braman, "More

Statistics, Less Persuasion: A Cultural Theory of Gun-Risk Perceptions," *University of Pennsylvania Law Review* 151:4 (2003): 1291–1327; and Imber, *Trusting Doctors,* 107–122.

48. Kahan, "Is the Person Relaying an Argument More Important than the Argument Itself?"

49. Kahan, "Is the Person Relaying an Argument More Important than the Argument Itself?"

50. Kahan, "Is the Person Relaying an Argument More Important than the Argument Itself?"

51. Brendan Nyhan and Jason Reifler, "When Corrections Fail: The Persistence of Political Misperceptions," *Political Behavior* 32:2 (2010): 303–330. James H. Kuklinski, Paul J. Quirk, Jennifer Jerit, David Schwieder, and Robert F. Rich, "Misinformation and the Currency of Democratic Citizenship," *Journal of Politics* 62 (2000): 790–816.

52. Michael Shermer, *Why People Believe Weird Things* (New York: Henry Holt, 2002).

53. Ken Ham, "Science Cannot Judge the Bible," October 25, 2008, available at http://blog.beliefnet.com/blogalogue/2008/10/science-cannot-judge-the-bible.html.

54. Broward Liston, "Interview: Missionary Work in Iraq," *Time,* April 15, 2003.

55. Albert Mohler, "Why Does the Universe Look So Old?" speech delivered June 19, 2010, transcript available at http://www.biologos.org/resources/albert-mohler-why-does-the-universe-look-so-old.

56. James A. Beverley, "Thinking Straighter: Why the World's Most Famous Atheist Now Believes in God," *Christianity Today,* April 8, 2005. Mark Oppenheimer, "The Turning of an Atheist," *New York Times,* November 4, 2007.

57. Stephen Garrard Post, Lynn G. Underwood, Jeffrey P. Schloss, and William B. Hurlbut, eds., *Altruism and Altruistic Love: Science, Philosophy, and Religion in Dialogue* (Oxford: Oxford University Press, 2002). Kristen Renwick Monroe, *The Heart of Altruism: Perceptions of a Common Humanity* (Princeton: Princeton University Press, 1996), 161–178. E. O. Wilson, *Sociobiology: The New Synthesis* (Cambridge, MA: Belknap Press of Harvard University Press, 2000), 117–120.

58. J. B. S. Haldane's 1974 quote in Kevin J. Connolly and Margaret Martlew, *Psychologically Speaking: A Book of Quotations* (Leicester: British Psychological Society, 1999), 10.

59. Steven Pinker, *The Blank Slate: The Modern Denial of Human Nature* (New York:

Penguin Books, 2002), 284–286. Richard Dawkins, *The Extended Phenotype: The Long Reach of the Gene* (New York: Oxford University Press, 1999), 35–36.

60. Stephen Crane, *The Open Boat and Other Tales of Adventure* (New York: Doubleday and McClure, 1898), 16.

61. Elliott Sober and David Sloan Wilson, *Unto Others: The Evolution and Psychology of Unselfish Behavior* (Cambridge, MA: Harvard University Press, 1999), 335–336.

62. Michael Gazzaniga, *Human: The Science Behind What Makes Us Unique* (New York: HarperCollins, 2008), 136. On animals and empathy see David Dobbs, "Do Animals Feel Empathy?" *Scientific American,* July 24, 2007.

63. Malcolm Gladwell, *The Tipping Point: How Little Things Can Make a Big Difference* (New York: Little, Brown, 2002), 182.

64. National Congregations Study, Data Wave 2 (2006–2007), available at http://www.soc.duke.edu/natcong/how_to_use.html#f (accessed March 17, 2011).

65. Christian Smith, *American Evangelicalism: Embattled and Thriving* (Chicago: University of Chicago Press, 1998), 32–36. Randall Balmer, *Mine Eyes Have Seen the Glory: A Journey into the Evangelical Subculture in America* (1989; repr., New York: Oxford University Press, 2006), 12–22. Robert Wuthnow, *Sharing the Journey: Support Groups and America's New Quest for Community* (New York: Free Press, 1994), 144–154.

66. Francis Schaeffer, *Plan for Action: An Action Alternative Handbook for Whatever Happened to the Human Race?* (Grand Rapids, MI: Fleming H. Revell, 1980), 68.

67. Marilynn B. Brewer, "Psychology of Prejudice: Ingroup Love or Outgroup Hate?" *Journal of Social Issues* 55:3 (1999): 435–436.

68. Tom Rees, "Why Religion Can Lead to Racism," *Epiphenom,* April 18, 2010, available at http://epiphenom.fieldofscience.com/2010/04/why-religion-can-lead-to-racism.html.

69. Lynne M. Jackson and Bruce Hunsberger, "An Intergroup Perspective on Religion and Prejudice," *Journal for the Scientific Study of Religion* 38:4 (1999): 521, 515. See also Christian Smith with Michael Emerson, Sally Gallagher, Paul Kennedy, and David Sikkink, *American Evangelicalism: Embattled and Thriving* (Chicago: University of Chicago Press, 1998); Michael O. Emerson and Christian Smith, *Divided by Faith: Evangelical Religion and the Problem of Race in America* (Oxford: Oxford University Press, 2000); Jay R. Feierman, *The Biology of Religious Behavior* (Santa Barbara: ABC-CLIO, 2009); and Jeffrey R. Seul, "'Ours Is the Way of God': Reli-

gion, Identity, and Intergroup Conflict," *Journal of Peace Research* 36:5 (1999): 553–569.

70. Charles Colson and Richard Neuhaus, eds., *Evangelicals and Catholics Together: Toward a Common Mission* (Nashville: Thomas Nelson, 1995), back cover.

71. Robert Wuthnow, *The Restructuring of American Religion: Society and Faith since World War II* (Princeton: Princeton University Press, 1988), 87–99. WallBuilders, "Overview," n.d., available at http://www.wallbuilders.com/ABTOverview.asp (accessed July 20, 2010).

72. Nancy Tatom Ammerman, *Baptist Battles: Social Change and Religious Conflict in the Southern Baptist Convention* (New Brunswick, NJ: Rutgers University Press, 1990), 123–125. Answers in Genesis, PowerPoint presentations on various topics, n.d., available at http://www.answersingenesis.org/home/area/overheads/TOC.asp (accessed August 15, 2010).

73. Smith, *American Evangelicalism,* 120–126. Harold J. Ockenga, "The Great Revival," *Bibliotheca Sacra* 104:414 (April–June 1947), 228.

74. Ken Ham, quoted in Michelle Goldberg, *Kingdom Coming: The Rise of Christian Nationalism* (New York: W. W. Norton, 2007), 96. On themes of light and darkness, see Nancy Tatom Ammerman, *Bible Believers: Fundamentalists in the Modern World* (New Brunswick, NJ: Rutgers University Press, 1987), 72–102.

75. Roy Moore, "Will America Choose to Acknowledge God?" World Net Daily, July 26, 2006, available at http://www.wnd.com/news/article.asp?ARTICLE_ID=51226.

76. Steven Pinker, quoted in Lisa Miller, "Harvard's Crisis of Faith: Can a Secular University Embrace Religion without Sacrificing Its Soul?" *Newsweek,* February 11, 2010.

77. Tim LaHaye, *Battle for the Mind* (Old Tappan, NJ: Fleming H. Revell, 1980), 9.

78. Ken Ham, "State of the Nation 2" (webcast), February 16, 2010, available at http://www.answerslive.org/.

79. Ham, "State of the Nation 2."

80. Chris Hedges, *American Fascists: The Christian Right and the War on America* (New York: Free Press, 2006), 27.

81. "'Creation' Witness Testifies about UFOs Sent by Satan," *San Francisco Chronicle,* December 12, 1981.

82. Henry M. Morris, *The Long War against God: The History and Impact of the Creation/Evolution Conflict* (Grand Rapids, MI: Baker Book House, 1989), 256.

83. Morris, *Long War against God,* 173–174.

84. Ed Stoddard, "Poll Finds More Americans Believe in Devil than Darwin," Reuters, November 29, 2007, available at http://www.reuters.com/article/2007/11/29/us-usa-religion-beliefs-idUSN2922875820071129.

85. Joseph Baker, "Who Believes in Religious Evil? An Investigation of Sociological Patterns of Belief in Satan, Hell, and Demons," *Review of Religious Research* 50:2 (2008): 206. Charles Honey, "Belief in Hell Dips, But Some Say They've Already Been There," Pew Forum on Religion and Public Life, August 14, 2008, available at http://pewforum.org/Religion-News/Belief-in-hell-dips-but-some-say-theyve-already-been-there.aspx. Pew Forum on Religion and Public Life, U.S. Religious Landscape Survey, Report," February 2008, Q.36 "Do you think there is a hell . . . ," p. 169, available at http://religions.pewforum.org/pdf/report-religious-landscape-study-full.pdf.

86. Peter Marshall, "The Secularist Wolves and Religious Freedom," February 4, 2010, available at http://www.petermarshallministries.com/commentary.cfm?commentary=245. See also D. James Kennedy and Jerry Newcombe, *Lord of All: Developing a Christian World-and-Life View* (Wheaton, IL: Crossway Books, 2005), 109, 210; Louis Gifford Parkhurst, *Francis Schaeffer: The Man and His Message in Honor of the 30th Anniversary of L'Abri Fellowship, June 5, 1955–June 5, 1985* (Wheaton, IL: Tyndale House, 1985), 53; Lane T. Dennis, *Letters of Francis A. Schaeffer: Spiritual Reality in the Personal Christian* (Wheaton, IL: Crossway Books, 1985), 92, 144, 146, 208; and Tim LaHaye and Edward E. Hindson, *The Popular Bible Prophecy Workbook: An Interactive Guide to Understanding the End Times* (Eugene, OR: Harvest House, 2006), 53, 55. Noll, *Scandal of the Evangelical Mind,* 140–142.

87. Quote from "Far Right: Focus on Their Faults," *The Advocate,* December 19, 2000, 18.

88. Ken Ham, "Creating Doubt—Satan's Best Tactic?" (audio recording), April 5, 2010, available at http://www.answersingenesis.org/media/audio/answers-daily/volume-090/creating-doubt-satans-best-tactic.

89. Ken Ham, *The Lie: Evolution* (Colorado Springs: Master Books, 1987), 44.

90. Nancy M. Tischler, *Encyclopedia of Contemporary Christian Fiction: From C. S. Lewis to Left Behind* (Santa Barbara, CA: ABC-CLIO, 2009), 251–253. Jason C. Bivins, *Religion of Fear: The Politics of Horror in Conservative Evangelicalism* (New York: Oxford University Press, 2008), 5, 18, 32–34, 178. Jay R. Howard, "Vilifying the Enemy: The Christian Right and the Novels of Frank Peretti," *Journal of Popular Culture* 28:3 (1994): 195–199.

91. Alissa Rubin, "Power Angels," *New Republic,* November 20, 1995, 21–22.
92. Ken Ham, "Are You Certain about Certainty?" October 23, 2008, available at http://blog.beliefnet.com/blogalogue/2008/10/are-you-certain-about-certaint.html.
93. Pew Center, U.S. Religious Landscape Survey, Report 2008, Vincent Crapanzano, *Serving the Word: Literalism in America from the Pulpit to the Bench* (New York: New Press, 2000), 18–24.
94. "David Barton at Work," youtube.com, January 24, 2008. David Barton, "Congress, the Culture, and Christian Voting," WallBuilders, November 2007, available at http://www.wallbuilders.com/LIBissuesArticles.asp?id=3930.
95. David Barton, "Is America a Christian Nation? (5/5)" youtube.com (accessed August 18, 2010).
96. Sixty-one percent of evangelicals surveyed by Pew in 2007 believed that "Miracles still occur today as in ancient times." Pew Forum, U.S. Religious Landscape Survey, Report 2008, q. 39a, p. 171.
97. Benny Hinn Ministries, "About Us," n.d., available at http://www.bennyhinn.org/aboutus/articledesc.cfm?id=1386 (accessed November 23, 2010).
98. Answers in Genesis, "Designers Working on Museum Project!" August 1999, available at http://www.answersingenesis.org/docs/4100.asp.
99. D. Michael Lindsay, *Faith in the Halls of Power: How Evangelicals Joined the American Elite* (New York: Oxford University Press, 2007), 4.
100. David Barton, "God: Missing in Action from American History," WallBuilders, June 2005, available at http://www.wallbuilders.com/LIBissuesArticles.asp?id=100.
101. David Halbrook, "Hodel Center Dedication a Tribute to a Beloved Friend," Patrick Henry College, October 13, 2009, available at http://www.phc.edu/20091013_hodel.php.
102. Douglas James Schuurman, *Vocation: Discerning Our Callings in Life* (Grand Rapids, MI: William B. Eerdmans, 2004), 1–16.
103. Uffe Schjoedt, Hans Stødkilde-Jørgensen, Armin W. Geertz, Torben E. Lund, and Andreas Roepstorff, "The Power of Charisma: Perceived Charisma Inhibits the Frontal Executive Network of Believers in Intercessory Prayer," *Social Cognitive and Affective Neuroscience Advance Access* (March 2010): 2.
104. Schjoedt et al., "The Power of Charisma," 124–125.
105. Francis Collins, "Creating a Community to Explore the Harmony of Sci-

ence and Faith," *BioLogos Forum,* June 1, 2009, available at http://biologos.org/blog/creating-a-community-to-explore-the-harmony-of-science-and-faith/.

106. Answers in Genesis, "God Makes Dreams Out of Nothing," March 2001, available at http://www.answersingenesis.org/creation/v23/i2/dreams.asp.

107. Harding, *The Book of Jerry Falwell,* 12.

Acknowledgments

Without the support of individuals, groups, and institutions, this project could not have been completed. We are extremely grateful for all the advice and assistance we received.

Each chapter benefited from careful readers and critics. Scholars of science and religion offered helpful suggestions and edits. Among those were Jon Roberts, Michael Ruse, and Eugenie Scott. Many provided keen insight into American religion, spending time reading chapters and making suggestions on what we have called the parallel culture of evangelicalism. Thanks to Peggy Bendroth, Daniel Vaca, Grant Wacker, John Turner, Jonathan Ebel, Barry Hankins, and Rachel Held Evans for being such wonderful critics. We especially appreciate that Paul Miller spent so much time with us discussing his life, faith, and college career. Our chapter on history benefited from the advice and wisdom of John Fea, Thomas Kidd, Chris Beneke, Maura Jane Farrelly, and Bland Whitley. Melani McAlister and Paul Boyer read the millennialism chapter and helped us better navigate the twists and turns, sidetracks and mysterious back roads of apocalypticism. A special thanks goes to Ronald Numbers and Randall Balmer, who read the entire manuscript and were crucial in helping us frame our argument and fine-tune the chapters—as well as convince HUP to publish our book. The arguments in this book have been developed over the course of many years in conversation with colleagues at Eastern Nazarene College (ENC). We would especially like to thank Bill McCoy, Philip LaFountain, Lowell Hall, Eric Severson, and Donald Yerxa.

Other individuals offered guidance on the larger themes presented in the book. In that regard thanks are due to Joe Lucas, Scott Hovey, Brian Ward, John Wilson, Bertram and Anne Wyatt-Brown, Paul Nyce, Michael Lynn, Kevin Taylor, Del Case, David Mislin, Hilde Løvdal, and Bryan Zimmerman.

The John Templeton Foundation provided financial support for this project, for which we are very appreciative.

We presented several chapters at conferences and seminars. For the comments of many participants and copanelists, we are significantly indebted. Gordon College hosted a 2009 conference titled "The *Scandal of the Evangelical Mind,* Fifteen Years Later." We appreciate Mark Noll's insight and the counsel of others at the event who helped us think through our work. Art Remillard and participants in the St. Francis University Faculty Writing Circle provided feedback on the introduction to our book.

Larry Friedman and all who took part in the Second Annual Conference on Public Intellectuals at Harvard University (April 2011) provided suggestions on the chapter dealing with history. That chapter benefited from the wisdom of two other seminars as well. Paul Harvey, Amanda Porterfield, and Philip Goff, who led and organized the 2007–2009 Young Scholars in American Religion program (hosted by the Center for the Study of Religion and American Culture at Indiana University–Purdue University Indianapolis and sponsored by the Lilly Endowment) assisted us in thinking through the argument and the content. Early-career scholars who took part in the program with Randall—Edward Blum, Darren Dochuk, Kate Engel, Spencer Fluhman, Rebecca Goetz, Charles Irons, Kathryn Lofton, Matthew Sutton, and Tisa Wenger—lent their ears, gave encouragement, and provided much-appreciated criticism. The history chapter also benefited enormously from a March 2011 seminar of the American Political History Institute at Boston University led by Bruce Schulman. Stephen Berry, Lynn Lyerly, and others in the Boston-Area American Religious History Group at Boston University read and critiqued the chapter on millennialism. Mark Mann, Jennifer Rogers, Sharon Bowles, and Silvia Cortez at Point Loma Nazarene University were wonderful hosts while Randall spent part of a summer on a fellowship at the school's Wesleyan Center for Twenty-first Century Studies.

In the last stages Carissa Schutz at ENC was an able proofreader, note checker, and all around indispensable assistant. Over the years a number of ENC students labored tirelessly to assist us on the project. Among them were Brooke Sword, Matt LeBlanc, Joshua Donovan, and Cameron Young.

Joyce Seltzer, our editor at Harvard University Press, gave us indispensable guidance and helped us craft the overarching themes. Lunch and breakfast meetings with her, as well as dozens of conversations over email and by phone, were tremendously beneficial. Without her assistance and that of Jeannette Estruth this book would not have seen the light of day. In addition, Christine Thorsteinsson, also of Harvard, was a crack copyeditor, spotting grammatical infelicities and syntactical troubles that had, despite our best efforts, eluded us.

Finally, we would like to thank our families for their support.

Randall thanks his wife, Beth, who was always willing to offer advice on the project and was patient with the time he spent hunched over a laptop, red eyes fixed on the screen. Family members back in Kansas and California also deserve special recognition, among them Janice Stephens, Phil and Nicole White, Dave and Nicole Stephens, Bill and Solveig Cagwin, Nora and Jarrod Whitcomb, and Inger Austad. For the hours of fun Thomas the Tank Engine playtime and healthy distraction, thanks are also due to Johnny and Harry Stephens and Will and Annika Whitcomb.

Karl thanks his wife, Myrna, and daughters, Sara and Laura, for tolerating his seclusion in the family sunroom, where he loves to write while looking out at the woods. Karl especially thanks his mother, Ursula, who raised him to appreciate books and writing. She passed away while this book was being written and is dearly missed.

Index